Legacies of Departed African Women Writers

Legacies of Departed African Women Writers

Matrix of Creativity and Power

Edited by Helen O. Chukwuma
and Chioma Carol Opara

LEXINGTON BOOKS
Lanham • Boulder • New York • London

Published by Lexington Books
An imprint of The Rowman & Littlefield Publishing Group, Inc.

4501 Forbes Boulevard, Suite 200, Lanham, Maryland 20706

www.rowman.com

86-90 Paul Street, London EC2A 4NE

Copyright © 2022 by The Rowman & Littlefield Publishing Group, Inc.

All rights reserved. No part of this book may be reproduced in any form or by any electronic or mechanical means, including information storage and retrieval systems, without written permission from the publisher, except by a reviewer who may quote passages in a review.

Chapter 5 was previously published as Perp St. Remy Asiegbu's "Forces and Flaws in Flora Nwapa's Efuru and Idu" in International Journal of Arts and Humanities, vol. 9 (2), S/NO 32, January 2019, ISSN: 2225-8590 (Print) 2227-5452 (Online), DOI: http://dx.doi.org/10.4314/ijah.v9i1.10. Published with permission.

British Library Cataloguing in Publication Information Available

Library of Congress Cataloging-in-Publication Data

Names: Chukwuma, Helen, editor. | Opara, Chioma Carol, editor.
  Title: Legacies of departed African women writers : matrix of creativity and power / edited by Helen O. Chukwuma and Chioma Carol Opara.
  Description: Lanham : Lexington Books, 2022. | Includes bibliographical references and index. | Summary: "Legacies of Passed African Writers analyzes and celebrates the resounding contributions of ten deceased African female writers of contemporary African literature and feminist scholarship, examining the ideologies, thematic concerns, and stylistic devices which constitute the fabrics of the legacies left by these iconic pacesetters"-- Provided by publisher.
Identifiers: LCCN 2022026077 (print) | LCCN 2022026078 (ebook) | ISBN 9781666914658 (cloth) | ISBN 9781666914672 (paper) | ISBN 9781666914665 (epub)
Subjects: LCSH: African literature--Women authors--History and criticism. | African literature--20th century--History and criticism. | African literature--21st century--History and criticism. | Women in literature.
Classification: LCC PL8010 .L387 2022 (print) | LCC PL8010 (ebook) | DDC 809.89287096--dc23/eng/20220608
LC record available at https://lccn.loc.gov/2022026077
LC ebook record available at https://lccn.loc.gov/2022026078

To all women of valor, virtue, and vision who have distinctly lent their voices, brains, and brawn to the validation of the dignity and visibility of woman on the African continent and the diaspora.

Acknowledgments

The editors would like to acknowledge the scholarly contributions of the authors of the chapters in this volume. They have, over the years of production, not only confided their essays to us but also patiently awaited the publication of the seminal work

Profound thanks are due to our dear colleague and friend, Professor Blessing Diala-Ogamba, who in the wake of daunting obstacles and varied challenges which we encountered, displayed unstinting sisterhood by facilitating the completion of this project.

Finally, we would like to record our gratitude to our respective families, associates and friends who palpably constituted sturdy crutches when unforeseen circumstances weighted against laudable aspirations, spirited efforts as well as set deadlines.

Contents

Acknowledgments — vii

Introduction: The Resounding Gongs of Fallen Female Heroes — 1
   Chioma Carol Opara and Helen O. Chukwuma

PART 1: AFFIRMING THE CHARISMATIC PATHFINDER: FLORA NWAPA — 13

Chapter 1: Flora Nwapa: The One Who Dwells in Wealth — 15
   Anthonia Kalu

Chapter 2: Uwa Umunwanyi, Uwa Oma: Flora Nwapa and Women's History and Culture in *Efuru* and *Idu* — 33
   Akachi Adimora-Ezeigbo

Chapter 3: Flora Nwapa, Feminism, and the Burden of History — 47
   Kemi Wale-Olaitan

Chapter 4: Flora Nwapa's Efuru: The Personified Goddess — 61
   Anthonia Adadevoh

Chapter 5: Forces and Flaws in Flora Nwapa's *Efuru* and *Idu* — 77
   Perp St. Remy Asiegbu

PART 2: ORALITY AND ROOTEDNESS IN CULTURE AND TRADITION — 89

Chapter 6: Wolof Taasu Genre as Narrative Device in Mariama Ba's *So Long a Letter* — 91
   Ada Uzoamaka Azodo

Chapter 7: Non-Verbalized Communication of True Love in
   Traditional Dholuo in Grace Ogot's *The Promised Land*   101
   Eunita Ochola

Chapter 8: Validation of Culture: A Re-reading of Zulu Sofola's
   Wedlock of the Gods and *King Emene: A Tragedy of Rebellion*   115
   Nkem Okoh

PART 3: INTERROGATING IDENTITY, AUTONOMY, AND HISTORY   135

Chapter 9: Archetypes of the Mother and the Scapegoat in Grace
   Ogot's Fiction   137
   Onyemaechi Udumukwu

Chapter 10: Bessie Head: A World Writer from Africa   153
   Mary S. Lederer

Chapter 11: Narrating Hybridity: The Synthesis of Tradition and
   Modernity in Emecheta's *Double Yoke*   167
   Solomon Omatsola Azumurana

Chapter 12: Depravity and Mental Torture in Nawal El Saadawi's
   Two Women in One and *Woman at Point Zero*   185
   Queen Albert and Onyemechi Nwaeke

Chapter 13: Resurrecting Women from the Margins of History:
   Feminist Synergy in Selected Works by Assia Djebar   199
   Rose A. Sackeyfio

PART 4: CONFRONTING CONTAINMENT WITH RESISTANCE AND FREEDOM   215

Chapter 14: From Passivity to Defiance: The Portrayal of Women
   in Yvonne Vera's Novels   217
   Blessing Diala-Ogamba

Chapter 15: The Buchi Emecheta Phenomenon   231
   Austine Amanze Akpuda

Chapter 16: Twin Kernels in One Pod: Naming of Nawal and
   Firdaus in Nawal El Saadawi's *A Daughter of Isis* and *Woman
   at Point Zero*   245
   Chinyere Grace Okafor

Chapter 17: Women, Tradition, and Resistance in Zulu Sofola's
Wedlock of the Gods 261
Irene Isoken Salami-Agunloye

Chapter 18: Nadine Gordimer's Multiplex Legacy 281
Ikeogu Oke

PART 5: DYNAMICS OF POWER AND NARRATIVE VOICE 297

Chapter 19: Language Use in the Discourse of Otherness in Bessie
Head's *Maru* 299
Omeh Obasi Ngwoke and Okwudiri Anasiudu

Chapter 20: Synthesis of Binaries: The Mediating Voice in
Mariama Ba's Novels 313
Chioma Carol Opara

Epilogue: Un Cri De Coeur 333
Marie Umeh

Index 335

About the Editors and Contributors 341

Introduction

The Resounding Gongs of Fallen Female Heroes

Chioma Carol Opara and Helen O. Chukwuma

African female writers, the inalienable progeny of oral female performers, have in almost six decades established a fertile female literary terrain. Essentially, the post-colonial African female writer has taken her cue from her artistic and talented foremother. Versed in oral tradition, the female performer set out to regale as well as instruct her pre-literate audience in a pristine, simple milieu. Underlining the import of the performer in her classic, *Oral Literature in Africa*, Ruth Finnegan expatiates upon the significance of performance in orality, "Oral literature is by definition dependent on a performer who formulates it in words on a specific occasion—there is no other way in which it can be realized as a literary product" (2). Since the female artistes—the *griottes*—excelled as performers in songs, tales and dance they stood out starkly as the live wire of African unwritten literature.

    The rise of African written literature can be traced to the 1960s with the publication of Chinua Achebe's *Things Fall Apart* (1958) which is a distinct refutation of the racist sentiments of colonial literature as expressed in the works of Joyce Cary, William Boyd and Joseph Conrad. African literature thereafter morphed into protest literature decrying colonial as well as neocolonial oppressions and dehumanization. The female stentorian voice joined the fray when in 1966 Flora Nwapa's *Efuru* was added to the panoply of African literary missiles. Toeing the line of her pre-literate foremother, the highly skilled *griotte,* Nwapa, displayed a measure of performance in her rendition of the lives of rural women as well as the numinous existence of the goddess of the lake and her ability to enrich her worshipers. Female characters are given significant roles in Nwapa's works. As Helen Chukwuma deftly puts it:

For the first time, the woman character took center stage and the reader was invited into the world of women and shared her true nature of her concerns, fears, joys, sorrows, and aspirations. Nwapa wrote to correct the disparaged image of women in male-authored fiction. She, the pioneer woman writer, opened the sluice gates, and African women have not stopped writing since. (xiii)

Much as African female writers have dexterously produced numerous works in various genres—fiction, drama, poetry—they have not been given commensurate critical attention both within and outside Africa. Adducing the marginality of black women writers to "the multi-layered oppression—gender, race, and class," Jennifer Thorington Springer and Obioma Nnaemeka have rued the grim fact that black feminist writers were practically sidelined in the 2007 anthology, *Feminist Literary Theory and Criticism,* edited by Sandra M. Gilbert and Susan Gubar which traces the literary outputs in English of feminist writers from the Middle Ages to the twenty-first century. In their own words, "Whether consciously or unconsciously, a few token black American women writers were included but there is no inclusion of feminist scholarship by African women" (xv). It is their express contention that it is an act of deliberate exclusion of feminist scholarship by African women. They also decry the obvious blindness of some male scholars to black female experiences. Such marginality is analogous to what Chioma Opara has dubbed a "death sentence" on African female writers in the critical judgment of a number of male critics (2). The corollary is outright cynicism evinced by male readers, gleaned from patronizing, prejudiced and even disdainful evaluations of feminist texts. Essentially, the peripheral status of female-authored texts on the African literary landscape is a palpable function of hegemony which stifles as it negates and represses with a crushing grip and tenacity. James Lull has deftly noted that, "Hegemony is more than social power itself; it is a method for gaining and maintaining power" (34). The dominance held by male scholars over "the other" is writ large in the selection of only thirteen female texts—twelve works of fiction and one play—among the constellation of one hundred best books at the 2002 Zimbabwe International Book Fair. It is significant to note that the selection committee consisted of only two women and fourteen men. Irrespective of the obvious gender asymmetry, Chikwenye Okonjo Ogunyemi posits that it was a distinct acknowledgement of "female literary endeavor, bringing it into a privileged circle. This point of departure of including women at a celebratory moment is noteworthy for establishing a female literary canon" (1).

What would appear to be a lopsided canonization notwithstanding, an established female literary canon, in one part sets in motion the continual celebration of female artistry and in another, strives at countering the diminished station of women in the African literary arena. In light of this, *Legacies of Departed African Female Writers*, in the vein of other feminist texts devoted to African women writers, aims at underscoring and boosting the female literary canon. Focused solely on ten departed women writers, who have patently left legacies of strength, creativity, and power, it foregrounds female thoughts, innovations, and artistry. The volume spans the entire African continent. The ten deceased female writers selected are: Nawal El Saadawi (1931–2021) and Assia Njebar (1936–2015) from North Africa; Bessie Head (1937–1986) and Nadine Gordimer (1923–2014) from South Africa; Yvonne Vera (1964–2005) from Southern Africa; Grace Ogot (1930–2015) from East Africa; Flora Nwapa (1931–1993), Buchi Emecheta (1944–2017), Zulu Sofola (1935–1995) and Mariama Ba (1929–1981) from West Africa. It is salient to note that seven out of the ten writers are among the thirteen female writers "singled out" at the 2002 Zimbabwe International Book Fair and ranked on the canonical list. They are: Bessie Head, Nawal El Saadawi, Nadine Gordimer, Buchi Emecheta, Mariama Ba, Assia Djebar and Yvonne Vera. In addition, Nadine Gordimer had received the Nobel Prize in Literature in 1991.

The contextual, theoretical, and textual analyses of the works of these women writers are insightfully effected by the contributors of this anthology, which comprises twenty chapters grouped in five sections. This is premised on the diverse perspectives adopted in the varied hermeneutics of texts. The commonality of thoughts inheres in the invaluable inputs of the departed women writers to the literary tradition on the African continent. These literary amazons are undeniably the foremothers of contemporary female writers such as Chimamanda Ngozi Adichie, Kaine Agary, Chika Unigwe, Yewande Omotosho, Susan Kiguli, Sefi Atta, Veronique Tadjo, and Chibundu Onuzo. The impact, in effect, runs across the three generations of writers. Consider for example the intertextual engagement between Flora Nwapa and her contemporary, Buchi Emecheta, on the joys of motherhood; third-generation writers such as Chimamanda Adichie have joined the conversation and defied tradition by casting successful, albeit childless, women basking in self-fulfillment. Again, the metaphors of self-identification, such as the mirror, used in Nawal El Saadawi's *Two Women in One (1985)* are echoed later in Tsitsi Dangarembga's novel *Nervous Conditions (1988)*. Also, the cultural atmosphere of women sharing kolanuts in Nwapa's rural novels is signified upon by a second-generation writer, Chinyere Okafor, in her collection of short stories *He Wants to Marry Me Again (1996)*. It is pertinent to note that the conciliatory and moderate tone in most of the writings of the departed heroes has invariably permeated the general tenor of the majority of the variants of African feminist theory which is, in the main, inscribed with the hallmarks of negotiation, accommodation, and conciliation.

The first part of this volume celebrates the dynamic and charismatic first female Nigerian writer, Flora Nwapa, who heroically cleared the path to the thorny terrain of African female literary production. Anthonia Kalu opens discourse on Nwapa with her essay titled "Flora Nwapa: The One Who dwells in Wealth" which explores the intertextual engagement between Nwapa and Chinua Achebe in some of their works. She notes the similarity in the plot trajectories in both *Efuru* and *Things Fall Apart*. In her critical survey of the vast majority of Nwapa's fiction, Kalu observes that Nwapa fuses oral narrative style with the Western form in her works. Applauding the author's creative output, she contends that it is employed effectively to underline an enduring Igbo legacy of self-assertion. Kalu accords Nwapa the title, "The Mother of African Literature" and affirms that in her writings she creatively used "her knowledge of Igbo narrative arts, cosmology, socio-political craft and her strong power of observation about the lives and experiences of Igbo women." Her power of observation and eye for details cap her oratorical skills as a *griotte*.

Akachi Adimora-Ezeigbo presents *uwa umunwanyi*, or world of women, in Nwapa's early novels—*Efuru* and *Idu*. Chinyere Okafor has stated elsewhere that *uwa umunwanyi* delineates otherness. In her own words, "*Uwa umunwanyi* which translates as 'women's world' is an expression that signifies separation from the mainstream, which is male" (60). Ezeigbo, nevertheless, portrays it as *uwa oma*—a beautiful world of women's culture and patterns of existence. She further defines *uwa umunwanyi* as the world of services and industry. In her refreshing analysis, Nwapa repositions the Igbo woman's identity in this space where the minutiae of women's lives are painstakingly recorded. Innovative and original in the choice of subject matter and form, Nwapa is lauded for breaking the silence and charting a course for women-centeredness in African literature. Ezeigbo expressly submits to Nwapa's legacy of empowerment to African women writers across generations as well as the reconstruction of women's culture, social and economic history.

The question of power hinged on the burden of history and identity is palpably interrogated in Kemi Wale-Olaitan's chapter. She asserts that Nwapa rewrites history when the female gender, that hitherto in men's works had been cast as silent or absent, is rendered visible and autonomous. Accordingly, 1966 became the watershed in the history of African literature, particularly in women's writing. The burden of history on Nwapa consists in upholding the realities of African life and depicting the varied manifestations of the quest for individual autonomy in her texts. In documenting the different moments of the historical development, the varied reactions of the apprised women to the patriarchal structure are bared. She submits that Nwapa has glaringly set the pace for contemporary female writers. Other female writers have followed in her stride and striven to restore the individuality of woman since she has made it possible for African women to retrieve their voices. The burden placed on the female African writer today is the appreciation of this perspective as well as Nwapa's works especially *Efuru* which is considered the mother text.

In a similar vein, Anthonia Adadevoh's "Flora Nwapa's Efuru: A Personified Goddess" extols Nwapa's transformation of the female figure. She contends that Nwapa personifies Uhamiri, the goddess of Oguta Lake, through the eponymous heroine of the novel, *Efuru*. Drawing on the Jungian theory of the collective unconscious, she asserts that in adopting the archetypal pattern, Nwapa "came to terms with her 'animus' the archetypal masculine symbolism within a woman's consciousness." Mythical figures are used to challenge stereotypical patterns, thus re-affirming the primary position of woman closely associated with nature. Where the average woman in the pristine milieu of the novel leads a humdrum life, Uhamiri's worshippers are set apart, liberated and wealthy albeit barren. She concludes that Nwapa uses the mythological sphere to link women with nature and elevate them beyond the realm of the mundane. Moving beyond the mundane to the esoteric, Perp St. Remy Asiegbu interrogates the dynamics of some supernatural forces with regard to Flora Nwapa's artistic delineation of the Nigerian/Ugwuta woman's experience in her first two novels—*Efuru* and *Idu*. Probing the intrinsic and extrinsic forces surrounding the protagonists as well as their creator, Nwapa, as an avant-garde African female writer, she examines the means employed to circumvent these clogs in plot development in these novels. In her well-balanced critique of the texts, she highlights the flaws in Nwapa's narrative structure that derive from the author's deliberate or unconscious efforts to handle both the natural and supernatural forces that arguably dominate her life. These deficiencies notwithstanding, Nwapa succeeds in creating a unique style of writing that glaringly projects women's lives and experiences.

The second part of the book is focused on the depiction of African tradition and culture on which the oral mode is hinged. Orality is deftly woven into the epistolary form in Ada Azodo's analysis of Ba's *So Long a Letter*. Providing a fresh insight into the novel, she unravels some elements of traditional Wolof (Senegalese) culture embedded in the text, by employing the sub-genre of taasu. This ultimately renders the text as a modified form of a traditional Wolof oral genre. As narrator, Ramatoulaye's own taasu unfurls, and the reader is apprised with her traumatic experience in marriage. Accordingly, the oral and traditional Wolof taasu genre is modified through the written form of "contemporary professionalism which further modifies the understanding of notions of culture and autobiography." Orality is similarly employed as a tool of exegesis by Eunita Ochola as she draws a nexus between verbal communication and nonverbal communication of traditional love in both traditional and modern African literature. She locates this form of communication in objects such as food, dance, song, and the semiotics of oral love in Luo culture of Kenya. Examples of such expressions of romantic love abound in post-colonial texts including Grace Ogot's *The Promised Land*. She posits that Ogot's legacy resides in exploring and illuminating non-verbalized love in Luo culture in order to explain some unwholesome tendencies in modern verbalized love.

A putative daughter of African tradition, Zulu Sofola, is presented in the garb of transformative feminism as Nkem Okoh's intervention diverges from most other critical reviews of her works. Taking a deconstructive stance, Okoh challenges the widely held view that Sofola is a diehard traditionalist. He rather dismantles binaries and asserts that the author is a westernized African who is not enslaved by tradition, much as she recreates Enuani Igbo oral tradition of the Niger Delta region of Nigeria in her plays. This includes the use of language, speech reality, cultural accoutrements and its performance. She has in her writings, revalidated indigenous African culture in the recreation of society through its oral literature. She, however, prescribes what Okoh terms coalescing of the two worlds of modernity and tradition that should work together. Differently stated, in Sofola's consciousness a balanced fusion is preferred to a return to the past. Okoh maintains that the playwright has, in effect, made a bold statement against retrogressive norms in her portrayal of forward-looking female protagonists who symbolize change which is duly propelled by the dynamics of female resistance and liberation. He concludes that the legacy of the first published female Nigerian playwright lies in her striking use of language.

The third section of *Legacies* deals with identity, consciousness-raising and history. The history of the migration of Luo ethnic group across nations in East Africa is not lost on Grace Ogot who unequivocally writes from the standpoint of cultural as well as national identity. Onyemaechi Udumukwu posits that Ogot is the inaugurator of a female novelistic and fictional tradition in East Africa. Dwelling on the psychological import of her work, he applies the theory of collective unconscious and archetypal criticism in his analysis of her texts. The mother and scapegoat archetypes proffer a sense of identification and cohesion respectively. He expressly maintains that Ogot wrote from a cultural crucible that establishes a strong sense of identity. The quest for identity is further explored in Mary Lederer's "Bessie Head: World Writer from Africa," which is a biographical document of the highly traumatized bi-racial South African female writer. Lederer underscores Head's collections of letters and makes a valid submission that much as the author's life constituted a well-spring of inspiration for her writings, she reworked the elements of her life in order to reproduce the idea in her work. Her unique style is the reason she is read and re-read from different perspectives. Head, in effect, balked at any limitation emanating from race, gender and class as she dwelt on universal themes. She is adjudged to be unquestionably ahead of her time.

The conflation of traditional and Western values has over the years bred palpable alienation as well as anomie in post-colonial African society. This conflict becomes a major concern in *Double Yoke* for Buchi Emecheta, whose works not only record important historical moments such as slavery, colonialism, post-colonialism, and Nigerian civil war but also woman's relentless struggle for identity in her autobiographical narratives which dominate her writings. Solomon Azuramana interrogates Emecheta's *Double Yoke* as an intervention in the debate of tradition versus modernity continuum. Embracing a hybrid stance, Emecheta uses some characters as sub-texts to illustrate the import of the synthesis of tradition and modernity in a hybrid culture This should be achieved by creating a third estate which is not completely western or traditional. Hybridity thus connotes the melding of disparate components. The hybrid woman. Nko, reconstitutes her identity to confront patriarchy as well as changing socio-cultural realities. This is effected in deft manoeuvers verging on the balancing and synthesis of tradition and modernity.

Debilitating Muslim traditions impinge on the identity formation of Nawal El Saadawi's female protagonists in the Arab world of two of her novels. In her capacity as a psychiatrist as well as psychoanalyst, she presents, in the main, schizophrenic female characters battling with stifling patriarchal institutions. Queen Albert and Onyemechi Nwaeke in their contribution discuss the identity crisis of the desolate and demonized heroines of *Two Women in One* and *Woman at Point Zero*. They contend that the crushing weight of deprivation, deviance and sheer depravity of the oppressive male, psychologically encumber the two protagonists—Bahiah and Firdaus. Overwhelmed by the shackles of a monolithic Muslim Arab culture, they ultimately become intrepid, vengeful, suicidal, and murderous. Such are the offshoots of sexist patriarchal tenets reeking of misogyny; the aftermath is the tragic decimation of female dreams.

In the same vein, Rose Sackeyfio's intervention dwells on the reconfiguration of female identity in the works of another committed Arab woman writer, Assia Djebar. She posits that the autobiographical features in her works establish her commitment to delineate the myriad of drawbacks that have retarded the actualization of women in the unalloyed Islamic culture of the Arab world in the course of their quest for parity. Some of the encumbrances consist in patriarchal oppression inscribed on the female body by means of various forms of violence and marginalization. Djebar portrays the reality of the Arab woman's subjugation as well as her resistance. This is adroitly juxtaposed with the colonization of Algeria by France, Algeria's revolution and subsequent independence. Sackeyfio concludes that the patently committed author underscores Algerian women's identities which were silenced by their omission from French colonial history. Essentially, Djebar has excelled at rewriting the subjugated woman's history formerly written from the white male's colored perspective.

Various facets of containment as well as resistance are dwelt upon in the fourth section. Blessing Diala-Ogamba's chapter deals with various shades of patriarchal subjugation in some of Yvonne Vera's novels. She underlines the author's unique narrative style shrouded in disguise. Form and structure are deftly deconstructed as Vera unfurls the narrative of the deprived and repressed masses in Zimbabwe, Southern Africa. Haunted by the realities of sexism, racism, and censorship, she adopts a feminist approach as she loosens the monstrous chains of silence by arming her female protagonists with the voice accessorized with the articulate tongue. This becomes the essential weapon and metaphor for freedom. The palpable transformation of her women is consistent in her works. Taking a rebellious stance, they jettison passivity for defiance which may take a tragic turn and, in some cases, may manifest in breaking glasses in public places as a measure of freedom.

Another progressive author, Buchi Emecheta, is arguably in the forefront of African women writers who exhort women to break the glass ceiling. The Westernized Nigerian female writer living in exile appropriated the ways of the West and was not in the least bashful in her brand of feminism. Her autobiographical novels attest to this submission. Austine Akpuda in "The Buchi Emecheta Phenomenon" argues that the highly accomplished writer was one of the first to stoke the awareness of women to the reality of the atrocities which they have championed, and which ultimately have impeded their growth. He further underscores the intertext in Emecheta's early novels especially *The Slave Girl* and her ability to probe the depths of her female character's mind as she struggles for self-autonomy. Akpuda uses ample historical sources to validate his claims about the socio-cultural reality of Emecheta's Delta Igbo region. In his opinion, her phenomenal stature, as well as her strident voice, has paved the way for a robust African feminist scholarship. Emecheta's success as a writer resides in her relentless quest and her capability to keep her head well above water, transcending from amateurish beginnings to canonical heights laden with numberless accolades and laurels.

In the vein of Emecheta, the iconic female writer Nawal El Saadawi, also plumbs the inmost thoughts of her female protagonists thus eliciting enormous repression. Her dogged fight for women is deemed personal and focused on the eradication of circumcision which she views as the basis of the oppression of women. It is Chinyere Okafor's contention that Nawal's commitment to writing 'woman' is personal, cultural and strategic. She asserts that the naming of Nawal in the author's autobiography *A Daughter of Isis* is as political as it is confrontational. The author takes issue with a patriarchal institution that has striven to exclude female names in the entire process of naming. Similarly, the title of the Egyptian writer's most popular novel, *Woman at Point Zero* or *Firdaus* as it was originally titled, was influenced by the author's disaffection with blatant patriarchal erasure of women's names. She avers that Firdaus is Nawal on a divergent path. Differently put, Nawal and her alter ego, Firdaus are two daughters of Egypt whose lives intersected like twins in a pod of gender construction but separated by a class structure that hurled them on different paths of life.

Irene Salami-Agunloye in her submission argues that much as Zulu Sofola has over time been pummeled by critics for holding tenaciously to hidebound traditional practices without making any effort at remodeling them to fit into modern institutions, this could be a function of the tradition of first generation set of writers who in their bid to protest against colonial hegemony, unwittingly encroached on the individuality as well as the dignity of the African woman. Sofola has, in effect, decried the jostling of African culture by the incursion of western values. According to her the African system of governance was superimposed with "European/Arabian male system of authority and governance. That was the first death blow to our psyche and the beginning of the dewomanization of the African woman" (61). It is not then surprising that the author accents traditional beliefs and values in her play *Wedlock of the Gods*. It is against this background that Salami-Agunloye explores the import of tradition in the play. Her defiant protagonists challenge sexist normative patterns and ultimately pay a price for their rebellion which is an apparent poetic justice. This appears to be a significant index to Sofola's rootedness in African cultural patterns and institutions. Her stricken protagonists, nonetheless, tower above retrogressive cultural norms in a feat of heroic resistance.

Ikeogu Oke's intervention is a commendation of the patent creative prowess and activism of 1991 Nobel Laureate in Literature, Nadine Gordimer the "lioness of literary activism," who championed racial and social justice in both Apartheid and New South Africa. Her legacy of exceptionality, which complements her legacy of corpus, consists chiefly in the unique markers of her literary style. He argues that Gordimer left a legacy of activism far beyond the sphere of politics. Her coinage "freedom of the WORD" consists in the unmitigated rights of all human beings to express themselves using words as the medium of communication. Accordingly, she fought for those rights through her works in social commitment. Her distinct commitment to freedom from injustice and racial discrimination is depicted in the dogged defiance, subversion and resistance displayed by her protagonists in *My Son's Story*. Oke is convinced that through her writings, South Africa as well as the world became a sort of laboratory for experimenting on the sociopolitical effect of literature globally while testing its capability to consciousness-raising and the attendant commitment to freedom

The politics of power and narrative voice are the major concerns in the fifth part of this volume. Bessie Head in most of her works, strategically narrates her own story as well as the experiences of women in Botswana, Southern Africa. Convinced that language is focal and integral in the discourse formation in the construction of the novel as an art and genre of discourse, Omeh Ngwoke and Okwudiri Anasiudu in their submission, unravel the use of language and discourse of otherness in Head's *Maru*. Language is examined in the service of a writer's reconstruction of otherness. The study adopts analytic and descriptive approach within Norman Fairclough's variant of Critical Discourse Analysis that underlines the regime and complexities of social power relations. Otherness, which is socially constructed, becomes an institutionalized social practice and results in the flagrant discrimination against Margaret Cadmore, the Masarwa in Dilepe. The linguistic labeling of a social group and female gender as the outsider is viewed as the encoding power of language and symptomatic of the politics and dynamics of a social power relation.

Likewise, the politics of power is foregrounded in Chioma Opara's chapter which discusses Mariama Ba's robust stylistic devices in her two political novels—*So Long a Letter* and *Scarlet Song*—which are structurally antithetical. Antonyms are bared in antitheses amd epigrams. In the catalogue of binaries, noise is delineated as an antonym of voice. Binaries are, nevertheless, ultimately blended and harmonized. This is indicative of Ba's liberal disposition which is hinged on the femalist philosophy patently antithetical to Western feminism. Essentially ambivalent in her posture and moderate in her thoughts, Ba probes the female psyche and excels in the subtle fusion of polarities—which evokes Sandra Gilbert's and Susan Gubar's "the angel and the devil" / maddened angel paradigm—in the variegated portrayal of woman. Her composite political thoughts are deftly articulated with phenomenal craft and artistry. Imagery of blending and the profusion of connectives are strategically deployed. Opara concludes that the enduring legacy of the politically conscious author inheres in her inspiring artistic innovations as well as her clarion call for gender complementarity. Marie Umeh's eulogy to Buchi Emecheta rounds off the thunderous ovation given to the ten iconic women writers who have made outstanding impacts in the domain of African literature.

Clearly the contributions in *Legacies of Departed African Female Writers* have proffered a collective testament of creativity and power generated by the ten deceased African female writers mostly of the first generation. The theoretical and thematic concerns as well as the varied stylistic devices examined in the exegeses of the writings of the celebrated *griottes* validate the indelible footprints they have etched on the African literary landscape. Flora Nwapa, in her capacity as the first African woman to publish a book in English, has been aptly dubbed the "Mother of African Literature." She has been an inspirational force to younger writers and even some of her contemporaries. This explains why a section composed of five chapters analyzed from different perspectives is devoted to her. A few other authors have double interventions with different focuses. Essentially, the positive impact of these writers on creative writing as well as theoretical formulations on African feminisms is very discernible in the burgeoning African women's literature. It is not then surprising that seven out of the ten selected writers have broken into the high ranks of canonization; one also clinched a Nobel Prize. May it be reiterated that the corpus of their works has lit up the artistic flame of African feminist scholarship and even far beyond.

It is our fervent hope that the conversation generated by reading this book will arouse more interest in African studies, particularly African women's literary tradition. Given the enduring legacies of these female heroes—the lionesses in the path cleared by Flora Nwapa herself—we also hope that this companion volume will disseminate the evidence of their invaluable contributions to African humanity in the areas of justice, parity, love, integrity, good governance, freedom, peace, and, of course, gender relations. It should also be a viable medium in lifting the limited visibility and attendant "Othering" of African feminist scholarship which has resulted in the perennial exclusion of most works in this area. Furthermore, *Legacies of Departed African Women Writers* proffers vibrant conversations and opens up vistas for further research in other areas which were not included in this volume such as texts in Lusophone literature. An engagement with works by Spanish speaking African women writers will unarguably further enrich the fertile African feminist literary terrain plowed, primed and propagated by the ten celebrated pace setters.

WORKS CITED

Chukwuma, Helen. "Introduction." *Meeting Points in Black/Africana Women's Literature.* Eds. Helen Chukwuma and Preselfannie McDaniels Trenton, NJ: Africa World Press, 2016: xi–xvi.

Finnegan, Ruth. *Oral Literature in Africa.* Nairobi: Oxford University, 1977.

Gilbert, Sandra and Susan Gubar.Eds. *The Madwoman in the Attic: The Woman Writer and the Nineteenth Century Literary Imagination.* New Haven and London: Yale University Press, 1979.

Lull, James. "Hegemony." *Gender, Race, and Class in Media.* Eds. Gail Dines et al. London: Sage Publications, 2018: 34–36.

Ogunyemi, Chikwenye Okonjo. "Prolepsis." *Twelve Best Books by African Women*. Eds. Chikwenye Okonjo Ogunyemi and Tuzyline Jita Allan. Ohio: Ohio University Press, 2009: 1–14.

Okafor, Chinyere G. "Modern African Literature and Beauvoirism." *Beyond the Marginal Land: Gender Perspective in African Writing*. Ed. Chioma Opara. Port Harcourt: Belpot (Nig) Co, 1999: 57–79.

Opara, Chioma Carol. *Her Mother's Daughter: The African Writer as Woman*. Port Harcourt: University of Port Harcourt Press: 2004.

Sofola, Zulu. "Feminism and African Womanhood." *Sisterhood, Feminisms and Power*. Ed. Obioma Nnaemeka. Trenton NJ: Africa World Press, 1998: 51–64.

Springer, Jennifer T. and Nnaemeka Obioma. "Introduction." *Unraveling Gender, Race and Diaspora*. Eds. Obioma Nnaemeka and Jennifer Thorington Springer. Trenton, NJ: Africa World Press, 2016: xi–xxviii.

PART 1

Affirming the Charismatic Pathfinder: Flora Nwapa

Chapter 1

Flora Nwapa
The One Who Dwells in Wealth

Anthonia Kalu

INTRODUCTION

Florence Nwanzuruahu Nkiru Nwapa (January 1931–October 1993) was born in Ugwuta, Nigeria. She was the oldest of six children born to Christopher Ijeoma and Martha Nwapa. She was the first female student to gain a direct entry admission to University College, Ibadan where she earned a Bachelor of Arts degree in 1957. Subsequently, she obtained a Diploma in Education in 1958 from University of Edinburgh. Nwapa's job positions early in her professional life include: working as an Education Officer in the Ministry of Education, Calabar; a teaching position at Queen's School, Enugu; Registrar at the University of Lagos; Commissioner for Health and Social Welfare (East Central State, 1970–1971); and, as Commisioner for Land, Survey and Urban Development (1971–1974). Later, she ventured into publishing, starting her own publishing companies—Tana Press (1974) and the Flora Nwapa Company in (1977). Nwapa's Tana Press was the first press owned and operated by an African woman. Its inauguration predicted and targeted the growing African female audience/readership that was developing based on the fact that books in the Heinemann's African Writers Series were required reading in the secondary school curricula of many of Africa's post-colonial nations.

Attending University College, Ibadan during the early Ibadan years placed Nwapa near the beginning of the list of Nigeria's pioneer writers like Chinua Achebe, Wole Soyinka, John Pepper Clark, Mabel Segun, and others. Although she attended University College Ibadan a little later than the writers on the above list, the narrative, style, and structural focus of Nwapa's early writing indicates that she knew them as colleagues and was familiar with their works. Unlike Achebe and Segun who acted as editor and assistant editor of the University College's student publications, Nwapa did not have the privilege of learning and honing her craft as a student writer during her college years. Her storytelling techniques rely heavily on her knowledge of the traditional oral narrative performance tradition. But like Mabel Segun, her writing also responds to the male voices that prevailed on campus during those early University College, Ibadan years as well as in the new and developing African literatures of the time. About the university female's experience at Ibadan, Mabel Segun says in her Introduction to *The Surrender and Other Stories* that in the first Nigerian university, then known as University College, Ibadan, there were about five hundred male students and only fourteen female students, "a proportion which made the women visible and therefore ready objects of vilification." Moreover, they were denied the "right to freedom of association and expression."

It would seem that Nwapa's experience at the University of Ibadan and the Girls' Secondary School that she attended In Elelenwa, Port Harcourt, provided some of the raw materials used in her short stories, poems, children's stories and novels, Flora Nwapa deployed the knowledge gained from the various job positions in southern Nigeria to speak out about women's issues in post-colonial Nigeria. Specifically, she did so by focusing her attention on Ugwuta and the surrounding Igbo communities. Her novel, *Efuru* (1966) was the first by a Nigerian (African) woman to receive wide international attention. In her keynote address at the 1991 African Literature Association conference in New Orleans, USA, Nwapa shared her story about sending the completed draft of *Efuru* to Chinua Achebe who, as editor of the African Writer's Series, chaperoned the book's publication by Heinemann Education Publishers, placing it in that publisher's growing list of works by African writers. Although, and in general, Nwapa's works place her in the group of early Ibadan writers; her decision to write fiction was firmly influenced by that of her fellow Igbo writer Chinua Achebe. As a trailblazer for African women writers in the early post-colonial era, she is usually mentioned alongside Kenya's Grace Ogot who's writing also draws the attention of both readers and critics to the works of these two women. However, and in significant ways, *Efuru* is Nwapa's initial response to the growing dominance of the educated African male elite whose narrative and political voices were quickly gaining authority across the continent and beyond.

Specifically, *Efuru*, a fictional book-length narrative about the Igbo people of Nigeria and Igbo land, was Nwapa's response to Achebe's *Things Fall Apart* (1958). In a different work, I have shown how she uses Efuru's story to engage Achebe's *Things Fall Apart*. (Kalu, 2000). Although she continues the intertextual conversations in her other works, most of that engagement is not as direct. Her other published works include the novels *Idu* (1967), *Never Again* (1975), *One is Enough* (1981), and *Women Are Different* (1986); two short story collections, *This is Lagos* (1971), and *Wives at War* (1992); a collection of poems, *Cassava Song and Rice Song* (1986); and some children's books. Nwapa's writings and writing life continue to generate scholarship in African literary studies as well as Women's Studies worldwide. During her lifetime, she was recognized for her sustained efforts to bring African women's voices into several different arenas of academic engagement. She attended African Literature Association (ALA) meetings, presenting papers, giving the occasional keynote addresses while steadfastly working hard at distributing her own books.[1] After her death in 1993, there was a great deal of effort within the African literary studies community to acknowledge her and pay tribute to her sustained efforts to use her passion for creative writing to include the African woman's perspective in African literature. Although African literary critics like Obioma Nnaemeka (1995) focus on the feminist contributions of Nwapa's works, and Chikwenye Okonjo-Ogunyemi (1995) provides a synopsis of those offers, much of the acclaim and criticism of Nwapa's works focus on the anthropological contributions of her creative works to African literary studies, while some examine her works as fictionalized autobiographical accounts. For example, Sabine Jell-Bahlsen sees Nwapa's works as contributions to the excavation of culturally identified Igbo practices among the Ugwuta Igbo while Marie Umeh contends that her fictional works are a window into her personal life. Umeh in her assay asserts,

> a re-reading of the novel and Nwapa's interviews with a number of critics, journalists, Nwapa's mother, brother, sisters, relations and friends, indicate that the story of Efuru is her story where Efuru plays the role of the author. In the late fifties, Nwapa's relationship with Gogo Nzeribe, a trade unionist, ended in disappointment, sadness, and anxiety. Gogo abandoned Flora after the birth of their child in 1959. . . . According to the plot, Efuru is a beautiful, successful, and kind trader who is unlucky in love and marriage. . . . Nwapa concludes that the success or failure of a relationship does not depend solely on the suitability of the bride, the bride price, or marriage ceremony, but rather on the man's maturity, character, social background, and inherited traits. (345–46)

Since *Efuru* is presented as a fictional work, it is difficult to draw a one-to-one relationship between its main character and the author. Although and because of interviews the author granted to journalists and literary critics, it is necessary to distinguish questions of verisimilitude in a fictional work from autobiographical accounts for a number of different reasons. For example, while *Efuru* addresses and examines questions about marriage relationships and customs, the novel also focuses on other types of relationships in the community. One such relationship that is central to Ugwuta people's lives in the novel is their relationship with both the lake and Uhamiri, the Woman of the Lake. The undisputed nature of the lake as part of every Ugwuta person's economic resource is further magnified by the community's assertion of the existence, in the lake, of Uhamiri, the Woman of the Lake who further enables access to that resource as a path to economic freedom for women without biological children. Especially, given the Igbo dictum that, "Wherever Something Stands; Something Else will Stand beside It," Nwapa's intertextual engagement of Achebe's *Things Fall Apart* makes it possible to see Efuru as having Uhamiri's authorization to this visible and female access to personal wealth and success. And, since according to Achebe, the Igbo "judged a man by the work of his hands" (19). then Nwapa's *Efuru* also provides some evidence of the workings of that worldview for the Igbo woman.

Anthropological research in this region has also identified some similarities that Ugwuta's Uhamiri bears to another water goddess, Ogbuide, known across most of Igbo land. Among some Igbo, Ogbuide is a full-fledged deity while in others, knowledge about this female deity has mostly retreated into dimly articulated socio-religious practices of the Igbo following colonial interference. Such withdrawals make it difficult to use only literary analytical frameworks to unravel the prevalence (or not) of this and other deities in the Igbo pantheon. While Ala, Ali, Ani or Ana, the Earth Goddess was re-introduced early in written creative works about the Igbo through Achebe's *Things Fall Apart* (1958), the Ugwuta female water deity Uhamiri was brought to readers' attention by Flora Nwapa in *Efuru*. Later, Achebe also presents the python of Idemili in *Arrow of God*; and later explores this deity in greater detail in *Anthills of the Savannah* (1987) using the character of Beatrice Nwanyibuife Okoh. However, this chapter is not about the intertextual dialogue between Achebe and Nwapa. Rather, I want to call attention to Nwapa's engagement of Igbo narrative arts and her use of relevant aspects of Igbo cosmology to address the Western-educated Igbo (Nigerian/African) woman's experiences in the new dispensation. This is not to say that there might not be any basis for Nwapa to have deployed her personal experiences through the questions she asks in all her works; creativity requires personal appraisal to inform the knowledge that enables a work's authenticity and success. At the time that Nwapa and other African women were gaining access to Western education in colonized African nations, the question of Africa's sons and daughters getting lost in western thought and culture was prevalent in many of those communities.

THE INVISIBLE AFRICAN FEMALE ELITE

Under special scrutiny, during this period, were the young women attending colonized Africa's secondary and tertiary educational institutions. However, although research and discussions about the growing community of Western-educated African men continue to note the connections between the men and their works as leaders in the new dispensation, there is scant discussion or information about linkages between the Western-educated women from that generation and their work or thinking about ongoing efforts for local and/or (inter)national advancement. For example, there is currently a growing body of work that continues to highlight the experiences and leadership trajectories of members of 'Old Boy's' networks (see: Nwakanma, 2010; Ochiagha, 2015). Much of ongoing research and consequent discussions focus on western-educated African men's experiences in early educational institutions like the Government Colleges in Nigeria and subsequent productivity (in all walks of life) of the men as individuals or groups. But infrequent mention is made about the ways in which female secondary school activities or university experiences are linked to the successes of the emerging populations of Western-educated African female elite. For example, although both Mabel Segun (a contemporary of Chinua Achebe) and Flora Nwapa attended University College, Ibadan, and have published their creative works, these two women are rarely mentioned in the same sentence in African (or Nigerian) literary studies. For the most part, Nigeria's female university graduates from that period suffered many anxieties as a result of their efforts to fit into the then quickly developing communities of Africa's Western-educated elite. Chinua Achebe addresses this problem in his second novel, *No Longer at Ease* (1960) through his portrayal of Clara Okeke's character. Obi Okonkwo does not marry Clara because she is an *osu* (an outcast group among some traditional Igbo communities). Although Obi Okonkwo's parents converted to Christianity, they strongly oppose the union because of Clara's identity as an *osu* in the tradition. While the *osu* system is part of Igbo socio-religious practice, the problem is also escalated by the fact that the new Igbo elite was also beginning to identify Western-educated Nigerian (Igbo/African) women as part of a group labeled "acada" (academic women) as different from the emerging and dominant voices of the new western-educated male elite. Functioning as a socio-economic label for excluding western-educated African females, the acada designation quickly identified educated girls and women (sometimes as early as late elementary school) who either aspired to, or acquired, a western education as unfit for marriage.

Frequently, that exclusion was supported using Western Christianity and access to a Christian school education where girls and young women were taught about the benefits of becoming good wives whose socio-economic well-being was supposed to depend on their husbands' successes. It is significant to note that formal socialization of female children as economic dependents of men in the framework of the new imperative was not supportive of traditional Igbo/African thought about a "good" wife as a hard-working woman. The notion of wives as economic dependents, stay-at-home women/mothers is one that still struggles to find a solid foothold (as a result of women's resistance!) in contemporary African communities. What is instructive is that, as the Ghanaian writer Ama Ata Aidoo and other Western-educated African women elite have indicated, via interviews and other works, female children's desire for and, sometimes entry into the western educational environments usually received strong support by their fathers. In her novel, *Nervous Conditions* (1986) Tsitsi Dangarembga takes the discussion further to examine a situation (familiar to elders who craft and maintain stability in many African communities), in which every family must find a way to continue in the absence of a male heir in the new Western-oriented, post-colonial dispensation. In *Nervous Conditions*, Tambu's education (after the death of Nhamo, her favored-for-Western-education-success brother) by Babamukuru and the subsequent examinations of women's eligibility in the evolving post-colonial African communities is instructive. Tambu's insertion into the evolving paradigm is in line with Ifi Amadiume's presentation about issues of (lineage and leadership) succession and collaboration in her seminal work about Nnobi Igbo in *Male Daughters, Female Husbands* (1987). A significant portion of early African women's creative works address this apparent conundrum as many newly Western-educated men and their tradition-oriented families (later, dissenting family members also included some western-educated women) found ways to exclude young Western-educated African women from the same spaces that the European colonizers had denied them access during colonization.

ON THE FEMALE SIDE OF THE NEW AFRICA

Flora Nwapa storms the male dominated literary terrain with many new and dangerous ideas including questions about the place of the Western-educated African woman in the new dispensation. She says that the character of Efuru was inspired by, "a woman [she] passed by while driving from Enugu to Onitsha, on the Agu Awka Road in Anambra State, Nigeria around 1961–1962" (Umeh 345). Nwapa's main narrative focuses on the apparently random nature and processes of inserting women into the new Africa. Significant in Nwapa's claim about that woman she passes by on the road is that she does not claim to know her—she is any woman that is on her way to somewhere.

In the traditional narrative format, the story would begin thus: "A woman came. And, she went to the market (or, to the farm); or, to the . . . " But here, Nwapa is writing a novel–a tradition of storytelling that does not recognize individual uniqueness in either the presentation or examination of that which is un-named. So, she names her character, Efuru–the lost (one?). Viewed from this perspective, then: Is Efuru lost as a woman, a wife, a mother, or a daughter of . . . in the evolving communities? Should her existence and experiences in the new spaces be appraised based on her own accomplishments only? What does her community think about women like her who embody most of their predominantly agrarian society's values but cannot or do not fulfil the ones about longevity in marriage relationships or childbearing in the family? These questions are important because Nwapa's exploration of Efuru's barrenness goes beyond her inability (as a daughter of Ugwuta and worshipper of Uhamiri) to have biological children; she does get pregnant and gives birth to a daughter Ogonim. Nwapa goes back to some of these questions in *Idu* (1970) in which the main character is able to maintain a lasting marriage relationship but does not have biological children. And the plot of *Idu* does not answer her questions about cultural clashes and the consolidation of different cosmologies that become more challenging as Nigeria rises to become a regional power.

Further, and similar to the plot trajectories in Achebe's works, Nwapa's works also begin to take on the challenges of the creation of national self-identity within ongoing projects of nation-building, advancement and success. Nwapa becomes more prominent in Nigeria's socio-political environment. She works as an educational officer in Calabar (southeastern Nigeria) and as Commissioner for Health and Social Welfare in eastern Nigeria.[2] Her different job postings to different parts of the country allow her to gain more insight and knowledge from those experiences and she continues to examine vexing questions about the evolution and roles of Ugwuta-, Igbo-and Nigerian womanhood from the precolonial period to contemporary times. Nwapa's creative use of her observations in this regard does not make Efuru a surrogate for Nwapa any more than Okonkwo is for Achebe in *Things Fall Apart*.

In her creative works, her narrative style, like those of her male contemporaries, fuses oral narrative and written (Western and African) fictional approaches by combining popular newspaper reporting and informal conversation forms. Her tone is direct and relies heavily on the oral modes. She engages the reader as though she or he is in the direct presence of the novel's narrator. This approach mimics the uncertain but authority-making approaches of the colonial and post-colonial leadership to storytelling. Although it makes for difficulty in gaining full access to point of view, this narrative style challenges both historical and narrative time as only the narrator (colonial administrators and teachers, the post-colonial African leadership?) seem to know certain information without a need to account for their sources. This narrative style is not the same one used in oral storytelling performances in which point of view is already built into various aspects of the story as well as the audience's culture. Nwapa's creative works engage an audience whose social perception is new but whose logic seems to both contradict and affirm itself as the narrator manipulates old and new metaphors in ways that emphasize the confusions and contradictions of the evolving new nation and its [potential] leaders.

For example, in *Women are Different* (1986), as Comfort and Rose wait for their three friends to come back to the train station, Comfort gossips about their school mate and communicates with Rose in pidgin English (6). In addition to the author's experimenting with pidgin English, Nwapa's narrator also points to the newness of pidgin English usage, especially in creative writing by women about women. Appropriately, only Comfort uses pidgin at this time in the story. Both the narrator's voice and tone position Comfort in a space that established her as someone who knows information that the other students do not have and is comfortable spreading the information while simultaneously seeking an entry point into their group. Comfort's character strengthens Nwapa's project about how women are at once different from men and different from each other; a perspective the author has been exploring since *Efuru*.

In *Women are Different*, the author begins to look at the differences between women by examining young female responses to the different opportunities they encounter early in life. Given the colonialists' normalization of sameness for Africans (for many Europeans at this time, Africans look alike!) and its consequences for African women during this period of socio-cultural and political transition, Nwapa eschews the examination of the individual girl-to-woman experience familiar in the bildungsroman by presenting to the reader, four different young women who enter a western, Christian-colonial boarding school for African females, and remain there, together, for several years. The four young women meet for the first time during the entrance examination the previous year. And three of them form a coherent but budding friendship before they meet Comfort again at the train station on their way to beginning their secondary school education. As they begin to get their bearings at the train station, their conversation is formal except for Comfort who speaks pidgin and "seemed to know everything about the school, and told the girls one story after another" (6).

Nwapa's narrative style enables the reader to share their sensation of arriving at a crossroads; a feeling that lasts for most of the novel's plot. Throughout the novel, and although Comfort's access to information pulls and keeps the young women together, it is difficult to ascertain how she knows what she knows. A plausible conclusion is that Nwapa deploys Comfort's character as a tool for the exploration and examination of the issues that the author finds necessary for a useful crafting and understanding of the female side of Nigeria's (Africa's) emerging communities during this resource-rich period in the history of African nations in conflict and transition. Comfort encompasses past and present knowledge as well as future expectations, including presentiments. But, as "Comfort," she is also an instance of the concept of "Nwaononaku," (the-One-Who-Dwells-in-Wealth)—Efuru's praise name—which Nwapa uses to both examine and underscore Efuru's approach and demeanor to the apparently conflicting experiences available to her in Ugwuta.

Nwapa's short stories examine women's responses in different types of relationships, including the institution of marriage. In *Wives at War and Other Stories* (1980), she uses the trope of the Nigeria–Biafra war to examine the lives of women. Although the stories in the collection do not all take place during the civil war, Nwapa engages the readers' imagination about the hostilities to evoke the idea of marriage and other types of male–female relationships as war. Many of the main women characters are western-educated and have attained a secondary- or university-level education; yet each woman ends up in a personal/domestic relationship in which she only possesses secondary roles and power, or none. While all the relationships do not end in marriage, each character works hard to assert personal authority in her life by observing the relationship's environment closely while listening intently for opportunities that enhance self-assertion. For example, in "Alpha," the story focuses on a male character, while the woman mostly functions as a listener—a sounding board for the male character's child-to-manhood dreams about the ideal male–female relationship. Alpha's narration of the desire he develops for the older Betty when he is a boy forms the backdrop for his unrequited feelings. As the story progresses, he develops a platonic relationship with Tonia to whom he tells the entire story of his erotic longings for Betty who he was hoping to marry. When, as a fully grown male, he finally tracks her down to her workplace, she does not recognize or acknowledge his devotion or desire for her. His narrative ends with the articulation of his disgust about Betty's independence, which is based on her personal and professional achievements.

Significant to Nwapa's engagement of the challenges facing women in the rapidly changing colonial and post-colonial societies is her focus on the ways in which her women characters' support each other through different experiences even when they have little or no opportunity for face-to-face interactions with each other. In "Alpha," Tonia's close observation of Alpha's relationship environments (she never meets Betty) enables her to decide whether or not she should marry him. In *Women are Different*, both Dora and

Rose are able to, through their close observation of and listening to different mutually intelligible relationship environments, decide whether to either stay in, or begin, a relationship with Dora's friend, Tunde.

TROUBLING QUESTIONS ON NEW IDENTITIES

Nwapa's creative works address some troubling questions about the challenges encountered by colonizing and colonized peoples, male–female relationships in a developing African nation, traditional African religions and Christianity, and intergenerational challenges in the socio-cultural arenas in a colonized nation as it becomes a post-colony. Engaging Nwapa's efforts to grapple with a multiethnic colonized nation makes it possible to begin to understand her creative agenda, especially with regard to her choices about style and voice. Of special interest is her decision, in all her works, to engage the reader directly in conversations about change. For example, where the missionaries (religion and social) and their cousins, the colonizers Politics and social), saw malleability in secondary-school-age young Nigerian women and the nation, respectively; Nwapa saw uniqueness and wealth arising from strength and difference.

Nwapa's *Efuru* begins her writing career by asking many of the inconvenient questions that remain of interest to practitioners of African literary studies. Buchi Emecheta's *The Joys of Motherhood* (1979) is at the top of the list of creative and literary analytical works that began to respond to some of Nwapa's questions about the polarization of women's lives and experiences when European cultures clash with Africa's. Over the years, literary critics have continued the discussions, engaging her insights and troubling questions. However, most of the conversations have focused on questions and portrayals of women, motherhood and marriage. But Nwapa continued to present the questions in different ways, undertaking her most creative responses to some of her own questions in the novel, *One is Enough* (1981). At first reading, the novel seems a continuation of the discussion about the consequences of childlessness for the new Igbo (Nigerian) woman—and unhappy marriage relationships. But Amaka's story also takes on questions about conflicts between traditional African practices, belief systems and Christianity in Africa. Beginning with the subject of woman-to-woman violence, Nwapa's narrator provides a detailed look into the ways in which women-as-mothers-in-law inflict emotional violence on their daughters-in-law. Even the dialog is emotionally violent and the childless Amaka is told that while she has been hoping to become a mother, her mother-in-law had already made sure that her son, Amaka's husband, had fathered two sons outside of what Amaka thought was still a happy and hope-filled marriage to Obiora. When she confronts her husband with the new (for her) information, Obiora not only confirms what his mother says but also begins to accuse Amaka of wanting to sleep with other men behind his back when she asks him about the mother of his two sons. She is relieved that she no longer has to worry about having children for him, especially sons. But she fights back when he tries to beat her. She eventually leaves him and moves to Lagos to start a new life for herself. When she meets Reverend Father McLaid, she decides that she likes him and begins a relationship with him.

Nwapa uses Father Mclaid's character to engage a number of questions that have been raised by other African writers of her generation, including Chinua Achebe. For example, where Achebe addresses the practice of the throwing away of twins among the Igbo, Nwapa goes further to explore what happens when twins are rescued by the missionaries. And, continuing with her practice of inter-textual conversations with Achebe's works, Nwapa takes the conversation one step further. In Achebe's *Things Fall Apart*, after Okonkwo's son Nwoye leaves home and joins the missionaries, he later becomes a catechist. Nwoye's son is Obi Okonkwo of *No Longer at Ease* (1960) who returns to a civil service job in Lagos, Nigeria after earning a degree in English Classics in England and is arrested on charges of bribery and corruption. Nwapa's creative and intertextual responses to the growing challenges of a post-colonial nation in crises take a closer look at emerging questions about the effects of colonialism's political patronage on the family and kinship systems in which Europe and Europeans claim African nations as extensions of their homelands (and part of their extended family systems?) based on colonization's efforts to re-create African nations' identity. As the family structure changes, Western Christianity also continues to work with the new European courts to encourage African women to be more feminine while discouraging their admission into the emerging socio-political leadership. In *One is Enough*, Nwapa explores the extent to which the combined efforts of the Christian mission, the Church and colonial imperatives were successful in crafting a new African identity through changing the family and kinship systems. Her explorations include the question: To what extent are African women's identities considered in the evolving new systems of patronage? In *One is Enough*, Father McLaid, the rescued twin who becomes a priest, tells Amaka how the Reverend Sisters take him to the Mission; "and . . . [he] became the property of the Roman Catholic church (sic) . . . Father Mclaid who was in charge of the parish gave me my name, Francis Ignatius Mclaid and adopted me" (71–72).

While the older Father McLaid is an adoptive parent, the younger Father McLaid is portrayed as both a member of the clergy (as a Reverend Father) and a biological father. The author asserts that based on Igbo (African) kinship system and practice, a father of any kind is not supposed to renege on his nurturing responsibilities—an idea that Achebe addresses in *Things Fall Apart* using Okonkwo's killing of Ikemefuna. After Okonkwo kills Ikemefuna and tries to absolve himself from blame by saying he was fulfilling the will of the Oracle, Obierika tells him, "It is the kind of action for which the goddess wipes out whole families . . . if the Oracle said that my son should be killed I would neither dispute it nor be the one to do it" (47). At issue here, are questions about adoption, surrogate parenting and other related arrangements used to protect and nurture children in the tradition and based on both religious and cultural beliefs and practices. The narrative also follows the older Reverend Father McLaid as he goes back to his native Ireland during the Biafra-Nigeria war, where eventually his adopted son is summoned to his deathbed. In that final deathbed scene, Nwapa focuses on the humanity of the clergy and the power that men have to install and reinforce rules as they encourage each other to "quit you like men" (I Corinthians 16:13, KJV). She confronts disturbing questions about the mutual humanity of European and Africans, including family relationships and resemblances, leadership succession practices and issues associated with both, similarities in kinship and other practices, mutual responsibilities for the futures of communities that come in contact with each other, including the future of the new nation as negotiations for developing local and international socio-political interactions devolve into "a shooting war" (72).

This novel also asks some difficult questions about African women's participation in the European and African communities' efforts to fulfil necessary "old-but-new" parenting (new nation-building project?) responsibilities. Nwapa's narrator engages the Western Christian Church's approaches to prevailing questions about the African family, especially parenting in general and, specifically, fatherhood. A significant aspect of the question revolves around the fact of the Church as a foreign entity whose rules authorize emerging post-colonial African family's understandings about marriage, parenting and beliefs and practices of worship and social justice. Some of the questions include: Should the citizens of colonized and post-colonial societies operate from the point of view of Christianity or local family and kinship traditions? Should local divorce proceedings favor long-standing traditional practices or those of the new Missions? Are the new "Cash Madams" better off when they stay in their marriages (modern or traditional); or, should they function within the confines of the new and evolving standards in which the leaders of the African churches collude with the colonizers (government and the new laws) to keep women outside of emerging leadership practices by insisting that they remain their husbands' dependents? Most of the questions remain unanswered as Nwapa steadily charts the different options available to Father Francis Ignatius McLaid (note the play on the names of Doctors of the Church), who although adopted by the Irish Reverend Father McLaid has no roots in either Nigeria or Ireland. As the older McLaid lies in his death bed in a hospital in Dublin, he tells his adopted son who has come to say his last goodbyes:

> My son . . . I am glad you have come to see me die. . . . Nigeria is different from Ireland in many ways. Many of us went into the order because there was nothing else to do. It's not so in your developing country. I should have given you a different kind of education if I had given it a thought at the time. You would have belonged more to your people, now you are neither here nor there. You have your own conscience; you should work out your own salvation . . . let your conscience guide you. (74)

Nwapa's portrayal of this deathbed scene packs the history of European adventurism that was part-fuel for the colonization scheme, the uncertainties of the colonizing enterprise and the different but difficult consequences for colonized African peoples. Father Francis Ignatius McLaid's mother converts to Christianity to give her twins a chance to life. She was the second wife of his biological father. His twin sister does not survive and his mother dies soon after. As the younger Reverend Father McLaid recounts the story, he and Amaka are lying next to each other in her bedroom. And, although she has been declared barren by both traditional healers and the European-trained doctors, their relationship results in Amaka's pregnancy. She eventually gives birth to identical twins; sons who look exactly like their father, the priest. Here, Nwapa plays with the idea of the twin heritage of colonized African nations: Are Amaka's children Irish or Igbo (Nigerian)? Which part of their inheritances should count toward their identities? Should they and their father, who is also a priest, claim their place in the old tradition or in the new and foreign imposition? Also, since their biological father must abandon them in order to fulfil his duties as a priest, how should their identity be constructed and nurtured? At the core of the conundrum of post-colonial African identities is the nature versus nurture debate. Abandoned by their Irish "grandfather" and his adopted son, their biological father, how should they proceed in the new post-colonial nation in which their mother must assert herself as a "Cash Madam" who has decided that one husband (as well as mother-in-law?) is enough.

The second part of Nwapa's exploration of these questions of traditional and the newly crafted African identities is Reverend Father McLaid's involvement with the soldiers. He is assigned as an adviser to the soldiers and he, ". . . ministered to their bodies and their souls" (75) at the army barracks. He uses his access to the military to help Amaka get contracts from the army officers. Eventually, he also becomes part of the new national government and is appointed a Federal Commissioner. His government portfolio evokes his alliances with the ex-colonial enterprise that enabled his adoption by the foreign missionaries. But his status within the new leadership also maintains the distance between him and his children. And, even though the Bishop gives him a dispensation, he decides not to leave the Mission or priesthood because he (and Amaka) interpret the fact that he does not die in the car accident as a sign of forgiveness that grants him the authority to finally accept Amaka's decision not to marry him; or, marry again.

Nwapa's engagement of the idea of African women and difference begins in *Efuru* and continues in her subsequent works. From the point of view of early Western feminisms, African women emanate from the same cultural place and praxis. Seen as essentially different from European and American women during this period, African women are mostly perceived and treated as looking and acting the same. Sometimes that perspective was also subscribed to by some newly Western-educated African women. Using Efuru, whose character was inspired by the woman on the Agu Awka Road, Nwapa's many-years-long discussion about differences between African men and women in general, and among African women, specifically, tries to unravel not just "where the rain began to beat us," to borrow Achebe's dictum, but also begins to identify and engage the rainmakers, local and foreign. Significant to Nwapa's explorations is the extent to which men-as-men, men-as-fathers, as well as men-as-husbands are known or knowable. And, even as her creative works encourage thinking about Igbo women's struggles to assert themselves in their communities, her examinations about marriage, family and community insist on the women's understandings about the fact that it is difficult to "know" the men they marry. The question of identity and identification arises early in *Efuru* during the main character's ceremonial visits to the market. In a conversation that ensues, the reader is told that the very beautiful bride, Efuru, is married to Adizua from a very humble background: "'He is not known. And nobody knows why she ever married him, and besides, not a cowrie has been paid on her head'" (18).

This conversation provides an early glimpse into inherent and niggling questions about women's choices and independence as the reader follows Efuru into a marriage relationship that she enters into and in defiance of custom and tradition. In *Efuru*, Nwapa introduces the fact that traditional Igbo communities are aware of the fact that women's individual lived experiences merit the development of coherent approaches to research (especially local) about women's social, political, economic and intellectual health. Nwapa portrays Efuru as having difficulty to marry and successfully have children. Ugwuta's Uhamiri, the Woman of the Lake, is Nwapa's main tool for the exploration of how the socio-religious experiences of traditional Ugwuta communities enabled their authorization of this particular consideration of women's individual differences and uniqueness as they make socio-economic choices that enhance their independence within the community. As she examines questions about barrenness at all levels throughout her works, Nwapa challenges accepted European and Western-educated Africans' notions of Africa as a barren continent—without history, culture and/or usable ideas. In *One is Enough*, Nwapa responds to Emecheta's use of *The Joys of Motherhood* to engage Efuru's thoughts about failed biological motherhood expressed in the novel's (*Efuru*) final paragraph.

Over the years, the more familiar (to the west and the Western-educated) arguments about African womanhood, childbearing and marriage presented in *The Joys of Motherhood* have gained prominence in Literary Studies, Anthropology, Women's and Social Studies classrooms across the West as well as in Africa's Western-style classrooms. This is not to say that Emecheta's work is off the mark. However, it does mean that there still is not enough information based on coherent research about traditional Igbo (African) thinking about women's lives and experiences. While Nwapa and Emecheta are both Igbo women, it is important to note here that Igbo cultural practices across Igbo land are nuanced and based on the specific practices of each sub-group.[3] In *One is Enough*, when Amaka goes back to Onitsha to present the twins to her people, some of the women who attend the party, ask if the twins were really Amaka's and begin to question their identity and authenticity, "It's the mystery of the father that baffles everyone, including Amaka's own people" (114). And, as with Efuru's character, the characters in *One is Enough* also, "speculated, they gossiped, yet they came to [Amaka], told her their problems and she gave them money" (116). About Amaka's wealth, the narrator says, "Their people believed that once God gave you wealth that you must share it with your relatives and in fact the whole village. The whole village had a right to your wealth because anybody among them could have had the wealth instead of you" (116).

Amaka's mother is happy with her success and refers to her as a lucky woman. The narrator says, "The kind of wealth she had was not bestowed on women at all, but men. . . . According to their belief, the two [wealth and children] did not go together. You either had children or you had wealth. Her own daughter had disproved this belief" (166–167). Throughout the novel *One is Enough*, the crucial use of Uhamiri as an alternate route to success for unique and different women is shelved. Instead, Nwapa links the contemporary women characters to both children and wealth, evoking discussions about the need for the women's independence, especially from men-as-husbands. This combined focus is frequently linked to the question of separation or divorce. After Amaka makes enough money to pay back the bride price so that she can be "absolutely free" (84).

In the meantime, the woman who gave birth to Obiora's two sons was also free of him because he had "refused to marry [her] conventionally (115) ... so she left with the boys" (84). But the social arrangements are such that Obiora can still bring his sons with him when he goes to visit Amaka during her visit home to present her twins (118). On the question of divorce and women's independence from marriage and husbands, Amaka ponders with Adaobi what would happen if she were to die before completely separating from Obiora. According to tradition, Amaka is still Obiora's wife despite the fact that they have not been living together for many years. She takes a crucial decision: "I will divorce him according to our custom, so when I die he will have no say. My property will go to my brothers or my uncles. He will have no claim whatsoever" (52).

Both Amaka's efforts to straddle the different cultures and processes that affect her life's decisions as well as the older Father McLaid's deathbed advice to his adopted son continue to go unheeded as post-colonial African nations and their leaders persist in ignoring the deep influences that European and African cultures have and continue to exert on each other and on the lives of their citizens; especially in Africa. Nwapa addresses this problem by entering a conversation with both Western Christianity and the legal systems that were imposed on African nations during the colonial era. Amaka's identical twins with Father Francis Ignatius McLaid inherit the mixed identities; they are offspring of both the old and new, the foreign and the local.

CONCLUSION

Flora Nwapa deserves the praise name, Nwaononaku (the One who Dwells in Wealth) as a complement to her given name Nwanzuruahu (the One-Who-is-Complete-in-Body). Given the Igbo practice of naming children to reflect and/or evoke circumstances for the named, Nwapa's creative endeavors show that she not only lived up to her name, but she used it effectively to affirm an enduring Igbo legacy of self-assertion. She deserves the title, "The Mother of African Literature." Using her knowledge of Igbo narrative arts, cosmology, socio-political craft, and her strong power of observation about the lives and experiences of Igbo women, she deserves her well-earned membership in the cult of Africa's educated elite among whom she left a legacy that makes her Ugwuta, Nigeria and her generation of Africa's knowledge seekers proud.

Her contributions to African literary studies will continue to inspire generations of Africa's female writers, Africanists, especially literary critics at home and abroad to look beneath the seemingly calm lake surfaces of Africa's encounters with Europe. Her innovative, expansive and instructive oeuvre will ensure that more women will join her in the search for further and coherent understanding of Igbo/African women's experiences within emerging post-colonial traditions in conflict and transition as African literary studies continues its engagement of the challenging journey toward understanding more of the Truth about African womanhood.

WORKS CITED

Achebe, Chinua. *Anthills of the Savannah*. Oxford, UK: Heinemann Educational Books,1987.
———. *No Longer at Ease*. Oxford, UK: Heinemann Educational Books Ltd, 1960.
———. *Things Fall Apart*. Oxford, UK: Heinemann Educational Books, 1958.
Amadiume, Ifi. *Male Daughters, Female Husband: Gender and Sex in an African Society*. London: Zed Books, 1987.
The Bible. I Corinthians 16:13. King James Version.
Dangarembga, Tsitsi. *Nervous Conditions*. Seattle: Seal Press, 1988.
Emecheta, Buchi. *The Joys of Motherhood*. Oxford, UK: Heinemann Educational Books Ltd, 1979.
Jell-Bahlsen, Sabine. "Flora Nwapa and Ugwuta's Lake goddess: Artistic liberty and Ethnography," *Dialectical Anthropology*, Vol. 31, 2007: 253–62.
Kalu, Anthonia. "Women in African Literature." Seminar. June 2000. (Special Issue: "African Transitions: A Symposium on the Continent's Engagement with Democracy").
Nnaemeka, Obioma. "Feminism, Rebellious Women, and Cultural Boundaries: Rereading Flora Nwapa and Her Compatriots." *Research in African Literatures*, Vol. 26, No. 2, Flora Nwapa (Summer, 1995): 80–113.
Nwakanma, Obi. *Thirsting for Sunlight*. UK: James Currey, 2010.
Nwapa, Flora. *Cassava Song and Rice Song*. Enugu, Nigeria: Tana Press, 1986.
———. *Efuru*. London, UK: Heinemann Educational Books, Ltd, 1966.
———. *One is Enough*. Enugu, Nigeria: Tana Press Ltd, 1981.
———. *Wives at War and Other Stories*. Enugu, Nigeria: Tana Press Ltd, 1980.
———. *Women are Different*. Enugu, Nigeria: Tana Press Ltd, 1986.
Nzeribe, Ejine Olga and Ebere Okereke. "Flora Nwapa: Pioneering Nigerian Administrator, Academic and Author," (April 21, 2016). Accessed on March 20, 2017. http://dangerouswomenproject.org/ at the Institute for Advanced Studies in the Humanities at the University of Edinburgh, Scotland. Accessed March 23, 2017.
Ochiagha, Terri. *Chinua Achebe and Friends at Umuahia: The Making of a Literary Elite*. UK: Boydell and Brewer; James Currey, 2015.
Okonjo-Ogunyemi, Chikwenye. "The Invalid, Dea(r)th, and the Author: The Case of Flora Nwapa, aka Professor (Mrs.) Flora Nwanzuruahu Nwakuche." *Research in African Literatures*, Vol. 26, No. 2, Flora Nwapa (Summer 1995): 1–16.
Segun, Mabel. *The Surrender and Other Stories*. Harlow: Longman Books, 1995.

Umeh, Marie. "Flora Nwapa as Author, Character, and Omniscient Narrator on 'The Family Romance' in an African Society." *Dialectical Anthropology*, Vol. 26, 2001: 343–55.

NOTES

1. Sometimes, at a few ALA conferences, Flora Nwapa would ask me to assist her in managing her book exhibit table and we would chat for a while. Other times, she asked me to manage the table for a few minutes when she needed to take a break. She was a great example, to me, of the hardworking Igbo woman as she accomplished her work—always with calmness, kind words and a smile.

2. Ejine Olga Nzeribe and Ebere Okereke. "Flora Nwapa: Pioneering Nigerian Administrator, Academic and Author," (21st April 2016). Accessed on March 20, 2017. http://dangerouswomenproject.org/ Institute for Advanced Studies in the Humanities at the University of Edinburgh, Scotland.

3. This is comparable to saying that British and American English evoke the same cultural norms. While both have the English language as a basic indicator for English-speaking cultures, history and other intervening variables provide markers for cultural and social differences between both cultures. This is comparable to the nuances between, for example, riverine Igbo on both sides of the River Niger, northern Igbo and south-eastern Igbo. Another consideration is that while Emecheta left Nigeria for Britain as a teenager, Nwapa did not.

Chapter 2

Uwa Umunwanyi, Uwa Oma

Flora Nwapa and Women's History and Culture in Efuru and Idu

Akachi Adimora-Ezeigbo

INTRODUCTION

Africa's literary history was given a remarkable boost and deeper resonance with the publication of *Efuru*, Flora Nwapa's debut novel that introduced and broadened African women's viewpoint in the burgeoning landscape of African literature. *Efuru* was number twenty-six in the African Writers Series (AWS) which was edited then by Chinua Achebe and published by Heinemann in London, in the United Kingdom. Her success in publishing the novel in 1966 brought the much-needed broader perspective to African literature, a gesture that meant the inclusion of women in the hitherto male-dominated literary culture. It is not difficult to imagine the passion that triggered and energized Nwapa's ambition to write a novel, a literary version of the great oral tales told and retold by her foremothers, the ordinary Ugwuta women, and passed on from one generation to another. It is exhilarating to reflect on the courage and determination that enabled her to go against the grain and create individualized, independent, and authentic women characters who were a match to the numerous strong male characters that populated the novels produced by her contemporaries, the celebrated male writers, such as Chinua Achebe, Cyprian Ekwensi, Ngugi Wa Thiong'o, T. M. Aluko, John Munonye, Elechi Amadi, Mongo Beti, and Ferdinand Oyono.

It is enlightening to ponder over Nwapa's words regarding her decision to write her groundbreaking novel. Nwapa was an interviewer's delight—a calm and attentive listener, a patient and confident speaker who made her points clearly and expressed her views lucidly and frankly. These were my impressions of her in 1989 when I interviewed her in the home of our mutual friend, late Nina Emma Mba, the distinguished feminist historian who was my colleague at the University of Lagos. Nina Mba was the author of the famous book, *Nigerian Women Mobilised: Women's Political Activity in Southern Nigeria, 1900–1965*. When I asked Nwapa the experience that inspired her writing of *Efuru*, her first novel, she replied:

> One day, on a drive from Enugu to Onitsha, the idea of *Efuru* came to me along that stretch of road called Agu Awka. I was cruising at a speed of 80 miles per hour. The idea came strongly and began to gestate. I started to write the story down at Onitsha. The urge to write was there and I went on and on. When I eventually finished writing it I got it typed. (*Gender Issues in Nigeria*, 89)

When I asked if she wrote it easily and rapidly, Nwapa immediately said she did and added:

> For me, the idea to begin writing was never consciously planned. It came suddenly. For me, writing was never chosen. Writing chose me. After writing, you don't know if you have written a good story. Sometimes you need courage to send it out; this is especially the case with new writers. After I had written *Efuru*, Chinua Achebe graciously accepted to read it and then sent it to Heinemann. I owe it to him—I mean the publication of the book. (89)

By writing and publishing *Efuru*, Nwapa made history and armed other women with the courage, the audacity and confidence to register their presence on the African literary scene. Her example provided a source of inspiration to other women—Buchi Emecheta is a good illustration—who courageously started writing. The "silence" was broken, inevitably. The long-drawn "absence" was finally exposed and remedied.

The voice of the traditional women artists returned to life again in the "written form" not only in Nwapa's voice, but also in the robust and confident voices of writers like Ama Ata Aidoo, Zaynab Alkali, Ifeoma Okoye, Tsitsi Dangarembga, Akachi Adimora-Ezeigbo, and so on. Indeed, her success is a legacy of empowerment to the African women writers across generations—from Buchi Emecheta, Zaynab Alkali, Yvonne Vera, Chimamanda Adichie, Chika Unigwe to Kaine Agary, Susan Kiguli and Yewande Omotoso. Today, the beneficiaries are hundreds of African women of all ages writing on the continent and in the African Diaspora since the publication of *Efuru* in 1966. "Their works seem to be a rewriting and reconstruction of the African woman in literature different from the construction of women's lives by their male counterparts" (Akachi Ezeigbo, "Options for Women's Development in Igbo Patriarchy . . . " 167).

Flora Nwapa could have chosen to write on any of the popular subjects such as culture conflict, politics, religious conflict, failure of leadership, communal or familial conflict and the struggle for power which preoccupied African male authors. Instead she chose to write about the lives and experiences of ordinary women from her community, exploring their activities in the home, on the farm, and in the marketplace as well as their relationships with fellow women and with men. Nwapa's peculiar choice of subject reminds one of Jane Austen's choice of subject for her remarkable novels in eighteenth-century England, when most male authors preferred to write about wars, religion, mercantile and territorial pursuits in foreign lands, great historical moments such as the French Revolution, crime, and the Industrial Revolution together with the upheavals that followed it. Interestingly, Nwapa's choice of subject for her fiction triggered similar thematic preoccupations in the works of female writers that wrote after her—Buchi Emecheta, Zaynab Alkali, Ama Ata Aidoo, Bessie Head, Mariama Ba, Ifeoma Okoye and a host of others. Her bold and innovative delineation of strong women characters and her remarkable recreation of the world of women—uwa umunwanyi—set her apart from all her male contemporaries, making her work, especially her early novels, a compelling site for the study or analysis of women's true condition and level of development in traditional Igbo society represented by the Ugwuta community. A researcher interested in the authentic lives of women in rural Igbo communities, their economic and social history must make Nwapa's *Efuru* and *Idu* primary texts to consult. When she began to write, the image and character of the African woman underwent a drastic change and became imbued with agency. Woman became a real human being who could think for herself, take independent and respectable actions and empower her people as well as her community. It is, therefore, my intention to analyze Nwapa's repositioning of the identity of Igbo women—which the male writers before her glossed over or misrepresented—by drawing a portrait of their lives that is historically and culturally authentic, especially in the pre-colonial and colonial period. *Efuru* and *Idu* are set in Nwapa's hometown, Ugwuta, where she was raised and received her early education. The social and economic history of the community, especially women's experience, is captured imaginatively with a powerful evocation of women's culture and patterns of existence in the areas of marriage, childbirth, motherhood, storytelling, worship of the lake goddess, Uhamiri, and commercial activities.

THEORETICAL AND PHILOSOPHICAL REFLECTIONS: NWAPA AND THE WORLD OF WOMEN

In Igbo culture, "uwa" literally means "the world"; but it also has a metaphorical as well as a symbolic meaning. In this paper, it is on the metaphorical meaning of the word that I focus and hinge my argument. There are different derivatives of the word—"uwa oma" (this is loaded with multiple meanings: beautiful world, good life, positive existence and experience); "uwa ojoo" and/or "chi ojoo" (bad world and/or bad luck, difficult life, misfortune); "uwa nmadu" (human existence or experience). My observations when I was growing up in my village coupled with some research I have done on the lives of Igbo women, especially in the Aguata Local Government Area where I come from, has enriched my understanding of the meanings of the concept of "uwa umunwanyi." My re-reading of Flora Nwapa's early novels, especially *Efuru*, based on the Igbo traditional society, using the concept enabled me to re-examine Nwapa's vision of women and women's existence, the motivation behind her graphic and authentic interpretation and recreation of their lives, and her revision and subversion of the interpretations by her male contemporaries.

Nwapa must have been disappointed when she read the novels by African male writers who wrote before her and encountered the "colourless women" (to use Emecheta's expression in an interview with me in 1989) that were portrayed in nearly every one of those novels. She must have told herself that the world of women (uwa umunwanyi) driven by the dynamic, individualistic and optimistic culture of Ndi-Igbo did not and could not engender self-effacing, dormant, dependent, and weak characters as she found in the novels she read. The women's story must be told by women, just as historians such as Nina Mba and Bolanle Awe were reconstructing African women's history. Predictably she resolved to do something about recreating women's lives, culture, and history in literature. She understood that there might be a few weak characters, but she was determined to give agency and active roles to her protagonists and other women they interacted with in her own novels; hence her delineation of strong characters like Efuru, the eponymous heroine of the novel *Efuru*, Ajanupu, Nkoyeni, Idu, the eponymous heroine of the novel *Idu*, Ojiugo, Uzoechi, and Nwasobi. Her symbolic use of the powerful lake goddess, Uhamiri (worshipped by divinely chosen women), to deepen the mythic content of her works is a strategy that gives importance and credibility to women. It shows that women are important and should be accorded respect and recognition. She was guided by the realization that Igbo women, especially Ugwuta women, were strong, economically active, independent-minded, and hard-working. As Nnolim bluntly and brutally puts it, "when Flora Nwapa started to write, she went on a demolition campaign of the main pillars of men's expectations of what constitutes decorum or approved manners on the part of women . . . as a feminist at heart, she must have been repelled, even horrified by Achebe's treatment of women. Women whom Achebe reduced to mere appendages to men, created helpless, dependent, and brutalized . . ." (6, 8).

In her desire to portray authentic women characters, Nwapa did not consider it out of place to include such details as women's banter and gossip which some male critics of her work found exasperating and "embarrassing" even. Charles Nnolim has this to say about Nwapa's style in her women-centered fiction:

> Flora Nwapa became the novelist of the traditional woman's point of view, the chronicler of their gossip and endless chatter. . . . It must also be pointed out that her early novels *Efuru* and *Idu* are crowded with innumerable characters engaged in wooden dialogue that tiresomely focuses on those "anthropological curiosities" that proved to be offensive to critics. (5, 16)

Incidentally these stylistic features of Nwapa's early novels which Nnolim denigrates in his speech have been commended by Ernest Emenyonu in an article published in *African Literature Today*. Describing what he calls Nwapa's "appropriateness of technique" in his essay, "Who Does Nwapa Write For?" Emenyonu praises "the way she reaches down to all her characters and communicates authentically at all their levels not excluding their idiosyncrasies and mannerisms which she manifests in their speech patterns to help reveal more and more the nature of the characters" (31). I have made similar commendable observations on Nwapa's "control of local colour, tonal inflections in dialogue and rhythms of rural lifestyle" in the two novels in an earlier article titled "Myth, History and Igbo Womanhood in Flora Nwapa's Novels" (68). As a reader of Nwapa's work, I find great delight in the light-hearted banter between women. They remind me so much of such friendly conversations when I was growing up in my village in which women made a lot of jokes with each other and threw in funny remarks when they were together. This mannerism is so characteristic of "uwa umunwanyi." There was a song women sang in my village then: "Umu nwanyi, jolibanu, na-aga; uwa unu bu nma nma" meaning, "Women, enjoy your lives, your world is a beautiful world."

It was the Ugandan feminist writer, Susan Kiguli, that said, "I am comfortable in the world of women" (15) while justifying the focus as well as the trends in Ugandan women's writing during the celebration of the 10th Anniversary of FEMRITE, the women writers' association in Uganda in 2006. I dare say that Kiguli is a writer who must have benefitted from

Nwapa's laudable example. Another young Ugandan woman writer, Goretti Kyomuhendo, must have been indirectly influenced by Nwapa's work as her assertion in the following excerpt indicates:

> As for my role as a woman writer, I can say that I am inclined to tell women stories and define them in their own voices and perspectives, so that other people can understand who they are. In my writings, I do not relegate the female writers to the peripheries of the narratives but rather make them active participants in the story being told. I also strive to highlight those "trivialities" that afflict the womenfolk so that I can bring them to the fore for the understanding and appreciation of society. (23)

It is right and logical to argue that Flora Nwapa is a writer that basks in the "sunshine" of the world of women. Her affection for and attention to women in her work is incontrovertible. She makes everyone have a say—both the pleasant and kind (Efuru and Idu) and the unpleasant and selfish (Omirima and Nwabuzo) characters. She has a profound understanding of the world of the women of Ugwuta, their joys, sorrows, agonies, frustrations, weaknesses, strengths, and triumphs. She recreates these natural, social, and historical phenomena with deep insight and imagination in *Efuru* and *Idu* and in some of her other novels and short stories. Her approach and achievement have proved infectious and inspirational, judging by the faithfulness and commitment of subsequent African women writers to issues relating to women. Perhaps the only exception to this rule is the enigmatic but prolific and now hardly discussed and almost forgotten novelist, Adaora Lily Ulasi, whose vision is essentially political and nationalistic, and whose interest has focused mostly on crime or detective fiction. Ulasi began publishing her works in 1970, four years after Nwapa brought out her first novel. Her thematic preoccupations tow a different line, as I observed in my article on her work and that of Nwapa (Ezeigbo, "From Absence to Presence: The Writings of Flora Nwapa and Adaora Lily Ulasi"). Though Ulasi has not focused on women specifically, Nwapa's publication of *Efuru* in 1966 must have motivated her (as it did Emecheta) to start writing, just as the publication of Achebe's *Things Fall Apart* inspired other African writers to embark on writing and telling their people's "story." In fact, this development gave rise to some critics categorizing some writers—John Munonye, Elechi Amadi, T.M. Aluko, Ngugi wa Thiong'o, I.N.C. Aniebo, etc.—as belonging to "the Achebe school."

No critic has used the expression "the Flora Nwapa school" to describe female writers that began to write after Nwapa. Perhaps this is on account of the divergence in technique and use of language in the works of African women writers, especially Buchi Emecheta, Ama Ata Aidoo, Bessie Head and Mariama Ba, to mention but a few. These writers focus on women's experience like Nwapa but use different approaches. A popular approach that women have used which Nwapa did not use in any of her five novels is the autobiographical technique or the diary mode used, for instance, by Mariama Ba in her award-winning novel, *So Long a Letter*. In the interview I had with Emecheta in 1990, she admitted that she wrote about "women's experience, the reality of women's lives and raising children" (103) but added, "My style is different from Flora Nwapa's, though both of us are from the same place. And there are peculiarities to certain areas and zones" (96).

The ideal women's world in Nwapa's fiction is one of perpetual activity, a beehive of industry in which a woman's hands find useful work to do. Idleness is a taboo and attracts severe censure. In *Efuru*, Omirima complains to Amede, Efuru's mother-in-law, that her own educated daughter-in-law is lazy and sleeps "until the sun is up" (193). Their disapproval and abhorrence of a life of idleness is starkly illustrated in the text.

> "This is bad. She is unlike our women. Where did she learn this foreign bad behavior?
>
> I thank God my daughter-in-law does not sleep till sunrise."
>
> "She learnt it from the white woman. That's what I told her . . . An idle
>
> woman is dangerous, so I told her to her face." (193–194)

In Nwapa's fictional world, as indeed in the Ugwuta community, keeping busy with work gives meaning to life, dignifies women's lives, and makes them economically independent.

UWA UMUNWANYI: THE WORLD OF SERVICE AND INDUSTRY

Uwa umunwanyi is a world of continuous activity—one activity blending into another from dawn to dusk. Nwapa captures this in her novels. For instance, women in *Efuru* wake up at dawn, prepare meals for their families, feed their children, and then go to the farm or to the market to sell their goods. When they return from the market, they go in pursuit of debtors who owe them money, as Efuru and Ajanupu do routinely. The omniscient narrator tells us that when Ajanupu goes to collect Efuru's money from Nwabuzo, she "sat down on the mat and stretched her legs. She was determined to stay there till doomsday" (*Efuru*, 47). She refuses to leave Nwabuzo's house until she collects the debt. After visiting their debtors, the women return home to prepare evening meals for the family or to attend other pressing engagements. Nwapa recreates the day-to-day activities of the women in minute details. What comes out most forcefully is their industry and unrelenting effort to live a life committed to service. Leith-Ross who lived in Eastern Nigeria had observed this resilience and diligence among Igbo women, even before Nwapa began to write, and had described Igbo women as a "rare and invaluable force, thousands upon thousands of ambitious, go-ahead, courageous, self-reliant, hardworking, independent women" (337). This is the type of women Nwapa recreates in her works.

Uwa umunwanyi also connotes the life of service in Nwapa's works. This rendering of service is not limited to the women's families. In the two novels under study, one sees several instances where women give service to the community or to individuals in the town. Efuru and Idu are famous for their philanthropy. Efuru gives financial support to people, especially to Nwosu and Nwabata, Ogea's parents, whom she lends money without interest and provides their other needs. She also pays the bills for Nwosu's surgery and for Nnona's protracted treatment in the hospital. It is important to note, although this is outside the scope of this paper, that the finest illustrations of women's life of service are explored in Nwapa's fiction on the Nigerian Civil War—also known as the Biafran War. Nwapa concentrates on women's activities and win-the-war efforts in her novel, *Never Again*, and in her collection of short stories based on the war, *Girls at War and other Stories*. She recreates women's efforts to grow food as members of a parallel force called the land army, their provision of food and other services to the armed forces during the war. Nwapa gives the impression that uwa umunwany, the world of women, recognizes the dignity of labor, and sees service as a prerequisite for a self-fulfilled life. Efuru, for instance, derives enormous satisfaction from her life of service to her people and her total devotion to the worship of Uhamiri so much so that when her second marriage breaks down like the first and she returns to her father's house, she finds consolation in these two self-fulfilling activities, in spite of her childlessness.

The impression one comes away with after reading Nwapa's novels is that Ugwuta women would not expect their husbands to be sole breadwinners, rather they believe in the Igbo proverb that says, "Aka wete, aka wete, o ju onu" meaning "When different hands fetch food, the mouth is filled." This proverb underscores the fact that both husband and wife must contribute to the maintenance of the family. In the two novels, some of the women support their husbands in economic activities—Efuru is the brain behind the success of the trading she did with her first husband, Adizua, and later with her second husband, Eneberi. Idu also joins forces with her husband, Adiewere, and their trade prospers. In the same vein, Nwabata is fully involved in Nwosu's business and encourages him. The women are not only the custodians and watchdogs of culture and tradition but also give their men useful advice and assistance. For instance, Efuru is apprehensive that Eneberi's imprisonment might be a result of his involvement in a case of theft and only regains her peace of mind after he assures her of his innocence. Conversely, the younger wife, Nkoyeni, is doubtful of Eneberi's moral probity and makes trouble for him on account of this.

In the novels, the world of women goes beyond economic and domestic activities to include social engagements and recreational preoccupations. Efuru and other women are fully involved in their age-group activities, especially in bonding and supporting one another in times of bereavement and other personal traumas and misfortunes. When Efuru loses her only child, Ogonim, her age group consoles her, takes her to the stream to have her body thoroughly cleansed, wash her clothes and feed her (77). Much later, when Eneberi charges her with adultery, she is strongly supported by members of her age-group who take her to the shrine of the goddess, Utuosu, where she is absolved of the offense.

Another aspect of the world of women that Nwapa gives much attention is their involvement in recreational activities. The lake inhabited by the goddess, Uhamiri, is strategic in the women's lives for life sustenance (as a source of fish and drinking water). It is equally important as a place of recreation where the women, their men and children go regularly to swim, to keep fit and clean their bodies. It is also a site for relaxation. Some of Efuru's most happy moments in the novel are the times she goes swimming first with Adizua and later with Eneberi. Omirima and a few other women gossip, criticizing Efuru for the enjoyment she derives from indulging in this exercise with her first and second husbands. Another recreational activity is dancing—both men and women go dancing in *Efuru*.

UWA OJOO: FLORA NWAPA'S TRAGIC VISION

There is ample evidence that Nwapa sees uwa umunwanyi—the world of women—as essentially a beautiful one. The pleasure of bonding, the joy of living life fully and looking out for one another in sometimes a very affectionate manner are ways that the beauty of the women's world is felt in the novels. However, Nwapa also shows that even in this beautiful and busy world, tragedy strikes, sorrow and pain are all too visible. They intrude from time to time to remind the people that life is full of ups and downs. They affirm that life is a mixture of pleasure and pain, joy and sorrow, and peace and strife. The novels have their fair share of misfortunes as well as successes and triumphs. In spite of happy beginnings, Efuru's two marriages end badly and each time she returns to her father's house where she began. Disappointed a second time, this time by Eneberi, Efuru is angry because she has once more loved in vain. She is ultimately infused with rancor and resentment which are traits alien to her nature (209). She loses her only child, but her husband Adizua does not return home even though he is sent for. Again, when her father dies, Eneberi is nowhere to be found and thus fails to play the vital role of a son-in-law at Efuru's father's funeral. Responding to a question I asked during our interview about Adizua's treatment of Efuru, Nwapa says, "There are people who are irresponsible . . . Efuru's tragedy is that she gave her love to a worthless man. It is a calamity for such a fate to befall such a splendid woman" (92). This is a case of bad luck, uwa ojoo/chi ojoo.

Other women suffer one form of misfortune or another. The pregnant Idu loses her beloved husband, Adiewere, and consequently loses interest in life and wills herself to die. In the interview, Nwapa comments thus: "Human behavior is not always guided by logic. Sometimes things happen in life that seem unnatural. Having lost her husband, certain things that seemed important to Idu before now lost their significance" (91). Other misfortunes in the novels include the experience of Nwosu and Nwabata who always lose money at each farming season, especially when it comes to selling the farm produce. They work so hard, yet they are always in debt; Amede, Adizua's mother, is beset by misfortune in the type of man she married and the type of worthless son that is the only fruit of that most unhappy marriage. In *Idu*, Ojiugo's childlessness compels her to leave her beloved husband, Amarajeme, for a more virile man who gets her pregnant. In utter humiliation and despair, Amarajeme commits suicide. Nwabuzo and her husband lose their merchandise in the Great River when their boat capsizes and when they change to trading in "gari," all their bags of "gari" are ruined by an unusually heavy rain.

I am of the view that the tragic occurrences in Nwapa's novels are a confirmation of the Igbo philosophy that "onweghi onye uwa zuru" meaning "there is no one in the world that has a perfect life." The Igbo believe that no one can completely escape from life's misfortunes. There is a song that says: "O dighi onye odiri na nma n'uwa; ezi enyim, gwam onye obu ka nkuoro ya aka" meaning "There is no one for whom everything is perfect in this world; my good friend, show me such a person and I will applaud him/her." In spite of the troubles they encounter in their lives, Nwapa's women remain optimistic and strive to overcome them, seeing the troubles as "uwa ojoo"—life trial or bad luck—that afflicts people in the course of their earthly journeys.

As a reaction to these devastating experiences and situations in Nwapa's novels, Nnolim describes her as "a writer of the tragic vision" (15). Nnolim is entitled to his opinion, but it is baffling that he goes on to make some other comments which seem misplaced in relation to Nwapa's novels, especially the two we have analyzed in this paper:

> In sum, a reappraisal of Nwapa's canon leads inevitably to the conclusion that her works devoid of humor, both in style and content. There are no moments of general laughter in Nwapa, no sly digs that elicit a chuckle as we see in Achebe or Munonye . . . Nwapa is not a novelist of the comic vision, for comedy celebrates a world at peace which finds its apotheosis in laughter and cheer. And there is little to cheer in Nwapa . . . Nwapa never finds the spectacle of human life either amusing or entertaining. (14)

On the contrary, there is humour in Nwapa's works. I would like to draw one or two illustrations from *Efuru*. The first occurs when Nwosu and Nwabata visit Efuru and find her laughing heartily with Ogea. It was all about the joke on the little boy, Emska, who burst into tears because he had been granted permission to go home when he was actually looking forward to a hot meal, No sooner had the food been offered to Emeka wiped his eyes quickly gulped down the food (98–99).

In another instance, Efuru and Ajanupu are bantering about the doctor, Difu, who has gone abroad to study again at his advanced age. They are discussing the terrible cold in the country that the doctor has to endure. Ajanupu prays that God would not allow her to ever go overseas. Efuru bursts out laughing, telling her that God has already answered her prayer for neither of them can go there as they do not "know book." Ajanupu also laughs heartily saying, "That's it, you are right" (164). Moreover, there is infectious humor in the scene where Eneberi and Sunday, his soldier friend, banter, teasing each other and recalling the experiences of their youth (188–191). The final illustration is the time Ajanupu's little daughter clutches a piece of yam in her sleep so that her brother, Ifeanyi, will not eat it (82). These are hilarious scenes but, for want of space, it is not possible to give the full details of the incidents. I disagree with Nnolim's verdict that Nwapa's work is "devoid of humor" and that "Nwapa never finds the spectacle of human life either amusing or entertaining" (verdict in an unpublished lecture).

CONCLUSION

The year 1966 when Flora Nwapa's *Efuru* was published represents a watershed in African literature. Nwapa is historically, thematically, and stylistically important in not only Nigerian but also African literature. She shattered the wall of silence that excluded African women from joining the men in the creation of the nascent African literature. For this she will always be remembered and celebrated. She was the first female writer from Nigeria and after her a harvest of literary productions was garnered in the next two or three decades. Her work has been innovative and original in the choice of subject matter, form, and style. She made fashionable what was then considered unnecessary and unappealing—the recreation of strong and economically independent female characters. Her work is women-centered, and her perspective is feminine. Nwapa's fictional universe that I call uwa umunwanyi—the world of women—is a dynamic one where women live their lives fully, plying their trade and taking care of their families.

Perhaps Nwapa's greatest contribution to African literature is the fact that she started an alternative tradition which complemented and enriched the literary tradition put in place by such prominent writers as Chinua Achebe, Wole Soyinka, Ngugi wa Thiong'o, Cyprian Ekwensi, Camara Laye, Mongo Beti, Sembene Ousmane, and others. She introduced the voice of women into the literary terrain and threw the door wide open for those coming behind her to enter. Being deeply rooted in Igbo culture, she has been able to explore with remarkable insight the world of women and recreate authentically women's lives and vicarious experiences, to give them agency in works where they are protagonists. Her major legacy is creating an opportunity and a good environment for other women writers to emerge and grow, chart a direction for their writing and delineate characters who are confident and who know what they want from life. Her work was not appreciated initially by male critics, but this did not deter her as she had a vision to inspire and empower women, as writers and characters. By so doing she made the emergence of a crop of women writers possible and the reconstruction of women's culture, social and economic history. By setting her first two novels on the solid ground of her Ugwuta homeland, she imbued her work with realism and authenticity.

WORKS CITED

Achebe, Chinua. *Things Fall Apart*. London: Heinemann, 1958.

Awe, Bolanle. Ed. *Nigerian Women in Historical Perspectives*. Nigeria: Sankora Publishers, 1992.

Ba, Mariama. *So Long a Letter*. Trans. Modupe Bode-Thomas. Ibadan: 1981.

Emenyonu, Ernest. "Who Does Flora Nwapa Write For?" *African Literature Today*, No. 7 (1975): 28–33.

Ezeigbo, Akachi. "A Chat with Flora Nwapa" in *Gender Issues in Nigeria: A Feminine Perspective*. Lagos: Vista Books, 1996.

———. "Conversation with Buchi Emecheta" in *Gender Issues in Nigeria: A Feminine Perspective*. Lagos: Vista Books, 1996.

———. "From Absence to Presence: The Writings of Flora Nwapa and Adaora Lily Ulasi." A paper presented at the Women Writers of Nigeria (WRITA) Creative Writing Workshop and the Celebration of the 70th Birthday of Mabel Segun, sponsored by the British Council in Lagos, 1999.

———. "Myth, History and Igbo Womanhood in Flora Nwapa's Novels." Marie Umeh Ed. *Emerging Perspectives on Flora Nwapa*. Trenton, NJ: Africa World Press, 1998: 51–75.

———. "Options for Women's Development in Igbo Patriarchy: The Dynamics of Flora Nwapa's Womanist Interventions."*Unraveling Gender, Race and Diaspora*. Eds. Obioma Nnaemeka and Jennifer Thorington Springer. Trenton, NJ: Africa World Press, 2016: 165–177.

Kiguli, Susan. "FEMRITE and the Woman Writer's Position in Uganda: Personal Reflections." A Presentation at the 10th Anniversary of Femrite, the Ugandan women writers' association, in Kampala, Uganda, in 2006.

Leith-Ross, S. *African Women*. London: Faber and Faber, 1939.

Mba, Emma Nina. *Nigerian Women Mobilized: Women's Political Activity in Southern Nigeria, 1900–1965*. Berkeley: University of California Press, 1982.

Nnolim, Charles. "Flora Nwapa: Writer as Woman." An unpublished Lecture delivered to the members of the National Association of Students of English Language and Literature (NASSELL), University of Port Harcourt, November 22, 1996.

Nwapa, Flora. *Efuru*. London: Heinemann. 1966.

———. *Idu*. London: Heinemann, 1970.

———. *Never Again*. Enugu; Nwamife, 1975.

———. *One is Enough*. Enugu: Tana Press, 1982.

———. *Wives at War and Other Stories*. Enugu: Tana Press, 1980.

———. *Women Are Different*. Enugu: Tana Press, 1981.

Ulasi, Adaora Lily. *Many thing You No Understand*. London: Michael Joseph, 1970.

———. *Many Thing Begin for Change*. London: Michael Joseph, 1971.

———. *The Man From Sagamu*. Glasgow: Fontana, 1978.

———. *The Night Harry Died*. Lagos: Educational Research Institute, Nigeria, 1974.

———. *Who is Jonah?* Ibadan: Onibonoje, 1978.

Chapter 3

Flora Nwapa, Feminism, and the Burden of History

Kemi Wale-Olaitan

INTRODUCTION

Flora Nwapa remains the acclaimed mother of female African writings; any study of the development of African literature cannot be complete without the acknowledgement of the contribution of this major female voice that changed the perspective of African writings with the publication of her eponymous novel, *Efuru*, in 1966. This intervention became necessary because of the long domination of the literary firmament by male writers. A female scholar, Chikwenye Okonjo-Ogunyemi once observed that African writings at the initial stage consisted of male writers who had no sisters (60). Another scholar, Lloyd Brown, a male, actually commented that "African literature has to be understood as a literature by African men," and he lamented the fact that the "ignoring of African women writers on the continent has become a tradition, implicit, rather than formerly stated, but a tradition nonetheless-and a rather unfortunate one at that" (3). The fact that women were not given the opportunity to get education early affected their output, such that female writings came on the literary scene later than the writings of their male counterpart. The writings of the males focused more on male issues, while feminine issues and female characters were not their concern. According to Bryce, feminine issues were couched in "absences" and "silences" (3). Thus, the coming of Nwapa onto the literary scene changed all that, and she was able to write back into existence the reality of life of the African woman. She thereby, "subvert(s) and demythologize(s) indigenous male writings and traditions which seek to label [women]" (Nfah-Abbenyi, 6). This notable achievement, however, is yet to be given enough critical attention. Not only has the first work not been appropriately situated among the literary canons in African literature, controversy still rages on whether Nwapa's works or in fact any female African literary work could be accepted as feminist writing or not.

When Flora Nwapa started out on her writing journey, it was to respond to the male writers who were writing about their unique African experiences from the male perspectives, depicting only male characters who were heroes of their society. In the works of these male writers, female characters were "absent" or "silent" and issues of concern to the female gender were nowhere to be found. Therefore, Nwapa took it upon herself to rewrite history, as it were, by writing a feminine novel with a major character who is a female, and the main issues of concern as feminine issues. Thus, 1966 became a turning point in the history of African Literature and remains a critical date in the history of female writings in Africa.

No doubt, Nwapa has done well in highlighting women issues and bringing it to the front burner; she has written the female gender "back to life," as it were, and this is an effort that cannot be over-emphasised. However, she writes within the confines of patriarchy, and struggles to highlight those issues that denigrate women, thereby leading the unofficial movement against the oppression of women. This action presents Nwapa in a bright light manifesting her activist zeal and earning her the label of a feminist.

However, Flora Nwapa lived at a time when feminism was just making an inroad into African scholarship, so many female scholars then were sceptical about the label and a few others rejected the idea of being labeled. While Ghanaian female writer, Ama Ata Aidoo, is of the opinion that African foremothers were feminists, Nwapa on her part was not so keen on being labeled as one. The focus here is to re-examine the writings of Nwapa, especially the seminal work, with a view to re-assessing the impact of her writing on the literary works of other female African writers; but more importantly, to call attention of contemporary scholars to the need to "rethink" the ideological position of the author, more than fifty-five years after the publication of her novel, *Efuru*. It is also necessary to appropriately (re)locate her works among the literary canons conditioned by the African environment, rather than allow them to continue to be bogged down by Western hegemonic ideas. This is the focus of this chapter.

BACKGROUND

In today's rapidly changing world, especially with the fast development of the globalized world system, every aspect of life has been influenced by globalization; the world has truly become a village. No part can lay claim to any separate idea that is unique to its locale; and feminine issues have gone beyond the moral sensitivity to a more concrete specificity within the global system. There are diverse interests in feminine issues now, and the concerns and experiences of women now receive more attention, yet the interplay of culture, history and socio-economic differences is making the realities more complex and difficult to comprehend. However, to understand the tapestry of views, especially when it concerns women in developing countries, especially African women, it is important to go back in time, as it were, to examine the background in order to be able to ground the realities. This is why such works as Flora Nwapa's fictional writings are very important in helping to present the view from the past and the perspectives of the cultural society, against the backdrop of an ever-changing society. In the particular case of Nwapa, it is important to acknowledge that she has infused into the African literary discourse, what Nfah-Abbenyi, quoting Gay Wilentz, refers to as "generational and cultural continuity" of and for African women" (6).

The ambivalent stance of Nwapa on the issue of feminism was not peculiar to her, but was a position taken by many of the female scholars then. The point truly is that the definition and perception of the idea was not really grounded in African values. While some of the females believed that the concept actually negated the cultural values of Africans, others believed that as long as it presents the woman in a positive light, then it can be accepted. However, when put in proper perspective, it is possible for female scholars to embrace feminism and actually relate the concept to women development. Little wonder Nwapa eventually embraced the idea because of what she perceived as "possibilities" that could aid women's "choices." She stated, in a write up later, that her interest was simply to project the females in positive light and highlight the good roles of the females within the African society. She explains that

> [W]hile some Nigerian male writers failed to see this power base, this strength of character, this independence, I tried in Efuru and Idu to elevate the woman to her rightful place. Unlike African male writers, I could overlook neither the safeguards with which custom surrounds the woman in her community nor the weight of women's opinions. I tried to analyze the woman's independent economic position and the power she wields by the mere fact that she controls the pestle and the cooking pots. ("Women" 93)

Thus, from the perspective of the emerging scholarship at the time, Nwapa's work manifests feminism as she tries to "elevate the woman to her rightful place" and this fits the variety of agitation for different demands made by women at the initial stage of the feminist movement.

Feminism itself has continued to attract controversies as a result of the historical development that presents variety of perspectives of the idea. When it first developed, it was a sociological movement, described as "a wide and changing movement, seeking in various ways to raise women's social status" (Randall, 4). It should be noted that the idea was not presented as a single perspective, as there existed, through historical developments, many variants of the woman question and the response to it. The idea took off as a movement which began fighting the unfavorable treatment of women and debating the need to ascribe intelligence and humanity to them. It was developed by women in the West, with leading names like Mary Astell, Catherine Cockburn and others. Later, the likes of Mary Wollstonecraft introduced the political dimension during the French Revolution, which led to the development of the Suffragette movement in the United States. And finally, Betty Friedan came up with the economic perspective by leading the female movement against the Industrial Revolution which made women redundant. This is to suggest that the movement and idea for the promotion of women interests could take many forms particularly depending on what the women consider as pressing at any point and also relating to those organizing the agitation and movement. According to Jaggar, "Feminists are united by a belief that the unequal and inferior social status of women is unjust and needs to be changed. But they are deeply divided about why changes are required (and how to effect them)" (5).

These varieties of perspectives about the unequal and inferior status manifest also in the different literatures of the people. For African female writers, the "silences" and "invisibility" that characterize male presentations of females in the early writings needed to be confronted and corrected; and this was what Nwapa did with such candor. It was such "invisibility" (a denigration of the humanity of the female), that feminism came to address, when African women writers began to write their gender into existence in the 1970s and 1980s (Rege, 4556). Therefore, Nwapa' s label as a feminist could be accepted as a manifestation of the idea in her work. She thus, set a unique example for other female writers to emerge and continue the tradition. It should therefore be expected that the incursion of the feminist tradition and sensibility into the literary field would produce diverse viewpoints on what constitutes a feminist reading in literature particularly as feminism is no more than a recent but growing addition to the canons of literary criticism.

What is and should be important is that other female writers took a cue from Nwapa and thus started the corpus of writing by African women all demonstrating not just an awareness of the denigrating position of women, but consistently canvassing various ways of overcoming them such that women could have a positive image in society. This is why, in her description of the uniqueness of Nwapa's works, Marie Umeh explains that "Nwapa unleashed a vibrant creative energy and began a female tradition in African letters that successfully confronted the one-dimensional, stereotypical portrayal of women as 'femmes fatales and ne'er do wells'" (118). As a matter of fact, the novel of Nwapa changed the literary landscape of Africa and actually began the process of "feminizing" the literature as she portrayed varied female characters—devoted mothers, dutiful wives, committed priestesses, enterprising market women and dynamic womenfolk propelled by diverse goals and aspirations. We undoubtedly cannot deny a central place for Flora Nwapa and her Efuru in the corpus of African literature to the extent that the representation of female characters changed as a result of her incursion.

NWAPA AND THE FEMINIST CRITICS

In their reaction to both the unfair treatment faced under patriarchy and the misrepresentation of their works by western critics, female African scholars started writing more about the experiences of their lives; this attracted more critical attention to the works. In this regard, many critics have called attention to many shortcomings in the writings of Nwapa, Most especially, they have critiqued the absence of deep feminist instinct while suggesting that her works do not approach helping to raise the bar genuinely for African women. What is clear however is that these critics, rather than analyzing the African writings based on the realities that are being experienced and which they were writing about, mainly seek to impose the western kind of feminism on the writings of African women. In her unabashed criticism of the theoretical imposition of Western analysis on African writings, Obioma Nnaemeka expresses deep concerns about the blatant distortions of the works of African women writers by feminist critics in the name of "feminist criticism" (81). She criticizes the feminist analysis of African writings without the consideration of the reality of the African experience; and being "outsiders" without the understanding of the inner workings of the African traditional societies, Nnaemeka sees no justification for the arrogation of the authority as a "savior" to rescue African women from the "patriarchal bondage." Indeed, this is the sense in which African female scholars have criticized the feminist theory as a tool of cultural imperialism and many have rejected its imposition. However, in the absence of a widely acceptable framework that could take into consideration all the ideas and issues bothering on cultural values raised by critics of feminism, African scholars remain stuck with the idea. However, some have decided to modify feminism to suit the African worldview, creating African feminism, African womanism, stiwanism, negofeminism, femalism, motherism and suchlike.

FLORA NWAPA AND THE FEMINIST PERSPECTIVE

Feminism became an issue in the discussion of female writings in African literature in the early days of analyzing such works and continues to occupy a significant position; yet, the debate is ongoing, and scholars still remain "in the trenches" as it were, trying to figure out the best possible way to address the issue. The controversy generated among scholars and writers alike became a major issue which obfuscated almost all other issues that were of concern to African women. In fact, the debate ensued then on whether Feminism should be accepted by African women; or whether African women could adopt the idea that issued from the Western context.

Nfah-Abbenyi, a female African scholar, puts the argument in proper perspective:

> Owing to the diverse nature of these voices, it becomes problematic for African women to adopt the word "feminist" that does not adequately speak their experiences but those of a particular Western/privileged group of women, a word that, when used in their African socio-cultural contexts, is often loaded with pejorative connotations. Often, when an African woman is associated with feminism or directly labelled as a "feminist," such labelling incongruously defines her as Western, meaning that she is either condemned of not credited for what she is or does because she is said to be deviant or simply imitating Western women (a negative statement). (11)

This statement encapsulates the situation the African woman finds herself at this period; and while the controversy rages on, Flora Nwapa could not help but be caught up in the debate and eventually, she became confused and could not choose consistent side in the debate, as noted in the quotation earlier. This apparent inconsistency arose as a result of the lack of clear understanding of what the full idea of feminism means for the African woman.

Many female African scholars continue to argue that the idea of feminism is not holistic enough to be able to explicate the unique experiences of the African woman with her myriads of "mountains"/problems and oppressions. Some others believe it is another form of imperialism but directed at African women. However, our interest here is not in the analysis of feminist theory for African literature, but the examination of the influence of feminism on the works of Nwapa and the need for re-evaluating and repositioning her works.

After the publication of the much-acclaimed female response to male domination of African literature by Nwapa, there was a rise in the interest of African feminist ideology and African scholars were not left out in the digestion and the promotion of the idea. Thus, it was not long before Nwapa's work became the focus of feminist propagandists who were determined to present it to the world as the much-awaited feminist text from Africa, as noted by the analysis above. These so-called critics with their claim to understanding and projecting the substance in the works of Nwapa failed to see the varied issues of concern for African women, raised by Nwapa in her rural novels; some of which were also her focus in later works. Nnaemeka addresses this issue in her criticism of the proliferation of feminist misinterpretation of African texts by some Western scholars. In her own words:

> So long as feminist critics of African literature insist on substituting highfalutin feminist verbiage for serious engagements with the cultural and material conditions that prevail in African literary texts, they will continue to produce irrelevancies and misrepresentations. Feminist theory and literary criticism should not be constituted into a wrecking ball with which to demolish and do violence to or initiate the demise of African literary texts; rather, it should be fashioned as the key or map with which to unlock or decipher meanings in their multiplicity and paradoxes; it should be put in the service of cultural productions by increasing our understanding of them. (81)

It is the cultural context of Nwapa's writing that form the basis for the major ideas of the works. Essentially, it is the lack of understanding of this focus that has led to the perceived inconsistency in the position of Nwapa on the issue of feminism.

As far as Nwapa, "an ordinary woman" is concerned, she is merely projecting "a more balanced image of African womanhood" that male authors "understandably neglect to point out" (Nnaemeka 90). For Nwapa belonged to the group of activists who believed that African women had a strong role within the African society which did not really need to be overhauled; what was really at stake was the dire need of critical attention by male writers and critics on female works. In fact, in her Keynote address delivered at the WAAD Conference in Nsukka in 1992, and published in 1998, Nwapa mentioned a few male African writers who she claimed "project an objective image of women, an image that actually reflects the reality of women's role in society." She also points to the powerful "Umuada" traditional group among the Igbo people and the powerful role and function the group performs in the Igbo society. Mention is also made of their spiritual roles in some areas as priestesses of certain deities in some parts of Nigeria. She goes further to add, "In my first two novels, I tried to recreate the experiences of women in the traditional African society—their social and economic activities and above all their preoccupation with the problems of procreation, infertility, and child-rearing" (92).

Surely, from the background analyzed so far, it is possible to conclude that Nwapa was not really interested in any confrontation or the dismantling of the existing structures. From the outset she apparently jus wanted to write about the African woman and her experiences. This is why the controversy rages on, whether feminism is truly applicable to the African experience and whether African women can be placed in the straitjacket of the feminist ideology. Nwapa, in an interview with Marie Umeh advises all those who wish to write to "read and listen" Nnaemeka on her part goes further to admonish the "all-knowing, all-talking, and never-listening" feminist critic of African literature. As far as Nwapa's works are concerned, the feminist critic should pay less attention to Helene Cixous, Luce Irigaray, and ecriture feminine and listen more to the rhythm and heartbeat of Igboland. (84)

The arguments have been made extensively, on both sides, and several books and journals are out there as proof; however, the new perspectives on the Woman Question still have not been able to accommodate the Nwapa experience or African scholars have not yet re-evaluated her important works within the context of the changing world order and the gender scholarship.

NWAPA AND THE BURDEN OF HISTORY

Most African women have reached the conclusion that feminism does not adequately describe their sociocultural reality, and many have pitched their tents with the modified model, especially, Alice Walker's term, "Womanism." Actually, Nwapa herself does not disagree with Alice Walker's term in showing her allegiance to the struggle of black women and men in Africa and the diaspora against racism, sexism, and ageism (Perry, 1262). The Womanist model, according to Umeh, "celebrates male-female relationships, family stability, and the healing of black nations torn asunder by colonialism, ethnicity, corruption, individualism, and innumerable social ills" (121). This "poetics" is adapted by Nwapa, manifesting the African value, involving the coming together of males and females to work for the development of society. Clearly, African society is heterogeneous, and the differences are celebrated; which is why the African woman is very passionate about her "place," her "location," her own space; and this explains why many have rejected the homogeneous label of "Third World," as the basis of feminist critics' appreciation of African literary texts. African feminist critics such as Mary Kolawole have observed that there are variations in the reality of the experiences of African women based on, regional differences, ethnicity, political exigencies, religion and other variables which all hinge on the reality of plurality.

This is yet another crux of the matter: the need for female African scholars to celebrate the local, in this case our own canonical works, in order to "foreground non-Western epistemic standpoints" (Herr 2013, Schutte 2002, Parekh 2014). This is one way of apprehending the major preoccupation of

Nwapa in her writings, which focused on dismantling masculine codes from the writings of Africans. This also explains why Nwapa tends to reject or rather become ambivalent toward the feminist label and chosen to remain with "what she knows" (Nnaemeka, 84). "What she knows," of course, has to do with the inner willpower of the female, which gives her the determination to make a way, even under very harsh realities. This is why the economic and historical context of the Igbo society presented to us by Nwapa provides a perspective that explains the female intelligent strategy in coping with the existing situation in the society especially through joint action with her husband. For example, Efuru quickly changes her business when her present one is no longer doing well; this deft move resulted in their netting a huge profit and they recovered their capital.

The burden of history on Flora Nwapa is not in being dragged into the controversy of contemporary African scholars, or whether Feminism should be the appropriate theory to explicate the African woman experiences, but in remaining true to the realities of the African life and leaving the issue of characterization to others. Thus, in all her works, Nwapa demonstrates the different varieties of African perspectives on the Woman Question, manifesting the variants of the historical development of the female reaction to the patriarchal system. Nwapa's systematic response to the patriarchal culture of her day, reflects the different and various actions of all the early feminist forerunners put together.

When she wrote *Efuru*, it was a reaction to the unfair treatment of female characters by male writers; so, she was operating still within the dominant patriarchal system, but came out to register her displeasure and set the record straight literarily. But, in subsequent texts, Nwapa reacts against the patriarchal system directly; after dealing with the village setting in *Efuru*, she turns to the fast modem life of the city in *One is Enough*, with a postcolonial treatment and a touch of modernity; Nwapa is still able to isolate the "local practices" that are peculiar to African society, while creating a female character that is different. Her character, Amaka, in this text, is a strong female who challenges patriarchy and still stands her ground as an individual with focus. Amaka questions the reasoning behind certain patriarchal conventions, "Was a woman nothing because she was unmarried or barren?" (*One is Enough* 22). This is one interesting question that reflects Amaka's self-doubt, yet it is a pointer to her gradual steps to self-awareness. Unlike Efuru who does not have such radical objection but rather operates quietly within the confines of the patriarchal system, Amaka interrogates the system, and takes radical steps to change her situation when it becomes unbearable for her. In spite of her effort in performing her "wifely duties," Amaka's mother-in-law is not satisfied with her because she is barren; so, she makes life unbearable for her. When Amaka is informed by her mother-in-law that her husband has two sons by another woman who would soon be moving in with her children, she becomes so enraged that she takes a drastic decision to divorce her husband, Obiora, because she feels it's time for her to move on with her life. And in moving on, Amaka becomes a wealthy businesswoman. In an ironic twist to her life, she bears a set of twins for her lover, a Catholic priest, whom she later refuses to marry for one marriage is enough. She is convinced that marriage is one of the obnoxious customs that hold "females in bondage" (*One is Enough* 105). She rather opts to be a single parent.

Amaka is undoubtedly the most independent female character in Nwapa's eight books; yet one could still point to the awareness of the "post-colonial thought" in the settings and the characteristics exhibited by the personalities created by Nwapa. Amaka leaves her place in the hinterland of Nigeria, the Eastern town of Onitsha, and moves to Lagos, the national capital. This action portrays the urban migration issue that was the reality of life then, in the post-independence years in Nigeria. The life in Lagos was liberal, and women were offered opportunities for self-improvement and economic development. With the outbreak of the Nigerian civil war, the opportunity to get involved in what is called the "attack trade" opens. Some women from the Biafran side actively participate in the trade by buying items from Nigerian soldiers and selling them to fellow Biafrans. Fully engaged in that business, Amaka prospers; living her own life and enjoying her independence, showing that a woman can be sharp and shrewd.

Where *Efuru* and *One is Enough* depict the post-colonial experience of women, *Women are Different* actually exposes the misleading influence of the West, through the missionary education on young women, at the period. The diverse life experiences of the three girls, Rose, Agnes, Doris, and their flippant friend Comfort are laid bare from their school days. They all had their education in the "same school where missionaries taught them all they needed to learn to live 'a good Christian life'" (*Women* 35). Unlike Amaka who defied her mother—a symbol of patriarchal subjugation of womankind—two of the female protagonists in *Women are Different* have no mothers. They are thus strategically removed from the indirect traditional influence and patriarchal control within the family, The girls whose mothers were alive could not take counsel from them, for they have been taught in western modes of "gender definitions" which do not conform to the standard female experience of the African culture. With their lack of maternal support and guidance, they are left to follow the dictates of "the good missionaries." This, nonetheless, does not save them from going through the pain of "adolescence" and the hurt of the realities of life in a post-colonial space (Stratton, 104). The lesson here, then, is that "gender definitions," whether in the mode of Western perspective or through the lens of African traditions, still remain strongly influenced by the strong patriarchal system and need to be confronted directly. Thus, as the early Western foremothers of feminism fought the patriarchal system through systematic actions, African fore-mothers also confronted the system through subtle reactions and systematic actions.

As the acclaimed first female writer in Africa, Nwapa "assumes control of the identity construction of African women characters, creating in the whole of her fiction lives that change and grow within and outside of the social, economic, and moral/spiritual traditions of Igbo society" (Tarver, 58). Thus, Nwapa foregrounds the female African writings with African traditions and values.

Flora Nwapa remains the dominant voice in the wilderness, in the African female's bid to counter the hegemonic stance of patriarchy displays in the dominant early works of African literature. As noted by Andrade, Nwapa has inaugurated "an African woman's literary history" (97) that can only be built on by emerging female writers. And truly, she already has "younger sisters" building on her foundation, notable among them is Buchi Emecheta whose works, The *Bride Price*, *The Joys of Motherhood* and others have been described as following Nwapa's "literary tradition." Nwapa's writings are rooted in the culture of her people and so, her perception of the traditional system of her people is not that of a demeaning structure with an overly oppressive system; but that of an evolving structure with a potential for growth and progress. Thus, her belief in the dignity of the female persona even within the patriarchal system remains positive and unshaken. This is why her female characters could hold their own within the society and "fight back" when the need arises, to maintain their dignity and still retain their position within the traditional society. Therefore, Nwapa's first feminine text, *Efuru*, remains the "mother text" for all female literary writings, and many emerging feminine texts develop a dialogue with the "mother text" in a way that help guide the development of the new female writings. And these new female authors continue the tradition of creating dignified African female characters against the backdrop of frequently pejorative representations of female characters by male authors, without actually demanding a destruction of the traditional system. Nwapa has set in motion an emerging female literary tradition that is unique and authentic, true to the African tradition while still pointing out a way for a progressive society that can grow to accommodate all members and fight for their equal development. Thus, while female writers continue to create new stories and ideas to present to the world the feminine perspectives, female African scholars continue to search for new framework to actually put these ideas in proper perspectives, even within the purview of the academic. Indeed, a powerful feminist structure has been set up by a historical figure that simply set history in motion by erecting a foundation on which others could build on.

However, contemporary female African scholars and writers also have a responsibility to locate this historical effort of the African literary matriarch appropriately, placing the works on a concrete pedestal in order to be firmly rooted in this rapidly changing and dynamic world. No doubt, Flora Nwapa has written women back into the literary discourse, setting the pace for other women, especially contemporary female writers to come out to express themselves in whatever way they care to do so, without fear of being denigrated.

There are, nevertheless, few critical issues raised by some scholars which reveal the weaknesses of Nwapa's major text as a good representation of a feminist text, advocating the promotion of the ideals of the African woman. For example, a notable Nigerian feminist scholar, Molara Ogundipe-Leslie seems to support Nwapa's presentation of the female image, yet, her other critical ideas point to a weak female presentation and an apologetic text of the patriarchal order, particularly that of marriage institution. According to Ogundipe-Leslie, who is convinced that some African traditions are not favorable to women—for example, the idea of a woman losing her identity in marriage is not agreeable to her. For it is within the marriage that the woman becomes a possession of the man and turns voiceless and right-less in the husband's family, unlike in her own family where she retains her rights and status as daughter or sister. She is empowered within her own family and disempowered in her husband's family; although in some communities, she can claim her rights through her children (75).

CONCLUSION

Given the understanding of the historical background of the work of Nwapa, we would not negatively criticize her works from this radical perspective; rather, the burden of history is on contemporary female scholars to appreciate Nwapa' s historical development. It is significant to note that Nwapa developed this point in *One is Enough*, when she presents her character, Amaka, as a woman who experienced marriage and eventually regretted and hated the experience. Whichever framework, in today's dynamic world, must be employed in analyzing Nwapa's works, it is important to appreciate where she was coming from; her unapologetic view that African men and women must stand together to fight oppression. A view also shared by another notable female scholar, Mary E. Kolawole, which she describes as "the totality of feminine self-expression, self-retrieval, and self-assertion in positive cultural ways" (*Womanism* 10).

It is these ideals that Nwapa has been promoting in her works since the very first publication of her text, *Efuru*, in 1966. Thus, whether the women reach a consensus or not, the fact that African women have "retrieved" their voices; the fact that they are now presenting a positive gender; and the fact that the scholars are carrying on research for further studies on new ideas/ theories to explicate their unique position, all point to their resilience. These are the main issues addressed by the brave act of Nwapa in publishing her first novel, *Efuru*, which has thus become a mother-text for African creative gender writing. The burden placed on contemporary writers and scholars is that of pursuing, relentlessly, the appreciation of this perspective of Nwapa as a writer and her works, especially *Efuru*, as the "mother text" that all female writings in Africa have been building on.

WORKS CITED

Andrade, Susan Z. "Rewriting History, Motherhood and Rebellion: Naming an African Woman's Literary Tradition." *Research in African Literatures,* 21.1 (1990): 91–110.

Brown, Lloyd W. *Women Writers in Black Africa*. Westport, Connecticut: Greenwood, 1981.

Bryce, Jane. "A Feminist study of fiction by Nigerian Women Writers." An unpublished Ph. D Thesis, Obafemi Awolowo University, Ile-Ife, 1988.

Carter, April. *The Politics of Women's Rights*. London: Longman, 1988.

Frank, K. "Feminist Criticism and the African Novel." *African Literature Today* (14): Insiders and Outsiders London, Heinemann, 1984.

Friedan, Betty. *The Feminine Mystique*. Harmondsworth, Middlesex: Penguin, 1984.

Friedman, Susan Standford. "Making History: Reflections on Feminism, Narrative, and Desire." *Feminism Beside Itself*. Eds. Diane Elam and Robyn Wiegman. New York: Routledge, 1995.

Herr, R. S. "The Possibility of Nationalist Feminism," *Hypatia: A Journal of Feminist Philosophy,* 18, 3 (2003): 135–160. Print.

Jaggar, Alison. "Political Philosophies of Women Liberation." *Feminism and Philosophy*. Eds. Vitterlin-Braggin, Mary, et al., New Jersey: Littlefield, Adams, 1977.

Kolawole, Modupe Mary E. (2002) "Transcending Incongruities: Rethinking *for Gender Equity F*eminisms and the Dynamics of Identity in Africa." *Agenda: Empowering Women,* 54 (2002): 92–98.

———. *Womanism and African Consciousness*. Trenton NJ: African World Press, Inc., 1997.

Mojola, Yemi I. "The Works of Flora Nwapa." *Nigerian Female Writers*: *A Critical Perspective*. Eds.Henrietta C. Otokunefor and Obiageli C. Nwodo. Ikeja: Malthouse Press Limited, 1989: 19–29.

Nfah-Abbenyi, Juliana Makuchi. *Gender in African Women's Writing: Identity, Sexuality, and Difference*. Bloomington: Indiana University Press, 1997.

Nnaemeka, Obioma. "Feminism, Rebellious Women, and Cultural Boundaries: Rereading Flora Nwapa and Her Compatriots" Research in African Literatures, 26, 2 (1995): 80–113. URL: http://www.jstor.org/stable/3820273 Web.

Nwapa, Flora. *Efuru*. London: Heinemann Educational Books, 1966.

———. *One Is Enough*. London: Heinemann Educational Books. 1981.

———. "Women and Creative Writing in Africa.," Sisterhood, Feminisms and Power: From Africa to the Diaspora. Ed. Obioma Nnaemeka. Trenton: Africa World Press, Inc., 1998.

———. *Women Are Different*. Trenton, NJ: Africa World Press. 1992.

Ogundipe-Leslie, Molara. *Recreating Ourselves: African Women and Critical Transformation*, Trenton, New Jersey: Africa World Press. 1994.

Ogunyemi-Okonjo, Chikwenye. "Womanism: The Dynamics of the Contemporary Black Female Novel in English," *Signs: Journal of Women in Culture and Society*. 11.1 (1985): 63–80.

———. "Women and Nigerian Literature." *Perspectives on Nigerian Literature: 1700 to the Present*. Ed. Yemi Ogunbiyi. Lagos: Guardian Books, 1988.

Parekh, Serena and Wilcox, Shelley. "Feminist Perspectives on Globalization," *The Stanford Encyclopedia of Philosophy* (Winter Edition), Ed. Edward N. Zalta. 2014, URL = <http://plato.stanford.edu/archives/win201 4/entries/feminism-globalization!>. Web.

Perry, Alison. "Meeting Flora Nwapa." *West Africa* 18 June 1984. 1262.

Randall, Vicky. *Women and Politics*. London: Macmillan,1982.

Rege Sharmil "More than Just Tacking Women on to the 'Macropicture':Feminist Contributions to Globalisation Discourses." *Economic and Political Weekly*, 38, 43 (2003):.4555–4563. http://www.jstor.org/stable/4414189. Accessed: 19/01/2015 06:5 5 Web.

Schutte, O, "Feminism and Globalization Processes in Latin America." *Latin American Perspectives on Globalization. Ethics, Politics, and Alternative Visions*. Ed. M.Saenz, New York: Rowman & Littlefield Publishing Group, 2002: 185–199.

Soyinka, Wole. *Myth, Literature and the African World*. London: Cambridge University Press, 1976.

Stratton, Florence. *Contemporary African Literature and the Politics of Gender*. London: Routledge, 1994.

Tarver, Australia. "Coming Home to Herself: Autonomy and Self-Conversion in Flora Nwapa's *One Is Enough*." *Africana Women In Contemporary Literature* Eds. Janice Liddell and Yakini Belinda Kemp. Arms Akimbo. Gainesville: University Press of Florida, 1999.

Umeh, Marie and Flora Nwapa. "The Poetics of Economic Independence for Female Empowerment: An Interview with Flora Nwapa." *Research in African Literatures*, 26, 2 (1995): 114–123. http://www.jstor.org/stable/3820268. Web.

Chapter 4

Flora Nwapa's Efuru
The Personified Goddess

Anthonia Adadevoh

INTRODUCTION

With *Efuru* the first novel published by a Nigerian woman, Flora Nwapa became black Africa's first internationally published female novelist in the English language. This earned her a respectable position in modern African literature. Although Nwapa wrote about women and their lives, in an interview with Marie Umeh in 1993, Nwapa refused to be called a feminist. In her own words, "I don't even accept that I'm a feminist. I accept that I'm an ordinary woman who is writing about what she knows. I try to project the image of women positively" (Umeh 27). Inspired by the resilience of African women, Nwapa constructs the female protagonists of her novels based on an African religious cultural perspective. Against this backdrop, she portrays her protagonists as wise, resilient, decisive, and independent; through their self-discovery journey, these female characters develop non-oppositional relationships with the males in their lives. In Nwapa's early novels *Idu* and *Efuru*, Uhamiri, the goddess of Oguta Lake, is foregrounded as a supernatural agent, directing the affairs of human beings. In *Efuru*, Nwapa personifies Uhamiri, a goddess of the Igbo cosmology, through the novel's eponymous protagonist, Efuru. The author adopts this archetypal pattern of a personified African goddess to characterize her protagonist as a strong African woman. In her article, titled "Women and Creative Writing in Africa," Nwapa states, "In my two heroines, Efuru and Idu, I was inspired by the women around me when I was growing up. They were solid and superior women who held their own in society. They were not only wives and mothers, but successful traders who took care of their children and their husbands as well" (Olaniyan 28). At the time of her death, Nwapa had completed *The Lake Goddess*, her final novel. This work focuses on the lake goddess Uhamiri (Mami-Wata), the eternal spring and mythical inspirer of Nwapa's fiction.

Nwapa's use of myth in fiction is as ancient as time. The unlearned knowledge of women stored in their subconscious becomes visible through the mythological. Therefore, it was natural for her to draw from the spiritual realm to anchor what she wishes to portray in the physical world. Thus, her work seems to draw on Jungian theory of the collective unconscious. This inherited knowledge is the residue of repeated kinds of experiences in the lives of our ancestors, and are buried deep in man's psyche, beneath the suppressed memories belonging to the individual. The mythic elements in Nwapa's novels often seem impossible in real life. She uses myths to deliver a message about the worth of women in multi-faceted forms. Since humans create the life of today that becomes myths tomorrow, humans send back to themselves that which becomes the archetypes. This means the message from within is sent back to the outer self.

The treatment of inner strength surfacing in the outward is the essence of Nwapa's message about African women in her use of the goddess archetype. Nwapa uses the strong personality of women in African mythological stories to challenge stereotypical images of African women in fiction. In many male-authored African fictional works, these women are usually represented in negative terms or in weaker positions that place them in opposition to men in society. While her message is explicit to some readers, there are others who cannot get the message because they are unfamiliar with her constructed cultural symbols and images; they may also be quite detached from nature that symbols and images appear unrealistic or even preposterous.

The author characterizes Efuru as a strong, assertive, resilient, independent, decision-making woman who is not predictably entrenched in a hostile gender dichotomy. Based on the Jungian figurative mother archetype, Efuru's personality is contrary to the Eurocentric representation of African women as docile, oppressed, and submissive. The goddess Uhamiri

(Ogbuide) is a symbol of benevolence and creativity. She is strong, wise, independent, and deeply involved in the lives of the people in Oguta. Uhamiri is also beautiful and has long dreadlocks. Sabine Jell-Bahisen, who has carried out some research on this goddess as far back as 1978, confirms Uhamiri's importance to the community, "The concept of the 'mother water' goddess, mammywater, is more than a divinity. She embodies and manifests important aspects of womanhood in pre-colonial Igbo culture and society" (164). Nwapa aligns Efuru's character with Uhamiri through a self-discovery journey. The writer uses physical attributes and personality traits of Uhamiri to characterize Efuru. These physical attributes denote a spiritual dimension to the character's identity; further, they are outward representations of the goddess's ability to dispense fertility and magic to her worshippers and to draw those she wishes to initiate into her rarefied world.

BIOGRAPHICAL INFORMATION

Some biographical information about the author is necessary to understand why she chose an African goddess as a prototype of the protagonist of her novel. Nwapa was born in 1931 in Oguta, a village in eastern Nigeria. Like her parents, she was educated in the British system—one that is dominated by a Eurocentric perspective. After graduating from Archdeacon Crowther's Memorial Girl's School, Elelenwa, Port Harcourt, she went on to earn a bachelor's degree from the University of Ibadan, Nigeria in 1957. Nwapa continued her studies in England, earning in 1958 a degree in education from the University of Edinburgh.

Nwapa became increasingly critical of foreign intrusions, especially the detrimental impact of Christianity on African spirituality, African identity, and African women. Nwapa personally struggled with the mixed blessings of Christianity and westernization in Igbo society, positioned as she was culturally as a native of Ugwuta and socially within Ugwuta's and Nigeria's upper class and Christian elite (Umeh,78). Acknowledging some of the negative influences of colonialism in her life, helped Nwapa come to terms with her shadow. According to the displacement theory of Edward Said, a literary theorist and cultural critic, Nwapa suffered two displacements, cultural and linguistic, in the vein of other Africans who were educated under the British system. Because she was only taught in English, her African culture was foreign to her total British educational process.

Despite her educational achievements, the question "Who am I" dominated her consciousness. To answer that question, she first had to identify and understand her shadow. As Jung explains, "The meeting with oneself is, at first, the meeting with one's shadow. The shadow is a tight passage, a narrow door, whose painful constriction no one is spared who goes down to the deep well. But one must learn to know oneself in order to know who one is" (21). Her shadow was her dislike of how the British and their Christian spirituality took over her African identity. In time, because she was not static in where her formal Western education led her, she began to understand her culture.

As a possible protest to this cultural invasion, Nwapa in her "grown up" years observed the overt hybrid culture in Nigeria that blended Christianity with African religious culture. In this accepted syncretic culture of Nigerians, she did not see a conflict between two religious ideologies. For example, in her village Oguta there was no conflict in churchgoers also believing in the goddess Uhamiri. Consequently, she confronted her shadow and reconciled her "masculine" and "feminine" qualities in order to self-actualize. Her self-actualization is portrayed in her first two novels where she explicitly creates her main female characters using the goddess Uhamiri as the prototype:

Nwapa builds a structure of ideas adequate for interpreting female experience. She generates a new tradition in which women are the center of focus and draws largely from the mythic reservoir to explore every aspect of female experience. Efuru and Idu embody references to mythic symbols and themes and, in this way, make Nwapa's earliest novels relevant to her time. (Umeh 112)

The new tradition that Nwapa generates uses nature to elevate women to their primordial position. Therefore, even though her Western formal education relegates nature to the background and associates its acknowledgement with backwardness, this is not the case with Nwapa who employs myth as a tool for the projection of female strength and solidarity in the workings of female realities and experience.

THE PERSONIFIED GODDESS

Against the background of Oguta mythology, Efuru, Nwapa's eponymous heroine, is elevated to a plane higher than that of a human being when she is chosen to be a worshipper of Uhamiri, the goddess of the lake. In this story, Nwapa explicitly presents her main character as a mirror image of Uhamiri alongside another strong female character, Ajanupu. As an author, Nwapa prefers to write stories that affirm women. She portrays women as strong with their "inherent vitality, independence of views, courage, self-confidence, and of course their desire for gain and high social status" (qtd. in Umeh 17). This is, beyond question, a negation of the negative image of Nigerian women portrayed by several male writers in their works, Nwapa believes that women's history must be recreated in fiction. In the paper she read at a conference in the United States in 1984 she asserts:

> The Nigerian male writers fail to elevate women to their rightful plane. They overlook the safeguards with which custom surround her: the weight of feminine opinion, the independence of her economic position, the power she wields by the mere fact that she holds the pestle and the cooking pots. They fail to see all these things because they are men and are influenced by the colonial administration's Victorian-type prejudices against women. (14)

Unlike her male counterparts, Nwapa prefers to portray women from the perception of strength, and also from a woman's point of view. She embeds into her fiction the customs that approve of women's leadership roles. For example, she sees the role of the woman as the provider of the meal for the family, even if she just cooks it, to be a leadership position. All persons in the community have to eat for sustenance; therefore, the provider of the meal occupies an important position which she can use to her advantage. This is what leaders do. Nwapa discovered that Uhamiri, as a goddess, has dominion over a spectrum of roles in which women can excel as leaders, and she explores these different options in her works. Uhamiri is often regarded as Nwapa's own alter ego. Marie Umeh contends that:

> Nwapa's theory of female existence and situation in her early fiction is based on the practical experience of her life in Ugwuta as she grew up. The mystical influence of the "beautiful blue Ugwuta lake" which the community depended upon for food, transportation, and . . . sustenance was decisive in Nwapa's mythopoeia when she began to create her women-centered fiction. Her mythic imagination derives its force from the spiritual being that controls this body of water—Uhamiri. (54)

Nwapa revealed that if she had written a sequel to *Efuru*, she would have titled it Efuru in Her Glory. In addition to the portrayal of the strong aspects of women, Nwapa's work often focuses mainly on the positive effects of African values on the lives of African women. She believed that African women's cultural reality, such as those pertaining to their spiritual belief system, should be used to judge their worth to their community. Even though she is from a Christian household, Nwapa has come to understand the cosmology of her people, and she is able to make the choice to pattern Efuru' s character after the Igbo deity. The shifting personalities of the deity are part of the appeal; she is evasive, flexible, and multidimensional (Umeh 40). So, Nwapa decides that the characteristics of Uhamiri would best inform her female protagonist, Efuru. She saw women as humans who exist first as independent beings and secondly, as humans who complement one another and can also be in interchangeable roles.

After sifting through her "colonial mentality" and her African traditions, Nwapa made informed decisions about what best fulfills her role as a woman. She became a voice for women through her fiction. She came to terms with her "animus," the archetypal masculine symbolism within a woman's consciousness; and hence she wrote *Efuru* and later started a publishing company, Tana Press. Furthermore, she accepted the goddess Uhamiri, a cultural icon that had been tucked away in her personal unconscious as she went through her Westernized educational process. Her acceptance of the goddess is an acceptance of self. What makes Uhamiri qualify as a prototype for the creation of her female protagonist is contingent on her mythical story.

The mythological beginning of this goddess is said to be from the moon. The goddess descended into the lake in Oguta and has resided there since. Her physical appearance is that of a mermaid, known as Mami-Wata—a mermaid who is beautiful and has long hair. Uhamiri has long dreadlocks that signify her spiritual power. This spiritual power is shown through her ability to dispense fertility and feminine magic. Uhamiri brings health and well-being to her followers, but this often comes with a price. To women who seek her, she brings beauty and wealth, but few or no children. This goddess also has a dark side which can be destructive when provoked. The personality traits contained in this archetype are portrayed in a cultural context on both the personal unconscious and the conscious levels: "The archetype is essentially an unconscious content that is altered by becoming conscious and by being perceived, and it takes its color from the individual consciousness in which it happens to appear" (Jung 5).

The goddess's strength is tempered with vulnerability, yet her focused essence helps her to achieve her goals. Her wisdom builds her confidence, and she attains independence through a balance of her inner self. In Umeh's critical analysis, she quotes the exact words of Onyemuru Uzonwanne, a local ferry woman from Oguta, who ferries people across the lake where Uhamiri resides, and she refers to her with one of her other names, Iyi: "Iyi comes from the moon. Iyi has followers. Iyi killed a person's son and used ram to pay back. Anyone who wants to go well on his way must offer a ram to her. If anyone drowns, you must give her a ram. Ogbuide has twisted hair; she has a big head. Iyi is good. The Woman King is fine" (78).

Again, it is reiterated by the woman from Oguta that Uhamiri is an essential part of the lives of the people in Oguta. Nwapa brings Uhamiri from the spiritual realm to the physical realm and personifies her through Efuru as a woman who has strength coupled with weaknesses that ultimately humanize her as she sets out on her journey of self-actualization.

CULTURAL SETTING

The story in *Efuru* is set in a rural community, Oguta, an Igbo village in postcolonial Nigeria in the 1960s. The setting for this story is one that actually exists. This is a place that Nwapa knows: she has firsthand knowledge of the reality of the dual society that colonialism forced on Nigeria. This enables her to skillfully weave that knowledge into the fabric of the story among the static and evolving indigenous traditions. In explaining his theory of the collective unconscious, Jung alludes to the connection of the so-called primitive man to nature: "Primitive man impresses us so strongly with his subjectivity that we should really have guessed long ago that myths refer to something psychic" (Jung 6–7). This inclusion of nature in the African religious culture makes the acceptance of the merging of the mythological and physical world possible. Nwapa establishes the connection of this place with nature and religion. Therefore, the importance of water, the lake as the habitat of Uhamiri, becomes the norm rather than the exception. Uhamiri descended from the moon into the lake in the village and stays in the subconscious.

This setting creates the authentic sense of place where Efuru the female protagonist thrives with Uhamiri. The personification of Uhamiri as Efuru is explicitly portrayed through the alignment of physical attributes with personality traits that embody decisiveness, wisdom, and independence with both good and dark sides as in the figurative mother archetype. Jung describes a goddess as the embodiment of many qualities: maternal, magic, wisdom, instinct, growth, rebirth, secret, and seduction all condensed into strength, wisdom and independence presented as the mirror image of Uhamiri from her outward physical appearance to her personality. She is beautiful with very long hair, and she has a good personality. When people wonder why Adizua always goes home from the farm, the response is that he married a very beautiful woman. We are told that others pay special attention to Efuru because of her looks. The woman who comes to perform her circumcision tells her, "You are beautiful, my daughter. I will be gentle with you"' (*Efuru* 13). People acknowledge her beauty the same way they do Uhamiri at the lake and her shrine. Every time the villagers cross the lake either to go fishing or to go to Uhamiri's shrine, they adorn her with praises for her beauty. She is often addressed as, "the most beautiful of women" (200), "the great woman of the lake; the most beautiful of women; the kindest of women" (202). However, Uhamiri's physical attributes are not just for adornment, they serve a purpose. Her beauty draws people to her, and her hair is symbolic of fertility and magic. Fertility in this case is not just in reference to childbearing but also fruitfulness in other areas. Igbo women of Oguta refer to Uhamiri as Nwanyiishiajakaja, woman of thick hair. Bell-Bahlsen explains, "Uhamiri: Ogbuide is often described as 'the embodiment of beauty,' the epitome of fertile giving. Her hair is described as long, thick, and at times twisted. Her beauty is awful, a 'killer beauty,' who kills with excess and may take the life of those who refuse to follow her" (82). Efuru shifts from one personality to another, but her goodness is constant. Therefore, the dark side that must be realized is manifest through Ajanupu, another female character in the story.

MAJOR THEMES AND COMPARATIVE ANALYSIS

Efuru is a beautiful, intelligent, and independent-thinking young woman who defies local custom when she marries Adizua, a man who could not afford to pay her bride price at the outset of the marriage. She suffers the loss of a child and the failure of two marriages before she starts to have dreams about the goddess of the lake, Uhamiri. At the end, she becomes a worshipper of this lake goddess, who is a mirror image of her. Efuru is blessed with beauty and wealth, and the story ends at the threshold of her self-actualization. However, in the course of the story, this coming actualization that is assumed is already witnessed through the person of Ajanupu, the independent, outspoken older woman of wisdom in the story.

Nwapa uses Joseph Campbell's template of the hero's journey as a prototype of the departure, initiation, and return plot of the story. Secondly, Efuru's beauty, long hair and the gentle side of her personality are shown to be identical to Uhamiri's. However, to portray the tough side of Efuru, Nwapa partners Efuru's character with that of Ajanupu who is a symbol of what she intends to accomplish in Efuru, "the grown woman." The combination of these two characters produces the true picture of Uhamiri. In creating this protagonist, the author's personal unconscious, which constitutes her repressed memories of African religious culture, is revealed. A comparative study of Efuru and Ajanupu shows the former as the gentler part of two personalities and the latter projects the forceful part. When merged into one, both become a perfect Efuru revered for her beauty, and throughout the story there is reference to both her beauty and long hair. She recognizes that her hair and beauty are her endearing physical assets, for her and, perhaps for other women. Consequently, when she suspects there is another woman in her husband's life, she wonders if the woman possesses physical attributes similar to hers: "Perhaps she is very beautiful and has long hair like mine" (*Efuru* 54).

In the personification process, Nwapa aligns the strong decisive persona of Uhamiri with that of Efuru whose strength reveals itself in the singular manner in which she makes the decision to marry Adizua before her bride price is paid. She works out a deal on how and when her father will be paid. At the beginning of Efuru's grown-up life, she biologically and emotionally craves an attachment to someone. This craving can be attributed to an unlearned knowledge existing in the collective unconscious. Nwapa uses this natural process to initiate the call for Efuru to set out on her journey into the world.

The world is represented by her marriage. She leaves her natal home and ventures into the world when she makes the decision to marry Adizua, her first husband. Although Adizua cannot pay her bride price, she discards this important aspect of Igbo tradition and moves in with him. This behavior characterizes Efuru as a non-conformist. In her action, she places herself above the conventions of her society even though the bride price is one mechanism that tradition puts in place to test the economic capacity of the prospective husband to maintain a wife. It is also a means of gauging the future husband's respect for the bride's family as he is expected to overcome the challenges placed before him. In making the decision to marry him, Efuru may not have discerned a profound weakness in her husband's character—that is, his tendency to take the easy way out. This is established through his reply to her question with regard to the bride price he opts for. Take a few clothes with you and come to me. "We shall talk about the dowry after" (1). Therefore, Efuru did not marry him for his chivalry, but for his love and companionship. Others wonder how a beautiful and intelligent woman like Efuru ends up marrying a man they refer to as an "imbecile" (6). At the outset of the relationship, Efuru ignores Adizua's personality flaws, but her capacity to focus is the saving grace that balances her bad judgment in choosing a partner she thought would complete her. In keeping with Uhamiri, Efuru imitates a decision-making goddess "whose rules determine the norms of daily life" (Bell-Bahisen 138), and Efuru makes a decision to marry and carry on with her life. This is an important first step in her journey to self-actualization. She makes another important decision that is not to go to the farm with her husband. She rather opts to trade. (*Efuru* 10). She recognizes early that the marketplace, not the farm, is where she can attain economic success. This innate knowledge is in alignment with her psychological attachment with Uhamiri who as a goddess presides over the affairs of women in the marketplace and her followers and those she decides to bless in the marketplace. Efuru tries to include Adizua in this circle of financial endowment when she makes the decision for him to leave farming: "both of us can trade together" (20).

After Adizua leaves her, Ossai, her mother-in-law, tells her to be patient. She says she went through the same predicament with Adizua's father, and that she is proud that she stayed true to a husband who left her. Nwapa uses this scene between these two women to give the reader an access into the inner thoughts of Efuru. The character's thought process shows that she is always in touch with her collective unconscious. The goddess qualities in her silently revolt against her mother-in-law's self-sacrificing response to her marital problem that is expected of Igbo women. This is when Efuru begins to define herself, and her transformation starts. She immediately decides that unnecessary self-sacrifice is not the way she wants to show her strength by wasting away on an irresponsible husband. It is very obvious that such "self-imposed suffering" does not appeal to her She affirms that her "own suffering will be noble" (61–62).

The divine union Efuru envisions when she marries Adizua does not materialize. Even though this marriage proves to be an error in judgment, it provides the opportunity for her to evolve. Jung says, "'The eternal child' in man is an indescribable experience, an incongruity, a handicap, and a divine prerogative; an imponderable that determines the ultimate worth or worthlessness of a personality" (Jung 179). This is Efuru's first introspective analysis of her life as Adizua's wife. Efuru's ability to evolve displays her strength. She makes the choice to leave her marriage at the appropriate time that she sets for herself, thus informing her mother-in-law about her decision to not wait indefinitely for Adizua (88). Her statement to her mother-in-law further demonstrates her continuing desire to seek a divine union to another man through marriage, even as her first marriage crumbles irrespective of her love and commitment.

Efuru's second marriage to Gilbert, an educated man, is slightly better than her first marriage. Again, as in her first marriage, Gilbert leaves her after a brief period of marital bliss. Margaret Laurence, essayist, novelist and author of Long Drums and Canon, may be right when she points out that Efuru's goodness to both men may be what scares them away (187). The radiance of her inner spiritual being "blinds" these men. She is not a whining, helpless person who wants to lean perpetually on others. Her kindness seems to "kill" her relationship with men. This may be because her kindness is not a reciprocal act to the action of the men. Efuru's kindness, which recalls that of Uhamiri, is innate. Both husbands apparently exploited this distinct virtue. In a similar vein, Uhamiri is also married twice. However, unlike Efuru, Uhamiri remains married to the two water gods, Urashi and Njaba. Through this act of marriage to two men, Uhamiri as a goddess defies tradition that assigns only one husband at a time to women, while men in her culture can marry multiple women at the same time.

Therefore, the contrast between Efuru the human and Uhamiri the goddess is drawn through the structure of marriage. Obviously, the lake goddess, Uhamiri, exists as a supernatural being who dwells in extremes that ordinary women may not easily attain. It is also possible that in a human form, Uhamiri does not want to be married because she is already married to two gods in the spiritual world. Whatever the case, Nwapa uses this difference in the marital status of Efuru and Uhamiri's to humanize the former and give her the opportunity to evolve. So, Efuru's decisive personality that gets her into two disastrous marriages also rescues her. Since her love and economic capabilities do not endear her to her two husbands, she picks up the pieces and forges ahead. From the African feminist perspective, Efuru is a woman who is fulfilling her part of the bargain, trying to complement her husband, but her role does not yield any reciprocal dividends. However, as a goddess, this is the path her spiritual journey must take in order for her to attain divine union and be spiritualized. Her relationship with men, especially through marriage, is not important to her spiritualization. If the relation is at all necessary, it is used as a means to an end.

The marriages furnish the story with varied challenges for Efuru to face in order to grow as a person in her initiation into the world. Nwapa skillfully uses Efuru's failed marriages and the death of her only child to create a path for her protagonist to be independently female outside of the traditional roles of wife and mother. This, by no means suggests that she is not feminine. There is a probability that her natural cravings to love a man and nurture a child are not her path to womanhood. It may have been instinctive for Efuru to want to be a wife and a mother, because her subconscious furnished her with that information at a specific time in her life, but it can be argued that in that same collective unconscious that informed her of her biological needs, there are other options from which to choose. However, she makes the choice of marriage and motherhood which replicates those other choices made by women that surround her.

The author at first allows Efuru these two "normal" choices to exist for her to function as a normal woman; then she changes the development of Efuru's life journey to fashion for her a unique life. Her husbands, unknowingly to her, are hindrances to a destiny she will later attain. In consequence, they are dropped off after fulfilling their roles of providing her with challenges. Again, her role as a mother is terminated when she loses her only child. After Efuru is severed from traditional roles, one after the other, she is then viewed through other lenses. Her female authority as a mother archetype is "fruitfulness and fertility" which is defined through her economic prowess and her generosity and kindness to others in her community, rather than in her roles as wife and mother. The men are released from the story, not because of their bad behavior but because their use is complete. This is not a gender obstacle, but an elemental one for her status as a goddess. Efuru's child Ogonim is also removed from the story because it is a commonly known fact that even though Uhamiri gives children to those who want them, she does not have any children of her own. Therefore, if Efuru is the mirror image of Uhamiri as already noted through their physical resemblance, other areas of her life in conjunction with those of Ajanupu must also align with those of the goddess.

Efuru's decision to marry Adizua who could not pay her bride price is a mistake; however, the marriage resulted in Efuru meeting Ajanupu, her mother-in-law's sister, who is also the omniscient pillar of strength in the village. From their first meeting they become inseparable. Her character is ever present in all the crevices of the story, pulling things together as she is always within Efuru's reach. However, while Ajanupu's actions are elaborate throughout the story, Nwapa never describes her physical attributes as she does those of Uhamiri and Efuru. Therefore, she lets only Ajanupu's actions and words define her. Nwapa, in creating Ajanupu alongside Efuru, blurs the former, so that when she merges with Efuru at the end of the story, there is no picture image of her features to leave her hovering in the story. She is not a worshipper of Uhamiri; that role is left for Efuru. She is the manifestation of what Efuru will become.

Furthermore, Ajanupu is seen as Uhamiri herself separated from the humanized Efuru; however, they become united at the end of the journey. In contrast to Uhamiri, Ajanupu has many children and Uhamiri has none. This may be a rnaneuver Nwapa uses to stop the reader from perfectly matching Ajanupu with Uhamiri at the outset of the story. Ajanupu's important influence is seen in the way she shoves herself into Efuru's life and remains there. Even after Efuru is no longer married to Ajanupu's nephew, Adizua, Efuru and Ajanupu continue their relationship, uninterrupted by any incidents. Efuru starts to see her as a mother figure, As Jung has put it, "Although the figure of the mother as it appears in folklore is more or less universal, this image changes markedly when it appears in the individual psyche" (82). For Efuru, Ajanupu's role spans many possibilities beyond the mother–daughter relationship that covers the length of the story. Ajanupu is strong, knowledgeable, courageous, and outspoken. In the physical realm she displays Uhamiri's medicinal knowledge. Since the initiation process takes a while, spanning many years chronologically and psychologically, Nwapa shows Efuru in her glory through Ajanupu. All the things Efuru would not or cannot do are done by Ajanupu on her behalf.

Efuru's independence is portrayed through her legendary business acumen. She is not formally educated in Western capitalism, but she has a firm grasp of economic structures and the shrewdness and tenacity for business. Her feminine magic is defined by her trading skills. Jung points out that for the figurative mother archetype, there is "the magic authority of the female" (82). Efuru has a Midas touch in her business; this can be attributed to Uhamiri who is also the goddess of the marketplace. On this issue Bell-Bahisen offers the following insight:

> Ogbuide, Oguta's ancient patron of people in general, and of women and their wealth in particular, prevails in the market. The goddess' association with the market is not accidental. The market is the Oru-Igbo women's realm. A major venue, preoccupation, and source of women's wealth, the market has maintained its importance to women. (244)

So, it can be assumed that Efuru's success as a trader is not coincidental; it becomes obvious that Uhamiri prospers Efuru with wealth but not children, as the only child she gives birth to dies in infancy. Efuru's economic success is continuous throughout the story. Her wealth is the vehicle through which her "fertility and fruitfulness" is realized, so she supports people in the community with it. She teaches her first husband, Adizua, to trade, but he fails to keep up with the wife's skills.

As Efuru begins to dream about Uhamiri, she becomes her worshipper. Women of the town feel that the step she takes to be the goddess' worshipper seals her fate as a barren woman. The usual female view of womanhood is that for a woman to be fulfilled, she must have children. The females project what they think or what society expects a woman should want in Efuru, but that does not deter Efuru from becoming Uhamiri's follower. Jell-Baishen rightly points out that, "The water goddess protects, encourages, and empowers those who cannot or would not live up to society's norms, ancestral customs and the laws of the land" (39). Efuru is protected by Uhamiri and her spiritual centering is at its prime. She gets closer to water because water represents all that Uhamiri is in her subconscious. Uhamiri resides in water, and from her Efuru will complete her journey to self-actualization.

Although Nwapa unfolds this tale explicitly, yet some underlying meaning remains in the unconscious. This unconscious begins to manifest through dreams as Efuru is about to get to know herself. With the dream experience that emerges, the dots start to connect. Efuru's ethereal beauty mirrors that of the unearthly goddess, Uhamiri. Efuru's status as a goddess in the physical realm exemplifies the extreme goodness that is not human. Laurence remarks that, "Efuru's tragedy is partly that she cannot permit herself the mistakes of ordinary people" (189) within her relationships. Her beauty matches her goodness; she is described as a good woman who always greets people and as good words for all: a "woman with a clean heart, who respects her elders" (77). Her good attributes make her unreal in a very real world. Her high standards may have scared away her two husbands. Ajanupu also reiterates her goodness and adds, "There is no woman like you" (83). Nwapa could not bring herself to "taint" the integrity of her alter ego. However, for a complete representation of this humanized goddess, a dark side must be part of her personality repertoire, so Nwapa develops an alternate way to show her protagonist's dark side in the form of Ajanupu and her first marriage. Efuru is humanized through the incidents that crowd her life at the beginning of her self-actualizing journey. Her strength, her ability to make decisions, and her self-sufficiency on the physical level remain constant. Jung says that in order to arrive at self, two other steps must be sequentially followed. First, there is the meeting of one's shadow and secondly the reconciliation of the "masculine" and "feminine" before the divine union.

CONCLUSION

Throughout the novel *Efuru*, Uhamiri's personalities are manifested through Efuru and Ajanupu. In the former, her gentle strength is made obvious through her two marriages and her survival after the death of her only child. She evolves, but her full evolution is not seen in the story; it is assumed through the understanding of Ajanupu's role in the story. The strength and wisdom that Efuru uses to navigate her journey to self-actualization are embedded in her personalities since Nwapa usually represents women from a space of positive self-definition, revelation, rediscovery, and relocation.

It is now understood that Efuru's journey is not meant to culminate in a happy union with a man; it is a journey that would end in the attainment of the divine union in the subconscious that manifests as contentment in the conscious. Her connection to Uhamiri is explicitly obvious from her dreams Nwapa ends this powerful womanhood story with a nagging question in the unconscious state of Efuru's dreams (221). Clearly, Nwapa uses the archetypal pattern to create some female characters as personified goddesses in order to enable the women represented in her fiction to have an alternative recourse from which to choose their roles in society. The iconic author uses the mythological sphere to elevate women through connections with nature where distinctions of the capabilities of men and women are not grouped by gender rules of opposition. This is the case with Efuru, the personified goddess.

WORKS CITED

Adadevoh, Anthonia. "Personified Goddesses: An Archetypal Pattern of Female Protagonists in the Works of Two Black Women Writers." Diss. Clark Atlanta U. 2013.

Campbell Joseph. *The Hero with a Thousand Faces*. Princeton, NJ: Princeton University Press. 1990.

Jahn, Janheinz. *Muntu*. New York: Grove Press, Inc., 1990.

Jell-Bahisen, Sabine. *The Water Goddess in Igbo Cosmology: Ogbuide of Oguta Lake*. Trenton, NJ: Africa World Press, Inc., 2008.

Jung, Carl G. *Memories, Dreams, and Reflections*. Trans. R. and C. Winston. New York: Random House, 1961.

———. *The Archetypes and the Collective Unconscious*. Princeton, NJ; Princeton University Press, 1990.

Laurence, Margaret. *Long Drums and Canon*. Edmonton, Canada: The University of Alberta Press, 2001.

Nwapa, Flora. *Efuru*. London: Heinemann, 1978.

Olaniyan, Tejumola. "God's Weeping Eyes: Hurston and the Anti-Patriarchal Form." *Obsidian II: Black Literature in Review*, 5 (Summer 1990): 30–45(16).
Said, Edward W. *Orientalism*. London: Routledge & Kegan Paul Ltd., 1978.
Umeh, Marie. "The Poetics of Economic Independence for Female Empowerment: An Interview with Flora Nwapa." *Research in African Literatures* 26.2 (1995): 22–29. Web. 8 Jan. 2012.
———. Ed. *Emerging Perspectives on Flora Nwapa*. Trenton: Africa World Press, 1998.

Chapter 5

Forces and Flaws in Flora Nwapa's *Efuru* and *Idu*

Perp St. Remy Asiegbu

INTRODUCTION

In his biting comment on Nwapa's works, Bernth Lindfors observes that her stories of distressed Igbo women are told monotonously; this deprives them of life and variety and parades characters that rarely perform. He further adds, "When her characters do act, they say and do things of little importance. Every chapter is littered with trivia, the detritus of an inexperienced novelist" (31). Although one of the concerns of this chapter is to show Nwapa's oversights in the narration of her foremost works—*Efuru* and *Idu*—it does not aim at totally dismissing her works as Lindfors has done above. Conversely, it affirms her pronounced legacy in the domain of African feminist literature. Nwapa's *Efuru* and *Idu* succeed in recounting the ordinary experiences of ordinary women in a third world community. It is, therefore, absurd for anyone to expect such works to be thrillers. A story of distress, as Lindfors notes, cannot sustain its thematic preoccupation if told with much excitement and color. Virginia Woolf would appear to come to Nwapa's rescue with this observation, "in dealing with women as writers, as much elasticity as possible is desirable, it is necessary to leave oneself room to deal with other things besides their work, so much has that work been influenced by conditions that have nothing whatever to do with art" (580). Commenting on the expectations of African fiction to appeal to international audience, Achebe recalls a tale he read:

> In a recent anthology a Hausa folktale, having recounted the usual fabulous incidents, ends with these words: "They all came and they lived happily together. He had several sons and daughters who grew up and helped in raising the standard of education of the country." As I said elsewhere, if you consider this ending a naïve anti-climax then you cannot know very much about Africa. ("The Novelist as Teacher" 105–6)

Mary Balogun and Remy Oriaku opine that *Efuru* and *Idu* are "compendiums of cultural practices as undergone by women in pristine Nigerian society with the main purpose of recreating the experiences of women in the traditional society with minor infiltration of other cultures in the assessment of the people" (118). Nwapa herself explains:

> In my first two novels, I tried to recreate the experiences of women in the traditional African society - their social and economic activities and above all their pre-occupation with the problems of recreation, infertility, and childbearing. Apart from exposing the pain, misery, and humiliation which childless or barren women suffer in the traditional society, the two novels (I hope) give insight into the resourcefulness and industriousness of women which often made them successful, respected, and influential people in the community. ("Women" 528)

Apart from the tradition of her people which, obviously, influences Nwapa's works, we will look at other forces outside and inside of Nwapa as a writer and how they manifest in Efuru and Idu, while at the same time noting the prevalence of certain flaws in the narration of the stories.

Reflecting on forces and the spirit world, Thomas Cromwell observes: "The reality of the spirit world can best be understood by recognizing the reality of intangible forces in life, such as the power of love to influence people through the invisible bonds of family, friendship, nationality, race, and religion. It is fair to say that most peoples' lives are governed by invisible influences stemming from belief, relationship, tradition, and culture. The world of humanity's physical environment is shaped by these internal forces because the activities of the body are directed by the mind. The realm of mind and spirit is causal to the world of body. ("Essentials of The Unification Principle" n. pag.)

The word "force" carries different connotations. However, all the meanings ascribed to it are connected to strength and power. Given the various definitions of force that border on "the strong effect or influence of something," force is described in this chapter as an influence, physical or spiritual, that controls and affects a person or thing and causes situations and circumstances to change. A. O. Kime has observed that, "The forces within the spirit world may not breathe but they're nonetheless lifelike. Who can say it isn't true? After all, science has no idea yet what constitutes life . . .

much less the possible parameters. Secondly, all of life's functions are living forces whether having a scientific (mechanical) explanation or not . . . and that applies to inspiration coming from out of the blue" ("The Muse of Greek Mythology" n. pag.).

The inspiration, thus spoken about, is celebrated in the creative world as the muse. Greek mythology has it that there are nine muses, otherwise referred to as "the muse." These are Greek goddesses who are daughters of Zeus and Mnemosyne. They are believed to inspire writers, musicians, and other artists. The goddesses and their domains of inspiration are as follows: Calliope—Epic Poetry; Clio—History; Erato—Song and Love poetry; Euterpe—Lyric Poetry and Music; Melpomene—Tragedy; Polyhymnia—Sacred poetry; Terpsichore—Dance; Thalia—Comedy; Urania—Astrology. For thousands of years, artists have acknowledged the existence and influence of the muse. Not even modern civilization with its amazing technological breakthrough in recent years has done anything to discredit the reality of muse among artists. This is explained on the basis that science cannot explain a lot about the subconscious mind; it knows nothing at all about the spirit world. Writers and other artists worldwide have chosen other archetypes and gods as their own individual muses or forces that inspire and influence their writing. Ogun is known as the muse of Nigeria's Nobel Laureate in literature, Wole Soyinka, for Ogun is Soyinka's muse and patron god, and his thyrsus is the stave made from the palm-wine (Macebuh 210).

This study, as hinted earlier, shall concern itself with the forces and flaws prevalent in Flora Nwapa's Efuru and Idu. It is noted and acknowledged, by some critics, that tradition is a major influence in Nwapa's foremost works. Here, besides tradition, emphasis is laid on certain supernatural forces surrounding Nwapa which are beyond her full comprehension and control. While this paper does not claim to know the force or muse behind Nwapa's works, it will point out some issues in the works that show the presence of certain forces. The flaws which are pointed out result, partly, from Nwapa's conscious or unconscious attempt to handle the forces some of which she is, most probably, vaguely aware of. Although, I would later criticize Nwapa's use of gossip, by mostly minor characters, to develop her plots, that and other observations do not write her stories off, considering that she is still able to sustain her subject matter revolving round the simple life of an ordinary African woman living out her experiences in a typical African setting.

THE REALITY OF FORCES IN *IDU* AND *EFURU*

Efuru is a self-respecting, self-assertive, and resilient woman. She builds up her husband's finances and makes him become more of a man in the sight of people. Adizua is a lazy farmer whose harvest comes to little or nothing at the end of the harvest season. His fellow farmers are amazed that Nwashike Ogene is "the man whose daughter that imbecile married" (Efuru 11). But, with the help of Efuru, Adizua makes a lot of money in trading. Efuru provides the strategies and advice that improve their economic wellbeing and, finally, he is able to pay the bride price. It may be said, therefore, that Efuru paid her own bride price, showing that where a man fails, a woman can succeed. That Efuru and Adizua "felt really married" (24) after paying the bride price shows the force of tradition at work on Nwapa. This, clearly, describes the writer as a custodian of traditional practices which uphold the dignity of womanhood. Efuru's defiant attitude in running off to Adizua without the latter paying the bride price has been attributed to Nwapa's feminist disposition. It is said to be "the first feminist statement of the book . . ." (Davies 249). Imo Eshiet affirms that it is Nwapa's way of condemning "an obsolete custom which ensnares women and keeps them as chattel in a male culture" (22). Efuru's attitude, rather than show disregard for tradition is, perhaps, the first sign of Uhamiri's interest in her. In Igbo land, those who are under the influence of some gods or spirits are known to exhibit some queer characteristics. Stubbornness or a defiant attitude is one of such character traits. This, most probably, explains Efuru's elopement with a man of Adizua's low status. Thus, Efuru's attitude of living with Adizua without observing the custom is a familiar characteristic of one possessed by the water spirit.

Efuru's beauty is such that prompts a character to quip, "She is so beautiful. You would think that the woman of the lake is her mother." The other character agrees: "After seeing this type of woman, one hisses when one sees one's wife" (*Efuru* 12). Unless Adizua is the Oguta version of the Greek Adonis, the reason why such a rare beauty (who later shows that she is not a woman to be treated shabbily), runs off to him, can be explained on the basis that she is under the influence of some strange force which is beyond her control; a power which is bigger than Nwashike Ogene, her father. This is why he does nothing but sends men to bring his daughter back, and this also explains the rather strange and effortless manner with which the men handle the case. Uhamiri's influence, therefore, more than Nwabuzo's gin, compels the men to leave Efuru to remain in Adizua's house. The spokesman says: "We shall go, our daughter . . . you seem to be happy here and we wonder why your father wants us to bring you back" (*Efuru* 9). Nwashike Ogene dissatisfied with the outcome, "sent another batch of young men from his village. But nothing came out of it" (*Efuru* 10). It is not out of place, therefore, to say that Uhamiri's choice of Efuru as her priestess does not just happen towards the end. There has been something of the Uhamiri spirit in her. Thus, Efuru's inane attitude in the beginning of the story serves, perhaps, as a prologue of the narrative; in the epilogue she is chosen as Uhamiri's devotee.

The great love that exists between Idu and Adiewere, around which Idu as a story revolves, is a significant force in the novel. The story of Idu as a character starts with her show of concern for her sick husband: "He had a headache yesterday, so he took some purgative medicine which I bought from the market. He has had a tummy upset since this morning" (*Idu* 1). This sickness, like Efuru's stubbornness in Efuru, is perhaps inauspicious to Adiewere's death. The cause of death is supposedly a brief illness or poison (208, 209). At the beginning of the story, the indescribable love between Adiewere and Idu is revealed to us through Uzoechi and Nwasobi's gossip: "'Sometimes when I see them, I am filled with happiness. Have you ever seen two people so happy before?' 'No, I never have. God created them as good people and God gave them to each other. You never see them quarrel, don't they ever quarrel?'" (2). Adiewere echoes the above statements: "God meant us for each other, and we were lucky to find each other" (206). Uzoechi and Nwasobi tell us, when Adiewere is ill again: "Well if something happens to Adiewere, Idu will be finished. I have never seen anyone lose weight as Idu has done recently. God created the two of them together and said they must be husband and wife. Do you know that if one is sick the other one becomes sick too. It is strange . . ." (150). This is a foreshadowing on the death of Adiewere and, consequently, Idu. Their love is very strong and their union is characterized by mutual respect and understanding so that even when Idu challenges her husband about his extramarital affair with Izukanane, he shows his great regard for her feelings by apologizing thus: "Leave it, my wife, forgive me. We men are like that . . . I want peace. There is no woman in the whole world like you" (207).

Love is so influential in Idu that wives die after their husbands' death. It is observed that Ojiugo died, in a way, after the death of Amarajeme: "She 'died' the day her husband died. The day Amarajeme died, that was the day she 'died'" (216). At the knowledge of her husband's death, Idu suffers mixed anxiety depressive disorder which is as a result of the shock and the burden of realizing that she is going to live without Adiewere. Her reaction is worthy of note. As he was lying face downwards on the floor. "She turned him over, called his name many times, but she could not reach him. He was already dead. She then went to Nwasobi's house to break the news. The calmness of Idu made Nwasobi's blood run cold" (209). Idu remains in this schizophrenic state; not eating; not sleeping; not crying, until she finally eats her last meal, lies down, and dies. Her love for Adiewere is so strong that she forsakes her only beloved son (Ijoma), her only sister (Anamadi), and her very good friend (Nwasobi), and dies for her husband (Adiewere). The force of love in this novel cannot be overemphasized.

The intrinsic force at work in creative writers is largely referred to as muse, as noted earlier. Writers, consciously or unconsciously, struggle with their muse in the course of developing their plots. This conflict often arises as a disagreement between one and oneself. It is a confused state in which a writer is indecisive about the next subplot or detail that the story should expose. This excerpt buttresses this point. It is from Deanna Mascle's witty testimony on the muse captioned "Why I Killed My Muse and You Should Too":

> It started out quietly. As I would sit at my keyboard or curl up with a notebook, she would perch on my shoulder as was her wont to do. "I don't think you meant to write that sentence," she would whisper in my ear. "That doesn't sound like the best description," she would snipe. "Is that the best you can do?" she would sneer. I took to sneaking my writing in when I knew she was occupied elsewhere. She never could resist critiquing the writing in the morning paper if it was left spread on the kitchen table. That way I could sometimes write several pages before she began her commentary. "Surely you can find a better way to approach this topic," her mocking voice would interrupt. "That has been so done." Soon I was spending more time arguing with her, defending my words, than I was writing. Then my production slowed to a crawl as I would overanalyze each word choice and sentence formation before committing it to screen or paper. All that did was give her more time to find fault with the few words I did write. . . . (n. pag.)

It appears that Nwapa does not allow the creative force behind her writing to have the final say in *Efuru* and *Idu*. This is noticeable in the final chapters. But it is hard to say who wants what. For instance, it is difficult to decipher whether it is her inspiration that must have a quarrel between Adiewere and Idu, or if Nwapa insists. Notice that Idu and Adiewere rarely disagree, they live very happily with Adiewere showering praises on Idu at every opportunity as has been observed before. They, indeed, quarrel only once and this is towards the end of the novel. This misunderstanding heats up to the extent that Adiewere refuses to eat Idu's food for days and even raises his hand to beat her. Idu exclaims: "A human being like yourself will not beat me for nothing. It is not really me you want to beat. Go and look for men like yourself to beat. It is here where I am that you have strength" (168). The only explanation to this bitter quarrel is that "The men-folk lorded it over their women-folk. Adiewere was merely making a fuss. All he had wanted was some petting from his wife it seemed. He was unable to hold anything concrete against Idu" (174). One would expect that what causes such a fight between such lovebirds will be something almost inexcusable. But, surprisingly enough, the cause of this huge disagreement is little or nothing. Moreover, there are no instances of "men lording it over their women" in Idu. Thus, it seems Nwapa is about to end the tale when suddenly, it occurs to her that it would appear larger than life if Adiewere and Idu do not quarrel even for once. So, she creates a fight which appears as fake as its cause.

There is, most probably, a force surrounding Idu's childlessness which Nwapa fails to expatiate upon. We see her conscious, and rather artistic, pairing of Ojiugo and Idu: "They had plenty of things in common as both had devoted husbands, but neither had borne her husband children" (37). This pairing becomes important to show that childlessness in a marriage is not always the fault of the woman because Ojiugo later leaves her husband, Amarajeme, when she realizes that she is pregnant with his friend's child. Thus, Ojiugo's childlessness is her husband's fault, and Idu's is her fault, or her chi's? This makes one wonder why Idu gets pregnant only when her husband takes another wife or is having an affair with another woman. It is to be noted that she becomes pregnant after many years of childlessness only when her husband marries the "small wife" (49). Also, when her husband begins an affair with Izukanane, she conceives again (204, 206). Could it be that there is something deeper about Idu's chi that Nwapa fails to lay emphasis on? A force which, most probably, is responsible for Adiewere's strange and untimely death especially as Nwapa has no explanation for his death as will be shown later.

FLAWS AND OVERSIGHTS IN THE NARRATION OF *EFURU* AND *IDU*

Nwapa uses what may be termed as a telltale technique in developing her plots. The stories are informed by a number of gossip by different characters—mostly minor characters in the novels whose opinions should not count. There is also too much dialogue and too little narrative. Furthermore, the stories are told in fragments of different people's lives with Idu's and Efuru's at the center. Those minor plots, unfortunately, fail to come together in the end and are not interlinked.

Nwapa makes it clear that Uhamiri does not intentionally deny her devotees children. In point of fact, she cannot give what she does not have. She has beauty and riches, and she gives them freely. Given her supernatural power, Uhamiri could cause the beauty and wealth of these women to make up, adequately, for their childlessness. But they still suffer, especially in the case of Efuru. When Efuru leaves Adizua, she has a company—her slave, Ogea. And her father is still alive. But, when she leaves Gilbert, she is a lonely woman, her father is dead, and Ogea is about to marry Gilbert. Why does she suffer so much? Efuru's ugly experience, as it is, is not as a result of her childlessness; Gilbert accepts her, childless or not. If, therefore, her tragic end is not connected to her childlessness; not for an evil she committed in the novel; then could it be her destined end as an Uhamiri devotee? Uhamiri seems to, purposely, deny her devotees personal fulfillment—when they are happily married, they are childless; when they have children, they lose their husbands and or children. What Efuru, for instance, gains in beauty and economic well-being, she loses in unhappy marriages and childlessness. This makes true an Igbo adage especially among non-worshippers of the water spirit—"Wete isi bia were isi, onyinye mammy water." This means that the water spirit's modus operandi is that she gives you something precious and takes an equally precious thing from you. This is arguably how Nwapa sets out to depict Uhamiri considering the way she (Uhamiri) is celebrated in these works. The facts are revealed in the stories.

Efuru's "washing" (female circumcision), for which Nwapa has been criticized, no doubt is an aberration. But we see the force of tradition at work again in Nwapa. The entire ritual is in concert with the dictates of traditional ethos. As the author reveals the reality of women's life in the Igbo tradition, we are intimated that Efuru "screamed and screamed" (14) while the circumcision was going on. This is Nwapa's way of exposing the torture that women undergo under certain traditional practices. The writer seems to show her approval for traditional practices as long as they do not bring so much pain or inhibit women. The ceremony that follows is celebrated not because the writer intends to put circumcision in good light, but, because she wishes to celebrate womanhood. However, in so doing, the ills of circumcision are not highlighted. Nwapa might have succeeded in this if she had given a different reason for the death of the baby whose mother failed to be circumcised (*Efuru* 14). By failing to do this, she approves of circumcision, albeit unconsciously.

Furthermore, Ajanupu is supposed to be an exemplary character. She speaks the truth bluntly and condemns injustice. She is strong, independent, assertive and a custodian of tradition. But Nwapa contradicts her character when she tells us that Ajanupu owes another woman and refuses to pay until the woman creates a scene: "'It is Ajanupu,' the woman said. '. . . She bought some yams from me three months ago. She gave me one pound and asked me to come the next day for five shillings. I have gone to her house nearly every day for the money but she refused to pay'" (49). The embarrassing part is that Ajanupu even has the money and would not pay until other women urge her to. Worse still, she has just returned from Nwabuzo, who owed Efuru, and has collected the money rather aggressively. Refusing to pay her own debt is, therefore, a conduct unbecoming of a woman of Ajanupu's character. It may be argued that Nwapa is only being realistic considering that no one is perfect but presenting Ajanupu in this manner confuses her character. She is a flat character, maintaining a wholesome attitude of strength, sisterhood, justice and fairness. Her fight with Gilbert, even, goes further to solidify her character. But the quarrel with this creditor is like a square shape in a round whole—unsuitable.

Again, Ajanupu discusses her children as if they were still very young. This is rather strange since she should be old enough to be a grandmother given the fact that she is older than Ossai, Efuru's mother-in-law (*Efuru* 176). It may, however, be possible that she might not have borne children until much later in life. Nevertheless, nothing in her depiction suggests that.

Another flaw is in the detail of Gilbert's first meeting with Efuru through a flashback. We are told that Gilbert had first seen Efuru in the stream and asked questions about her and "he was told that she had married but had left her husband" (117). But Nwapa forgets that Efuru had known Gilbert before. They were in the same age group, and as young boys and girls they had danced together and that he had visited Efuru before in Adizua's house (84–85).

In *Idu*, Adiewere is ill from the beginning of the story. When he finally dies, Nwapa mentions that "He had died of poison." But it is not clear if this is what the people think, or if it is the truth. Nwapa does not expatiate upon this. This is how she puts it: "What else could it be if not poison? That's not the way to die. One cannot return from the beach and die having one's bath, after vomiting and passing out blood. It is not natural" (*Idu* 209). If indeed he is poisoned, Nwapa should have told us how and why, if not she should have made it clear that the sickness which he suffers from in the beginning of the story, or some other thing, killed him. Adiewere's death is a significant event in the novel, so the readers ought to be fully informed about the cause.

Furthermore, one cannot but wonder why Efuru does not, as a devotee of the woman of the lake, consult and implore her when she is sick. And nobody really knows the cause of her illness. It seems that as in Idu, Nwapa comes up, suddenly, with a fuss without a cause. Efuru suddenly takes ill, a sickness that lasts for quite a long time and defies every effort to get her healed. She, who takes others to the doctor, could not request to be taken to a clinic. And then, the cause of this illness for which she is accused of adultery is not made clear, at least, to exonerate her from such a false allegation. Perhaps the reason Nwapa strikes Efuru with such an illness is to cause a misunderstanding between her and Gilbert, to create a reason for Efuru to go back to her father's house—an end which makes her childlessness more significant and agonizing. She goes back to her father's house alone, without a child to comfort her, without Ogea to assist her, not even with her father alive anymore to keep her company. Thus, Efuru ends up a sad, lonely, and suffering woman. Yet she has not committed any atrocity in the novel to warrant such a miserable end. Her fate is, therefore, worse than that of Idu, for the latter dies gallantly for love, rejecting a traditional practice that would impose on her a nonentity as a husband. Efuru's sad end is completely arbitrary unless it is explained on the basis of her destined end as Uhamiri's devotee.

If Nwapa has intended, however, to make Efuru an independent, happy woman by letting her become separated from her second husband, then she

(Nwapa) did not succeed in that because Efuru does not strike one as a successful, happy, and contented single woman, but as a lonely, forsaken, and suffering woman. Her end evokes pity from the reader, not "eureka!" This sympathy for her strikes the reader more at the point when Gilbert is absent at Efuru's father's burial. The irate Efuru refuses to talk about Gilbert: "Efuru hissed when Ajanupu mentioned Gilbert. She did not want to discuss it. She was very sad. Gilbert was not at the burial of Efuru's father" (204). This incident undoubtedly opens the wound inflicted by Adizua's absence at their daughter's burial. The pity for Efuru begins with Adizua's elopement with his lover, it gathers momentum when Gilbert accuses her of adultery and climaxes when she leaves his house. One begins to wonder why Efuru is very unfortunate in marriage. Fate, perhaps, or could it be that Uhamiri frustrates her purposely so that she could worship her with undivided attention? Future researchers on Nwapa may want to address this question and also unravel why Uhamiri is so celebrated, her inability to give the much wanted children notwithstanding. Even Nwapa wonders at this. The last three lines of Efuru read thus: "She gave women beauty and wealth, but she had no child. She had never experienced the joy of motherhood. Why then did the women worship her?" (221).

CONCLUSION

Nwapa's narration of the intricate and intriguing experiences of the Igbo woman in a world controlled by tradition and man—the custodian of tradition—is surrounded by a number of forces. Some of these influences, besides tradition and Uhamiri, which have been extensively treated include, love, fate, and other abstract, unnamed powers that control some of the experiences of her female characters and, of course, the force within her as a writer, otherwise known as a muse. The great affinity between Idu and her husband, Adiewere, indubitably, portrays the force of love in *Idu*. Idu's demise from grief over the loss of her husband lends credence to the power of love in this novel among other instances. The love professed to Efuru by both husbands, even though it fails to stand the test of time, also betrays the influence of love in *Efuru*.

The power of the unnamed forces is evidenced by Adiewere's death, of which no substantial reason is given, and also in Idu's rather strange struggle with childbearing. Idu's conceptions during odd situations in her marriage expose the influence of some weird forces. The two times that she gets pregnant is when her husband takes a second wife and when he is having an affair with his inamorata, Izukanane. It is not absurd to assume that the spiritual power behind the death of her husband is, most probably, responsible for her difficulty in conceiving, granting her heart's desire only when she had to contend with another woman for her husband's attention. This force is perhaps a spirit husband, though Nwapa does not make mention of it nor did she clearly explain the cause of Adiewere's death and Idu's uncanny conceptions.

Arguably, the power of Uhamiri as a force in Efuru, is first felt in Efuru's elopement with Adizua, who is evidently a nonentity. Such defiant, inexplicable, and uncontrollable characteristics are known traits of those possessed by the water spirit or some other forces. However, Nwapa's failure to link the unfair experiences of Efuru to the influence of Uhamiri establishes that the force of fate is integral to Efuru's sad ending. It is obvious that the writer's struggle with tradition is seen in her presentation of circumcision, her regard for bride price, and her romance with polygamy although she ensures that the second wives come to no good.

A writer's battle with her muse is clearly evident in Nwapa's sudden and impromptu creation of heated quarrels among the major couples in these works. The disagreements are caused by little or nothing. Hence, the squabbles are afterthoughts decided upon at the last minute, perhaps to make the stories more realistic. The many subplots that lack unification at the end of the story are also offshoots of this struggle. Nwapa's attempt, intentionally or unintentionally, at managing these forces leads to certain flaws to which no explanation has been given.

Be that as it may, Flora Nwapa succeeds in telling stories of her female folks by showing that they are not mere appendages to men; that they are worthy, hardworking, and dignified women, their sufferings as wives, mothers, and childless women notwithstanding. Nwapa's Efuru and Idu, therefore, "set the stage for many of her contemporary women writers to define the African reality" (Sridevi, 16).

WORKS CITED

Achebe, Chinua. "The Novelist as a Teacher." *African Literature: An Anthology of Criticism and Theory*. Eds. T. Olaniyan and Ato Quayson. Blackwell Publishing, 2007: 103–106.

Balogun, Mary and Remy Oriaku. "Charting the Growth of Gyno-Texts in Nigerian Prose Fiction." *Journal of Pan African Studies,* Vol. 6, No. 9 (May 2014): 117–133.

Cromwell, Thomas. "Essentials of the Unification Principle." Tparents.org. n.p. 21 Jul. 2015.

Davies, Carole Boyce. "Motherhood in the Works of Male and Female Igbo Writers: Achebe, Emecheta, Nwapa and Nzekwu." *Ngambika: Studies of Women in African Literature*. Eds. Carole B. Davies and Anne A Graves. Africa World Press, 1986: 241–256.

Eshiet, Imo. "Flora Nwapa as a Disruptive Pathfinder in a Male Dominated Literature." *Flora Nwapa: Critical Perspectives*. Eds. Ebele Eko et al. University of Calabar Press, 199: 21–32.

Lindfors, Bernth. "Nigerian Novel of 1966." *Africa Today*, Vol. 14, No. 5, 1967: 2731.

Macebuh, Stanley. "Poetics and The Mythic Imagination." *Critical Perspective on Wole Soyinka*. Ed. James Gibbs. Three Continents Press, 1980, 200–211.

Mascle, Deanna. "Why I killed My Muse and You Should Too." Fictionfactor.com. Testimonials to the Muse. n.d. 12 Nov. 2010.

Nwapa, Flora. *Efuru*. London: Heinemann Publishers, 1966.

———. *Idu*. London: Heinemann Publishers, 1970.

———. "Women and Creative Writing in Africa." *African Literature: An Anthology of Criticism and Theory*. Eds. Tejumola Olaniyan and Ato Quayson. Blackwell Publishing, 2007: 526–532.

Sridevi, Lalitha M. "Revival of Usable Past: Use of Myth and Folktales in Selected Works of Flora Nwapa." *International Journal of English Language, Literature and Translation Studies*, Vol. 2, No. 2, April–June 2015: 14–17.

Woolf, Virginia. "Women and Fiction." *The Novel: An Anthology of Criticism and Theory*. Ed. Dorothy Hale. Blackwell Publishing, 2006: 579–585.

PART 2

Orality and Rootedness in Culture and Tradition

Chapter 6

Wolof Taasu Genre as Narrative Device in Mariama Ba's *So Long a Letter*

Ada Uzoamaka Azodo

INTRODUCTION

This chapter seeks to unearth aspects of traditional Wolof culture embedded in Mariama Ba's seminal novel, *So Long a Letter* (*Une si longue lettre*). Attention is drawn to the role of the creative artist as a performer and to the creative art as performance. In addition, the performer's choice in characterization, language, style, and contexts of audience and occasion with any given performance is significant (Harding xiii). If this experimentation proves compelling and convincing, then Mariama Ba's novel is a work of art which underlines the legacy of its writer a producer of work of art, albeit one of an ephemeral existence, for as long as a particular reader is willing or able to recognize the said writer as an artist and her work as an art object. The recognition of the artist and her art require then that the reader pay attention to the physical self and presence of the artist, which is the condition *sine qua non* of any performance. According to Frances Harding:

> Each "reality" which appears—seems—to exist and which appears in order to exist, does so only for the duration of a performance. After the performance, there remains only the memory of a performance. Each performance is unique, each perhaps a "subsequent performance" (Miller 1986) of a familiar text, each neither an original nor a final product, but a reproduction, a representation of previous actions. Performance means: never for the first time. It means: for the

second to the nth time (Schechner 1985: 36). With such absolute centrality of the living self in a never original, never completed and always to be repeated act, what is the experience of performing for the performer? (. . .) There is a two-layered presentation of the self as performer, firstly as "body" (i.e. the physical presence) and secondly either as a "character" (a fictional persona) or as an extension of one's own persona (non-fictional). A distinction therefore can be made between the extent to which performers are the performance and the extent to which it is what they do that is the performance. As well as this, we can ask, to what extent do they present another? Within the presentation of self, in ceremonial performances (. . .), imaginative interpretation and reinterpretation—creativity—is not absent in these performances. (3)

Mariama Ba's *Une si longue letter (So Long a Letter)* can be read as the narrator Ramatoulaye's own Taasu. Through this genre, she details her crisis of a good wife, mother, and community member, who's mean husband destroyed their romantic relationship by introducing another woman into their relationship. Ramatoulaye's aim is that her hearers and readers should sympathize with her, offer her their understanding and compassion, and see the wisdom in her decision to stay in the polygynist household, and according to her personal principles of religious faith and ideals, despite the advice of friends and family to the contrary. We shall argue that Mariama Ba's *So Long a Letter* modifies the oral and traditional Wolof taasu genre, through a written form of contemporary professionalism, which further modifies the understanding of notions of culture and autobiography.

Ngone Mbaay's *taasu*, a laudatory and self-referential prose-poetry, most probably told at a naming ceremony of her son encapsulated in the refrain: "Ngone Mbaay, What burned in your fire?"[1] This version was related to Radio Television Senegal, and so bears contemporary marks of the oral artist's profession, like repetition of question lines—"Ngone Mbaay, What burned in your fire?"—that may not have been there in the spontaneous and regular version (McNee 46). Mbaay has since died; apparently there was a fire that gutted the couple's belongings, but we are not privileged to check on the veracity of this aspect of the story. Perhaps another way of reading it, as Lisa McNee has suggested, since competition is the basis of all taasu performance (56), is to see the symbolism of fire as a metaphor for conjugal problems that devoured the relationship between Mbaay and her husband. The fire then is her husband's passion for another woman, which passion and its concretization in the presence of another woman and wife have destroyed Mbaay's home.

The insertion of another woman between them caused a rupture in the couple's relationship, and this is the subject theme of the taasu. The taasu is used by the taasukat, performer, in a competitive mode to complain about her hurt, and more importantly to vaunt and elevate herself over her rival. In this instance, Ngone Mbaay goes on to detail her qualities of a good wife, good mother, and good community member. The long list of goods lost in the fire is meant to convey to the listener her virtues of a wife, who works hard to contribute to the family wealth and well-being. She has lived with her husband for several years and has not hindered him in any way, not in his goings and comings in the family. She has sons for her husband. In her capacity as a good mother, she has taken care of her children. She has provided her husband the wherewithal to assure his immortality. As a good community member, she has contributed to peace and harmony in the community, for she does not quarrel with anyone. Then why did her husband introduce another woman into their family? This is the problem that the taasu addresses.

Ngone Mbaay's husband is cast implicitly as a bad man for treating a good woman so shabbily. He is a womanizer, a skirt chaser, for in spite of his wife's goodness, he marries another wife, whose wedding ceremony is conducted as she, the first wife, is having the circumcision ceremony of her last-born son. The taasukat wants to share this issue as a gift with her friends and family, because she is overwhelmed with despair. The structure of the taasu with chorus and dialogue allows Mbaay to express her feelings openly. She nonetheless continually wards off evil that could fall on her at this vulnerable moment by exclaiming: "Laaw la cat! Kaar!" In the call-and-response, which is a mirror of a typical Wolof formal communication structure, the reader or listener sees a circular dynamic of exchange, which pushes along the story line. The taasukat expects from her friends and family a moral gift of compassion and understanding and other material gifts such as money.

THEORETICAL FRAMEWORK

The indigenous Wolof taasu genre forms part of the general self-praise, created and performed by the subject herself. In the performance of the taasu, the taasukat articulates her relationship with individuals and the community. In Wolof taxonomy, states Lisa McNee, the taasu is marked by gender in that it is almost exclusively performed by women, although some men have performed and still do as comic performers, mbàndkatt, such as clowns, buffoons, actors, what the Wolof call the géwel.

Moreover, the taasu is not a high art form given that the subject speaks for herself, like the Rwandan ukwivuga (speaking for oneself) or the Yoruba oriki, in which a new bride, Iyawo, reflects and speaks to call attention to her new status as a married woman (McNee 58). This taasu self is in opposition to the subject of such a high art as formal praise poetry by a professional bard or griot for an individual. In this instance, the praise consists of the family genealogical tree, lineage, which is accompanied with appropriate epithets, what the Wolof would call tàgget As McNee has noted,

> Since genres like praise songs and proverbs demonstrate that textual meaning is dependent on the context, it is necessary to modify the meaning of autobiography in the context of the taasu, to show that the performance of the taasu gives rise to the exchange between reader and text, and that the exchange between reader and text in turn engenders the performance. This modified model of articulations of self and community relies on a dynamic relationship. This Wolof genre differentiates the autobiographical exchange in the particular text from totalizing models that assume deterministic one-for-all exchange for all renditions. (56)

So, as in all cases of reader-response theory, this study depends on the critic's style of reading. Everything depends on the interpretative contexts and frameworks, which do not nullify previous readings of the same text. There is no attempt on our part as the present readers of Mariama Ba's text to collectivize Africa. On the contrary, this study seeks to construct a particular identity of the performer or autobiographer of *So Long a Letter* in a Wolof context. We shall explore how she represents herself in written form (a letter or a diary, depending on individual understanding), which becomes a public discourse, because it is published as an epistolary novel (Azodo 2). Our work in this study is an attempt to apply Lisa McNee's groundbreaking study of Senegalese women's autobiographical discourses, through coming to grips with the elusive Wolof cultural context of this most important novel in African literature, *Une si longue lettre*. We hope to open up thereby a rethinking of our understanding of Mariama Ba and our theoretical conceptions of the genre of autobiography in the African context.

In the textual study of Mariama Ba's *So Long a Letter,* Mariama Ba's narrator Ramatoulaye's mirasse (Moslem funeral ritual of stripping the dead to facilitate its entry into salvation) is a gift exchange to her audience as she searches for happiness. She hopes for an understanding of her plight as a betrayed and abandoned wife and mother, now widowed. She also hopes for an understanding of her earlier decision to remain with a betraying husband, and her subsequent decision to mourn him fully according to the tenets of Islam to which they both adhered. Furthermore, she has hopes for an understanding of why she decided to remain a single mother, raising some difficult children, rather than choose the easier way out of marrying a rich husband as her friends and family advice. Ramatoulaye valorizes, ultimately, a personal philosophy, according to which one must not run away from the blows of fate and destiny, but rather work them out with Voltaire-like diligence and determination. She states: "The word 'happiness' does indeed have meaning, doesn't it? I shall go out in search of it. Too bad for me if once again I have to write you so long a letter" (89).

In tracing Ramatoulaye's taasu, we shall adopt the same model used above in Ngone Mbaay's taasu. We shall explore Ramatoulaye's identities as wife, mother, and community member.

RAMATOULAYE AS WIFE

Ramatoulaye details her qualities of an excellent wife, such that even her sisters-in-law acknowledge this (19), for after Modou's death they treat her and her co-wife Binétou well. They had been generous and welcoming of the extended family, the sisters-in-law say. Ramatoulaye, particularly, had sometimes inconvenienced herself to accommodate the sisters-in-law who would desert their own homes to encumber her own. Not only did she accommodate the extended family (19–20), she made peace with them (56), gave more than she received (55), and loved her home (56). As a schoolteacher, she brought in extra money that helped to make the home as complete as possible. She could afford electronic gadgets for her kitchen, which meant that food was prepared faster. She had maids to help with the house chores. That meant that Modou, even if he was minded to help out, simply because he had lived in France and might have acquired the Western culture of men helping out at home—African men are not so socialized—did not have to do so. What is more, Ramatoulaye did not encumber Modou, who was free to come and go as he liked. Some women insist that their men must not go out without them. Ironically, perhaps, it was Ramatoulaye's largeness of heart that led to her betrayal. She would be the last to suspect that her husband was playing around with the young girl, a friend of their daughter, who often came home to study. As it happened, sometimes Modou suggested that he take her home when it was late. So, whereas Ramatoulaye had an open and sincere mind, it was Modou who had a sick and corrupt mind.

Yet in spite of thirty years of marriage, Modou deserts his family, morally and materially. What Ramatoulaye wants her listeners to understand is the extent of Modou's betrayal, his calumny and the complexities of her loss and problem:

> And to think that I loved this man passionately, to think that I gave him thirty years of my life, to think that twelve times over I carried his child. The addition of a rival to my life was not enough for him. In loving someone else, he burned his past, both morally and materially. He dared to commit such an act of disavowal. And yet, what didn't he do to make me his wife! (12)

In spite of everything, Ramatoulaye decides to remain and not leave the conjugal fold, seeing her decision as the "right" and "dignified" solution. Still Modou was wanting, for he left the family fold, rather than see through the relationship into which he willingly went: She continually lamented their broken relationship, and she rued the fact that she "was left with empty hands" (46).

Nonetheless, Ramatoulaye displays her superior qualities over the fickle-mindedness of Modou, by deciding again to mourn his death, as if he had been a good husband. She was not going to descend to his level by paying him back in his own coins. She was determined to carry out her duties fully by complying with the demands of Islamic religion and remain confined in mourning for four months and ten days (8–9).

RAMATOULAYE AS MOTHER

Ramatoulaye is not only a wife, but also a mother of twelve children from eleven pregnancies; she has one set of twins and four sons and eight daughters. After Modou's death, she quickly trains herself to take over his duties as husband and father of the household, in order to ensure continuity for her children. She learns to pay bills, change locks, and do all other manly duties as much as possible (51). Modou on his own part, while he is still alive has the effrontery to abandon his children for the love of another child, the friend of their first daughter, Daba. Still Ramatoulaye has decency and would disagree with Daba's attempts to confront their father in the night club with his new wife. Ramatoulaye would also disagree with Daba's attempts to confront Lady Mother-in-Law, her co-wife Binetou's mother, after the funeral, when the latter thought that the payments Modou made to them while he was alive would continue.

Ramatoulaye demonstrates resentment of her dead husband Modou when she finds out that he mortgaged the Villa Fallene where she lived with all their children, which he had earlier abandoned, for a whopping sum of four million francs, to pay for his excesses, a pilgrimage to Mecca for his new parents-in-law, and Alfa Romeos for his new wife at the slightest dent. Modu's betrayal and abandonment of Ramatoulaye was indicative of a preference for a new life adorned with a much younger wife (9).

RAMATOULAYE AS COMMUNITY MEMBER

The virtues of being a good wife and mother in Wolof culture go hand in hand with being a peaceful and harmonious member of the community as well.

Ramatoulaye tells her readers that she has been a submissive woman according to Islam and the Qur'an. She accepted the new wife as she was expected to do, despite the insults to her human dignity by Modou in not following tradition; she was not informed before her co-wife was chosen and was not allowed to have a say in who was chosen. Then again, she was ready to take turns as expected, but that was also denied her. Parents of her schoolchildren turned out in great numbers to console her when her husband died, because she was a good teacher in accord with them all. Furthermore, being from a large and notable family in town, she had always conducted herself as a true woman of upper class should, never descending to the level of her oppressors:

> As I come from a large family in this town, with acquaintances at all levels of society, as I am a schoolteacher on friendly terms with the pupils' parents, and as I have been Modou's companion for thirty years, I receive the greater share of money and many envelopes. The regard shown me raises me in the eyes of the others and it is Lady Mother-in-Law's turn to be annoyed. (6)

Ramatoulaye's taasu, as it were, continues with her avowal that she also well understood her husband's position as a fighter for the poor people's rights, and so supported him in every way to make his task easy, so that the people could always get what was possible for them. Ramatoulaye opines that, "Aggression and condescension in a woman arouse contempt and hatred for her husband. If she is gracious, even without appealing to any ideology, she can summon support for any action. In a word, a man's success depends on feminine support" (56).

Ramatoulaye decides to blame none other than her fate and destiny for her downfall. Her condition, she rationalizes, is more like that of the handicapped of society, the unrecognized heroes: "Your stoicism has made you not violent or subversive but true heroes, unknown in the mainstream of history, never upsetting established order, despite your miserable condition," she says (11). If anyone is bad, Ramatoulaye rationalizes again, it was Modou, and after Modou, it is Lady Mother-in-Law and then her daughter Binetou, in that descending order of culpability. As for herself, Ramatoulaye, she is above board, idealistic, honorable, free of selfishness and greed, and she is steadfast. These are distinctly her creator's virtues which are inscribed in her philosophies.

These are the messages Ramatoulaye/Ba as taasukat transmits to her readers in her taasu, messages written in her widow's hut over the period of the days of seclusion and confinement. It is now up to the interlocutors to judge who is a better human being, she or her aggressors.

CONCLUSION

The subgenre of the taasu applied to Mariama Ba's *So Long a Letter* renders her text as a modified form of a traditional Wolof oral genre. It is important to recall at this juncture that the indigenous Wolof taasu genre has one aim only, namely, to allow the taasukat to express her innermost feelings publicly, without inhibition. Furthermore, to help the performer to talk about herself in opposition to her rivals and adversaries as better off and worthy. Mariama Ba's narrator-heroine, Ramatoulaye, becomes a modern-day taasukat able to use this aspect of traditional Wolof culture to talk about her betrayal, her widowhood and all the attendant social problems of her community, not to mention the part that post-independentceSenegal plays in condoning the oppression of women. Clearly, her adversaries are three and more. Ramatoulaye assumes agency for herself. She was quite unwilling to act as she was urged, in order not to call herself into question. She would neither submit to the pressure nor to supernatural power. She opted to look reality in the face (49).

Accordingly, she refuses to consult marabouts, but rather sees her problem for what it is; she must have a better grip on her life, in order to change it for the better. By extension, she would like the entire Senegalese society to look at itself in the mirror and change its mores regarding the treatment of women in particular, and their views of gender and power in general. Ramatoulaye's lucidity and courage in many ways change our perception of autobiography, especially African autobiography, as a less than serious genre, and demonstrates that the Wolof taasu genre is a solid and valid oral literary genre that is adaptable in written form and can promote individual and collective identities.

WORKS CITED

Azodo, Ada Uzoamaka. "Lettre senégalaise de Ramatoulaye: Writing as Action in Mariama Ba's *Une si longue lettre.*" *Emerging Perspectives on Mariama Ba.* Ed. Ada Uzoamaka Azodo. Trenton, NJ: Africa World Press, 3.

Ba, Mariama. *Une si longue lettre* (1981, Heinemann). Dakar: Edition Serpent a plumes, 2002.

———. *So Long a Letter*. Portsmouth N.H.: Heinemann, 1989.

Harding, Frances. Ed. *The Performance Arts in Africa: A Reader*. London and New York: Routledge, 2002.

McNee, Lisa. *Selfish Gifts: Senegalese Women's Autobiographical Discourses*. Albany: State University of New York Press, 2000.

NOTE

1. This is a segment of an excerpt of Ngone Mbaay's taasu:

. . . —Ngone Mbaay, What has burned in your fire? . . .

I lost so much! . . .

(Extract from the Taasu of Ngone Mbaay of the Colom Fall village of Senegal, produced on April 4, 1969, and lodged in the Archives culturelles du Sénégal, and in the Archives of Radio Television Senegal (McNee 2000: 50–55).

Chapter 7

Non-Verbalized Communication of True Love in Traditional Dholuo in Grace Ogot's *The Promised Land*

Eunita Ochola

INTRODUCTION

Non-verbalized communication of romantic love in traditional Luo and other African languages and cultures remains a very interesting and intriguing topic in oral and modern African literature. (Dholuo is a western Nilotic language spoken by the Luo people along the shores of Lake Victoria in western Kenya, Tanzania, and Uganda). Equally interesting are misconceptions of the existence of romantic love in oral African culture.

In this chapter, I employ an integrated approach of semiotics theory of communication as proposed by Charles Sanders Pierce and cultural theory by Hall and Thompson et al., to explore the non-verbalized expression of romantic love in oral African literature and its carry-over into modern African literature. Primarily, I look at the way the Luo people expressed feelings of true love in Dholuo, during courtship and in marriage in Grace Ogot's *The Promised Land*, and how this type of communication of true love is changing/ evolving among the emerging new urbanized Luo people (Ogot 3). Although the article is focused on Ogot and the Luo culture, references are made to the cultural conflict between non-verbalized love depicted in Okot p'Bitek's *Song of Lawino* and Chinua Achebe's *Things Fall Apart*.

I argue that the non-verbalized communication of true love in the traditional Dholuo language was an integral part of the traditional oral Luo culture.

I show how the Luo people communicated romantic feelings through objects such as food, a third party, song, metaphorical, and proverbial expressions. More importantly, I claim that non-verbalization communication of love in this culture was a means of preserving love, because the Luo people believed that love was secretive, if not sacred. Finally, I believe that understanding the nature of non-verbalized communication of love in traditional Luo culture may help explain some questionable behavioral patterns in modern love relations among urbanized Luo husbands and wives, especially among those Luo husbands who hardly tell their wives *aheri*—"I love you."

In traditional Luo culture, like in some traditional African cultures, romantic feelings were not verbalized directly, and non-verbal expressions, such as kissing in public, which are typical of western and some urbanized African romance, were regarded with scorn, derided and severely satirized. Thus, many western people and some urbanized African people today may not understand why some African lovers are not verbally very expressive.

Yet there is no question as to the presence of words of love, such as *hera* "love," in Dholuo, or *upendo*, "love," in Swahili, and many traditional African languages. Furthermore, songs, such as *"Jeber yaye ang'o machandi* . . . Oh, the beautiful one what is bothering you . . ."* in Dholuo, or *"Malaika, nakupenda Malaika* . . . Angel, I love you Angel . . .*"* in Swahili are just a few examples of love songs that expressed *love* verbally in many African languages.

Moreover, the traditional Luo man and woman believed that they understood romantic love in every sense. p'Bitek, a famous post-colonial Ugandan writer, expresses this better when he writes in his *Song of Lawino*, "Women hunt for men. // And men want women" (27). At the same time, Achebe in *Things Fall Apart* summarizes communicating non-verbalized love between African lovers as follows:

> If I hold her hand,
> She says, don't touch me.
> If I hold her foot,
> She says don't touch me
> But if I hold her waistband
> She pretends not to know. (123)

BIOGRAPHY OF GRACE OGOT

Grace Emily Akinyi Ogot was born on May 15, 1930, in central Nyanza in Kenya. She was a well-known Kenyan author, nurse, journalist, politician, and diplomat. She was one of the first to author and publish several short stories about the Luo people of Kenya and their traditions in pre- and post-colonial periods in Kenya. She was also the first woman to have her fiction published by the East African Publishing House. Her stories, which appeared in European and African journals such as *Black Orpheus* and *Transition* and in collections such as *Land Without Thunder* (1968), *The Other Woman* (1976), and *The Island of Tears* (1980), give an inside view of traditional Luo life and society and the conflict of traditional with colonial and modern cultures. Her novel *The Promised Land* (1966) tells of Luo pioneers in Tanzania and western Kenya. Encyclopedia Britannica names Ogot among 100 trailblazers and extraordinary women who strove to promote issues of female concern. She died on March 18, 2015.

DEFINITION OF TERMS

Non-verbalized communication of love is used in this paper to refer to expressing romantic feelings indirectly through objects such as food, song, and dance in the oral Luo culture. Oral literature refers to the literature delivered by the word of mouth—"utterances, whether spoken, recited or sung, "whose composition and performance exhibit an appreciable degree the artistic characteristics of accurate observation, vivid imagination and ingenious expression" (Nandwa and Bukenya 19); traditional oral African literature is literature that is handed down from one generation to another by word of mouth (Okpewho 5); folklore consists of "what the people traditionally say (e.g. song, proverbs, tales) and what they traditionally do (e.g., weaving, dance, rituals)" (Okpewho 4–5); and "culture consists of the channels of communication used by people in regular interaction and the messages conveyed in them" (Parkin 2).

RESEARCH METHODOLOGY

Population

Data used in this paper came from ten elderly rural Luo men and women, between the ages of 60 and 70, three men and two women from Asembo and the other three men and two women from Nyakach. Another data came from ten rural Luo young men and women, between the ages of 30 and 50, three from rural Nyakach and seven from rural Asembo. There are also data from ten young, urbanized Nairobi Luo men and women (five each) and eleven adult first-language speakers of Dholuo living in the United States while pursuing further education. Data were also collected from five postgraduate first speakers of Dholuo, three women and two men, who were studying at Lancaster University, United Kingdom, in 1990 and 1991. The urbanized younger generation and graduate students were between the ages of 20 and 30.

Data Collection

I started collecting tape-recorded data on Dholuo in 1989 when I was enrolled in postgraduate degree program at Kenyatta University, Kenya. I tape recorded discussions of ten elderly rural Luo men and women on two separate occasions in April 1991, with each recording lasting at least two hours. My interest in studying the Dholuo language and culture continued when I came to the United States for my Ph.D. studies in linguistics in 1995, at the University of South Carolina. Between 1996 and 1997, I tape recorded informal conversations among my Luo friends on the Dholuo language and culture, during birthday parties and other social occasions. The data from the email messages were collected between 2000 and 2001, from email correspondence among twenty, first speakers of Dholuo, including me, who belong to *Jokiseru*, a global network group of elite Luo people globally. Most of the topics discussed in this forum ranged from the future of the Dholuo language and its culture, against the influence of the Western culture and urbanization.

BACKGROUND ON THE DHOLUO CULTURE AND LANGUAGE

The traditional Luo culture, like some African cultures, was largely polygamous and patriarchal. The traditional Luo man was allowed to marry as many wives as he could, so long as he was rich enough to pay the bride price for all the wives, and the man was the head of the home. Today, kinship in the Luo culture is still patrilinear (kinship is traced through the man), and the Luo society as a whole is a segmentary lineage (the society is organized into segments), and still remains localized in *dala* "the rural village" (see Parkins 9).

The patrilinear kinship and rural localization in traditional Luo culture helps in understanding the cultural changes in the modern Luo culture as well as understanding the current changes in communicating romantic feelings in modern Dholuo. According to Southall, "It is the rural localization of poly segmentary lineage that is the main factor facilitating [the Luo people's] modified but recognizable cultural continuity under urban conditions." This means the urbanized Luo people "tend to become bilateral as they settle in town" (Cohen 209).

SOCIALIZATION AND MORAL VALUES IN TRADITIONAL LUO CULTURE

Maintaining the good image of one's clan was very important in traditional Luo culture. At the age of seven both girls and boys were considered grown-ups, and they were told not to sleep together. At that age, a girl slept in *siwidhe* "an old woman's house." This house belongs to any woman who was past child-bearing age and no longer slept with a man. Young boys slept in an older boy's *simba,* "a bachelor/boy's hut."

Every night, *Pim* taught the girls moral values and the laws of the land, which the girls were expected to observe when they met or visited boys whom they might marry. Specifically, "*Pim* taught the girls to be careful not to lose their virginity whenever they slept near boys. The girls also learned and practiced *oigo* 'love songs' that every Luo girl was expected to know, and which the girls sang on their way to visit the young boys in their *simba*" (Ndisi 65).

All girls sleeping in *siwidhe* had to report their movements during the day to *Pim*, who also had to examine their dresses and ornaments, especially if the girls had visited a possible suitor's village. In the *simba*, the senior boy taught the younger ones to avoid rowdy behavior, such as starting fights, especially when they accepted the bride price for their future sisters-in-law, since such behavior could spoil/damage the name of the clan (Ndisi 66).

THE LANGUAGE OF TRUE LOVE IN THE DHOLUO LANGUAGE

The Dholuo language, like many other African languages, has a rich vocabulary and phrases that express romantic feelings. For example, the following Dholuo words are commonly used in romantic relations: *hera* "love," *osiep* "friend," *ja-hera* "lover," *ber* "beauty," *chuny* "heart," *gomb* "longing for," *ndi* "a lot/very much," *ma-tek/ma-thoth* "very much," *hero* "liking/loving," and others. These words also appear in romantic phrases, such as *jahera-n-a* "my lover," *osiep-n-a* "my friend," *osiep chuny-a* "my sweetheart/darling." These words are also used in romantic sentences.

The central issue of this paper is that in spite of the presence of the means to express romantic love verbally in the Dholuo language, the traditional Luo man and woman expressed such feelings non-verbally to each other for various cultural reasons.

SELECTED LITERATURE

There are many studies on traditional oral African literature (Okpewho 1992; Nandwa and Bukenya 1983; Babalola 1966). There are also many modern/post-colonial African writers (Achebe 1959; p'Bitek 1966; Ogot 1966; Radin 1957) whose works are referenced extensively in this study, because they present evidence of non-verbalized expression of love in traditional oral African literature. For example, although their works are written in English, the underlying structure of the discourse and choice of words in these post-colonial works are that of the African languages in which the stories are told, for example: "She had failed to start a baby in two months" (Ogot 19).

It would, however, seem that there are no substantial studies on the non-verbalized communication of romantic love in traditional oral African literature and languages like traditional Dholuo. This is probably because the language of love in traditional African cultures is so deeply rooted in cultural ideology that it requires only researchers well versed in these cultures to understand them. Note that many studies on African cultures were embarked upon mostly by foreign scholars who relied on translations, and as Okpewho has also pointed out, the literary qualities of oral African literature suffered from inadequate understanding of the African languages by foreign scholars and from sociological misunderstanding (Babalola 19).

The present study is an extension to the ongoing research on African languages and cultures by African and other scholars. The purpose of the study is to provide additional literature needed on non-verbalized communication of romantic love in traditional oral Dholuo language and other African languages. Moreover, investing non-verbalized communication of romantic love in traditional Luo culture also forms a backbone on understanding the root of some questionable behaviors in some romantic relations involving the urbanized Luo people specifically and African people in general.

FRAMEWORKS

This study adapts semiotic theory, which explores linguistic signs and how meaning is transmitted and understood; more important, semiotics has also come to imply any cultural product, including non-verbal communication, such as gestures, clothing, and other signs. According to Deely, "At the heart of semiotics is the realization that the whole of human experience, without exception, is an interpretive structure mediated and sustained by signs" (5; see also Barthes (1967), Saussure (1960), Pierce (1878)). The paper also employs the view of critical socio-cultural theory (Thompson et al 1990, Hall 1990), which assumes that cultural change is gradual, and that cultural features include kinship, esthetics, historical backgrounds. I use these frameworks to demonstrate how traditional Dholuo language and culture expressed non-verbalized communication of love, and how aspects of this expression of love have remained among the urbanized Luo lovers today. However, I should point out that the current debate on semiotics and critical social cultural theory are beyond the scope of this paper.

ANALYSIS OF TRUE ROMANTIC LOVE

As already pointed out, the traditional Luo people, like those people in many traditional African cultures believed that true romantic love was something very special, discreet, secretive, and almost sacred. Grace Ogot, a prolific Kenyan female writer, implicates this idea in several instances in her portrayal of the romantic love between Ochola and Nyapol in her 1966 novel, *The Promised Land*. In one particular instance, Ochola, Nyapol's suitor, and his people have just come from Nyapol's home where Nyapol's people tell Ochola that he is not fit to marry their daughter. Although Ochola and Nyapol are longing for and are desperate to hold each other, they have to wait until they are hidden away from the others. Ogot writes that as they were leaving the village:

> Nyapol and Ochola kept a little behind. They said nothing. When a small bush hid them from the others, Ochola grabbed Nyapol hungrily and crashed her to him. Then he pushed her roughly away and faced her. . . . "Nyapol, listen! No one shall take you away from me." (9)

In this excerpt, "they said nothing" signifies the fact that even when alone, neither Ochola nor Nyapol can tell the other, *aheri ahinya* "I love you very much." However, to show his undying love and desire for his bride, "Ochola grabbed Nyapol hungrily and crashed her to him." Nyapol's non-resistance to Ochola's roughness and non-verbalized response must be interpreted to mean that she is also telling Ochola: *An bende aheri gi chunya te* "I also love you with all my heart." Ndisi corroborates this when he notes that even when the traditional Luo man and woman danced together at beer parties, "They never danced hand in hand" (93).

LOVE WAS SECRETIVE; IT WAS NOT FOR PUBLIC CONSUMPTION

The idea that romantic love in the traditional oral Dholuo was secretive, sacred, and therefore not meant for public consumption is further revealed through Ochola and Nyapol's love affair, "The secret Ochola had made her keep smoldered in her flesh. The sensation she felt when Ochola crushed her to his chest was still alive in her young, erected breast. . . . Yes, this was the secret Ochola would not let her tell. Nyapol had not yet known a man and the burning fire within her could only be extinguished by a man she loved" (10–11). By "secret," Ogot implies the unquenched feeling of true love that both Ochola and Nyapol are experiencing during their courtship and the burning desire to hold each other.

Yet Ochola and Nyapol cannot even verbalize *jaherana* "sweetheart." To do so during courtship, Ochola would consider Nyapol a "girl with loose morals," something no traditional Luo girl wanted to hear, and Nyaopl would consider Ochola emotionally weak, a label every traditional Luo man avoided at all costs. In the main, Luo girls were taught that it was considered immoral to say to a boy, *jaherana* "my lover/sweetheart," or *aheri gi chunya te* "I love you with all my heart," directly. In the same vein, traditional Luo boys were taught that expressing their true romantic feelings to a girl publicly and verbally/directly was a sign of emotional weakness.

Achebe also shows this non-verbalized love through his main character, Okonkwo in *Thtngs Fall Apart* when he states, "Okonkwo ruled his household with a heavy hand. His wives, especially the youngest, lived in constant fear of his fiery temper. . . . Perhaps down deep in his heart Okonkwo was not a cruel man. But his whole life was dominated by fear, the fear of failure and of weakness" (14).

In the same vein, Ogot also shows how Ochola's actions are motivated by his fear of being considered weak. Nyapol is angry with Ochola for staying out late and Ochola, though guilty, tries to justify his staying out late as a "manly thing." After all, it was a wife's duty to open the door for a husband who keeps late night. Ochola knows full well he has to be home early to attend to the calves. "But to apologize now would set a precedent and then each time he came home late, he would have to explain where he had been" (*Promised Land* 12–13).

It can be argued that Ochola and Okonkwo's actions should not be interpreted as lack of caring and cruelty, these actions must rather be seen as non-verbalized communication of true love. After all, the traditional women were happy to talk about such "manly" actions with other women. Viewed from an egoistic perspective, it was a means of self-dignity for the man. For what woman would love a man who was a laughingstock in society?

Today, some urbanized Luo men support the traditional non-verbalized expression of romantic love. They believe that romantic love among the Luo people is still not a public affair nor is it for public consumption and "for your eye."

NON-VERBALIZED LOVE IS LOVE PRESERVED

The traditional Luo people also believed that true love was to be consumed in small doses. The Luo people also believe that verbalizing and showing romantic feelings of true love directly and over and over weakened and wore out love prematurely. When love is worn out, it withers and dies quickly. This view of love can be seen in the contrast between Ogot's portrayal of Nyapol's relationship with Ochola in *The Promised Land* and her depiction of Mr. Jimbo's relationship with Elizabeth in her collction of short stories *Land without Thunder*. For example, as had been earlier stated, when Ochola saw that he and Nyapol were hidden from the others, he had lustfully grabbed Nyapol but roughly released her as he did not want to be tempted into demanding sex from her. He would rather show her how much he loved and longed for her. In her short story, Ogot compares Ochola's gentility in ruthlessness with Nyapol to the harshness of Mr. Jimbo (a married man) towards Elizabeth in verbalized love. For instance, Mr. Jimbo tells Elizabeth, "I care too much about you. No, Liz, you are so lovable" (196). The fact that Ochola does not force Nyapol to have sex with him while Mr. Jimbo ends up raping Elizabeth, because she refuses to have sex with him, underscores Ogot's belief that non-verbalized expression of romantic love was still more acceptable among the post-colonial urbanized Luo people.

NON-VERBALIZED LOVE WAS AGGRESSIVE, BUT ALSO GENTLE

Non-verbalized expression of romantic feelings of love in traditional Luo and other African cultures was aggressive and even very rough at times; however, it was also viewed as very gentle. The argument here is that most western colonial writers, scholars, and Christian missionaries did not understand the local culture and language and misreported the non-verbalized expression of romantic love among the indigenous Africans. For example, *yuecho* "pulling" among the traditional Luo people appeared ruthless and rough, but it was the Luo people's marriage custom. I argue that the roughness in *ywecho* and the girl's "pretentious" screaming and resistance during *ywecho* symbolized years of muffled burning fire of love within the girl "wife-to-be," a fire that had just been waiting for the right time to erupt, like a volcanic eruption. Ogot's portrayal of Ochola's roughness to Nyapol in the brief moment the two lovers find themselves alone illustrates this better, "Ochola grabbed Nyapol hungrily and crashed her to him. Then he pushed her roughly away and faced her" *(Promised Land* 9).

The urgency and fear in Ochola's voice, at the thought of losing his bride, is revealed in "'Tell me quickly why you have stabbed me in the back! How can you put a calabash of water to my lips and suddenly remove it, leaving me to die of thirst?'" (10). Ogot's metaphorical use of "calabash of water," "my lips," and *the death of love* from *the thirst of love* signifies her prejudice for non-verbalized love.

Ogot's view of *aggressive love* in non-violent love is supported by Liyong who also notes the aggressive nature of romantic love during courtship among the Luhya people. Liyong illustrates this provocative and aggressive nature of love in the traditional Luhya culture (18–19).

DIFFERENT WAYS OF EXPRESSING LOVE NON-VERBALLY IN THE TRADITIONAL LUO CULTURE

Expressing *Hera Mar Chuny* "Deep Love from the Heart" through Food

The traditional Luo people expressed non-verbalized romantic love through food. Traditionally, the Luo man was expected to look for food and bring it home to the family, while the woman was expected to cook the food. However, occasionally, a man went out of his way to look for the best food there was to bring home when he wanted to show his wife how much he appreciated her. At the same time, when a wife wanted to show her romantic love for the man, she cooked the food in a special way and served.

The role of food in expressing non-verbalized romantic love is also delineated by Achebe in *Things Fall Apart*. Ekwefi prepares Okonkwo's meal in a special way: "Okonkwo had not tested any food for two days. On the third day, he asked his second wife, Ekwefi, to roast plantains for him. She prepared it the way he liked—with slices of oil-bean and fish" (66). Achebe shows how Ekwefi communicated her non-verbalized love for Okonkwo by preparing her husband's food the way he liked his meals prepared.

Essentially, in many traditional African cultures, a woman could tell that the man loved her by how much he liked her food and how much of her food he ate. Ogot shows this through Nyapol's complaint to Ochola when he does not eat her food: "You treat me as if you only picked me up from the marketplace. You don't eat the food I put before you" (18). However, when Ochola eats up all his breakfast, Nyapol tells Ochola about her earlier apprehension that he did not want to eat breakfast. To acknowledge her non-verbalized expression of love, Ochola assured her he would never miss breakfast. Then, he drank a mouthful and said, "'Mm, this porridge is good.' 'I'm glad' Nyapol responded" (23). This dialogue also illustrates how couples could use food to create light moments in traditional Luo culture.

How a Man and a Woman Told Each Other *Aheri* "I Love You" through Stubbornness

Traditionally, a Luo man was expected to go out with his male friends every evening and not to be back home until late at night. But sometimes some men stayed out too late into the night. This is illustrated by Ogot when Ochola leaves his bride home alone at night to visit with his neighbor's friends from Tanzania. Much as he felt guilty when he came back, he brushed it off with "the proud voice of a man in him" wondering why a man should not stay out as long as he wanted (12–13). This is an instance of stubborn love among the traditional Luo with the strong conviction that men had to act as real men.

Similarly, the women showed romantic love through stubbornness. This is evident when Nyapol also shows Ochola that she can be stubborn by refusing to ask him where he had been. Although she was not sleepy, she went straight to bed, very angry (19). Ogot allows the reader to see the stubborn love between Ochola and Nyapol, as true love expressed in small doses, through Nyapol and Ochola's thoughts:

> Nyapol wondered sadly what had turned Ochola against her so much . . . she *too* grew moody and refused to talk . . . Ochola remained smoking and staring into nothing. . . . Her heart was sore and the desire *to have a child burned within her womb.* She had failed to start a baby in two months running. (19)

This shows that both Ochola and Nyapol are sizing each other up, as if they are waiting to see who would fold in first. To her mind, Ochola has recently been cold and indifferent. When she started sobbing, "*To her surprise*, Ochola suddenly jumped to his feet and went to her. He put his arms around her and *asked tenderly*, 'What bothers you? Have you received bad news from home?'" (19).

In addition, Nyapol's rudeness toward Ochola when Ochola comes home late at night and finds her wrestling with the calves which had run loose should be interpreted as an indirect expression of her love for Ochola. In the scene below, Nyapol is furious with Ochola for being away when the calves are loose and when he should be home sleeping next to her. "Who is it?" Ochola's voice asks. When Nyapol recognizes the voice, she does not hide her anger, "'Who did you expect to be here at such an hour?' Nyapol asked, her own voice trembling and tears blinding her eye. 'What are you doing alone in the cow-pen at such an hour?' Ochola asked. Instead of replying, Nyapol *dragged* the second calf away from its mother and tied it roughly on to a peg. Resentment still filled her heart and she refused to look in her husband's direction" (12).

The line, "her own voice trembling and tears blinding her eye" can also be interpreted as Nyapol's volcanic love, ready to explode consume Ochola. At the same time, the excerpt above is also an illustration of why the traditional Luo people believed in consuming love in small dosages. For example, though Ochola and Nyapol just got married, it is clear that they have not had much sex like most newlyweds would at this time. Especially when Nyapol confesses, "'You don't talk to me and at night you forget that I am a woman longing to hold a baby in my arms'" (12). Ogot indicates that Nyapol is reminding Ochola that it was about time they slept together more often so as to "start a baby" (19).

CONCLUSION

This study shows that there is a connection between non-verbalized communication of romantic love in traditional and modern African literature. It indicates that an understanding of this form of romantic love is necessary in analyzing the depiction of characters in post-colonial and modern African literature and understanding the direction of African literature. Ogot's characters in Ochola and Nyapol have also indicated that cultural change in traditional Luo culture and the Dholuo language, like in other oral African cultures and languages, is already taking place. For this reason, I conclude that a study on specialized topics such as this is necessary, if not for anything else, but for the preservation of the traditional African cultures and languages. In addition, given the amount of interest currently shown in African languages, this kind of study will help foreign and African scholars better to understanding the research they are undertaking in African languages and cultures.

In sum, many urbanized Luo people, like some African people, have maintained strong connections with the extended rural kinship (*jodala* "the home people"). Thus, a study like this will help explain non-verbalized behaviors of some married urbanized Luo people. The fact that "many Luo urban family settlements (like other urbanized African people) occur in conjunction with and not to the exclusion of strong rural lineage involvement" (Parkin 1978, 8–9) means that the urbanized Luo people remain largely bilateral through rural location. This is probably why p'Bitek seems to be suggesting a compromise, when Lawino says one can eat the white man's food so long as the ultimate goal is freedom.

> To have freedom. . . .
> To eat what one wants? (78–80)

Eating the white man's food, which is definitely not forced down one's throat, implies a seamless integration of tradition and modernity—the new and the old.

Finally, one of the problems I encountered during this research is the lack of the older population (80 years and older) among the Luo people and other African ethnic groups. There are very few Luo men and women in this age group, and even the few who are there are hard to track down because they are scattered all over the place. Thus, although strongly recommended, this type of research requires time and money. With the availability of the two, I believe very strongly that non-verbalized communication of true love in traditional oral African cultures can be reconstructed and formalized into verbalized language of love for a comparative study, and/or just for preservation purposes. Moreover, younger authors should follow in the footsteps of Grace Ogot who has left a legacy by striving to accentuate some aspects of tradition and orality in her works.

WORKS CITED

Achebe, Chinua. *Things Fall Apart*. London: Heinemann. 1959.

Babalola, Adibaye S. *The Content and Form of Yoruba Ijala*. Oxford: Clarendon Press, 1966.

Cohen, A. *Politics and Customs in Urban Africa*. London: Routledge and Kegan Paul, 1969.

Deely, J. *Basics of Semiotics*. Bloomington, IN: Indiana University Press, 1990.

Donahoe, J.W. and D. C. Palmer. *Learning and Complex Behavior*, Allyn and Bacon, 1993.

Dundes, A et al.(ed) *The Study of Folklore*, Englewood Cliff: Prentice Hall, 1965.

Hall, Stuart. "Culture, Identity, and Diaspora." In *Rutherford Identity, Community, and Cultural Differences*. London: Lawrence & Wishhard, 1990.

Kokwaro, John O. and Johns Timothy ed. *Luo Biological Dictionary*. Nairobi: East African Educational Publisher, 1998.

Liyong, Taban Lo. *Popular Cultures of East Africa: Oral Literature*. Nairobi: Longman, 1972.

Marley, Bob. "No, Woman, No Cry." *Natty Dread*, 1975, http://www.leoslyrics.com/listlyrics.php.

Nandwa, Jane, and Bukenya Austin. *African Oral Literature for Schools*. Nairobi: Longman Kenya, 1983.

Ndisi, John W. *A Study in the Economic and Social Life of the Luo of Kenya*. UPPSALA, 1973.

Ogot, B. A. *History of the Southern Luo*. London: Heinemann, 1967.

Ogot, Grace. *Land without Thunder and Other Stories*. Nairobi: East African Educational Publishers, 1988.

———. *The Promised Land: A True Fantasy*. Nairobi: East African Publishing House, 1966.

———. *The Strange Bride*, Trans.Okoth Okombo. Nairobi: Heinemann, 1966.

Okpewho, Isidore, ed. *African Oral Literature*. Bloomington: Indiana University Press, 1992.

p'Bitek, Okot. *Song of Lawino and Song of Ocol*, London: Heinemann,1966. London: Academic Press.

Parkin, David. *Cultural Definition of Political Response: Lineal Destiny among the Luo*. London: Academic Press, 1989.

Pierce, Charles S. "Deduction, Induction, and Hypothesis." In *Writings of Charles S. Pierce: A Chronological Edition*, vol. 3, pp. 1872–1878. Bloomington: Indiana University Press.

Thompson, et al. *Cultural Theory*. Oxford: Westview Press, 1990.

"100 Women Trailblazers." Britannica, https://www.britannica.com/biography/Grace-Ogot. Accessed Apr. 11, 2021.

Wilson, Gordon. *Luo Customary Laws and Marriage Law Customs*, 1961, Nairobi: Government Printer.

Chapter 8

Validation of Culture
A Re-reading of Zulu Sofola's Wedlock of the Gods *and* King Emene: A Tragedy of Rebellion

Nkem Okoh

INTRODUCTION

Having established itself as a veritably viable scholarly domain, African literature today can be seen as espousing such concerns as post-modernism and post-colonialism. Despite the enormous progress recorded by modern African literature up to and into the twenty-first century, however, this literature cannot necessarily be associated with rosy beginnings. Even for its founding father, it was far from smooth sailing, whether in terms of establishing" where the rain began to beat us" or pursuing the fundamental theme in order to put away the complexes and years of denigration. Nor was it an easy ride for the other first generation African writers, who were generally male.

Against this background, it becomes even more pertinent to study an artist who is not only a major African writer, but also the continent's first female playwright: 'Zulu Sofola. In spite of the progress by modern African literature, as evidenced by the present proliferation of posts seen above, it is vital to cast some backward glances at what may conversely be called the early or pre-days of this literature, an era to which Sofola justifiably imperiously belongs. Such glances are worthwhile, since time is of the essence. The fact that more female African writers have emerged since the heyday of African literature and over fifty years after Flora Nwapa's *Efuru* also makes it even imperative to consider African female writing from a retrospective standpoint.

The image of Sofola clearly looms large on the Nigerian literary landscape, while her pioneering role in the development of Nigerian drama remains undeniable. This chapter is not concerned with her dramaturgy, her particular conception of the stage or technical understanding of theatre, especially as the present writer is not a theatre practitioner. Rather, the paper examines Sofola's exploration, indeed re-creation, of Enuani culture. Thus, we focus on her particular attention to the linguistic and literary aspects of her craft, that is, the major means by which she endeavors to achieve an authentic and successful depiction of this society.

To consider a playwright's work from such a perspective necessitates no hairsplitting, as drama also represents a literary domain. Not only is there a great interconnection between literature and linguistic expression, language itself constitutes the foremost medium by which the artist (poet, novelist, or dramatist) strives to encode or communicate his message to an audience. While we have underscored the largely literary leanings of this study, we focus specifically on Sofola's use of Enuani oral literature. It is a common misconception to associate African literature with only the modern or written. In our context, therefore, the term literary by no means refers exclusively to written literature, as we are actually concerned with the oral. Okoh clearly justifies investigating a culture via its oral literature: "Whether in a nonliterate or highly technologized context, oral literature . . . can provide any society with a potent tool for introspection, reflection, regeneration, or reform" ("Regal" 22).

The discourse here centers specifically on *Wedlock of the Gods* (1972) and *King Emene: Tragedy of a Rebellion* (1974). Not only are both works tragic compositions, they sufficiently fit into the overall drift of this chapter. Considering when they were both published, an era in which disposing of the fundamental theme was particularly critical, the paper argues that as a writer and especially in both works, Sofola is concerned with exposing and, more importantly, validating, the Enuani culture in general, and oral literature in particular. Okoh considers both the culture and oral literature as "insufficiently exposed," then adds, "Whereas a substantial body of scholarly literature exists on the arts and culture of the east Niger Igbo, comparatively little research has been done on the Enuani Igbo" ("Categories" 73). A sub-thesis here is that Sofola's concern with validation is propelled and propped by an intimate understanding of this culture. As will be shown, such deep knowledge is unmistakably demonstrated in her creative incorporation of the people's oral literature and overall discourse behavior in both works.

SOFOLA ON ASPECTS OF ENUANI CULTURE

We have posited that Sofola is especially concerned with exposing and, more importantly, validating, an indigenous African culture. While her work concerns literature, not history or sociology, we further argue that her overriding artistic motivation or objective, namely the recreation of a society through its oral literature, remains a clearly profitable undertaking. As will be shown, Sofola's work, like oral literature and its performance, involves what Okoh calls a "coalescing of tradition and modernity" ("Synergies" 29). Thus, by the instrumentality of such link, contemporary Nigerian society can see the past, live the present, then plan for the future, that is, by studying its oral literature. In Nigeria's quest for national cohesion and development, oral literature provides some profoundly wholesome messages which are potentially of benefit to the country.

No doubt, Africa has generally been perceived by Europe as a backward and barren continent. African writers have contributed greatly to destroying "the specter of misconceptions, distortions and negative stereotyping . . . perennially pursuing Africa" (Okoh, "Big Brother" 411), leading to a better understanding of the continent and her peoples. As Okoh also comments, "Chinua Achebe's declaration of a fundamental theme was like a salvo or battle cry for other African writers to confront and overturn the perverted Western conception of the African as a benighted, barbaric and inferior specimen of humanity" ("Father and Son" 211).

Of course, there were claims by Europe that Africans had neither history, philosophy nor religion. In the last-named domain, for example, it was claimed that Africans were ignorant about God. The reality, of course, remains that the people considered Chukwu (Chi ukwu = "the big God") too mighty to be approached by humans. For this reason, such smaller intermediaries or gods as Mkpitime were approached. Sofola clearly illuminates this aspect of the culture, even in view of the fundamental theme. Before the palace altar, the Mother of King Emene prays for her son, a prayer she directs simultaneously to both God and Mkpitime, the Merciful Mother:

> NNEOBI: . . . Oh Mkpitime, who understands all things,
>   Have mercy on me . . .
>   Merciful Mother, dry my tears. (*Emene* 39)

The reader also encounters such other prayers as:

> QUEEN: Goddess of Life, bless your children;
>   God of all, bless my husband. (*Emene* 1)

In praying for the young king to see reason, his godfather, Ojei, makes references to both the almighty God and the indigenous gods: "The person whose god does not want him to see is the one who has a blind man for a godparent. I am not blind. I have seen and I have advised you. If you see, then God be thanked; but if not, then God will see that I have done my part" (34).

The foregoing prayers are plainly replete with parallel references or simultaneous invocations to both the Almighty God and the gods of the indigenous pantheon. With such frequent juxtaposition, Sofola may be accused of advocating syncretistic tendencies, but she is actually presenting a basic religious reality. Such parallel portrayal also points to her intimate understanding of the culture, especially as the iba-nzu (Peace Week) is central to the entire action in *King Emene*. In addition to the prayers, Sofola incorporates such other aspects of the people's religious life as ancestors, libation, divination, shrines, and oracles. In both plays, she accurately depicts such religious paraphernalia of the people as palm wine, kola nuts, the ikenga, okwa (wooden tray), otulaka (horn), deer horn (for drinking palm wine), ofo (short wooden staff), afa (divination equipment), goatskin bag, and nzu (white chalk). Thus, any director on production of the plays will be careful not to ignore such central Enuani cultural accoutrements.

Another important dimension of the culture which Sofola depicts concerns the political and how the Enuani conceive of their kings. The question of governance is important to the Enuani, as it is to virtually all societies of the world. Thomas Paine captures this reality thus: "There is no subject more interesting to every man than the subject of government. His security, be he rich or poor, and in great measure his prosperity, are connected therewith" (*First Principles* 135–136). Sofola provides an authentic portrayal of the Enuani political configuration, that is, with its democratic and egalitarian leanings. While the king has enormous powers over his subjects and expects allegiance from them, he necessarily upholds the democratic ideals of the society. It is exactly the violation of this code that provokes a confrontation, which is played out early in Act 1, Scene One (*Emene*). In the following, there is a prevailing air of inevitability, as the people contend with a king who is not only recalcitrant, but also suspects everybody.

Because the king failed in this important regard and, in spite of his enormous powers, the people stage a protest. A mob action follows, as the people demand the abdication of the king:

1ST Voice: . . . Let everybody tell him that he is not fit to pray to Mkpitime for us.

2ND Voice: . . . who are you that you must do only what pleases you?

1ST Voice: We don't want you to pray for us . . .

1ST 2nd Voice: He is not our King! (41–42)

Indeed, the whole commotion attains a climax here as they not only reject him as their King but also chase him away:

MOB: [In a frenzy] Open the door and get that King out! (43)

The overall picture here shows that in olden days, the king wielded considerable power. Sofola's contention at this point is that political change has become imperative. In other words, power should be shared; the king, rather than being greater than the people, should be accountable to them. It is such seemingly simple stipulation that Achebe's towering and intellectual character, Ezeulu, rejects, leading to his downfall in *Arrow of God*. From this viewpoint, the end of *King Emene* deserves further comment. The play can be considered as concluding with a message which cannot be disregarded, apart from being congruent with the following assertion: "[S]uch [the king's] powers should be . . . used to protect, not marginalize the populace . . . no consequences can be too grave for tyrannizing rather than protecting the people. And since [the King] is not above the law, he pays the supreme penalty for abusing his powers" (Okoh, "Regal" 29). This, in fact, can be seen as succinctly capturing the very conclusion of Sofola's *King Emene*.

SOFOLA AND THE LINGUISTIC ESSENCE

This section endeavors to demonstrate that in her use of language, Sofola has contributed greatly, not only to African literature, but also to African women's writing. Any keen reading of Sofola promptly reveals the sheer beauty of her language, while the two works here clearly bristle with a sparklingly delightful use of language. Anwasia deems Ogwoma's pregnancy quite offensive, as the latter should be mourning her late husband instead of being emotionally or sexually involved with a lover (*Wedlock of the Gods* 8). Far from being perturbed, Ogwoma is, of course, adamant.

Thus, to denote Ogwoma's iron determination, even in committing what members of her community consider an abomination, Sofola deploys language in a striking fashion; the language is condensed and distinctly delightful. In fact, the expression here is not only particularly poetic, but it evidently captures the feeling of love and encapsulates the very language of love:

OGWOMA: Let the moon turn into blood; let the rain become fire;
Ogwoma loves and Ogwoma will do it again! (9–10)

In both plays, we find, not a fortuitous depiction, but a genuine artist and craftsman at work. Sofola's language is particularly poignant, as she further endeavors to paint a picture of the supremacy, obduracy and durability of genuine, passionate, consuming love, as Uloko declares: "Come, my love . . . I love you dearly . . . and that seed which is in you shall make our joy complete. The stars are on our side" (*Wedlock* 14).

Like Charlotte Brontë in *Jane Eyre*, Sofola is concerned with depicting a truly enduring love story. Ogwoma is not afraid to stand alone or swim against the very tide of tradition. Her resistance is not motivated by a desire to be recalcitrant or nonconformist, but by genuine love. It is a peculiarly persistent love which the society simply cannot fathom. As Odi accurately comments, "The theme of Ogwoma and Uloko's love breaks all traditional and cultural constructs and exposes an existentialist individualism that the society cannot come to terms with" (46). Sofola endeavors to demonstrate that even in a traditional African setting, true love can deliberately and decidedly defy all odds. More importantly, the language here attains an artistic zenith as the playwright paints some really exhilarating love scenes:

> OGWOMA: Oh God, Uloko has blinded me. / I go to the market,
> It is Uloko I see in every stall . . . (10)

Nor is such profession and profusion of love one-sided. Thus, Sofola not only depicts a man fiercely in love, but more importantly, employs appropriately poetic and emotional language: "ULOKO: Ogwoma, please, don't make my heart bleed . . ." (12). In fact, Sofola raises the intensity of the language, as *Wedlock of the Gods*' very concluding lines, which are highly emotive and evocative:

> ULOKO: Ours is the wedlock of the gods.
> Together we shall forever be lightning
> And thunder—inseparable. (55–56)

Such delightfully expressed and aesthetically pleasing lines are even further embellished by a striking use of parallelism, highly reminiscent of Churchill's war time speech stressing his determination to fight.

Not only is the language of the following clearly measured and moving, it is further heightened by its very metaphorical exquisiteness:

> DIOKPA: When your father was with us, we saw the best of things . . .
> Our old men had crowns of silver . . .
> Our young men moved mountains;
> The rivers laughed and the trees clapped their hands! (*Emene* 19–20)

This was how your father left us, and this is what we want to retain. Things were much better in the community then. The young King's coronation ushered in strife and destruction. Still, to posit that one of Sofola's contributions to African literature lies in her remarkable use of language is to demonstrate only one dimension of her creative endeavors. It is thus imperative to consider another crucial linguistic component of her work, namely proverbs.

While it is true that modern African literature "hardly stands alone, but remains inextricably linked with the different Nigerian oral literatures" (Okoh, "Fear of" 358), in no other area is such interlocking relationship more apparent than in the use of proverbs. Chukwuma calls the proverb "'the basic genre' as well as 'the core' of Igbo oral literature" (28). Not only is her comment easily applicable to virtually all African societies, it also suggests the prominence of proverbs in African writing. It must rank as a cliché to either state that African writers borrow extensively from their oral traditions or that they copiously incorporate proverbs in their works.

While the Enuani culture boasts several techniques for "sweetening" speech, proverbs constitute a foremost means of enriching discourse in this society. Sofola demonstrates the well-known Enuani love of discourse, even the Pan-Igbo palm oil/proverb analogy. Okoh calls proverbs "a crucial means of communication in Igbo" ("Direction" 254), then adds as follows: "[P]roverbs and indirection provide an effective safety valve for avoiding danger and direct confrontation, or circumventing language that can easily give offence" (255).

Thus, Ibekwe addresses the Onowu family meeting in proverbial language: by saying that the tortoise takes responsibility of his problems which would never crush him. He therefore goes around carrying those problems on his back. (*Wedlock* 28). This is a particularly apt proverb in the context, as Ibekwe covertly but justifiably accuses his brethren of not doing enough to help him when it mattered most. As the Onowu family meeting rapidly reaches a rancorous climax, Ibekwe is concerned with telling members the hard truth: "Some people here make the evil in godly men rise up" (32).

A few more examples will suffice here of making a delicate point in covert fashion, that is, by recourse to proverbial expression. Of course, the overall objective of the interlocutor is to stay out of trouble, in other words, not to offend the listener. Nneobi speaks to the King: "Ogugua my son, listen to me. The rat did not fall from the ceiling for nothing" (*Emene* 44). This is clearly an appropriate recreation of the Enuani proverb *Ife kwa-tu oke n'enu*.

Far from being employed in a haphazard or fortuitous fashion, Sofola's proverbs demonstrate diverse cultural, artistic and stylistic dimensions. Proverbs are used to variously advance the dramatic action or comment appropriately on it, as in the following: "OTUBO: A man who plays the flute also blows his nose" (*Wedlock* 6). This proverb is quite apposite and gives some clear indication of the playwright's position on tradition. By this proverb, in fact, Sofola reinforces her view that despite the seeming abomination Ogwoma is accused of, she deserves some respite, especially as a woman. Another proverb is introduced as Jigide emphasizes his pedigree: "It is a castrated man who shudders at the sight of a woman. A man like me who has led the royal lineage for so many years cannot act like a castrated man at a time when these people are throwing such an insult into our face" (*Emene* 27). This proverb represents an important comment by Sofola on dictatorship, as the King relishes Jigide's advice. The sycophantic Leader of the royal lineage clearly eggs the headstrong King on, even when such a path of stubbornness will lead to the downfall of both the King and his lineage. In the play, in fact, Sofola actually contrasts the enormous knowledge and wise statesmanship of Ojei, the King's godfather, with the naivete, ignorance and impertinence of the young king: "The earth says that a corpse is not a new thing to her" (Emene 32).

Ojei employs another proverb in addressing the King: "It has often been said that a parcel is like a wife, while the cord used to tie it is like a husband. If the cord breaks, the parcel falls into pieces. If you break, I will fall into pieces" (34). Again, Sofola's choice is apt: Ojei's proverb fittingly cautions the King that his individual failure, if he disregards the message of the Oracle, will spell doom for the entire royal lineage. This proverb aptly reinforces the point that the King must do the right thing before entering the Peace Week, namely confront his mother on the evil she has committed. Of course, the impetuous King remains adamant, a development which advances the plot, propelling it precipitously to its inevitably tragic or disastrous destination.

While individual proverbs can effectively convey the intended point, serve the purpose of commenting on the plot or moving it forward, it is interesting that Sofola sometimes employs a concatenation of them. Diokpa Ata addresses the family meeting summoned to discuss the "abomination" by Ogwoma: "The news about Ogwoma's behavior has punctured our eyes but it has not blinded us . . ." while Ike, Ibekwe's brother, adds cryptically: "No one knows why the snail sighs" (*Wedlock* 26).

Similarly, the entire discourse here is built on and powerfully propelled by proverbs:

> ATA: . . . we say that it is the one who has a sore that hops to where he can get a cure. (*Wedlock* 32–33)

On his own, Ibekwe lashes out further at his unhelpful extended family, following the Enuani discourse style of employing language in covert fashion: "There are teeth among us here which are rotten inside even though they are white outside" (30).

In the following, there is also a striking stringing together of proverbs by Okolo, one of Diokpa's Assistants, as the former foresees a situation in which the people will perish for the sake of one man, that is, the unyielding young King:

> OKOLO: We pray you to hear our appeal ... You are our father and must cover the rubbish to take the fruit. If we don't eat yam for the sake of the palm oil, we eat the palm oil for the sake of the yam ... listen to our cry and save us, save yourself, and save Oligbo. (*Emene* 20)

As if not to be outdone by his subjects, the King replies in striking, proverbial language: "I have heard you. It is the way a child opens his hand that a piece of meat is given to him" (20). By this proverb, the King attempts to justify his uncompromising fire for fire posture in his address to the elders, who really meant well for him.

It is interesting and instructive that proverbs are not only the means by which Sofola aims at a true portrayal of speech in this society. In both plays, she also captures another crucial speech reality: the Enuani speech code stipulates occasions for sheer bluntness, even others for couching one's message in covert or euphemistic expression. In an attempt to establish "the parameters for communicative competence, even appropriateness, within given interactional settings," or that "verbal behavior is essentially culturally determined, differing from society to society," Okoh establishes a "long and short index of Igbo speech" ("Two Faces" 107–8).

Sofola realistically depicts the Enuani linguistic repertoire, clearly capturing such alternation between blunt speech and donning the euphemistic garb. Elders in this culture claim considerable poetic license, not only declaring the truth, but also doing so in highly blunt, forthright fashion. Ojei, the King's godfather, speaks to him frankly: "Anyone who toys with his god toys with his destiny. And as your godfather I must do right and speak the truth without fear and without favor" *(Emene* 34). And when the impetuous young King asks him to leave, Ojei is not deterred, but fires back: "I will leave when I am finished" (34). Early in the play, Ezedibie, the Palace medical doctor, confronts the King: "It has been rumored all over the kingdom that your youth troubles you, but I think it's worse than that. It is madness" (5).

The following is easily the most interesting demonstration of uncompromisingly blunt speech. Quite angry, Odogwu barks at the King: "Ta! Ta! small boy! Ta! Listen to the good advice of the elders. I said listen to the words of the men who saw the hairs in your father's anus!" (25). Even before the King replies, Odogwu fires back: "Ta! small boy! I say listen to good sense" (25) and later, "[to the audience] 'A small boy enthroned only yesterday does not want any advice. An upstart whose umbilical cord is not yet cut wants to eat meat before he grows teeth.' [To the King] 'I tell you, we had enough of your father and we don't want any shit from you at all. If the sense of your lineage was put in their anuses and not in their heads, then, for God's sake, step down and let better people step in'" (25–26). Sofola's portrayal features what is essentially command English. It is suitable and justifiable for Odogwu, the Commander-in-chief of the Military in Oligbo Kingdom, to bark his orders, especially at an errant junior. By the choice of the exclamation "Ta!," Sofola has pithily implied a myriad of expletives such as "Shut up! Keep quiet, Listen to me, Keep your mouth shut!," as Odogwu exercises his license as an adult to rain insults on his young and recalcitrant king.

Conversely, a few examples will suffice of language that is not blunt but euphemistic. Anwasia reprimands Ogwoma for sleeping with during the three months of mourning. Resolute as ever, Ogwoma retorts she could not wait any longer "before letting him in" nor would she for "another blink of the eye" (8–9). Sofola's intimate knowledge of the society is again evident, while her depiction of the euphemistic mode of speech is significant, as women do not generally engage in language that is even remotely sexually explicit or offensive. But while the men may expectedly break such euphemizing rule, they now choose to follow the pattern laid down by the women, as Odibei states that, "not all cutlasses that went to the farm are used. Some just don't cut that deep. A man is not a man simply because he parades an okra sprout" (14). Uloko, contending that not all husbands are virile, remarks thus: "You should have discovered what type of cutlass your son had that even in mourning his wife clings to me" (15–16). The blunt/euphemistic speech index is seen as Ogoli speaks: "A man goes to a woman; it is the woman who opens the door" and Anwasia replies: "But the man can force the door open if the woman refuses" (*Wedlock* 23). Sofola's language is really exciting here while the imagery is even more striking. The crux here is easily decipherable: in all the examples, no literal okra sprout, cutlasses, or doors are meant!

The final dimension we explore of Sofola's linguistic creativity concerns her deployment of Enuani speech rhythms; she is simply adept at weaving Enuani idioms and speech modes into her plot or narrative fabric. Ogwoma tells Nneka, her mother: ". . . you tied me like a goat and threw me away to a man I hated" (*Wedlock* 18), while the latter declares later: "If Uloko has worked medicine on you his head will carry it" (20). "His head will carry it" is Enuani for "He will face the music," or "There will be repercussions," while "medicine" has simply nothing to do with pharmaceutical industries or the Western idea of drugs, their production or prescription. Any keen translator or speaker proficient in Enuani and English will see Sofola's "He will carry it with his head" (Isi e k'o ji bu e) as approximating to, "He will pay for his crime," "There will be repercussions," or "He will not go scot-free."

The medicine imagery recurs as Nneka further threatens: "That Uloko will see... He will not disgrace me and go untouched" (*Wedlock* 20). When the Omu brings the message from the Mkpitime oracle, the king is unwilling to listen and, like all dictators, listens only to what he wants to hear: "Swallow the rest" (the imperative bu e no! = "swallow it!") and banishes her immediately: "From now on never more let a dead or a living person see you in Oligbo!" (*Emene* 5).

Diokpa Ata declares that Ogwoma's "shameful" behavior "has punctured our eyes but it has not blinded us" (25). Here, the playwright so effectively reworks a popular Enuani idiom that the native speaker can almost "hear" both Sofola and Ata declaring that what Ogwoma did "*tu m anya mana o tu-kpo na m* a" ("really hit my eyes but did not blind me!"). A few more examples will here suffice: Odibei announces, "I do not allow anything to end in my hands" (17), an effective rendition of the native idiom, O ma si aka ma na, while Ibekwe declares: "I knew that Okolie and his lot would have gone behind with their evil deeds and would have dragged my legs outside" (*Wedlock* 30). "To drag one's legs outside" (*Ilapu-ha mmadu or ilapu-ha mmadu (ukwu) n'ilo*) means to create trouble for one or to implicate one. As members of Ogwoma's family discuss, Diokpa Ata also declares: "Diokpa Okolie, your mouth has wisdom" (27), an indigenous idiom to say, "You are really wise," or "You have spoken wisely."

Of course, the circumlocutory "told you to tell them so" is characteristically oral Enuani speech. Sofola employs à la Armah, what may be termed the language of shit, as she consciously assaults the reader's sense of smell, while the use of parallelism ("Tell them... Tell them") is far from fortuitous. The use of such parallel structures further reveals a disciplined and artistically profound writer at work, apart from reinforcing the point Jigide is concerned with making. Ojei refers to the King thus: "He is a small child. He can only bathe his stomach," while in the words of Jigide, "These Olinzele people... will not allow us to drink water and put the cup down" (*Emene* 27–28), two expressions which typically belong to the Enuani oral idiomatic mode of communication. In these examples, indeed, Sofola artistically reproduces Enuani native idioms, with almost Achebean exactitude and mastery.

As the foregoing examples also demonstrate, a crucial component of Sofola's objective, that is, a validation of her indigenous culture, concerns her accurate incorporation of native idioms. By her re-creation of indigenous Enuani speech patterns, she arrives at a clearly authentic portrayal of this traditional milieu. Whether in her dialogic representations or character delineation, Sofola carefully captures the very essence of Enuani speech. Even the texture, as well as context is duly reflected in her use of proverbs, native idioms or diverse other dimensions of the indigenous oral repertoire. Thus, the literate indigenous Enuani speaker will without difficulty recognize in her portrayals, the very flavor of Enuani discourse.

Sofola's craft indeed demonstrates diverse dimensions. Her specific incorporation and re-creation of the indigenous speech patterns are highly effective as the two plays easily demonstrate "the rich, communal and vigorous voice of orality." To continue with some of Okoh's comments on p'Bitek's *Song of Lawino*, which are also quite applicable to Sofola's two plays, they are African works "whose readability, freshness and directness derive solely from [their] central concern with communicating in an oral 'communal' manner" (*Lawino* 51). All of this, of course, pertains to Sofola's language, which is readable and simple, but not simplistic. In all, she is an eloquent writer who employs language in highly vibrant fashion. Akinwale rightly observes the "harvest of words that abound" (73) in Sofola's works.

As this section concludes, it bears repetition that Sofola is a painstaking artist, whether regarding her use of language in general, or deployment of idioms and proverbs, in particular. One implication of both elements being carefully crafted and integrated is that even a foreign reader will appreciate the information provided regarding the applicability of the idiom or proverb to the given narrative situation. Conversely, the indigenous reader will not consider Sofola's approach boring or condescending, as he himself will also savor and appreciate the proper application of the given proverb or idiom.

SOFOLA'S STANCE ON TRADITION

The penultimate portion of this paper pursues two principal points. First, considering especially the period Sofola wrote, it is easy to misunderstand her conception of, even attitude to, tradition. Second, while no one anywhere encounters exactly a large corpus of critical material on Sofola, it is surprising and, as will be here shown, that much of the little which exists is generally not of a satisfactory quality. According to Obafemi: "Most of her [Sofola's] plays advocate a return to the past that could reasonably be regarded as decadent where magic, ritual, and a certain overdose of the tyranny of age tower oppressively" (61). Such an assessment rests solidly but sadly on a shallow and surprisingly inaccurate reading of Sofola. A thorough or deliberately discerning reading (or re-reading) of *Wedlock* and *Emene*, for example, will by no means support such logic of "a return to a decadent past" where magic reigns supreme. In fact, the so-called magic cannot be said to display an obtrusive presence in the latter work. Of course, it will be shown how Sofola treats the theme of the past, in other words, her interpretation or assessment of tradition. In the following, the discerning reader will promptly "hear" the voice of tradition and the society at large, as Anwasia underlines what is generally considered a taboo: "A woman being pregnant for another man while she is still in mourning for her dead husband?" (*Wedlock* 8).

Obafemi's critique of Sofola's rises to an even more intriguing crescendo: "We encounter in Sofola's plays, a simple and even simplistic plot all geared towards a thesis or advocating submission to the whims and caprices of age-old demi-gods or 'custodians' of bogus tradition, for those who kick, there is no restitution. There is no redemption from the tragic consequences of dissent" (62). But in reality, and as this chapter essentially argues, Sofola's central concern is with contesting the so-called bogus tradition. From the two plays, she neither embraces nor sides with its uncompromising custodians; this accounts for her appropriately "empowering" her protagonist, Ogwoma. But Anwasia, is unwaveringly traditional and consistently critical of her friend, who has mustered the courage to challenge the status quo. Anwasia, clearly donning her reactionary garb, reacts to such uncommon guts by reprimanding her friend, Ogwoma (*Wedlock* 21).

But the crux here, in fact, what every reader or critic must consider the inescapable reality, is that Ogwoma is simply not prepared—whether by her very temperament or by Sofola's particular artistic conception of her—to subject herself to this colossal and consuming what-our-people-do injunction. Thus, the playwright deliberately and deftly pitches modern love against what Obafemi calls the "bogus tradition." It is by Sofola's design that Anwasia continually pesters her rebellious but "liberated" friend to follow the dictates of the community as regards a leviratic marriage with her deceased husband's brother in order to bear a child for him (22).

It must be emphasized that only a careful reading of Sofola will reveal her meaning. Though Ogwoma carried her rebellion against tradition to the end and may not be said to have been entirely victorious, her stand represents an extremely bold statement. Sofola's meaning or message is that people should not be forced but allowed to marry who they wish. Thus, *Wedlock* propagates a divergent marriage-based-on-love-and-reciprocity message, which necessarily negates the tradition of marriage based on material or pecuniary considerations. Ogwoma's iron resolve is underlined thus: "Kill me if you like, but you cannot stop me from loving Uloko" (20). Akinwale rightly remarks that critics "who do not seek the undermeanings of her [Sofola's] writings are likely to misunderstand them," especially as "a lot of information about [her] background is . . . essential for a complete understanding" of her works (73).

Ogwoma's overall posture above unequivocally condemns the "selling" of one's daughters to the highest bidder in the name of marriage. Here we see the crux of her revolt (21). Ogwoma vehemently rejects being cast as an object, even a common commodity to be sold. She rebels against being bundled to some unloving and unlovable husband. In other words, she expresses her support for "progressive tradition" by being engrossed in an intense love affair, rather than mourning, who is, in her view, a so-called husband for the mandatory three-month period.

This constitutes an action about which modern feminists will make an artistic meal. But our concern here is to underline that one implication of Sofola's portrayal is that such rebellions or dissenting voices against the traditional shackles are actually a positive development. Not only is Sofola thus concerned with challenging the status quo, Ogwoma can be said to have sacrificed herself. For Sofola, then, such a sacrifice is really necessary, if change is to "happen." The implication here is that with more of such sacrifices, the oppressive traditions will capitulate to a new order, that is, a more humane, more egalitarian and more progressive society.

For Eni, Sofola is "a strong supporter of tradition and custom" (155). One may not jump to a conclusion that Eni's postulation views the playwright's work in essentially negative terms. The picture becomes much clearer as Eni asserts thus: "She is a reactionary writer who reacts to issues in her society. Her plays feature characteristically magic, ritual, myth, legend and tradition, but not with the same depth with which myth and ritual is employed by Soyinka in his plays" (155). In artistic matters, of course, it becomes futile setting up the Platos, Shakespeares or Soyinkas as absolute standards, since every writer is unique, often guided, to paraphrase Eliot, by tradition, creativity, or individual talent. Each writer pursues a "selfness," creates a niche, and devices his own lens for viewing originality. Indeed, if Sofola is a reactionary writer because she draws from her oral traditions, then the Achebes, Soyinkas and Amadis, like all first-generation African writers, must be top of any list of unrepentant and incurable reactionaries.

No doubt, most critics have tended to make a real meal out of Sofola's purported artistic "failings." But to accuse Sofola of too much attention to myth, taboo or ritual is to contradict the central contention here that her crucial artistic concern is with validating her indigenous culture. Clearly, myth and ritual constitute essential components of life in virtually every traditional African society. From our re-reading so far, then, Eni's "reactionary" accusation constitutes a gross misrepresentation. Such an erroneous assessment of Sofola's work presents only part of her artistic vision. Indeed, Eni falls into the same trap as Obafemi, of misjudging or making too much of Sofola's so-called "romance" with tradition or, in Obafemi's language, a decadent past.

From our re-reading also, promptly arises a question for "those critics who wrongly assert that [Sofola] is purely a traditionalist and nothing more" (Akinwale 73). Simply put: Does a strong supporter of tradition necessarily support its perpetuity and continuity in its entirety? Most critics fail to realize a basic reality: not only does Sofola have an intimate understanding of the society she is concerned with depicting, she is also a Westernized African. It is thus inconceivable that she will simultaneously be "enslaved" by tradition.

Indeed, this makes the charge of excessive support for the past the very height of implausibility. Critics must not allow Sofola's real meaning to elude them. It must be understood therefore, that she does not necessarily advocate in both plays a return to the past, but a marriage of both worlds or, as pointed out, a "coalescing of tradition and modernity." An underlying contention of Sofola which some critics deliberately ignore is that positive practices and values have to be maintained, while obsolete, hoary or retrogressive customs need to be jettisoned in favor of modern ones.

Another critic, Ezenwanaebe, talks about Sofola's "excessive focus on the so-called cultural violation," then adds: "Sofola deliberately sidetracks the gruesome reality of women oppression in the play *(Wedlock)* as if they are not worthy subjects for drama" (10). Ezenwanaebe makes the claim that in the works of the majority of African female playwrights "women's resistance to cultural oppression is [not] allowed to succeed on the stage" (10). More specifically, he posits that female voices in *Wedlock*, for example, are "represented as voices of evil and of cultural aberration," then adds: "They are represented only to be crushed as a warning to others" (10). By this, of course, he refers to the end of the play in which presumably both lovers have come to ruin. In his view, then, Sofola counsels that nobody can successfully confront or defy tradition. Such an interpretation, to be sure, verges vigorously on the vacuous.

Just as Eni accuses Sofola of not exploring myth and ritual in a profound manner like Soyinka, Ezenwanaebe complains about "the playwright's excessive focus on the so-called cultural violation" (10). If we recognize that this is a major theme in the play, then what exactly constitutes excessive focus? Still, it is instructive to consider Okwechime's and Eke's comments: "Regarded as the first female writer of modern Nigerian theater, Sofola brought psychological insights, provocative subject matter and social concerns to the Nigerian drama" (95). In the words of Akinwale, Sofola "now occupies the position Wole Soyinka is occupying amongst his male peers" (73), while according to a Saraba Review, her plays "challenge the political, spiritual, and traditional norms of Nigerian society" (4).

Indeed, considering the views of Obafemi, Eni and Ezenwanaebe, for example, we cannot but emphasize here that the logical starting point for appreciating Sofola's work lies in the recognition that they predominantly advocate change. In Sofola's view, the society must work towards the capitulation of such shackles as tradition, dictatorship, or political high-handedness, which hold men down. In *Emene,* Sofola "concedes" that the King has great powers by presenting what may be regarded as the old, while positing side by side, that which is modern, namely the reciprocity of power. In her view, then, while the king retains his original powers, the people themselves deserve more participation in important issues.

Critics of African literature sometimes rehash the cliché of whether or not the writer has proposed solutions at the end of a given work. But even the poorest critic must realize that Sofola did not set out to write a play that by some lightning magic or artistic diktat, will effectually rout the forces of patriarchy and male dominance, or end the problem of female subjugation in the traditional society. But by broaching such issues, she demands that society pursue the path of humaneness and civilized conduct by abrogating its negative practices. The death in *Wedlock* of the "rebels" against tradition must not be interpreted as a crushing of such a rebellion. As a writer or dramatist, Sofola indeed summons and encourages more "rebels," anticipating that with time, their dissenting stance will particularly provoke change. Customs that have held sway for donkey's years cannot be expected to vanish overnight, but such works as *Emene* and *Wedlock*, which address certain societal anomalies will considerably weaken the very foundations of such obnoxious traditions, or even force them to collapse completely. It is obvious that while supporting the culture, she contends that it must be dynamic. For this reason, she "opposes" the retrogressive aspects of the Enuani cultural milieu. In *Emene*, for example, one message reverberates: dictatorship or abuse of power is utterly reprehensible, whether in the microcosmic Oligbo kingdom or in the wider Nigerian context. In *Wedlock*, she anticipates and proposes transformation by mirroring the deleterious tradition of forced marriages, a dimension of the levirate institution.

Rather than advocating the perpetuity of unwholesome practices against the female folk in Africa as some critics claim, Sofola and her works give a voice to the downtrodden or oppressed female folk

CONCLUSION

This chapter has considered Zulu Sofola's work from a literary/linguistic perspective. More specifically, we have examined her cultural-cum-literary portrayal of an indigenous African culture, the Enuani. We have argued that in her artistic depiction of this culture, her concern is with exposing and thus, validating it, especially in the light of the fundamental theme. It has been shown that a critical means of validation, even a crucial component of Sofola's art, lies in her deployment of the people's oral culture. Regarding her literary-cum-cultural depiction of the society, we have also emphasized the kind of language in which such portrayal is couched.

As Okoh has rightly pointed out, "The question of how indigenous African experience may be conveyed in a non-African language constitutes a major problem for the writer" ("Translation" 18). From all our examples here, it is clear that Sofola effectively as well as creatively transposes and recreates the very spirit of Enuani speech patterns in both plays. There is a successful blending of her deep knowledge of the society and her artistic capabilities to achieve a highly accurate and convincing depiction of society. The proverbs and other forms of Enuani verbal behavior really come alive in both plays, being guaranteed, on account of their accuracy and authenticity, to appeal greatly to both Enuani-speaking and non-African readers.

Such an achievement is easily attributable to her original, sensitive, and compelling use of language. Not only is Sofola's language well-suited to her themes and setting, it is employed in a highly effective, even nativized manner. More importantly, then, various aspects of the discussion here have shown that not only is she an important forerunner of women's writing in Africa, her legacy lies in her striking use of language. Her language is clearly carefully controlled and crafted, whether to denote love, tradition and modernity in wedlock, or politics and dictatorship in Emene. Also, the characters in both works "speak" the appropriate language. In both plays, Sofola's portrayal of Enuani culture, oral literature, idioms and speech modes authentically captures the very texture and verbal flavor or setting of a rustic African community, Oligbo Kingdom. Her successful portrayal of a pristine and pre-colonial society remains a worthy contribution, as here involved is a culture which, as noted, is not so well known. Since Sofola is a major African artist, her contributions are far from limited to Enuani culture or oral literature. Indeed, she has made important pioneering, linguistic and literary contributions to female African writing and modern African literature. She truly deserves more critical acclaim, considering her status and overall creative output and towering stature. This paper has therefore offered a re-reading of the two plays, in order to put Sofola's work in proper perspective, to show its real worth, even her very place in modern African literature. Thus, against charges of being reactionary or unduly attached to the past, it has here been established that Sofola is on the contrary a revolutionary and visionary writer, especially considering when both works were published. As our re-reading has shown, her craft and portrayal in both works unequivocally mark her out as a highly realistic, sensible and sensitive writer. It has also been demonstrated that whether in terms of her characterization, subject matter, attention to aspects of the people's oral literature, or her overall conception of society and how it should operate, Sofola is a thoroughly balanced writer. In spite of her attachment to the Enuani culture, she achieves a particularly impartial portrayal, neither uncritically endorsing every dimension of the culture nor idealizing it.

WORKS CITED

Akinwale, Ayo. "Zulu Sofola Her Writings and their Undermeanings." *Nigerian Female Writers: A Critical Perspective.* Eds. Otokunefor, Henrietta, and Obiageli C. Nwodo. Lagos: Malthouse Press, 1989: 68–73.

Chukwuma, Helen. *Igbo Oral Literature.* Port Harcourt: Belpot (Nig.), 1994.

Eliot, T. S. "Tradition and the Individual Talent." *The Norton Anthology of English Literature.* Eds. Abrams, M. H., et al., New York: W. W. Norton, 1962: 1501–08.

Eni, Kenneth Efakponana. "Zulu Sofola and the Nigerian Theatre: Influences and Traditions." www.ajol.info/index.php/cajtms/article/download/76629/67077. Retrieved May 25, 2016.

Ezenwanebe, Osita C. "Feminist Consciousness and Nigerian Theatre." *Consciousness, Literature and the Arts,* Vol 7, No 1, 2006: 1–14. Retrieved September 19, 2016. http:/// blackboard.lincoln.ac.uk/bbcwebdav/users/dmeyerdinkgrafe.

Obafemi, Olu. "Zulu Sofola's Theatre." *Nigerian Female Writers: A Critical Perspective,* Eds. Otokunefor, Henrietta, and Obiageli C. Nwodo Lagos. Malthouse Press, 1989: 61–67.

Odi, Christine. "Wedlock of Nightmares: Narrating Motherhood in Sofola's *Wedlock of the Gods* and Binebai's *Beyond Nightmare.*" *Journal of the Literary Society of Nigeria,* Vol. 4 (2012): 41–53.

Olakitan, Yemi. Remembering Zulu Sofola. Blogspot.com.ng . . . remembering.zulu. March 10, 2010. Retrieved May 27, 2016.

Okoh, Nkem. "Categories of Igbo Oral Literature: The Enuani Example." *Journal of Asian and African Studies,* Vol. 35, 1988: 73–83.

———. "The Direction of Indirection in Chinua Achebe's Trilogy." *Neohelicon* 30.2: (2003): 241–56. Print. [also online at http://dx.doi.org/1023A:1026224324216].

———. "Father and Son: Pursuing an Unequal Relationship in African Literature." *Connecting Paths: Essays in Honour of Professor Ogude,* Ed. O. Ogaga, Bahiti/ Dalila, 2016: 211–31.

———. The Long and the Short of it: Chinua Achebe and Two Faces of Igbo Verbal Behaviour." *Uyo Online Journal of the Humanities,* Vol. 1, 2010: 107–25. http://udoca.org/index.php?option=com_jresearch&view=publication&task=show&id=14&I temid=176-.

———. "Of Synergies: Linking Literature, Language and English in Nigeria." Inaugural Lecture. Http://www.uniport.edu.ng/files/Inaugural%20Lectures/97th%20Inaugural%20Lecture_2012.

———. "Regal Repression versus Egalitarian Expectation in Enuani Igbo Tales." *Africana Marburgensia,* Vol 27, Nos 1/2, 1994: 21–31.

———. "'Translation' as Validation of Culture: The Example of Chinua Achebe." *Hemispheres: Studies on Cultures and Societies,* Vol. 30, No.3, 2015: 5–20.

———. "Writing African Oral Literature: A Re-reading of Okot p'Bitek's *Song of Lawino.*" *Bridges: An African Journal of English Studies,* No. 5, 1993: 35–53. [Reprinted in *Twentieth-Century Literary Criticism,* No. 149, 2004: 73–80; Reprinted also in *Tradition and the Dynamics of Women's Empowerment* Ed. M. Kandji. Dakar; Univ. of Dakar, 2006: 239–56.

Okwechime, Okey, and Kola Eke, "Protest Against Matchmaking: The Example of Zulu Sofola's *Song of a Maiden*," *African Women and Cultural Spaces* Eds. Falola, Toyin, and S. U. Fwatshak. New Jersey: Africa World Press, 2011: 95–109.

"Positive Review for *Wedlock of the Gods*" http:// www.sarabamag.co./positive-reviews-for-wedlock-of-the-gods/. Retrieved September 19, 2016.

Sofola, Zulu. *King Emene: Tragedy of a Rebellion*. London: Hetnemann, 1974.

———. *Wedlock of the Gods*. Nigeria: Evans Brothers, 1972.

Solanke, O. Stephen. "MythoSymbolic Representations: Assessing Heroism in Zulu Sofola's *Wedlock of the Gods*." *Journal of Postcolonial Cultures/Societies*, Vol. 4, No. 4, 2013: 117–36.

PART 3

Interrogating Identity, Autonomy, and History

Chapter 9

Archetypes of the Mother and the Scapegoat in Grace Ogot's Fiction

Onyemaechi Udumukwu

INTRODUCTION

Kenyan female author Grace Ogot is a pioneer in a number of ways. She, like Flora Nwapa, is an inaugurator of a vibrant female tradition in modern African literature. She is the first notable Kenyan female writer of Luo origin to publish a novel and also engage in public service up to the rank of Assistant Minister. But Grace Ogot is a writer who is misunderstood. The few critics that cared to glance at her work are quick to dismiss her as unserious. While even some other few, especially those writing within a feminist orientation, force her into a preconceived model of women's liberation. It is in fact because she is misunderstood that the way for this present reading. is paved. As C. G. Jung has underscored, "interpretations are only for those who don't understand; it is only the things we don't understand that have any meaning." In addition, "man woke up in a world he did not understand and that is why he tries to interpret it" (Jung, 31). Our basic proposition is that Grace Ogot wrote from a deep urge to tell the intimate link between the attachment to land understood not simply in terms of politics or as an economic tool, as we find in the works of other Kenyan writers.

Etymologically, land is defined as the solid surface of the earth where it is not covered with water. But it equally means a particular area of this solid surface distinguished from other areas by political, geographical, economic, or other considerations. Understood in this way, land has been subjected to many kinds of uses. Nations have gone and will continue to go to war in order to appropriate and preserve it. It is demarcated and shared on the basis of politics and economics. Elementary Malthusian economics teaches that land is a major factor of economic production. Agricultural production, sports, cities and urban planning result from the management or mismanagement of land. In fact land is at the root of the heinous crimes committed against vast population of human beings in the form of slavery, war, colonization of one form or the other, genocide, and internal displacement. The words "colonialism," "colonization" and the infinitive "to colonize" amount to a significant historical fact. This fact crystallizes in the occupation, seizure of power by a foreign power, and the imposition of a new system of authority over a territorial land and a people. It is a question of one dominant from a different territory moving its military, intellectual, business to rule over another dominant in another land by weakening the latter's claim to power. Accordingly, colonialism and the process of colonizing a land is not a spontaneous and haphazard activity. It requires planning, espionage, and investment. As V. Y. Mudimbe has explained, colonialism and colonization "basically mean organization and arrangement." The words, colonialism and colonization, he says, derive from the Latin word, *colere*, meaning to cultivate or to design (Mudimbe 1). As we have indicated earlier no other subject has elicited keen response from Kenyan writers as the question of land. At independence Kenya was plunged into a "land-hunger" precipitated by an imbalance in the pattern of resettlement of former African landowners. As such, large expanse of land remained in European hands, or through these Europeans, into the hand of the new elite. Oginga Odinga has stressed that this condition of land hunger is one of the obstacles to "Uhuru.". He says that: "Our government's land policy was hobbled from the start by wrong policies" (259). As we see in Ngugi's *Devil on the Cross*, the political elite represented by a character like Gitutu prospered on these wrong policies. Gitutu has prospered by engaging in a ruthless form of land alienation. Land and the politics of how it is shared form a core issue in Meja Mwangi's novel *Striving for the Wind*. In the relationship between two characters in the novel, Baba Pesa and Baba Baru, we witness how land forms the basis for the marginalization of some sections of the society.

Land, with its acquisition and use, constitutes a major motif in the novel *The Promised Land*. At the center of this motif are the inter-relationships between the individual Luo's access to land mostly through inheritance and the collective ethnic unconscious to land. From the collective ethnic basis, land is perceived as a source of life. Clearly, inter-village relationships manifesting in such forms as marriage and even death are tied to land, which is not only the place of abode. It is equally the place of work: the characters in the rural setting are mainly farmers. Just as land provides the foundation for social and individual life, the figure of the mother acquires even larger than life proportion. The role of mothers, understood in terms of personal mothers or figuratively as the homeland, forms the source of stability. By adopting the insight from Carl Jung's theory of the collective unconscious, we will examine and interpret how the relationship between land, as a force, unites with two archetypes—that of the mother and the archetype of the scapegoat to form the main legacy of Grace Ogot as a woman, a writer, a nurse and midwife, and a community leader. Through these two archetypes Ogot underscores the richness of her Luo cultural identity. For practical discussion we will focus on her novel, *The Promised Land*, and the collection of short stories, *The Land without Thunder and Other Stories*.

ROOTEDNESS IN THE LORE OF THE LUO ETHNIC GROUP

Grace Emily Akinyi Ogot was a politician, writer, and health specialist. She eventually served the government of Kenya as an Assistant Minister for Culture and Social Services. Until her death she was married to Professor Bethwell Allan Ogot. Grace Ogot's work can be best understood as an important part of the overall story of the Luo ethnic group of Kenya. The Luo in Kenya, who call themselves *Joluo* (aka *Jaluo*, "people of Luo"), are the fourth-largest ethnic community in Kenya after the Kikuyu, Kalenjin and Luhya. In 2010 their population was estimated to be 4 million. The Luo in Kenya and Tanzania call their language Dholuo, which is mutually intelligible (to varying degrees) with the languages of the Lango, Kumam and Padhola of Uganda, Acholi of Uganda and South Sudan and Alur of Uganda and Congo. The Luo ethnic group is characterized by two dominant tendencies which resonate in Grace Ogot's works. These tendencies are those of migration and the ability to assimilate members of other ethnic groups.

The question may be asked on whether this type of foray into the historic-cultural background of Ogot has any significance in our attempt to understand her contribution and her legacy. It is true that our approach in this study is not completely sociological, but sensitivity to the social forces at work in the writer's background is never out of place. It is pertinent therefore to recall the case made by Abiola Irele on the importance of sensitivity to a sociological context. According to Irele:

> A more truthful kind of sociological approach is that which attempts to correlate the work to the social background . . . to understand the work of each writer or how each group of writers captures a moment of the historical consciousness of society. (34)

The verbs "correlate" and "captures" in Irele's assertion are true representation of the understanding of society as a given, as an objective condition which the literary text names by capturing and taking into consideration "everything in our society" that has gone into the work. In her representation of the rural life of the Luo of Kenya and even their experience of migration into parts of Tanzania, Ogot can rightly be said to have captured a moment in the development of her people's story.

In spite of her sense of verisimilitude, Grace Ogot has suffered the misfortune of being ignored by critics. This is even surprising, given the fact that there are not many female authors from the East African sub-region. In his celebrated *Uhuru's Fire*, Adrian Roscoe indirectly mentions Grace Ogot's reflection of "the fertile lakeshore of the Luo" (Roscoe, 178). He goes to affirm, nevertheless, that Ogot's "undervalued novel *The Promised Land* . . . uses the motif of migration still resonant in the memory of a people who arrived in East Africa centuries ago after a traumatic exodus and who still say of themselves, 'we are like water . . .'" (25–26). It is significant that Roscoe alludes to these migratory tendencies among the Luo in his reference to Ogot's novel. Apart from Adrian Roscoe, O. R. Dathorne has praised Ogot's portrayal of Luo women especially in the novel, *The Promised Land*. Dathorne asserts that *The Promised Land* explores the theme of marriage and a woman's duties to her husband" (130). Dathorne focuses attention on Ogot's presentation of a major female character in the novel, Nyapol. Thus he applauds the author's "excellent portrayal of Nyapol." Such portrayal becomes emblematic of Ogot's general attitude to women. The female characters are true matriarchs in their own right. Supportive to their husbands and committed to the well-being of the marriage and family, they are a far cry from the separatist tendencies we witness in the works of Buchi Emecheta or in Nwapa's *One is Enough*. Gloria Chukukere rightly observes that Ogot's female characters reveal that Luo women are not "militant advocates of sexual equality" (220). Chukukere, nonetheless, identifies Ogot's legacy in "her adroit skill as a short story writer" (217).

In "The Nigerian Tradition in the Novel" Charles Nnolim has cautioned about the futility of hiding under the pretext that it is premature to discuss the Nigerian tradition, regarding the novel. He proceeds to stridently argue that a robust Nigerian tradition exits in the novel genre. It is true that this volume is on the legacies of African women authors. The key word here is legacy meaning "something resulting from and left behind by an action, an event or person," but connoting heritage, inheritance, and tradition, a custom, or a habit of expression or manner of presentation. In line with the case made by Nnolim for the Nigerian novel, the problem before this contribution is to pursue the case that Grace Ogot is an inaugurator of a female novelistic and fictional tradition in East Africa rooted in the lore of the Luo ethnic group.

Her modest attempt at novelistic creation, nonetheless, represents a sensitivity to domesticate the novel genre in order to narrate an experience that is rooted in the collective unconscious of her ethnic community. Also recalling the case made by T. S. Eliot in "Tradition and the Individual Talent" Nnolim further reiterates that apart from Achebe's *Things Fall Apart,* Ferdinand Oyono's *Houseboy* draws its breath from two traditions namely, Jungian psychology and Judaeo-Christian mythopoeia" (117). In the same vein, Ogot's novel *The Promised Land* draws from the traditional Luo myth of migration for which reason the ethnic group is dispersed across the great lake regions of East Africa with members of the ethnic group settling in countries like Uganda, Kenya, and Tanzania. The account of the novel is rooted in aspects of novelistic tradition such as the inevitability of contemporary experience, sense of magnitude, with the action shifting from one location to others, and realistic presentation of characters.

Ogot expresses a unique sensitivity to the experience of her people and especially the contribution of the women to the overall survival of the group. By going back to her rural roots; she reconstructs pristine elements of their cultural reality in a way that gives them solidity. Accordingly, we will adopt the insight from Carl Jung's theory of the collective unconscious in order to analyze the unique interplay between the characters that are typical of the Luo ethnic community in both contemporary Kenya and Tanzanian societies. Our point of departure is the interconnectedness between land, and the mother archetypes especially as the latter expresses the collective unconscious of the group.

THE SCAPEGOAT ARCHETYPE

Our discussion will begin with the short story "The Rain Came" because its underlying and unifying archetype of the scapegoat draws from the collective ethnic unconscious of the Joluluo people. "The Rain Came" begins at the moment of death. The atmosphere in the setting, a rural community, is described as "tense and confused. Everyone moved aimlessly and fussed in the yard without actually doing any work" (*Land without Thunder,* 116). The tension, confusion and lethargy are borne out of what a female character described as "this rain business." The effect of the "rain business" is felt as "our cattle lie dying in the fields." And the people fear that "soon it will be our children and then ourselves" (116). In other words, the absence of rain has brought about drought, the death of the cattle and the apprehension of potential death of the children. In his perplexity, the chief of the community, Labong'o, has gone to the chief priest to seek solution from the gods. The action begins with his expected return from the gods. But the solution is filled with foreboding. While on his way back the narrator places the chief side-by-side with his daughter, Oganda. The oracle has instructed the chief to sacrifice his only daughter, Oganda, so that the evil in the land would be taken away in order that rain might fall. The instruction from the oracle weighs heavily on him as he retreats to the interior of his hut without speaking to anyone. We are told: "Instead of calling the family together and giving them the news immediately, Labong'o went to his own hut, a sign that he was not to be disturbed" (116). Furthermore, we are told: "it was no longer a question of being the chief of hunger-stricken people that weighed Labong'o's heart. It was the life of his only daughter that was at stake" (116).

Later, however, Oganga goes to meet her father. But in its metaphysical import that meeting turns out to announce the fulfillment of the prophecy. We are told that there was a glittering chain shining around her waist when Oganga went to meet him. This chain becomes the sign, the bold thread that sutures and serves to fulfil the prophecy of the oracle. In his frenzy the priest laments: "It is Oganda, Oganda, my only daughter, who must die so young." After this outburst the narrator tells us that "Labongo'o did not care anymore . . . He loved his people, the Luo, but what were the Luo for him without Oganda?" (116).

We should observe the allegorical feature in the foregone assertion. This is what M. H. Abrams has described as "allegoric tableau" (6). Here the fictional character Labong'o in a fictional presentation directly makes statements that juxtapose his grief with the needs of the ethnic community, the Luo. In this regard he infuses his personal consciousness within the ethnic collective unconscious. This allegorical feature of representing characters who seemingly break the wall between fiction and reality; rather than being contained in the fictional world, they make statements that directly address the real community rooted in Luo experience. The allegorical insertion is one of the characteristics of Grace Ogot's writing.

We can further explain this feature from two perspectives. From the point of the character, a fictional creation, it serves to ground him within a realistic cultural ambience. The second perspective is that of the author. The bits of allegoric tableau are indicative of the writer's sense of social responsibility, her commitment or properly put her awareness of what she is answerable to. She is answerable to illuminating the Luo ethnic collective unconscious. This sense of commitment equally has its political underside. Grace Ogot, a woman of Luo origin, wrote within the context of multi-ethnic Kenya, especially at a time when the political equation in the country swayed between the Luo and the other three major ethnic groups, the Kikuyu, Kalenjin and Luhya. Ogot has not engaged this political equation frontally and directly. Nevertheless, the subtlety in her voice sounded from a base that has its foundation in an ethnic consciousness. Grace Ogot is not alone in this even though others may not have been as subtle.

The major Kenyan writer, Ngugi wa Thiong'o equally wrote about national and even continental issues from a definite ethnic base, that of the Gikuyi. Olakunle George has earlier described this feature in Ngugi and other major African writers including, Soyinka and Achebe, as "a polyvalent oscillation between multiple markers of identity and subject position" (279). According to George this implies that the consciousness of the ethnic doubles as a metonymy for the nation and equally for the continent. He concludes by affirming that the "rhetoric of cultural nationalism as we encounter in these writers is inevitably transnational" (279). In other words, there is transnational when the ethnic identity and its representation serve as a metonymy for the nation-state and for the continent.

The ethnic consciousness in Ogot's commitment is amplified in the work of another Luo political intellectual, Oginga Odinga. The first chapter in Odinga's autobiography, *Not Yet Uhuru* paints a tableau of ethnic consciousness titled, "At the Feet of the Village Elders." Odinga begins, "Among the Luo of Central Nyanza, the forecasters had said of the White people 'If you touch them the skin will remain in your hand because they are very soft. But they will come with thunderstorms and they will burn the people'" (1). Odinga's autobiography was published in 1967 and Ogot's collection of stories in 1968. It is easy to see that these two Luo intellectuals could not but have sat "at the feet of the village elders," possibly at about the same period.

It is also not a coincidence therefore, that at the center of the narrative of "The Rain Came" is the motif of the scapegoat archetype. First of all, the idea of the coming rain connotes positivity, freshness, and a new beginning after a period of negation and death. The freshness that comes with the coming rain contrasts with the softness "in the white man's skin" in Odinga's account. We will explain the meaning of scapegoat, and adopting Jung's model of the three elements of the psyche, account for how "The Rain Came" expresses the shared belief of the Luo. And following from this to understand how Ogot has created access to the archetypal images of her people.

In Jungian psychology, the archetype forms a part of the collective unconscious which is the third part of the psyche. The collective unconscious "does not derive from personal experience and is not a personal acquisition but is inborn" (Jung, 3). The collective unconscious is not personal but universal in nature. As Charles Bressler has explained, "this part of the psyche houses the cumulative knowledge, experiences, and images of the entire human race" (154). Another interpreter of Jung, Betinna Knapp describes the collective unconscious as "suprapersonal" and "non-individual," inaccessible to conscious awareness, that neither to the personal conscious nor personal unconscious. Although it is covered to these elements it manifests itself through archetypes and archetypal images. Archetypes are patterns or images derived from repeated human experiences manifesting in terms of birth, death, rebirth, the seasons, and motherhood. The function of a writer, such as Grace Ogot, in the face of the great force of the collective unconscious is to provide her readers access to the archetypal images buried in the ethno-racial memory and by so doing revitalize the aspects of the ethnic and racial identity.

The scapegoat archetype in "The Rain Came" is embodied in the female character Oganda. A scapegoat is a person made to bear the blame which should fall on others. According to *The New Webster's Dictionary of the English Language*, "in ancient Jewish ritual a goat on whose head the high priest symbolically laid the sins of the people on Yom Kippur, and which was then allowed to escape into the wilderness" (891). Apart from ancient Jewish ritual, James Frazer's account in *The Golden Bough* attests that the scapegoat archetype is deeply rooted in a vast majority of cultures all over the world. He has presented an account of the role of the public scapegoat in the face of communal evil. Thus we are told: "the evil influences are embodied in a visible form or are at least supposed to be loaded upon a material medium, which acts as a vehicle to draw them off from the people, village or town" (562). Frazer also confirms that the scapegoat can be either human or non-human. We will recall the account of an example of scapegoat by Frazer from Uganda because of its cultural proximity to the Luo. As he puts it:

> From time to time the gods used to warn the king of Uganda that his foes the Banyoro were working magic against him and his people to make them die of disease. To avert such a catastrophe the king would send a scapegoat to the frontier of Bunyaro, the land of the enemy. The scapegoat consisted of either a man and a boy or a woman and her child, *chosen because of some mark or bodily defect, which the gods had noted and by which the victims were to be recognized*. (565)

We have emphasized the last portion of the quotation due to its resemblance of the situation in the short story "The Rain Came." In this story, Oganda wears a chain around her waist. We are told: "he saw the glittering chain shining around her waist." It is that sign that completes the prophecy for the chief. But we don't quite understand is whether that chain can be described as some form of "bodily defect" in the eyes of the gods. Ogot does not give us a clue to this. Also in Frazer's account on the "King of Uganda" the mark on the body serves to clinch the prophecy and identify in human proportion the one chosen by the gods.

If Oganda is the chosen one, who exactly is she? And what is special about her? Oganda is the only daughter of Chief Labongo'o, a chief of a clan whose name is not given, but which is situated by the lake and shares boundary with another clan. She was conceived after the chief had married four other wives in addition to her mother as the fifth wife. She is the only daughter in a family of twenty children. This really makes her special. Her name means "beans" because we are told "her skin was special" (117). Strange enough, it is this special one that the gods have separated for themselves. The narrator tells us: "out of all the women in this land, we have chosen this one. Let her offer herself a sacrifice to the lake monster. And on that day the rain will come down in torrents" (118).

The fundamental aspect of Oganda is not the physical dimension of her life but the psychological import of the fact that she is a communal sacrifice. Basically, a sacrifice is an offering given over to an-*other*, especially a deity. But the psychological import lies in the fact that in a sacrifice the one that offers deprives himself of his right and therefore denies his individuality for that *other*. In her analysis of the American writer Flannery O'Connor's short story, "Everything That Rises Must Converge," Bettina Knapp asserts: "psychologically, sacrifice implies a divestiture of one's individuality in favor of another person, as well as a renunciation of one's personal claim over another individual. Sacrifice is a wholly altruistic act which does away with egoistic desires" (Knapp, 89). It is in this "divestiture" of the individual, the personal that sacrifice finds authenticity with a people's collective unconscious.

Ordinarily, Oganga is indeed precious not only to her father that loves her dearly. If we may recall the words of Chinua Achebe in *No Longer at Ease,* the girl is an only palm fruit that should not be allowed to get lost in the fire. That is, she is someone worthy to be preserved. But it is the same high value on her that makes her sacrifice worth the while. In this it is not only the girl that is divested of her individuality. Her father, Labongo'o, her poor and helpless mother and of course her numerous brothers, nineteen in all and her stepmothers will surely miss her.

The weight of Oganda's task is encapsulated in the lyrics of the song she sings as she walks the long path to death. Thus:

> The ancestors have said Oganga must die,
> The daughter of the chief must be sacrificed
> When the lake monster feed on my flesh
> The people will have rain. (122)

Beyond the psychological import, the sense of sacrifice in the short story "The Rain Came" equally has political significance. This political significance goes beyond the ethnic collective unconscious of the Luo to the nation of Kenya especially in the post-independence era. This political significance is embodied in the program of *Harambee*. In *Not Yet Uhuru*, Oginga Odinga provides an account of the principle of *Harambee* in a chapter entitled "Harambee for Independence." Thus:

> Kenyatta introduced our *Harambee* slogan. *Harambee* became our national cry from this time on, but I remember it had first been used by Omolo Onigiro . . . of Nyakach location in Central Nyanza. At every meeting he shouted "*Harambee-eeh*" and added "Let us all go to Lowar to pull Kenyatta from prison, pull together for independence." *Harambee* became Kenya's slogan for national unity, for cooperation in the building of a new country. It stood for one country, one destination, one Africa, one party, one policy, the unity of all tribes and people for a united free country. (Odinga, 238)

As we can see at the core of the *Harambee* is the spirit of mutual collectivism, of respect especially inter-ethnic respect rather than xenophobia or ethnocentrism. These ideals could be attained through a deliberate attempt at the investing of self, of individuality. The 2007–2008 political crises following the presidential election serve to put the ideals of *Harambee* to question. Some of these issues cannot be handled in the present discussion. The overall relevance of this for us is that the motif of sacrifice in Ogot's story is simply a truthful representation of an ideal that had national spread and acceptance.

Besides, the name of the major character and chief, Labongo'o, is resonant of the name of the mythical forefather of the Acholi and the Luo who separated from his brother at a place called Wang-Lei by the River Nile (Jeane 2). Grace Ogot does not provide this information about the mythical background of the story. But recall that the story is set in a place without a name. Perhaps, the author has assumed that immediate Luo and Acholi reading public will fill in the gaps since they would have known of the name from traditional oral tradition. Again, in the story the chief is an archetypal father figure. He is a biological father to his twenty-one children. That in itself is legendary, and he is symbolically a father to all inhabitants of the community. This is in spite of the fact that the community serves as a metonym for the ethnic group. From this perspective, therefore, the sense of responsibility ascribed to him is reinforced.

THE MOTHER ARCHETYPE

If the scapegoat archetype represents an ideal that must serve to cohere the society and the nation at large, the mother archetype serves to maintain a strong sense of identity. In other words, the idea of sacrifice is about the duty of the individual, his or her sense of commitment to the unity of the group. The mother archetype is about bonding, a commitment and recognition of belonging to a shared common identity. And for the Joluo, it is a plain reminder that in spite of their history of migration beginning with their forefather Labongo, they share a common identity as descendants from a common stock. This later sense of belongingness is represented in the novel, *The Promised Land*. The analysis that follows, therefore, will begin with an account on the action of the novel. This will be followed by an explanation on the mother archetype as enunciated by Jung in his *The Archetypes and the Collective Unconscious,* and the interpretation of selected passages and incidents from the novel.

The Promised Land is the story of a couple, Ochola and Nyapol, their marriage, their migration to Tanganyika, their period of prosperity and adversity following Ochola's strange illness. The simple plot structure begins in Nyapol's marriage hut. The action commences after a "fierce tropical thunderstorm" (1). From the outside we are led into the interior of the hut. As we enter into the hut we quickly observe that the fire is burning but the hut is cold, and some rain water seeped through the roof. Soon there is a shift from the physical interior of the hut to the character. Nyapol projects her inner fears, her apprehension, to the wind. That projection produces anxiety over her loneliness. Her loneliness as a bride shifts from the marriage hut to her loneliness as a married woman who is supposed to "wake up once in a while to open the door for a late-coming husband as part of her duty" (5).

The narrative line shifts from Nyapol to her husband, Ochola, in a new state of anxiety. The basis of the Ochola's anxiety is precipitated by an overwhelming urge to migrate to Tanganyika. We follow Ochola and his wife in their preparation and eventual migration to Tanganyika. Once there he sets to work, builds a new home, prospers as a wealthy farmer and a father. But Ochola's fortune changes on a fateful day as he makes a wrong turn on his way back home. That one turn changes everything in his life. We are told:

> One day, as Ochola was walking home from a visit to friends living on the other side of the hill, he took a wrong turning and suddenly came to the gate of a half-hidden village. (61)

With an open mind and apparent good intention, he goes to felicitate with the inhabitants in the neighborhood and that decision becomes, as Robert Frost would put it, the path he should not have taken. This is because that choice brings him in a collision course with evil. The rest of the account revolves around his madness, and the struggle to be delivered from the strange illness.

In a sense the narrative is the account of Nyapol's coming to maturity and individuation. She is the ideal wife and companion, the animus that completes and complements her husband. She is caring and steadfast, rebuking him sternly in his follies and miscalculations; the voice of reason, and yet standing by him. We have introduced two terms, "individuation" and "animus" which need to be explained. In Jung's psychoanalytical theory, the animus, together with its counterpart, anima, represents the first level of the manifestation of the personal unconscious of any individual. While the anima is the feminine image in the male psyche, the animus is a male image in the female psyche. The animus is an opposing or rival sexual drive in the female psyche. Betinna Knapp describes it as the "inner man" in the female psyche (Knapp, 4). The animus can have a positive attribute by functioning as a source of inspiration in the male and a stabilizing force in inter-gender relationships. It is in these two qualities that we can recognize the animus function in Nyapol. She is a source of inspiration to her husband who at critical moments in the narrative will recognize such qualities and will reward her by calling her the pet name, "daughter of the lake." Although Nyapol takes pleasure in such appellation at the conscious level, the manly quality she has exhibited that triggered the praise from her husband occurred at her unconscious. It is in this regard that Nyapol's animus complements and completes her husband.

As in archetypes generally the mother archetype forms and fosters an underlying structural principle. Accordingly, it provides a rationale for the pattern of presentation and organization of the action. Since it is non-personal, the mother archetype is not really focused on any individual perceivable mother but is derived from the general communal memory. As Jung has explained, "all those influences which the literature describes as being exerted on children do not come from the mother herself, but rather from the archetype projected upon her, gives her a mythological background and invests her with authority and numinosity" (Jung, 83). However, in a work of literature such as the novel, archetypal images are dramatized through a character or characters as the center of consciousness or even through a set of motifs associated with the central character. According to Jung, the mother archetype manifests under the following forms:

1. The personal mother
2. The grandmother
3. Stepmother
4. Mother-in-law
5. Mothers in a figurative sense

Mothers in a figurative sense include many things that arouse devotion and feelings of awe such as the church, university, or country. Also included in this figurative sense are things that stand for fertility, fruitfulness, including ploughed fields, farmlands, cave or rock. As Jung affirms in the quotation above, possible influences or effects associated with the mother may not necessarily originate from the personal mother but from the archetype as it exists in the collective unconscious beyond the idea of any individual child.

In *The Promised Land*, we witness a unique relationship that exists between Ochola and the recurrent manifestations of the mother archetype. He is a character who is surrounded by the shades of the mother figure. There is his personal mother who incidentally died when he was only ten years old. But her death does not erase her image from his psyche. His life as a character is dominated by the influence of the mother. Perhaps it is the loss of his physical mother at the age of ten that creates the gap in his psyche, a gap that finds fulfillment in the collective unconscious in the image of the mother archetype. The loss and its attendant gap create a longing for fulfillment in the character. His mother is first introduced by the narrator thus: "Ochola's mother was the daughter of a fisherman who lived in Uyoma near the Lake . . . She died when Ochola was ten years old . . . She left Owiti with two small sons and no one to look after the home" (19). The death of Achar, his mother, left a deep scar in Ochola's psyche. The more obvious effect of the gap created by the loss of the mother is that he develops a "Don Juan complex." Here we witness a clash between his consciousness of a female being and the content of his personal unconscious. This is because he unconsciously seeks his mother in every other woman around him. As a matter of course, his absent mother becomes the yardstick for measuring a genuine relationship with any other grown female subject. The first step-mother is described as "unkind." She beat the children, calling them names, and starved them as they toiled in the fields (19). In other words, the first stepmother is a disaster especially because from Ochola's perspective she does not measure up to his late mother. This gap is soon filled, albeit partially, with the second stepmother, Chila. Observe that the first stepmother is so below the mark that she does not have a name apart from simply being identified as "stepmother." Unlike this unnamed ghostly mother figure, the new stepmother, Chila, is more benign and Ochola calls her "mother." We are told, "Under the love of the devoted Chila, the boys started life anew. They went with her to the fields and helped her at home to her heart's satisfaction" (20). But we should observe that these two stepmothers exist as mere types. They lack any real motivation. Their characteristics tend to emanate from remote communal memory rather than from concrete patterns of characterization. In other words, one is simply presented as good while the other is utterly wicked. They are visibly two poles apart from each other and no reason is given for the difference.

> In the first night at Tanganyika, the image of his late mother appears to him. "His mind went back to Seme, his motherland. . . . He recalled his mother's grave under the siala tree, a shadow seemed to ve towards him. . . . The shadow slowly turned into the image of his mother. He closed his eyes tightly but the

image remained. He covered his face with a blanket, but the image would not go. Then he burst into tears. 'What message have you for me, mother?'" (46).

The immediate conscious context of this scene is his first night in the new land, on a bed with his wife in Tanganyika, the land of his dream. At the level of personal consciousness, he lies beside his wife who momentarily drifts to sleep. But his unconscious self-separates from the concrete, first as his mind wanders to his motherland, Seme. And then it rests on the grave of his mother. Soon he moves away from Seme and back to the room, with the image of his mother accompanying every movement of his thoughts. It is noteworthy that much as he closed his eyes tightly, the image of his mother remained. It is as if in this first night of his accomplishment, arriving in the land of his dream, his mind travels back to the motherland to invite his late mother. Soon she appears and he finally bursts into tears. Throughout the period of encounter his wife lies beside him oblivious of what is unfolding.

At this moment of fulfillment after the initial anxiety he had prior to his journey has dissipated, Ochola's inner sense of fulfillment tends to be projected towards his mother. Even though Ochola has arrived at his promised land, Tanganyika, his Canaan, the idyll is embodied in the metaphor of his mother. He constructs this Promised Land in the image of his mother. In other words, his senses construct his new environment reality as a virtual reality embodied in his mother. At work here is the psychological feature of projection. In Jung's psychoanalysis projection is a psychological defense mechanism where a person unconsciously denies his or her own attributes, thoughts, and emotions which are then ascribed to the outside world. But projection equally has positive attributes. In this regard, we tend to "assign characteristics we love onto others" (Knapp, 1). It is this positive quality of projection that is foregrounded in the character Ochola especially as evidenced in the passage above.

In order to understand how this is achieved, we will recall the case made by Raymond Gozzi, Jr. According to him, projection is a psychological metaphor that serves as a way of describing certain feelings about other people. Seen in this way, therefore, he underscores that projection is better as our construction through images of others and external reality (179). The view of projection as construction harmonizes with what Bettina Knapp has described as the positive quality of projection since it enables us to assign positive attributes to others and the external world. Ochola's encounter with the apparition of his late mother in the first night of his arrival at Tanganyika is a mere construction of his new Promised Land in the image of his late mother. But this quality essentially is his. Having constructed them in the image of his mother he reassures himself and then drifts to sleep.

The image of the late Achar appears to Abiero, Ochola's brother as he comes to Tanganyika to look for his brother. Abiero on that night had the same dream he had en route to Tanganyika. His mother asked him not to return to Seme until he found Ochola. He felt the presence of his mother in the room when he woke up (94). In this case we see projection working in a positive sense as Abiero transfers his desire to see his lost brother to his late mother. As it were, the image of the late mother becomes a construction of the inner desire of the character. The dream becomes a guide to Abiero and a motivating factor to continue in the search for the lost Ochola. But the fact that the same image appears to both brothers serves to reinforce the sense of belongingness which we had mentioned earlier. Their mother's womb which they share is a construction of the common identity which every Joluo shares. Ogot has used the archetype of the mother in order to construct a strong sense of bonding for members of her ethnic group. The optimism pays off the following morning as Abiero goes into the bush and Ochola calls out to him from a cave. We are told: "Ochola slowly emerged from a cave under the very rock on which Abiero had been sitting" (97). The cave is a manifestation of the mother archetype which has preserved the ailing Ochola for Abiero to find him.

CONCLUSION

Grace Ogot wrote from a cultural crucible that reinforces a strong sense of identity for members of her Luo ethnic group. This is a binding factor in their seasons of migration across the nations in East Africa. This contribution is alert to the fact that Ogot was a child of two traditions, the Luo oral tradition and the tradition of the novel. Our main concern is to explore how the archetype of the scapegoat and that of the mother have served as the basis for understanding the legacy of Ogot as a writer. We have shown that while the scapegoat archetype in her work provides a sense of cohesion in the ethnic group while eliciting from the members sensitivity to self-sacrifice, the mother archetype reinforces their ideal of belongingness. What is new in this study the fact that previous critics of Ogot have glossed over the deep psychological import of her works. The adoption of the insights of Carl Jung especially his theory of the collective unconscious and archetypes to study the contribution of a female writer from Kenya is indeed novel. And for as part of a volume that documents the legacy of female writers this contribution has moved away from the given feministic discourse in order to explore something different in the creativity of a pioneer female writer.

WORKS CITED

Achebe, Chinua. *No Longer at Ease*. London: Heinemann, 1964. Print.
Abrams, M. H., Geoffrey Galt Harpham. *A Glossary of Literary Terms*. Eight Edition. Boston: Thomson Higher Education, 2005.
Bressler, Charles E. *Literary Criticism: An Introduction to Theory and Practice*. Second Edition. Upper Saddle River, NJ: Simon & Schuster, 1999.
Chukukere, Gloria. *Gender Voices and Choices: Redefining Women in Contemporary African Fiction*. Enugu: Fourth Dimension Publishers, 1995.
Dathorne, O. R. *African Literature in the Twentieth Century*. London: Heinemann Educational Books Ltd, 1975.
Frazer, James. *The Golden Bough: A Study in Magic and Religion*. London: Wordsworth Edition Ltd, 1993.
Frye, Northrop. *Anatomy of Criticism*. Princeton, NJ: Princeton University Press, 1973.
George, Olakunle. "The National and the Transnational: Soyinka's *The Interpreters* and *Ake: The Years of Childhood*." *Novel: A Forum on Fiction*. Vol2. No. 3(2008): 279+ *eLibrary* Web. 3rd August 2016.
Gozzi, Jr, Raymond. "The Projection Metaphor in Psychology." *ETC: A Review of General Semantics* 52:2(Summer 1995):197+ *Academic OneFile,* Web. 3rd October 2016.
Irele, Abiola. *The African Experience in Literature and Ideology*. London: Heinemann, 1981.
Jean, Dear. "Wang-Lei, the place where Girpir, Labongo parted ways." *Daily Monitor* Saturday, 17th August 2013. www.monitor.co.ug.
Jung, Carl .G. *The Archetypes and the Collective Unconscious*. Trans. R. F. C. Hull. Princeton, NJ: Princeton University Press, 1990.
Knapp, Betinna. *Women in Twentieth Century Literature: A Jungian View*. University Park: Pennsylvania University Press, 1987.
Mudimbe, V. Y. *The Invention of Africa: Gnosis, Philosophy and the Order of Knowledge*. Bloomington: Indiana University Press, 1988.
Mwangi, Meja. *Striving for the Wind*. London: Heinemann: 1992.
Ngugi wa Thiong'O. *Devil on the Cross*. London: Heinemann, 1982.
Nnolim, Charles. "Jungian Archetypes in Oyono's *Houseboy*." *Approaches to the African Novel*. Port Harcourt: Saros International Publishers, 1992: 28–34.
———. "The Nigerian Tradition and the Novel." *Nigerian Literature in English: Emerging Critical Perspectives*. Ed. Onyemaechi Udumukwu. Port Harcourt: M & J. Grand Orbit Communications Ltd, 2007: 26–42.
Odinga, Oginga. *Not Yet Uhuru*. London: Heinemann Educational Books, 1975.
Ogot, Grace. *Land Without Thunder and Other Stories*. Nairobi: East African Educational Publishers, 1988. First Edition, 1968.
———. *The Promised Land*. Nairobi: East African Educational Publishers Ltd, 1990. First Edition 1966.
Roscoe, Adrian. *Uhuru's Fire: African Literature East to South*. Cambridge: Cambridge University Press, 1977.

Chapter 10

Bessie Head
A World Writer from Africa

Mary S. Lederer

INTRODUCTION

Bessie Amelia Emery Head (July 6, 1937–April 17, 1986) was an African writer of the universal human soul who resisted being labeled as any "type" of writer. She wrote about her discomfort with being called a feminist, and she disagreed very strongly with those who challenged her for not writing about "African issues." Lewis Nkosi famously criticized her for not engaging with the South African political situation (76). She insisted that she would not limit her characters to a narrow definition of "African," and that her most important literary influences were not African ("Why do I Write?", 57–59). However, she lived in Africa her whole life, and even though she frequently considered moving away from Africa, in the end she decided that, despite her universal worldview, her identity was African and she needed to remain in Africa. Her view of humanity, this worldview of the "brotherhood of man," as she articulated it in her most famous novel *A Question of Power*, was cultivated through her experiences growing up and working in South Africa and then moving to Botswana. She believed herself to have a writer's calling, and she began writing very early. Gillian Stead Eilersen, Head's biographer, notes that in 1951, at thirteen years of age, "Bessie broke into print for the first time. An organization called the Goodwill Council published short essays and poems from schoolchildren of all races in a small magazine" (23), and a piece by Bessie Emery was included.

Bessie Amelia Emery was born on July 6, 1937, in the Fort Napier Mental Institution in Pietermaritzburg, South Africa, where her mother was a patient. Her father was unknown. Although her mother was white, the baby Bessie early developed African physical characteristics, and so the local authorities had difficulty placing her because no white family wanted a baby that might be black. Finally she was placed with George and Nellie Heathcote, a poor Coloured family. Head believed the Heathcotes to be her biological parents, but when she was fourteen years old, she was abruptly taken to court, told that the Heathcotes were not her parents, and made a ward of St. Monica's Diocesan Home for Coloured Girls. Not surprisingly, these events had a profound impact on her life and her writing. Head herself narrated the story of her origins in her statement:

> The reason for my peculiar birthplace was that my mother was white, and she had acquired me from a black man. She was judged insane, and committed to the mental hospital while pregnant. Her name was Bessie Emery and I consider it the only honour South Africans ever did me—naming me after this unknown, lovely, and unpredictable woman. (Preface to "Witchcraft" 72)

This version is now known to be incorrect (see Tom Holzinger, "The Black Antecedents of Bessie Amelia Emery Head"). Nevertheless, Head's version of events is important in order to understand both her relationship to her mother and her own sense of isolation in life.

Head received her teaching credentials from a nearby high school while she was still a ward of St. Monica's, and when she finished, she moved to Durban and then Cape Town and Johannesburg to work first as a teacher and then as a journalist. She worked for a while at the *Golden City Post* writing an advice column for teenagers and contributing other short pieces. She was briefly involved in politics and was arrested for carrying a letter with incriminating information, but appears to have turned state witness. After this event (April 1960), she tried to commit suicide and then returned to Cape Town.

Back in Cape Town, among the journalists and activists Head was involved with, she met Harold Head, whom she soon married. The marriage was not happy, and Bessie eventually left him, taking their young son Howard with her. She went first to Johannesburg, then accepted a teaching post in Serowe, Botswana. She was only given an exit permit, so she and Howard left South Africa permanently in 1964. Serowe eventually became her permanent home, despite several attempts to leave Africa, and she received Botswana citizenship in 1979.

Head did most of her writing in Botswana, including her most famous novels *When Rain Clouds Gather* (1968), *Maru* (1971), and *A Question of Power* (1973). She also wrote a collection of short stories *The Collector of Treasures and other Botswana Village Tales* (1977), inspired by an oral history of Serowe, *Serowe: Village of the Rain Wind* (1981), that she was working on at the time. As her reputation grew, she began to receive invitations to travel to Europe, the United States, Nigeria, and Australia. While resident at the Iowa Writers' Workshop in the United States, she commenced the research for her final novel, a historical novel about the establishment of the Bechuanaland Protectorate in the late nineteenth century, titled *A Bewitched Crossroads* (1984). She contracted to write her autobiography but died before she began work on it. Two friends, a white man and his Motswana wife, were with her when she died. Eilerson writes, "firmly supported by one black hand and one white, [she] passed from life to death. 'In my end is my beginning'" (344). She was buried in Serowe.

HEAD'S PHILOSOPHIES AND GLOBAL INFLUENCES

Bessie Head's reading influences were very broad. After her experiences at St. Monica's, she firmly rejected Christianity. Nevertheless, she had a very solid education in Christian thought. She did religious studies at St. Monica's, which was an Anglican institution, and her writing reflects a deep knowledge of the Bible. All of her novels contain references to the Bible, sometimes direct references, but more often allusions or allegorical images. She was interested in Jesus Christ and what his life stood for, but she did not believe that there was a God somewhere controlling everything. Her own view was that every human being was God (an idea with some parallels in Christian thought), including but not exclusively Jesus Christ. In Head's view, giving one person that much power—whether religious, social, or political—was dangerous and, throughout history, had resulted over and over in human catastrophe and suffering. Her famous reference to Islam near the end of *A Question of Power* reflects her view:

> If there were any revelation whatsoever in her own suffering it seemed to be quite the reverse of Mohammed's dramatic statement. He had said: There is only one God and his name is Allah. And Mohammed is his prophet.
>
> She said: There is only one God and his name is Man. And Elizabeth is his prophet. (205–6)

These ideas appeared early in her letters and other writing. In her letter to Randolph Vigne dated June 11, 1969, she states, "People brought up on Christianity think God has nothing to do with them. He is someone who turns water into wine. They just go on shitting up the world and feel no responsibility for their character or anything they do" (*A Gesture of Belonging* 91). Again, she asserts, "I foresee a day when I will steal the title of God, the unseen Being in the sky, and offer it to mankind. From then onwards, people, as they pass each other in the street each day, will turn to each other and say: 'God-morning, God.' War will end. Human suffering will end" ("Why Do I Write?" 59). Despite her rejection of Christianity in its organized forms (as well as her skepticism about most organized forms of religion), she was very interested in questions of spirituality and the human soul.

While Head was in Durban, she began reading texts on Hindu and Buddhist thought at the M. L. Sultan Library (a private library designated for people of all races). The ideas she gathered from her reading there also influenced her thinking on human spirituality, and she incorporated them into her later work. (Later, when a Canadian group offered to send her some books, she specifically requested *The Gospel of Sri Ramakrishna*, and copied at least one passage out of it, the description of Mother Kali [Khama Memorial Museum file 457 Bessie Head Papers document 64, hereinafter KMM 457 BHP 64].) *A Question of Power* contains numerous references to and descriptions of some of the Hindu deities (see Rukmini Vanamali, "Bessie Head: The Mythic Dimension").

However, Head's interest in these various strands of religious philosophy did not move her to declare herself an adherent of one or the other form of organized religion, or a member of one or the other political party. The breadth of her reading, as well as her experiences in South Africa and Botswana, led her to a strongly anti-ideological stance. She had already become disillusioned with political ideology while she was in Cape Town, and in 1978 wrote that "political camps ... falsify truth" ("Some Notes on Novel Writing" 63). She stated firmly to Paddy Kitchen that she was not a feminist:

> All the mad, wild feminists of the world passionately love A Question of Power and Elizabeth but they make a mistake. Elizabeth is brutally assaulted but she remains in close intellectual communication with the two men, particularly Sello, and heeds their communication because it is important. . . . They make a mistake. Elizabeth is not women. The student [being referred to] . . . is WOMAN. (KMM 74 BHP 117)

Head called out injustice and inequality wherever she saw it, not just in relations between men and women but across ethnic and class lines, too. Ultimately, she developed her own philosophy of the "brotherhood of man," which includes aspects of many different philosophies. Head was opposed to power in any form, and her experience of human society showed her that anyone, white or black, male or female, could wield power over anyone else, not just black or white, female or male. She was deeply sensitive to the injustices suffered by women, blacks, and the poor, but that did not prevent her from understanding the roots of those injustices and writing about them in her letters and published work.

Head's reading habits in Botswana were somewhat haphazard. She read what she could get her hands on. She read things from the Serowe library, but she also asked her correspondents to send her books, and people would send her things they thought she might be interested in: D. H. Lawrence and Boris Pasternak, but also Bertolt Brecht, R. D. Laing, the "William" stories for Howard, Gabriel García Márquez, Ruth Benedict, George Padmore, and Alice Walker, to name but a few. She read some African writers, such as Chinua Achebe, Nadine Gordimer, and Doris Lessing, but her access to the full spectrum of African writing was limited to what she could find in journals that she occasionally received and the books that people sent her. She liked Ruth Benedict and Bertolt Brecht, but she disdained Doris Lessing and Nadine Gordimer; she found R. D. Laing frightening. D. H. Lawrence and Boris Pasternak influenced Head most strongly. She wrote that she kept copies of their novels *Sons and Lovers* and *Doctor Zhivago* next to her bed and read favorite passages from them repeatedly. She felt a strong affinity with what she saw as their examination of the human soul in its dual nature, especially what she saw as the writers' deep understanding of the character and place of evil in the world. Her own battle with evil, including the evil that she knew to be in herself and in every human being, drew her again and again to these two writers.

ON CORRESPONDENCE

There is not much material that remains from Head's early years in South Africa. Until recently, it was assumed that the only major work to come from that period was her novel (or novella) *The Cardinals*, which was published in 1993 along with some other short works. However, in 2014, papers were discovered in Munich in the home of Cordelia Guenther, with whom Head lived for a few months in 1961. The papers include letters that Head and Guenther wrote to each other (despite living in the same flat) as well as poems that Head wrote but never published and some pencil sketches of her by Guenther. Probably the most interesting information to come out of these papers concerns references to a manuscript, which Head and Guenther referred to as "*Das Buch*" ("The Book"). Descriptions of the plot and characters clearly establish that this manuscript is not an early version of *The Cardinals*. Unfortunately, the manuscript is probably lost (destroyed along with other papers that could not be saved), but the remaining documents shed light on how important writing was to Head and how important it was for her to get the words right. The brief correspondence with Guenther reveals discussions about how to cut out the things and words that don't matter in the story or to the characters (in "*Das Buch*"), and reiterations about how distracting some ideas, phrases, and passages can be. They can take the reader away from the most important thing: the *idea* in the writing.

The letters also show Head's early determination to understand someone else's writing by copying it down: in one letter to Guenther (undated, 1961) she wrote that she would be late getting home because she was trying to "get" a very difficult poem, and she included the words that she had to that point been able to follow (the poem appears to be the lyrics for the song "Black Coffee," which she might have been listening to in the library). She continued this habit for the rest of her life, writing down passages that were important to her, such as the description of Mother Kali from *The Gospel of Sri Ramakrishna* (mentioned earlier), passages from *Doctor Zhivago*, Lawrence's poems, and many other texts.

Another important correspondence that was not discovered until recently is one with Langston Hughes (October 1960 to February 1961). At this point, Head was unemployed in Cape Town, and she wished to establish contact with writers outside of Africa (because of the deteriorating conditions for writers inside South Africa). The correspondence was very brief: they exchanged only a few letters; Bessie sent him some of her poems, and Hughes sent her a couple of his books. Possibly Hughes was not prepared to participate in the kind of intense dialogue that Head craved; the last thing she received from him was a letter from his secretary.

Head is best known for her novels and stories, but the Khama III Memorial Museum in Serowe contains a collection of more than two thousand of her letters, manuscripts, interviews, notes, photographs, and other documents that were found in her house after she died. Head was a dedicated letter-writer—sometimes, famously, responding immediately on an aerogramme in the post office—and her papers contain correspondence that lasted many years. Some of her correspondents she never met. Some admired her work and struck up a written conversation with her about her ideas. Others were people who helped her through very difficult times. She responded to and saved every letter she received, and kept copies of her own replies, but since her house was very small, she was forced at one point to destroy many of the letters she had saved. What remains gives important insight into the writer, her style, her working methods, and her life.

Many of the letters in the papers deal with Head's problems with publishers and with getting royalties paid on time. For a poor woman in southern Africa, with no other source of income, these royalties were critical. Many of her correspondents became involved with her in discussions about gardening, since she worked on several co-operative gardening projects and growing vegetables was an activity close to her heart (see *Everyday Matters*, edited by M. J. Daymond). Some correspondents discussed Christianity (in some cases trying to convert her) and the nature of God, evil, and the human spirit (see letters to and from Mona Pehle, KMM 034 BHP, and Tom Carvlin, KMM 038 BHP). These ideas both informed her novel *A Question of Power* and led her to further investigations into the nature of the soul. She developed a large network of readers who sometimes also got to know each other through their connection to Bessie Head.

Some of these letters have been published in limited collections: *A Gesture of Belonging*, her letters to Randolph Vigne (1990), *Imaginative Trespasser*, her correspondence with Patrick and Wendy Cullinan (2005), and *Everyday Matters*, her correspondence with Paddy Kitchen (2015). Currently, another scholar is at work editing a longer volume that will include a greater set of the letters to many different people. The increasing interest in Head's letters points to an increasing understanding of the importance of reading them alongside her published work.

HEAD AS SUBJECT OF LITERARY CRITICISM

Bessie Head's writing has, since her death, attracted a great deal of critical attention. She has been most often examined within a post-colonial or feminist context, but given the breadth of her work, many other types of critiques are possible. Recently, work has been done on the eco-agricultural aspects of her novels, and her letters are fostering more and more examinations of autobiographical and spiritual aspects of her writing. Several studies have appeared since 2000 that look at the way Head writes about the natural world, whether she writes about the bush in Botswana, the problems of drought in a largely agricultural society, or the pleasures of small-scale gardening. However, there are very few studies of spirituality in her work. (Two important exceptions are June M. Campbell, "Beyond Duality: A Buddhist Reading of Bessie Head's *A Question of Power*," and Desiree Lewis, *Living on a Horizon: Bessie Head and the Politics of Imagining*.)

Head first began to attract critical attention with her novel *When Rain Clouds Gather*, but it was not until she published her third novel, *A Question of Power*, that her name began to appear commonly in the pages of literary criticism and her books on the syllabi of literature courses. Criticism of her novels dates back at least to the mid-1970s, but the first book-length study of her writing only appeared in 1990, after her death. *The Tragic Life: Bessie Head and Literature in Southern Africa* brings together a number of essays that deal with questions of race, sociology, psychology, women, and stylistic technique. These approaches anticipated the critical approaches of the next ten to fifteen years, during which time Head's writing was examined from the angle of the feminist critic, the black critic, and the psychological critic.

One of the most fascinating aspects of Head's writing is that many different critical approaches can be applied to it. And yet none of them seems satisfying, or complete. Desiree Lewis has described the difficulty of controlling Head's writing in a neat and organized way: "Much of the reading that *does* focus on the substance of her writing tends to continue an appropriating impulse" ("Bessie Head's Freedoms" 1), and Head's work seems to "defy conclusive interpretation" (*Living on a Horizon* 15). Very often critical analyses begin with a recitation of her biography, perhaps reflecting the impact her own life had on her writing. Yet with Bessie Head it is important always to separate fact from fiction. While her life story certainly influenced her ideas, and while it is true that she used aspects from her life in her writing, nevertheless, she carefully crafted story and character to use and reshape *only* what she needed. Perhaps the problem for many is that in her writing Head used her life and her surroundings to such an extent that it can be difficult to know the difference. Knowing *about* her is important, but it is important precisely because it is too easy to confuse her with her characters. Most crucially, because of her personal circumstances, she is still all too often labeled as a "mad" writer who used her madness to literary effect.

Another reason that these approaches seem unsatisfying rests in the fact that Head herself frequently contradicted others' assessments of her (as well as her own assessment of herself). Feminist criticism frequently overlooks the fact that many of her male characters reflect Head's ongoing development of the figure of the "great man": Makhaya develops into Maru, who develops into Sello, who develops into Paul Thebolo, until she is finally able to write about her hero, Khama III (the Great). Some have suggested that this development represents a search for a father figure. Perhaps this is true, and perhaps it is also true that the female characters—Paulina, Margaret, Elizabeth, and Dikeledi—represent an idealized figure of a mother who safeguards her children, even when she can no longer take care of them (as Head's own mother did). But Head frequently describes her mind as "masculine," and her responsibilities as Howard's mother were also very important to her.

Analyses based on racial–political understanding are equally unsatisfactory. Head was under no illusions about the guilt of whites in the oppression of Africans. On January 9, 1961, she wrote to Langston Hughes about John F. Kennedy that "I don't know whether I like him or not because I don't like and trust any White people" (Moore 14); this observation is hardly new or even surprising, given her background and where she lived. However, by the middle of 1961, she was sharing a flat with a white woman (the German woman Cordelia Guenther) in Cape Town, and by the time she wrote *When Rain*

Clouds Gather, she was looking at people's characters rather than their race. In Botswana she was stunned to discover that black people could speak about and treat other black people the way white people spoke about and treated black people in South Africa. In particular the language used by Batswana to speak about the San was very familiar to her, and she wrote *Maru* about a San woman in a rural Botswana village to expose those injustices and to remark on their similarities to what whites in South Africa said about blacks. And although critics often understand *A Question of Power* and Elizabeth's problems as stemming from her life in apartheid South Africa, Head herself was adamant that the characters of Dan and Sello were developed out of her experiences in Botswana, demonstrating what she perceived as the intrigues and plotting of a Botswana village. Elizabeth's, Margaret's, and Makhaya's tormentors are black, and their saviors are both white and black.

At least three critics have analyzed *A Question of Power* in an effort to understand the psychopathology of the main character, Elizabeth, and many others assume Elizabeth's situation to be madness as literary trope. However, these critics fall into the trap of trying to understand the novel as a quasi-realistic one, referring to the episodes with Dan and Sello, two of the main male characters, as literary representations of what is going on in Elizabeth's mind. But reading the text in this way misses many of the nuances that Head deliberately cultivates within the narrative. Head herself insisted that "The embarrassment of the book is that a part of it takes place on a spiritual level—people prefer to call it insanity but it is not a record of insanity as much as it is a record of the spirit (KMM 77 BHP 33, September 13, 1974, to Betsy Stephens; see also Sarah Mandow, "Boundaries and Beyond: Issues of Resistance and Control in the Work of Bessie Head").

Since the 1990s, Head's work has been examined from the post-colonial perspective, looking at situations of exile, the isolation of the outsider, and the ways in which colonial and post-independence political and social structures have served to perpetuate the oppression introduced during the colonial period in Africa. In particular, many critics are interested in how Head's early life under apartheid rule in South Africa reappears and is reshaped in her novels. Such analyses are interesting, but often fail to take into account the very contradictions (as suggested above) that bedevil any examination of her writing. Her exile and the exile of many of her characters offer opportunities to examine how she imagined societies without power relations and without any form of oppression, but at the same time it is important to understand that outsiders remain outsiders: there is no antidote to exile. Maria Olaussen, in *Forceful Creation in Harsh Terrain*, argues that the outsider must remain outside if positive change is to come about; change cannot come from within: Makhaya and Gilbert marry into a village of (internal) exiles; Margaret's marriage to Maru removes her from the very society her marriage is supposed to educate; and Elizabeth's famous gesture of belonging is made alone in a dark room on the edge of the village.

Most recently, as the existence of Head's papers and letters gets wider recognition, critics have begun to look at the role of autobiography in her writing and at the relationship of her letters to her published work. As noted earlier, three collections of her letters have already been published, and another major collection is in the final stages of preparation for publication. These letters give insight into how Head understood God, her struggles with the co-existence of good and evil, her deep understanding of the circumstances of poor women, and her keen observations of Botswana society as its dramas played out in Serowe. The most important impact that the letters have is to make clear the relationship between autobiography and fiction in Head's writing. Although her novels and stories contain autobiographical elements, the relationship between them is that of a bolt of fabric and a finished dress. Head's life provided ideas and inspiration for her writing, but she reworked the material from her life with the aim of creating the idea in her work.

Thus, with so many paths branching out of each text, one cannot help but wonder where a reader should begin. I believe that readers of Head should begin with themselves. If Head's letters demonstrate anything, they show the extent to which Head herself worked to create a network of readers and writers. She relished discussing and conversing with her correspondents, and her ideas about everything, including her own books, changed, often dramatically, over time. Consider for example that later in her life she felt that Makhaya was a weak character, a result of the weakness often exposed in a first novel. Again she considered *Maru* her masterpiece, although she grappled to the end of her life with the ideas in *A Question of Power*. She never wrote of *The Cardinals* or her poems from Cape Town. Many readers of Bessie Head experience similar feelings of "discussing" and reconsidering ideas with her as they read her books, stories, and essays. This uncertainty is central to Head's work, and it makes her works both easy and difficult to analyze, but it also gives the greatest pleasure.

LITERARY CONTRIBUTION

Bessie Head's contribution to African literature and to African women's literature is very difficult to measure, in large part because her writing is so unusual, particularly in her anti-ideology stance, and so to pigeonhole her as "African" or "woman" is to miss the universality of how she understands human experience. The variety of criticism about her writing demonstrates to some degree the difficulty of slotting her as a "type" of writer. She does not ignore the consequences of race or gender; indeed, her short stories in *The Collector of Treasures and Other Botswana Village Tales* examine in minute detail the ways that poverty and sexism affect the quality of women's lives, but her female characters may contribute to their own misfortune, such as Neo in the story "Snapshots of a Wedding" or MmaMompati in the story "The Village Saint." The stories are also filled with versions of the "great man" she so desired to create and find. The stranglehold of patriarchy is fatal for characters such as Life ("Life"), who returns from Johannesburg to her parents' village and tries to settle down, but whose husband receives only a very light sentence for her murder. Patriarchy also drives women to take drastic action, as it does in the case of Dikeledi in "The Collector of Treasures." But in prison she finds women—and even her male neighbor—who help her earn money and maintain her children's schooling. Head represents the situation of women and examines the power relationships that lead to poverty. She is also clear about the importance of men in sustaining equitable relationships and about the women who are complicit in their own oppression.

Head's writing is possibly unique, and the different ways of analyzing her work show the countless ways her books can be "read." She is not given to stereotypes: Sello is "both God and the Devil at the same time" (*A Question of Power* 176); Paul Thebolo in "The Collector of Treasures" is a "traditional" man who treats his wife and her friend as equals despite doing all the things that men do in traditional society; Gilbert is a white man who recognizes his own limitations and finds a complement to himself in Makhaya, an anti-apartheid activist who decides he would rather build dams than blow them up; Dan, while also having supernatural abilities, is a black African nationalist who demonstrates prejudice as well as any white person against a woman he decides is not African enough; Margaret is an outcast raised by a white woman to help her outcast people. These characters demonstrate the folly of allowing oneself to be limited by others' definitions of what they ought to be as well as the folly of trying to fit into those expectations. Bessie Head was an African woman by birth, and so realized that she belonged in Africa, but she claimed the whole world for herself and for her characters. In her own words:

> I admit that my reading background and influences are international, but I would worry if limitation could be placed on the African personality and that only certain kinds of writers could properly represent the African personality. All my characters are black, but I reserve for them the charm of being unpredictable and highly original. I would dread to be faced with a dark dungeon called the "proper" and recognisable African and that this should be the standard character one would find in an African novel. There is the urge towards a kind of closed-door nationalism in independent Africa, an urge to reject the colonial

experience. But this is not possible. The African personality has been enlarged and changed by the colonial experience. I am not bad on Western civilisation. I simply have a door that stands open and characters that startle and enchant my readers. ("Why Do I Write?" 58–59)

Given the fact that her reading background and influences are international, her characters are as a matter of course not typically African.

Desiree Lewis in "Bessie Head's Freedoms" has written about the problems of critical appropriation of a text, in this case Bessie Head's texts, to serve one's own critical purpose, or worse, one's own ideology. Lewis argues that Head's writing resists such appropriating impulses. While I agree with Lewis's statement regarding much literary criticism, I am also struck by the fact that there are so many possibilities in each of Head's novels and stories that appropriation, while in one sense exposing critical "power" over a text, in another sense reveals possibility for deep personal engagement with readers who come to her books with particular interests and ideas. I think one reason for this is that Head, in her fiction, nonfiction, and most particularly in her letters, speaks for herself in a way that invites readers to look at her ideas in the context of their own thoughts and ideas. In literary criticism, this not surprisingly takes the form of a critical approach, but for other readers, it takes the form of a conversation.

Thus critical writing *about* Head might seem bombastic or limp: bombastic when the critic tries to exert control over the text, to master it, and limp when the critic admits defeat or makes unsupportable claims about the writer's omissions and weaknesses. These kinds of analyses are hamstrung by the supposed power of criticism, either the bombastic exercise of it or the limp relinquishing of it. Head strongly resists that kind of relationship and insists that each reader approach her as a unique human being.

Head's work remains alive thirty-six years after her death because her ideas grab readers and bring them back to her over and over again. We read Bessie Head because she is a great writer. We re-read her because once we finish, we re-think, and then we have to re-read. I can think of few other writers whose ideas are as alive as Head's, because they contain so much of her own experience, because she draws from so much of life—and not just Botswana life or even African life, but *all* life—and because she does so with skill and humor.

CONCLUSION

Essentially, this is a never-ending conclusion because of course, if Bessie Head's writing does engage her readers repeatedly, then there can never truly be a conclusion. The conversation between the reader and the writer will go on.

But perhaps there is another way to conclude. Literature is becoming less national and more global in the modern world, so perhaps Bessie Head was ahead of her time. She wrote about universal themes and insisted that she would not be pigeonholed. African writers in the Diaspora are no longer limited to a narrow definition of Nigerian, or Ghanaian, or South African, or Ethiopian, or Sierra Leonean, or whatever identity. They write about what they know from home, but also what they know from wherever else they are, and what they imagine from their experience, just as Bessie Head did. Her location was "home," but her themes touched on universal questions of love, belonging, God, justice. Perhaps she has finally come into her own.

Perhaps, Bessie Head was the first, more than thirty-six years ago, of this new generation, and her legacy is just beginning to be written.

WORKS CITED

Abrahams, Cecil, Ed. *The Tragic Life: Bessie Head and Literature in Southern Africa*. Trenton, NJ: Africa World Press, 1990.
Campbell, June M. "Beyond Duality: A Buddhist Reading of Bessie Head's *A Question of Power*." *The Journal of Commonwealth Literature* 29.1 (1993): 64–81.
Eilersen, Gillian Stead. *Bessie Head: Thunder Behind Her Ears. Her Life and Writing*. 1995. Johannesburg: Wits UP, 2007.
Head, Bessie. "The Collector of Treasures." *The Collector of Treasures and other Botswana Village Tales* London: Heinemann, 1977: 87–103.
———. *Imaginative Trespasser: Letters between Bessie Head, Patrick and Wendy Cullinan 1963–1977*. Edited by Patrick Cullinan. Johannesburg and Trenton, NJ: Wits UP and Africa World Press, 2005
———. *A Gesture of Belonging: Letters from Bessie Head, 1965–1979*. Edited by Randolph Vigne. London and Portsmouth, NH: SA Writers and Heinemann, 1991.
———. Preface to "Witchcraft." MS 4 (1975): 72–73.
———. "Some Notes on Novel Writing." 1978. *A Woman Alone*. Oxford: Heinemann, 1990: 61–64.
———. *A Question of Power*. London: Heinemann, 1973.
———. "Why Do I Write?" 1985. *English in Africa* 28.1 (2001): 57–59.
———. *A Woman Alone: Autobiographical Writings*. Edited and introduced by Craig MacKenzie. Oxford: Heinemann, 1990.
Holzinger, Tom. "The Black Antecedents of Bessie Amelia Emery Head." *Writing Bessie Head in Botswana: An Anthology of Remembrance and Criticism*. Edited by Mary S. Lederer and Seatholo M. Tumedi. Gaborone, Botswana: Pentagon Publishers, 2007, 119–21.
Lewis, Desiree." Bessie Head's Freedoms." *Chimurenga Online*. Chimurenga, n.d. Web. May 8, 2010.

———. *Living on a Horizon: Bessie Head and the Politics of Imagining.* Trenton, NJ: Africa World Press, 2007.

Mandow, Sarah. "Boundaries and Beyond: Issues of Resistance and Control in the Work of Bessie Head." *The Life and Work of Bessie Head: A Celebration of the Seventieth Anniversary of her Birth.* Edited by Mary S. Lederer, Seatholo M. Tumedi, Leloba S. Molema, and M. J. Daymond. Gaborone, Botswana: Pentagon, 2008.

Moore, David C. ed. Introduction "The Bessie Head and Langston Hughes Correspondence, 1960–1961." *Research in African Literature*, 41.3 (2010): 1–20.

Nkosi, Lewis. "Southern Africa: Protest and Commitment." *Tasks and Masks: Themes and Styles of African Literature.* By Lewis Nkosi. Essex, UK: Longman, 1981, 76–106.

Olaussen, Maria. *Forceful Creation in Harsh Terrain: Place and Identity in Three Novels by Bessie Head.* Frankfurt/Main: Peter Lang, 1997.

Vanamali, Rukmini. "Bessie Head's *A Question of Power*: The Mythic Dimension." *The Literary Criterion* 23.1–2 (1988): 154–71.

Chapter 11

Narrating Hybridity

The Synthesis of Tradition and Modernity in Emecheta's Double Yoke

Solomon Omatsola Azumurana

INTRODUCTION

Arguably among Buchi Emecheta's novels, *Double Yoke* appears to be the least analyzed. This is in spite of the complexity of the story Emecheta tells and the topicality of the story within the framework of African modernity. In this chapter, I interrogate Emecheta's *Double Yoke* as an intervention in the debate of the tradition versus modernity continuum. Focusing on the major male and female characters of the novel. I then argue that while some African writers advocate a return to traditional culture, and others just show the crisis of identity that emanate as a result of the conflicting demand of tradition and modernity, Emecheta through her novel under consideration, advocates a synthesis of tradition and modernity. Although critics have insisted on the need to move beyond the understanding of tradition in opposition to modernity as the dichotomy between the past and the present, and the opposition between African and European value system, it is specifically through this demarcation/distinction that I approach the reading of Emecheta's *Double Yoke*. Exploiting Richard Bjornson's ideas in his "Alienation and Disalienation . . ." and that of Abiola Irele in his own "In Praise of Alienation" and relating them to *Double Yoke,* I show why and the ways Emecheta solicits the synthesis of tradition and modernity.

Yet by calling for the synthesis of tradition and modernity, Emecheta in the same spatial-temporal imaginative space also advocates the need for the African to embrace a hybrid culture following his/her encounter with colonial modernity. It is in this way that *Double Yoke* can be seen or taken as a novel that narrates hybridity. Within the frame of various definitions that have been provided, hybridity simply refers to a phenomenon or individual that is neither here nor there. It denotes a state of being in which a phenomenon or individual draws from two conflicting ideas to create a third estate of being that does not wholly belong to any of the conflicting phenomena or ideas.

THE CONTRIBUTION OF EMECHETA TO THE EVOLUTION OF NIGERIAN/ AFRICAN NOVEL TRADITION

Florence Onyebuchi Emecheta (1944–2017) by any given standard, is an accomplished and revered Nigerian/African/feminist novelist. When, for instance, she suggests as the imaginative Miss Bulewao in *Double Yoke* that her accomplishment as a creative writer is spoken about "not only in Nigeria, but abroad" (3), she was not exaggerating. There is no way that the evolution of the Nigerian/African novel tradition would be written/traced without Emecheta occupying a central position in terms of her contribution to such a development. As Chioma Opara observes in a tribute to her memory as well as her contribution to the evolution of the Nigerian novel tradition, "Not only are her stories very compelling, her 'racing, no nonsense, chatty style' is patently enthralling. . . . Essentially, she is the first African writer to dare render the private very public in her autobiographical works where she superbly melds the 'granite of facts' with the 'rainbow of dreams'" (250). In contrast to what most critics would allude to, Opara here locates and inserts Emecheta's contribution to the development of the African novel tradition beyond the sphere of feminist writings. Yet her greatest contribution is in the way she has used her creative writings in inaugurating a new model of African feminism, which according to her is a feminist brand with a lowercase "f." Arguably, she is among the first set of Nigerian/African women novelists who through their imaginative works hinted on the need for Nigerian/African women writers to craft an indigenous feminist aesthetics that is workable, realistic, and different from the Western model. It is, therefore, surprising that her novels have not received the kind of critical attention they deserve. This is even more so with her novel, *Double Yoke,* which appears to be the least analyzed among her creative works. While her *Bride Price* (1976); *Slave Girl* (1977); and *The Joys of Motherhood* (1979) have received some critical attention, the same cannot be said of *Double Yoke* (1982). Apart from scant reviews and one or two full length essays, there is very little or nothing about *Double Yoke*. And this is in spite of the complexity of the story Emecheta tells in that novel and the topicality of the story of the novel within the framework of African modernity.

THE GENERAL RECEPTION OF EMECHETA'S *DOUBLE YOKE*

Irrespective of some negative criticisms Emecheta's *Double Yoke* has received, it has elicited some interpretations in most scant reviews. There are, therefore, three reasons that recommend themselves as to the need for the present critical exercise. The first is the negative criticism Emecheta's *Double Yoke* has received; the second is that most of the critical attention it has attracted are in scant reviews; and the third is that most of the scant reviews even miss or ignore the fundamental theme of the novel, which is the synthesis of tradition and modernity. For instance, equating Emecheta's *Double Yoke* with Mariama Ba's *So Long a Letter* and Bessie Head's *The Collector of Treasures*, Yaba Badoe argues that Emecheta's novel, like the other two, treats "the theme of women demanding more fulfilling relationships with men in contemporary society" (103). Also establishing a parallel between Emecheta's and Head's works, Badoe also remarks that the aforementioned like the latter "is also about how a woman reacts to a man's desire to possess and dominate her" (104). Thus, what Badoe sets out to accomplish in his/her scant review of three pages is to show the ways in which Emecheta's *Double Yoke* can be equated with Head's short story and Mariama Ba's novella in terms of their thematic preoccupation, and not the way it intervenes in the tradition/modernity dichotomy.

Another critic who sets out to carry out a comparative study of Emecheta's *Double Yoke* like Badoe is Katherine Frank, who compares it with Flora Nwapa's *One is Enough*. She concludes that they do not "dabble in daydreaming about enlightened heroes or reformed, non-sexist societies" but show "a bitterness and cynicism born of the unflinching vision and hard struggle." Moreover, the two novels believe in "the solution of a world without men, men being the enemy, the exploiter and the oppressor." Therefore, the two novels see "no possibility of a compromise or even truce with the enemy." The "women spurn patriarchy in all its guises and create a safe, sane, supportive world of women: a world of mothers and daughters, sisters and friends—which means "feminist separatism . . ." (cited in Imafedia Okhamafe 74). Far from the thesis and observation of Katherine Frank, Emecheta in *Double Yoke* does not preach or advocate "feminist separatism." The ending that Emecheta hints at with the turn of events in the novel is a possible reunion between Nko and her lover, Ete Kamba. Thus, none of the major female characters in the novel compromises her relationship with the man in her life for a relationship with another woman—be it in the form of a mother, daughter, sister, or female friend. Thus, Katherine Frank's reading is one that misses the mark of what Emecheta's *Double Yoke* is all about.

In contrast to Badoe and Frank is Marie Linton Umeh who sees Emecheta's novel "as a study of an educated woman's frustration" (cited in Charlotte H. Bruner 69). But as the turn of events in the novel would reveal, the story of *Double Yoke* is not so much about Nko's frustration as it is about her emancipation in the face of African modernity. Yet, in her "Autobiography and the Autobiographical Novel: Fact and Fiction in Buchi Emecheta's Works," which is a full-length essay, Chioma Opara spares one paragraph to interrogate *Double Yoke* as one in a long line of works that show that Emecheta's novels are largely representations of her persona and personal life experience. According to Opara, "Although she [Emecheta] tries to present multiple viewpoints [in *Double Yoke*], the authorial point of view dominates since the novel is partly autobiographical. Her adulation for her persona, Miss Bulewao rings unctuous" (*Her Mother's Daughter* 252). As is already obvious, even though the essay is full-length, Opara's reading is still a scant review in which she relates *Double Yoke* to Emecheta's other novels to arrive at the conclusion that they are all largely autobiographical. Moreover, because of what is the focus of her study, she does not acknowledge the fundamental theme of *Double Yoke*, which is the synthesis of tradition and modernity.

It is, however, somewhat surprising that the foregoing readings do not acknowledge the fundamental theme of synthesis of tradition and modernity in Emecheta's novel taking into account the clue provided on the blurb by the synopsis of the novel itself that the story is about Nko (a university undergraduate student) who "tries to cope with the double yoke of tradition and that of modernity." Yet, as depicted in the novel, it is not only Nko who tries to cope with the tradition/modernity conflict. All the other major characters (both male and female) are also portrayed to be confronted with the same conflict, and they all appear to be able to reconcile the demands of tradition and modernity in their different circumstances.

This, however, does not mean that no critic has acknowledged or hinted at the conflict between tradition and modernity in Emecheta's *Double Yoke*. But the critical lens of interrogating the conflict between tradition and modernity is not the same with that of investigating the synthesis between both polemical positions. For instance, it is the view of Marilyn Richardson that "*Double Yoke* is an exploration of the ways in which . . . corruption, taken for granted in public and business matters, corrodes the integrity of even the most intimate aspects of private life as well. In her understanding of the intersection of

Narrating Hybridity 171

the public and the private in Nigerian life, Emecheta shows us the formidable adjustments facing young people, especially women, as they move from the traditions of village life to the independence of life in the university; from village social norms to the world of expediency and compromise beyond" (6). Apart from being a scant review of two pages in which Richardson expresses her view briefly about three novels of Emecheta (*Double Yoke, Rape of Shavi, and Destination Biafra*), she just pinpoints the tradition versus modernity dichotomy in *Double Yoke* without interrogating Emecheta's take on the conflict within the framework of the novel. Moreover, Richardson concentrates her critical lens on only Nko without investigating how the same phenomenon plays out in the lives of Emecheta's other characters (both male and female).

Yet, it is almost in the same vein that Jewelle Gomez in a scant review of about a page remarks that:

> Emecheta's new novel lays bare the schism between the limiting yet familiar comforts of traditional African roles, and the more expansive and sometimes dangerous choices offered by modern society. These forces buffet the lives of Ete Kamba and Nko, two young Nigerian university students who fall in love. Within the context of the most simple love story, Emecheta opens up the complex world of tribal life and is able to make real both the values of ancient customs and the urgent need to revise them; to learn to take the best from both the old and the new. (51)

Owing to the complexion of the write-up of Gomez, which is just a review, she just hints at Emecheta's stand in the schism between tradition and modernity without contextualizing it within the narrative world of *Double Yoke*. What is more, as would be seen shortly in the present study, it is not just in the lives of Nko and Ete Kamba that Emecheta exemplifies her theme of the synthesis of tradition and modernity in the novel under consideration. While they are the main characters through whom Emecheta presents her take on the demands of tradition in opposition to modernity, she (Emecheta) also uses other characters as sub-texts to concretize her aesthetic vision of showing the vitality and inevitability of synthesizing tradition and modernity.

Also, in her own full-fledged essay entitled "Class vs. Sex: The Problem of Values in the Modern Nigerian Novel," Rhonda Cobham-Sander observes that "Nko is not the only one caught between conflicting roles. Ete Kamba is equally confused about what manhood involves and what his ideal woman should be like" (24). Without specifically saying so, like Gomez, Cobham-Sander links Nko's dilemma to that of Ete Kamba on the platform of the confusion about which road to take in the tradition versus modernity dichotomy without contextualizing her observation within the framework of

Emecheta's novel. What is more, the focus of Cobham-Sander is not on the theme of the synthesis of tradition and modernity as it is on the manner in which Emecheta has a little edge in her artistic production in *Double Yoke* over and above Zaynab Alkali in the *Stillborn* and Ifeoma Okoye in *Behind the Clouds.*

Another full-fledged essay that has examined Emecheta's novel under consideration is Solomon Azumurana's "Creating Transgressive Space in Ezeigbo's *The Last of the Strong Ones* and Emecheta's *Double Yoke,*" in which "Jacques Lacan's structuralist polemics of the signifier and the signified and Luce Irigaray's counter-narrative of the feminine morphology" is exploited to "contend that the writers and their female characters by their narrative strategy, actions, and inactions transmute from being the signified to the signifiers" (125). Although Azumurana hints at the tradition and modernity continuum by contending that Ezeigbo's and Emecheta's female characters transcend gender stereotypical roles within their cultural milieu, paying particular attention to Ejimnaka and Onyekozuru in Ezeigbo's *The Last of the Strong Ones,* and Nko and Ete Kamba's mother in Emecheta's *Double Yoke,* he concludes that "against the background of their cultural environment, they are still illustrative of transgressive female behaviors" (139). Thus, in this study, Azumurana's interest is not so much on the synthesis of tradition and modernity as it is on the transgressive behaviors of Emecheta's female characters.

NARRATING HYBRIDITY: THE SYNTHESIS OF TRADITION AND MODERNITY IN EMECHETA'S *DOUBLE YOKE*

It is owing to this gap in the scholarship of Emecheta's *Double Yoke* that I interrogate the novel as an intervention in the debate of the tradition versus modernity continuum, and argue that while some African writers advocate a return to traditional culture, and others just show the identity crisis that emanate from the conflicting demand of tradition and modernity, Emecheta through her novel under consideration, advocates a synthesis of tradition and modernity. The conflict between tradition and modernity has engaged the attention of many scholars, especially on the African continent following its encounter with colonial modernity. Ann Elizabeth Willey says as much when she notes that, "The complex interplay of orality, literacy, cities, rural areas, technologies (modernity), and traditions that shape the twenty-first century in Africa is increasingly the subject of African cultural studies" (Willey 145). She also observes that "the nexus of modernity and tradition . . . trouble so many artists and scholars in Africa" (132). The confluence between the aforementioned excerpt and the latter is that the dichotomy between tradition and modernity is a subject of intense debate among African critics and imaginative writers. In responding to this subject, however, the debate has always been whether the African should return to traditional culture or embrace modernity. As already indicated, while some insist on the aforementioned, others opt for the latter.

Irrespective of the argument to the contrary, Amos Tutuola's *Palmwine Drinkard;* Chinua Achebe's *Things Fall Apart* and *Arrow of God*; Ngugi wa Thiongo's *The River Between*; Ferdinand Oyono's *Houseboy* and *The Old Man and the Medal*; and Camara Laye's *African Child* and *Radiance of the King*, for example, are all imaginative works that advocate the return to traditional culture. They all in one way or another criticize colonial modernity while eulogizing African traditional culture. It is apparently within the purview of African narratives such as these that Abiola Irele "links foreign material goods to 'modern' ideology that is fundamentally 'other' to African psyches and claims that, while modernity is inevitably part of the African landscape, it always signifies loss" (cited in Ann Elizabeth Willey 135). As portrayed in the identified novels, it is the encounter of the protagonists of the novels with European modernity that signals their tragic fall. Thus, modernity can be said to signify loss to most of the protagonists of these novels because their creators and writers eulogize the African glorious past in comparison to the African modernity as facilitated by Western civilization (or European modernity).

In contrast to these African writers are those who just show the crisis of identity that emanates from the conflicting demands of tradition and modernity without taking any definite position. In this category are works such as Wole Soyinka's *The Interpreters;* Achebe's *No Longer at Ease, A Man of the People,* and *Anthills of the Savannah;* Ngugi's *Petals of Blood* and *Wizard in the Crow;* Ayi Kwei Armah's *The Beautiful Ones Are Not Yet Born* and *Fragments;* Ezeigbo's *Children of the Eagle* and *Roses and Bullets;* Adichie's *Purple Hibiscus* and *Half of a Yellow Sun;* and Emecheta's *The Joys of Motherhood.*

But in contradistinction to these writers, and even her own depiction in *The Joys of Motherhood*, Emecheta advocates the synthesis of tradition and modernity in her novel, *Double Yoke.* Although critics have advocated the need to move beyond the understanding of tradition in opposition to modernity as the dichotomies between the past and the present, and the opposition between African and European value system, it is specifically through this demarcation/distinction that I approach the reading of Emecheta's *Double Yoke.* Eulogizing Brad Weiss's and Cati Coe's works respectively on the conflict between the demands of Western formal education and that of the African tradition which he reviews, Amy Stambach observes that they "share a basic framework of moving beyond understanding modernity in terms of differences between the 'local' and the 'national' or between the 'colonial' and the 'neoliberal,' the 'past' and the 'present,' and 'European' and 'African'" (292). The merit of Weiss' and Coe's works in the estimation of Stambach is in their ability to move beyond the static categories of what characterize tradition and modernity within African scholarship/modernity. Yet, it is through these "simple" polemical categories as supported by Richard Bjornson's ideas in his "Alienation and Disalienation: Themes of Yesterday, Promises of Tomorrow" and that of Abiola Irele in his own "In Praise of Alienation" that I interrogate Emecheta's novel with a view to reveal why and the ways in which she insists on the need to synthesize tradition and modernity.

Although Emecheta's novel was published in 1982, which is ten years before the publication of Bjornson's and Irele's ideas in 1992, I still exploit and re-appropriate their ideas because what they give vent to in their critical exercise and the reason for their position/argument is almost in tandem with what Emecheta has imaginatively expressed earlier in her novel. Moreover, the period that is covered by the critical intervention of the contributors to the volume in which Bjornson and Irele's ideas appear is from 1947 to 1987, which in a sense accommodates Emecheta's *Double Yoke* published in 1982. What is more, while they do not specifically speak/write of the synthesis of tradition and modernity, their arguments seem to point in that direction. Even though one might be tempted from a cursory reading of their works to conclude that what Bjornson and Irele are prescribing is the need to embrace European modernity and jettison African traditional values, a close reading would reveal that what they are in fact recommending is the synthesis of African tradition and European modernity. For instance, commenting on Oyono's novels in general, it is the view of Bjornson that what they reveal is that "neither traditional African values nor French colonialist rhetoric provides an adequate basis for forging a stable sense of identity" (154–155). While I disagree with Bjornson's argument especially as it relates to Oyono's *Old Man and the Medal*, what should be noted in Bjornson's argument (which altogether is valid) is that the whole-sale rejection of tradition for modernity or vice versa is not useful in forging a stable sense of identity. It then follows that what Bjornson advocates is a compromise between the two polemical positions, in which case there is going to be a balance/synthesis between tradition and modernity.

It is in a similar vein that Irele argues that "[t]he resources in ideas, techniques, and in certain respects values offered by our traditional cultures are simply not adequate for our contemporary needs and interests" (213). That an object or phenomenon is not adequate is not the same as saying that it is not useful. Therefore, what Irele insinuates is that African tradition is not fully sufficient, and thus needs adjustment, support or addition to be sufficient or adequate in the face of being confronted with African modernity as facilitated by European modernity. Hence, Irele's argument is very much the same as that of Bjornson which is that neither African tradition nor European modernity in isolation provides the basis for a stable sense of identity. In this way, it can be argued that Irele in a similar vein with Bjornson countenances the fusing of tradition with modernity.

It is also in the foregoing regard that Bjornson and Irele appear to have provided the precedent and justification for the adoption of the "simplistic" approach of the past versus the present and African versus European values such as I intend using to interrogate Emecheta's novel as against the supposition of Amy Stambach. For instance, in his explanation of what alienation is for Africans, Bjornson observes that it "is the condition that afflicted Africans who had become estranged from the values of traditional culture" (147). Without specifically saying so, what Bjornson's observation points to is the conflict between African tradition and European modernity in the lives of the African scholars about whom he writes. They have been alienated from the values of traditional African culture because of the fact that they have been introduced to colonial/European civilization. Abiola Irele also observes concerning the cultural productions on the African continent that "[t]he theme of alienation as an existential predicament runs through all our literature inspired by the colonial experience in one form or the other" (203). In the foregoing context, therefore, there is no way in which an imaginative work produced on the African continent can escape the depiction of the past versus the present as well as the African versus the European values. Irrespective of the fact that tradition together with modernity is continuously in a flux, what is traditional in contrast to what is modern to the African can still be apprehended and simultaneously deployed as tools of interrogation, especially in the case of texts that have been written from this perspective.

There is no equivocation that Emecheta's *Double Yoke* is one of such novels that have been written from the perspective of the past versus the present, and African versus European modernity. As the author poses on the blurb in the synopsis of the novel," Should Nko lose her identity in marriage and be a good woman in the traditional sense, or should she get a degree and be labelled feminist, rebellious . . . or is she expected to carry the two burdens on her shoulders? Which is the right way for the woman of Africa?" Emecheta's posers in the form of rhetorical questions leave no one in doubt as to the conversation she engages with her novel, *Double Yoke*. It is the conversation of the conflict between African tradition and European modernity as occasioned by the experience of colonialism. Although she does not reveal to her readers what her position is in this seeming irreconcilable conflict within the synopsis of the novel, the unfolding of events and incidents in the novel shows that the way out as far as she is concerned is to synthesize tradition and modernity, not only through or in the character of Nko as suggested by the synopsis, but also in the lives of the other, his characters (both male and female).

This can immediately be seen in the character or action of Ekpeyong, the shoemaker. As the narrator reveals, much as Ekpeyong's children played about with colorful bicycles and "real imported footballs" he rejected some aspects of modernity. He refused to cover his thatched house in corrugated iron sheets like some of his neighbors (51). Ekpeyong's action of building his house with blocks and having a thatched roof is a synthesis of traditional and modern architectural design. While the blocks in contrast to mud with which his house has been built symbolize modernity, the thatched roof is a symbol of tradition. And as can be seen, he is better off than his neighbours who have wholly embraced modern architectural design. It is significant that while the houses of his neighbours who have uncritically embraced modern architectural design to the detriment of the advantage of traditional design are "more like ovens," Ekpeyong's house that is the manifestation of the synthesis of both polar positions "was always cool." In this way, the character or action of Ekpeyong is a sub-text through which Emecheta drives home her aesthetic vision of demonstrating the need to synthesize tradition and modernity. By so doing also, she advocates the need for the African embracing a hybrid culture that combines aspects of the traditional and modern culture.

Another character whose action Emecheta deploys as a sub-text to illustrate the need for synthesizing tradition and modernity is Arit's father, who is just "a farmer, but a farmer with a difference" (20). Not only is he able to read and write, but also he exploits government policies on agriculture to enhance his farming business. He uses caterpillar to clear his farms, fertilizer on his soil, and even employs the services of a youth corps member to assist in his farming business. For this reason, the yams produced on his farm are bigger than the yams produced by other farmers; the result being that "Ete Kamba had since learnt that Arit's father had been right. If he were to be a farmer, he knew now that he would do even better" (20). For exploiting modern techniques of farming in his traditional farming business, Arit's father is a successful farmer. Not only is he able to throw birthday parties for his children, "[t]hey [his children] were always smartly dressed and always had the air of people who had everything" (20).

Writing about Paul Hazoume, the author of the novel *Doguicimi*, Bjornson observes that for him (Hazoume) "there was no contradiction between his respect for African traditional values and his support for the civilizing mission of French colonialism. His synthesizing worldview . . . provides a good example of how the dual alienation process can produce a heightened level of awareness" (149). The dual alienation that Bjornson speaks about is that of simultaneously being estranged from the African tradition and European modernity—being neither here nor there, and creating a third estate of being in which an individual draws from the past and the present and combines them to cope with the present reality. It is apparently in the same regard that Irele sees alienation as implying "a willed movement out of the self and a purposive quest for new horizons of life and experience" (215). This new horizon of life and experience is not contained in the wholesale jettisoning of tradition or past experience and embracing wholly the present or modernity but combining both worldviews to create a new worldview that can respond to new realities. Thus, the alienation of which Bjornson and Irele speak is the lot of Arit's father in Emecheta's *Double Yoke*. It is noteworthy that for synthesizing traditional and modern techniques of farming, Arit's father becomes a source of amusement to the children of the village, and an object of annoyance to the other farmers (20). It is obvious that it is as a result of Arit's father's "purposive quest for new horizons of life" in farming that he becomes a source of amusement and annoyance in the environment in which he operates. Yet, his synthesizing worldview makes his farming business a success—one to which Ete Kamba aspires and hopes to exceed by doing the same. This recalls the case of Ekpeyong, the shoemaker who synthesizes traditional and modern architecture and "succeeds" in so doing. Likewise, it is the synthesizing worldview of Arit's father in employing modern techniques of farming in his traditional farming business that produced in him a heightened level of awareness, which places him at the top of the ladder in comparison to other farmers in his community.

Equally important to the synthesizing perspective of Emecheta in *Double Yoke* are the children of Ekpeyong, the shoemaker and those of Arit's father who incidentally also bear Ekpeyong. Thus, there is Ekpeyong, the shoemaker and Ekpeyong, the farmer in Emecheta's *Double Yoke*. Mention must be made here of the epilogue of the textbook titled *The Social Anthropology of Africa,* The author Angulu Onwuejeogwu, in this epilogue, tells the story of two groups of children who to all intent and purposes are representative of traditional as against modern life. According to Onwuejeogwu:

> The children of the new elite (modern life) did not know that the teapots and teacups which they were using were made of clay, while all the local children knew this. Indeed, some of them helped their parents to make clay pots and cups and fire them. The children at home (traditional) could name all trees around, and talked about the palm trees, banana, and yam, while the children of the new elite knew nothing about them. They ate them and that was all. The children from the urban area talked about airplanes, television, hotels, birthday parties, fine dresses, and shoes. Those at home talked about masquerades, wrestling on the sand, making traps and fishing. (cited in Irele 213–214)

And commenting on this story, Irele takes a swipe at Onwuejeogwu that his "story is in fact tendentious and amounts to a prodigious begging of the question: he proves only what he wants to prove, which is that traditional culture produces children better adapted for life (214). It really depends on what life: in the village or in the city offers in terms of traditional culture or modern culture respectively (214). But unlike the two groups of children in Onwuejeogwu's story and against Irele's environmental proviso; the children of the two Ekpeyongs in *Double Yoke* are well adapted to both traditional and modern life since they live in the village and are also exposed to the luxury of city/modern life in the form of "noisy colorful tricycles," "real imported footballs," birthday parties, and smart dresses and shoes. Thus, in their case, the city/modernity has been brought to them in their village with its traditional culture, and both have been synthesized in their daily living.

Apart from the two Ekpeyongs and their children, Miss Bulewao, who can be regarded as the imaginative Buchi Emecheta, is another character who is also deployed as a sub-text in exemplifying the synthesizing perspective of Emecheta in *Double Yoke*. In her own case (Miss Bulewao), she is portrayed as the synthesis of the African and Western notion of female beauty. The narrator observes that although "Ete Kamba noticed that . . . she was not skinny, and though she was not the type of the New Woman they had been taught to regard as beautiful, she knew how to handle herself together" (6). What is enacted by Ete Kamba's observation is what should be the frame of reference for describing a woman as beautiful. Is it the traditional/African notion of a woman being plump or fleshy (going to the fattening room to become plump and round as depicted in *Double Yoke*) or is it the modern/Western notion of a woman being skinny? It is worthy of note that even though Miss Bulewao is plump and fleshy, she is agile.

Writing about Hazoume in relation to his novel, *Doguicimi*, it is the argument of Bjornson that "In seeking to reconcile his conflicting attitudes towards the Danhome (the setting of his novel), he (Hozoume) projected into his novel a worldview that combines French ideals of freedom and justice with traditional concepts of wisdom and nobility" (150). It is important to note that what enables Hazoume to achieve this synthesis, according to Bjornson, is his simultaneous exposure to Christian moral standards and secular Western education on one hand, and the traditional way of living in Danhome on the other. This is also true of Emecheta in relation to her novel *Double Yoke*. The only difference in the particular instance of being plump and fleshy while being agile is that what she synthesizes is the African and Western notion of beauty, which she is able to achieve (within the foregoing frame of reference) as a result of having lived in Nigeria and Britain. As pedestrian as this might sound, the majority of Emecheta's novels, including *Double Yoke,* give vent to it.

In her own tribute to Emecheta, following her (Emecheta's) death on January 25, 2017, in London, Chioma Opara insists that "[t]here can be no doubt that she [Emecheta] was an acculturated and emancipated Nigerian woman living in London" and that "she is the first African writer to dare render the private very public in . . . her works" (Tribute 250). This is in furtherance of an earlier argument by Opara in an earlier work that "Although (Emecheta) tries to present multiple viewpoints, the authorial point of view dominates since the novel is partly autobiographical. We are told that 'she (Emecheta/Miss Bulewao) was somebody who has actually made it in that field (creative writing) not only in Nigeria, but abroad'" (Opara Autobiography 139; Emecheta *Double Yoke* 3). If it is agreed that Miss Bulewao is the imaginative Buchi Emecheta who had lived most of her adult life in Britain, it can then be argued that what she projects is her ability to synthesize her plump nature as an African woman with the agility of a skinny woman, which is the expectation of the Western environment in which she had lived all her adult life.

In addition to Miss Bulewao is Arit who is portrayed to have gone to Aba to learn how to make women's hair. Her portrayal is also in line with the overall aesthetic vision of Emecheta's synthesizing perspective as Ete Kamba is reported by the narrator to have "heard Arit say very loudly that the lady who trained her in Aba was a been-to, and that she had been taught how to make African hair look European. She could straighten, she could blow, she could weave, she could curl and she could wash with shampoo" (16). According to Irele, "the axis of the world in which" the African "is living is shifting from its grounding in the institutions and values of the traditional culture towards a new point of orientation determined by the impact of an alien culture, specifically Western civilization" (207). It is certain that the contact between Africa and Europe introduces exotic hairstyles. Arit learns how to make African hair look European and vice versa. That she could weave (African) and at the same time straighten and curl (European) is because she has arrived at a new point of orientation that has been determined by the mixture of an African and alien culture in the form of Western civilization. Thus, even though Ete Kamba is depicted to have expressed reservation about how Arit is going to enjoy the patronage of women who are largely farmers in their village locality (*Double Yoke* 16), the point to note is that Arit learns and can make African hair look European or vice versa because of the urgent need to adapt to changes that have been occasioned by colonial modernity. The edge Arit, therefore, has for synthesizing African and European hair styles is not encapsulated in Ete Kamba's reservation but it is quite obvious. We are told that, "Many people opened their eyes" and concluded that "Arit had really made it" (16). It stands to reason that with her ability to combine African and European style of hairdo, she can function successfully in and outside the locality of her village. In this way, she is more adapted to present realities than someone who sticks just to the African or European style of making hair.

Ete Kamba's mother in her portrayal is also very much like Miss Bulewao and Arit in synthesizing tradition and modernity. The only difference is that while Miss Bulewao synthesizes the African and Western notion of female beauty, and Arit, her style of making women's hair; Ete Kamba's mother synthesizes tradition and modernity in her domestic duties and in her interactions with her husband and family in general. To illustrate, the narrator notes that Ete Kamba's mother "would serve them, the men of the house on a special collapsible table they had bought from a carpenter in Calabar. She would then spread on it her one clean tablecloth. Then she would bring their food, mainly garri and soup, in very clean but plain imported plates and a metal bowl of water to wash their hands with" (18). The collapsible table, clean tablecloth, imported plates, and metal bowl are all what Irele describes as the material furniture of European modernity. And it is on/in this/them that Ete Kamba's mother serves "garri and soup," which are manifestations of traditional culture. It then means that in carrying out her domestic duties, Ete Kamba's mother synthesizes tradition and modernity. Thus, contained in Ete Kamba's mother are both the characteristics of a traditional and modern woman, which also makes her in a sense to be a hybrid woman who draws on both the past and the present in her interactions with her husband.

That Emecheta's narrative in *Double Yoke* hinges on the need to synthesize tradition and modernity can also be seen through the character of Nko. In fact, it is fundamentally through her character/characterization that Emecheta pushes for this synthesis. It is Nko who fundamentally carries the burden of Emecheta's posers as questions in the synopsis, and it is also primarily through her character/characterization that she (Emecheta) provides the answers to the questions. Although Badoe argues that Nko is portrayed "as a passive agent reacting to a changing environment" (103), her words to her mother that she wants both worlds is not a statement of a passive agent. Rather, it is an expression of an agent of change who wants what her mother already has as a traditional woman and that which her mother does not have as a result of her not being a modern woman. In anguish Nko tells her mother, "I want to have both worlds. I want to be an academician and I want to be a quiet nice (sic) and obedient wife, the type you all want me to be. I want the two mother . . . I know I can be of more use to you and my brothers if I had these two worlds" (94). Here, it is evident that what Nko wants is to be a traditional as well as a modern woman. That she will be "of more use" to her family by synthesizing tradition and modernity is in itself an articulation of the advantage of such synthesizing perspective within Emecheta's imaginative world. Thus, Miss Bulewao's words, "Ete Kamba the question is—are you strong enough to be a modern African man? Nko is already a modern African lady, but you are still lagging . . . oh, so far, far behind" (162), should not be taken to mean that Nko in Emecheta's story embraced modernity wholesale in place of tradition. Rather, what it means within the moral economy of Emecheta's narrative is that Nko is new/modern to the limit that she inhabits in herself both traditional and modern values.

This even becomes very evident after Nko's discovery that she is pregnant with Prof. Ikot's child. It is the view of Bjornson, for instance, that "By adopting a perspective that is other than the one (Africans) presently hold," an African "may be reconstituting that identity in light of new knowledge and expanding horizons" (148). This is very true of Nko on discovering that she is pregnant with Prof. Ikot's child. Rather than aborting the pregnancy, she decides to keep it. According to her, "she is going to be a sure academician and a mother" (159). Here, Nko reconstitutes her identity in order to confront the new challenges in her life. Yet, it is a new identity in which tradition or modernity does not hold sway as an advantage over the other. By deciding to keep the pregnancy rather than abort it, she hints at a traditional disposition. Yet, by keeping the pregnancy with a view to fend for the child when she eventually gives birth to it without any male patronage or support smacks of a modern disposition. It is, therefore, not surprising that she tells herself that she is "going to have a double yoke to carry" and that she "can't escape it" since she is "a child of this age" of European modernity (159).

For all that has been said of Ete Kamba being a traditional man, it can still be argued that he is also an active agent of change like Nko in the face of European modernity. It is significant, for instance, that unlike the choice made by his father, Ete Kamba wants his future wife to be as traditional as his mother; but modern by being a little less educated than him. Like Nko, Ete Kamba's response here can be seen as an appropriate one to the changing environment in which he finds himself notwithstanding the fact that he still wants his future wife to be a little less educated than him. Bjornson seems to identify three facets of European modernity as Christianity/education, commerce/capitalism, and romantic love (154). Ete Kamba and Nko buy into and participate in these three facets of European modernity, while still retaining aspects of traditional culture. For instance, they are both Christians with a university education; and by obtaining Western education, it stands to reason that they will both engage in the commerce and capitalism of European modernity. What is more, their relationship is based on romantic love rather than any pre-arranged relationship as suggested by Missy—the nineteen year old American girl who is at Unical to study African culture (98–99).

It is the view of Cobham-Sander, for instance, that "the knowledge that Nko, as a graduate herself, will enhance his social standing if she becomes his wife, is an important factor in his (Ete Kamba's) decision to attempt to win her (Nko) back despite the fact that she is carrying another man's child" (26). In this regard, it can be argued that Ete Kamba is being pragmatic in the face of European modernity. He accepts Nko back, not so much as a result of her as a person but, for her exchange value and sign-exchange value. This, undoubtedly, is buying into and sustaining the commerce and capitalism of European modernity.

Equally important in terms of embracing European modernity is the romantic love between Ete Kamba and Nko. Rebecca Scherer in her attempt to make a distinction between tradition and modernity also makes a distinction between love as by-product of marriage, and love as the motivating force for marriage (8). While in the first instance, husband and wife come to love each other after marriage (tradition); in the second, it is love that propels a man and a woman to marry (modernity). While the first instance is the case with Nko's and Ete Kamba's parents, the second scenario is the case with Ete Kamba and Nko. That their relationship is predicated on romantic love is even evident from their first sexual encounter (51–52). It is important to note that this sexual encounter takes place by the wall of an unfinished building. Although it has been argued that to emphasize the novelty of her (Nko's) action, this sexual encounter can also be interpreted from both the perspective of Nko and Ete Kamba. In other words, by having sex by the wall of an unfinished building, it is not only Nko but also Ete Kamba who transcends the traditional notion of decent sex to have a modern-styled sex.

Yet, in a similar vein with Nko, Ete Kamba is as much traditional as he is modern. His grouse with Nko notwithstanding that "He wished Nko had not allowed him to do it" (have sex with her by the wall of an unfinished building) (53) is not so much that the latter allows him to have his way with her as it is the fact that she is not a virgin. The narrator reports Ete Kamba's ruminations thus: "Did he find her difficult to penetrate? He could not tell. He had forgotten, and he did not notice. They were so carried away. But what right had she got to be carried away? She was supposed to be in pain" (53–54). Although this scene in its entirety can be interpreted as encapsulating Ete Kamba's traditional disposition, what it also conveys is his modernity. By insisting on the virginity of Nko, Ete Kamba is traditional. Yet, by having sex with Nko by the wall of an unfinished building, he is also modern. What is more, towards the end of the narrative, the narrator hints at a possible reunion between Ete Kamba and Nko despite the latter's infidelity. Although Cobham-Sander argues that this initiative for a reunion on the part of Ete Kamba is predicated on a selfish motive (26), another way to see the initiative is as an enactment of Ete Kamba's maturity of synthesizing tradition and modernity. As Badoe rightly observes, "Ete Kamba and Nko at the end of the narrative manage to transcend the conflict between old and new in their relationship to achieve a better understanding of each other" (104).

CONCLUSION

Irele observes generally that the African is "wedged uncomfortably between the values of . . . traditional culture and those of the West" (212–213). While this is the case with all the major characters of Emecheta (male and female) in *Double Yoke,* they are still able to cope and even succeed by synthesizing tradition and modernity. For example, the house of Ekpeyong the shoemaker is cool while those of his neighbors are like oven because he synthesizes traditional and modern architectural techniques. Ekpeyong, the farmer, is also at the top of the ladder in his agrarian community because he combines the agrarian and industrial farming system. The foregoing is also the lot of Miss Bulewao who synthesizes the traditional and modern notions of beauty. Arit also becomes the cynosure of her village community because she learns and can make African hair look European and vice versa. Ete Kamba's mother also succeeds in her interactions with her husband and family in general by balancing the traditional and modern way of living. Nko and Ete Kamba also manage to transcend the conflict between the old and the new in their relationship to achieve a better understanding of each other. Thus, as far as Emecheta is concerned in the conflicting demand of tradition and modernity, the way out is not to embrace wholly one value at the expense of the other. Rather, it is to balance and synthesize aspects of both cultures as a way of creating a third estate, which is neither wholly traditional nor modern. It is in this way that Emecheta narrates hybridity as the only way out of the quagmire and quandary of the conflict between tradition and modernity.

WORKS CITED

Abiola, Irele. "In Praise of Alienation" *The Surreptitious Speech: Presence Africaine and the Politics of Otherness (1947–1987).* Ed. V.Y. Mudimbe. Chicago & London: UCP, (1992): 201–224.

Azumurana, Solomon Omatsola. "Creating Transgressive Space in Ezeigbo's *The Last of the Strong Ones* and Emecheta's *Double Yoke*." *Journal of the African Literature Association (JALA),* 7.1 (Summer/Fall 2012): 125–140.

Badoe, Yaba. "Review: Women in African Literature." *Feminist Review,* 17.(Autumn 1984): 102–105.

Bjornson, Richard. "Alienation and Disalienation: Themes of Yesterday, Promises of Tomorrow." *The Surreptitious Speech: Presence Africaine and the Politics of*

Otherness (1947 – 1987). Ed. V. Y. Mudimbe. Chicago & London: UCP, (1992): 147–156.

Bruner, Charlotte H. "Review" *Ngambika: Studies of Women in African Literature* Eds. Carole Boyce Davies and Anne Adams Graves *Africa Today,* 37.1 (1st Qtr. 1990): 69–70.

Cobham-Sander, Rhonda. "Class vs. Sex: The Problem of Values in the Modern Nigerian Novel." *The Black Scholar,* 17.4 (July/August 1986): 17–27.

Gomez, Jewelle. "Review of Emecheta's *Double Yoke.*" *The Black Scholar,* 16.6 (November/December 1985): 51.

Mason, David. "Fiction Chronicle" *The Hudson Review,* 44.4 (Winter 1992): 691–697.

Opara, Chioma. "Autobiography and the Autobiographical Novel: Fact and Fiction in Buchi Emecheta's Works." *Her Mother's Daughter: The African Writer as Woman.* Port Harcourt: University of Port Harcourt Press (2004): 131–142.

———. "Tribute—Buchi Emecheta (1944–2017): Beyond the Dingy Ditch." *Tydskrif VIR LETTERKUNDE,* 54. 1 (2017): 250–252.

Scherer, Rebecca. "Tradition Versus Modernity: Women's Rights in Marriage and Divorce in a Judeo-Spanish Novel." *Shofar,* 12,3 (Spring 1994): 1–16.

Stambach, Amy. "Review." *Comparative Education Review,* 50.2 (May 2006): 288–295.

Willey, Ann Elizabeth. "Reading Modernity in Mambety's *La petite vendeuse de soleil:* Orality, Literacy, and the Regional Imaginary." *Mosiac: An Interdisciplinary Critical Journal,* 45.2 (June 2012): 131–148.

Chapter 12

Depravity and Mental Torture in Nawal El Saadawi's *Two Women in One* and *Woman at Point Zero*

Queen Albert and Onyemechi Nwaeke

INTRODUCTION

African women, in the main, find themselves in societies that pose major threats to their existence and mental health through certain obnoxious cultural practices such as clitoridectomy, gender-based oppression, sexual slavery, rape, early marriage, among others. The thrust of this chapter is to examine the depiction of depravity and mental torture by Egyptian writer and psychiatrist, Nawal El Saadawi in her novels, *Two Women in One* and *Woman at Point Zero*. The essay investigates the disturbing and shocking ordeals of the two protagonists, Bahiah and Firdaus. It also examines the incalculable strain and overwhelming anguish they have to grapple with as young Arab women. The discourse establishes the high level of pain and suffering occasioned by perversion, degeneracy, and moral corruption. The effects of such deprivation, deviance and cruelty are reflected in the mental states of Bahiah and Firdaus. The psychological strain that these victims of cultural oppression have to put up with in the face of religion and patriarchy is excruciating and overwhelming. It is our contention that the two novels unearth the depth of human depravity that ultimately leaves Bahiah and Firdaus overly fearless, suicidal, and murderous. The continual perpetration of profound cruelty and large-scale brutality contributes to their mental state and eventually leads to their tragic end.

As an Egyptian female writer, psychoanalyst, and activist, Nawal El Saadawi bears witness to the myriad of injustice that has scorched women in the Arab world. She captures this succinctly in her works—*Two Women in One* and *Woman at Point Zero*. Having explored the effects of these sufferings on the Arab woman and the repulsive consequences that follow it, Saadawi lucidly unravels the depth of depravity and mental torture in her breath-taking narratives. Through these narratives, she discloses the mental torture that overwhelms the Egyptian girl child, and this can understandably be linked to the depravity that has engulfed every fabric of that society. This evil can be traced to traditions and male supremacy in a poverty-stricken society, neck deep in patriarchal beliefs, and sexist Islamic tenets.

Saadawi, a strong advocate and a powerful voice for women, has globally and visibly represented the international struggle for the liberation of African woman. She was born and raised in Egypt in a large Muslim family. Saadawi was the eldest daughter but the second of nine children from her mother. Through the encouragement she got from her parents, especially her mother, she was able to receive an education. She was trained in the University of Cairo Medical School in 1955. In 1966, she received a masters degree in Public Health at the Columbia University in New York. She had a stint with the Egyptian government for almost a decade but lost the job as a result of the political upheaval and pressure that rocked the nation at that time. She was imprisoned in Qanatir Prison by the then president, Anwar Sadat, but was subsequently released after his assassination.

Saadawi was totally blunt and outspoken on certain issues that affect women and devoted her time to exposing the ills of female genital mutilation and other retrogressive practices. She has faced series of troubles for this cause, having been censored, exiled, blasted, and imprisoned. She was a strong advocate of gender rights, and an activist against the oppression and objectification of women. As a psychiatrist, she maintains that imperialism, religion, and patriarchy are hugely responsible for mental health issues among women of the Arab region.

Her works include: *Memoirs of a Woman* (1960), *Searching* (1968), *God Dies by the Nile* (1974), *Woman at Point Zero* (1975), *The Hidden Face of Eve: Women in The Arab World* (1977), *The Circling Song* (1978), *Death of an Ex-Minister* (1980), *She Has No Place in Paradise* (1979), *Two Women in One* (1983), *The Fall of the Imam* (1987), *Memoirs from the Women's Prison* (1984), *The Innocence of the Devil* (1994), *North/South: The Nawal El Saadawi Reader* (1997), *A Daughter of Isis* (1999), *Love in the Kingdom of Oil* (2020), and *The Novel* (2009). Many of her works have been translated into many languages.

Depravity is perceived as moral perversion or a corrupt or degenerate act. In Saadawi's *Two Women in One* and *Woman at Point Zero*, there is evidence of large-scale mistreatment or abuse of womanhood in the patriarchal setting thus energized by adherence to Islamic religious practices. The male folk represent the bulk of the authority figures in the home, lecture hall, mosque, street, and workplace: they play key roles that lead to the mental torture of Bahiah and Firdaus. In these novels, Saadawi appears to suggest that the observable influential figures materialize in the shape of brothers, fathers, uncles, lecturers, husbands, pimps, imam among others. They all choose to behave in a way that is unreasonable and unacceptable thereby posing a threat to the mental health of these women.

Mental torture appears to swallow up the victim as a result of this moral perversion thereby leaving her to confront the demons. It is deliberate and systematic with the intention to inflict suffering on young women such as Bahiah and Firdaus, who are the main protagonists in the novels—*Two Women in One* and *Woman at Point Zero*, respectively. In *Two Women in One*, Bahiah finds herself in a situation where she cannot even acknowledge and embrace her sexuality. She appears caged in and forced to cope with emotional stress and upheavals. She is constantly faced with the impending "genital amputation" and an arranged marriage to a suitor who happens to be the family's "perfect" choice for her. The family heads disregard her opinion totally in the choice of a spouse or a career outside the medical field and this becomes a psychological distress for her.

In *Woman at Point Zero*, Firdaus is the victim of incest, child labour, early/forced marriage, sexual slavery, female circumcision, and domestic violence. Firdaus is inflicted with mental torture by her oppressors such as her uncle, parents, husband, and pimps. In her attempt to normalize her life or numb the pain, Firdaus embraces prostitution and ends up killing a man without feeling remorse for her action. She degenerates to a point of frustration, insatiability and suicidal tendency. Bahiah on her part is stifled and gagged to a point that she struggles mentally to express her sexuality in a system that degrades and humiliates women

This chapter is anchored on psychoanalytic theory. The literary approach emphasizes the study of the mind and how certain events can influence the mental functioning of the individual. The principal goal of this theory is to examine the human psyche by investigating the fears, conflicts, and mental health challenges that confront the characters in the novel. Austrian neurologist and founder of psychoanalysis, Sigmund Freud, puts forward the theory that human behavior is the product of the interactions among certain components of the mind. This approach places immense significance on the way conflicts among the parts of the mind help to shape behavior and personality. Freud is of the opinion that the sexuality of an individual is the main driver of human personality development. In these two novels, it appears that the women's psychological and physical problems are largely connected to the oppressive and domineering patriarchal structures they live in.

Using psychoanalytical theory to analyze a work of literature illuminates the mental torture of an agonized victim. This allows the reader to consider how writing represents the author's repressed desires, fears and impulses. Psychoanalysis also considers how literature presents the author's isolation from events or even the denial of the existence of certain events and circumstances through identification of the inner workings of the mind. Modern psychoanalytical theories, some of which are the rereading of Freud, provide the literary critic or theorist, with a guide to discovering, revealing and examining the truths that are hidden in literary works.

AGONY OF THE FEMALE VICTIM OF PATRIARCHAL DEPRAVITY IN *TWO WOMEN IN ONE*

In *Two Women in One*, Nawal El Saadawi portrays a Muslim post-colonial Egyptian society, exhibiting different structures of patriarchal authority upon which females are depraved, degraded, debased, and mentally tortured. The novel chronicles a series of agonies in the life of the girl-child who automatically is a victim of patriarchy in the Muslim post-colonial Egyptian society.

Traumatic circumcision rite is a very painful ordeal, which as it were, results in worm-like movement of young girls who are mandated by their culture, never to let their legs be parted. "These girls walk with a strange mechanical gait, their feet shuffling along while legs and knees remained clamped, as if they were pressing their thighs together to protect something they were afraid might fall" (*Two Women in One* 7). Their faltering steps would seem to connote passivity and difference—a patriarchal culture which expects women to be circumcised.

In the novel, Saadawi also explores the ordeal of forced marriage where young girls are given out in marriage by force to men they have no love or feelings for. This was portrayed when the protagonist, Bahiah Shaneen, a medical student was withdrawn from school by her father and given out in forced marriage to her cousin Yaseen, simply because she was involved in activism during the students' riot. There can be no doubt that Bahiah Shaheen's intelligible quest is not within the confines of marriage, especially a forced one, which is invariably sad and cheerless. Funeral and somber imagery are evoked in the description of the wedding scene:

> Her (the bride's) white silk dress stretched tightly over her chest, smothering her breasts. A long tail folded like a coffin around her bottom and legs, and dragged along to her feet, uncomfortable inelegant high heels to trip over. The

bridal stage, surrounded by rose located like the grave of an unknown soldier. The drums slow heavy beat sounded funeral strains. Her small cold hands lay in the bridegroom's large palm. His fingers were strange they coiled around her like the fingers of fate. Under the folds of the coffin her legs moved slowly as if she was heading for unknown disaster. (100)

The repletion of impending marital rites is as "lapidary" as it is "sepulchral." Chioma Opara observes that "the author likens the wedding procession to a cortege replete with funeral imagery of the grave and coffin" (*Her Mother's Daughter* 96). It is quite glaring that this is not what Bahiah Shaheen wants for herself. She wants to finish her education and embark properly on her career. She aspires to be a self-fulfilled woman, to gain self-attainment and self-independence. Little wonder Saadawi arms her with the privilege of the gaze. In her relentless quest for reality and self-identification, she continually takes recourse to gazing at herself in the mirror.

> She saw her unusual eyes examining her face as she herself examined it in the mirror, piercing her eyes through long, narrow corridors leading to her very depths. One more movement was all she needed to reach the end. But she jerked her head away. She was afraid of reaching ends. She feared arrival, the impossibility of returning to where she had been; she was afraid that by a magic touch, she would become somebody other than Bahiah Shaheen, somebody who was her real self. (36)

In the above paragraph, Saadawi portrays the struggles which her protagonist, Bahiah Shaheen goes through in order to attain self-fulfillment in a society dominated by patriarchy. According to Opara, "The mirror here serves as a tool of introspection, this evokes the Freudian mirror phase" (95). In her revision of Freud, Juliet Mitchell notes that, "The ramifications of the mirror phase spread beyond the strictly narcissistic movement of intra-subjectivity and the constitution of the ego for the infant in his own reflection" (cited in Opara 96). Simone de Beauvoir on her own part contends that, "Narcissism is a well-defined process of identification in which the ego is regarded as an absolute end and the subject takes refuge from himself in it" (cited in Opara 97). As the female subject stares in the mirror, she abruptly identifies with the image reflected, and constructs an "appropriate figure in imagination"—the unconventional Bahiah Shaheen, the real self who is not subjected to patriarchal authorities.

The world of the novel reflects a society where women are mostly veiled to accent their invisibility and marginality. Even the clothes girls put on are strictly recommended by culture. The female folk do not have the freedom and liberty to wear what they like; they must dress accordingly to the dictates of the Muslim culture:

> In those days, girls' dresses made it impossible for them to walk freely. Their skirts wound tightly round the thighs and narrowed at the knees, so that their legs remained bound together whether they were sitting, standing, or walking, producing an unnatural movement. (2)

The torture girls undergo in the Muslim post-colonial Egyptian society as portrayed by Saadawi is quite dehumanizing. In the novel, we are also intimated with the fact that girls have no right to their own bodies. As a child, Bahiah Shaheen's probing fingers had tried to define her body and she discovered she was a female by touching her sexual organs. Her mother had slapped her for doing that. Bahiah Shaheen's unnamed mother represents the voiceless women in Egypt who embody invisibility and passivity. When she told her mother that she hated God for creating bodies and sexual organs, she slapped her face for voicing such heresy. The perplexed mother also wondered whether her daughter was normal. Bahiah's mother, the dim-witted girls in the anatomy class, as well as the average women in the street—Allaih, Zakiah, Najah, and Yvonne—are as faceless as they are voiceless in the mechanical performances of culturally specified gender roles. This explains why Bahiah Shaheen is deemed an oddity. In the main, she is considered neither a woman nor a normal person. All the other faceless characters are examples of uniformity and repression resulting in utter agony under patriarchal manipulations.

One of the agents of patriarchy as portrayed in the novel, *Two Women in One,* is Bahiah Shaheen's father. Bahiah Shaheen is the unassuming and unpretentious eighteen-year-old medical student whose life is the subject matter in *Two Women in One*. As a result of the confinement and deprivation she is forced to contend with, Bahiah is psychologically distressed and miserable. She is raised by a domineering father, who happens to be a well-known Egyptian public health figure. His high-handedness and overbearing attitude does no good to Bahiah because she is made to do things against her will. This leaves Bahiah constantly frustrated and exasperated. Even her personal love for the art world is regularly challenged. Her father detests her artwork. He takes delight in crumpling her drawing with "his large fingers" and "broad palm" and ends up tossing it into the dustbin. Bahiah remains undaunted. Then she pulled out a fresh sheet of paper and with determination she drew her lines . . ." (26).

As a result of Bahiah's vulnerability and helplessness, manifested in "her small hand" contrasted with her father's "broad palm," Bahiah is increasingly faced with threats and intimidation as a young Arab woman living with a very strict and authoritarian father. He does not allow her to live her life as she had desired. She does not even have the freedom or liberty "to do" and "to be." Her father invades her privacy according to the dictates of culture. It is not surprising then that, "She felt defeated . . . she felt chains around her hands, feet, wrists, ankles, and neck pulling her mercilessly towards that small red house" (58).

That "small red house" is her father's house where the fettered Bahiah Shaheen is the distinct object of the gaze. Her father, the quintessential guard, sits on his bamboo chair watching her every movement. In her bedroom is also a red chair and a red desk. The dominance of the red color in a patriarchal household is indicative of a cultural violence that diminishes African womanhood (Opara 10). An aspect of this is made manifest in gory circumcision rites that leave the female mind and body writhing in pain and agony. El Saadawi remarks that the cries of her sister Fawziah still rang in her ears; there was a red panel of blood under her (970). The first spot of red blood the adolescent, Bahiah Shaheen had seen was on her white knickers—her first menstrual flow. "A deep red blood trickled down between her legs and onto the asphalt, it lay on the ground in a red circle that widened to grow as big as the sun" (28).

Drops and flow of blood would appear to establish the bloody trajectory of African womanhood in menstruation, genital mutilation and the rupture of the hymen on a nuptial white sheet. Woman's blood is accordingly, inextricably linked with what Opara deftly describes as woman's femalist role in fertility, maternity, and nurturance. She further observes that since these roles are ultimately manipulated by a monolithic culture, it is not surprising that an agent of patriarchy, the policeman, in a vein of a sniffer dog sniffs at Bahiah Shaheen's menstrual blood on the black and sticky asphalt. It is noteworthy that Bahiah Shaheen's portrait of her father could be that of the policeman. (*Her Mother's Daughter* 11). She gave her father "two red eyes and a black handlebar moustache, huge hands and fingers coiled round a long stick" (27). These are obvious features of patriarchal authority which has reduced the bodies of most women, including the female medical students in the Anatomy class to slow moving bodies practically like corpses in the dissecting room. These subdued bodies recall those of the wives of the men of Kafr El Teen in *God Dies by the Nile*.

This society places value on the girl's honor being based on chastity or sexual purity as a prerequisite for marriage. Young Arab girls are afraid of being declared outcast, dishonoring, or declared devalued; therefore they accept whatever choice that had been made on their behalf. As a way to control their sexual urges, they are circumcised and denied any form of sexual pleasure. Bahiah is astonished at the hypocrisy of her parents who refuse to allow her to embrace her sexuality but expect her to be ready to satisfy her spouse adequately. She is of the opinion that, they are probably convinced she must have undergone an internship in her mother's womb, on how to satisfy a spouse. She observes with disgust and chagrin on her wedding night that, "Women's tools in their married life are all sexual. A girl moves from her father's house to a husband's and suddenly changes from a non-sexual being with no sexual organs to a sexual creature who sleeps, wakes, eats, drinks and sex. With amazing stupidity, they think those parts that have been cut away can somehow return, and that murdered, dead, and satiate desire can be revived" (101).

Bahiah is increasingly disturbed and infuriated by the constant maltreatment and degrading way in which the women are handled. They are expected to lower their gaze at all times and to know their place in the presence of the male folks. Bahiah is frustrated and upset that she is expected to behave like someone without sexual desires and instincts, this becomes emotionally excruciating for her to bear. She constantly feels defeated when she considers her plight and every other privilege that she is being deprived of.

Another agent of depravity as portrayed in the novel is the Medical College Anatomy lecturer, Dr Alawi, He attempts to seduce Bahiah but she aggressively turns him down, insisting that she is not interested in that kind of 'normal' relationship. He held "both her wrists in one hand and started to undress her with the other. She kicked at him strongly and he fell. As he picked himself up, he stared at her in astonishment" (111). The assertive Bahiah was politically conscious and equipped to fight her oppressors who are visible agents of patriarchal depravity.

DEMONIZATION OF THE FEMALE VICTIM OF DEPRAVITY IN *WOMAN AT POINT ZERO*

Depravity is portrayed in any individual who exhibits a behavior that is corrupt, evil, and perverse. A depraved person is deficient of moral sense, integrity and uprightness thereby not showing any concern or regard for human life. He is outrageously mean and wicked to humans around him. Firdaus, unlike Bahiah, came from a very poor background. She grew up in a large household where she witnessed depravity, hardship and negligence. She points out her origins:

> My father, a poor peasant farmer, who could neither read nor write, knew very few things in life . . . How to be quicker than his neighbour in stealing from the fields once the crop was ripe. How to bend over the herdsman's hand and pretend to kiss it, how to beat his wife and make her bite the dust each night. (10)

She witnessed her father's miserly attitude and his tendency for wife battery. It was an occurrence in the home that was not hidden from the little child in the household. Both parents totally neglected the nutritional needs of their children and would rather feed the head of the home (father/husband) than consider their starving children. Food was exclusively reserved for the head of the home, while the rest of the household starve in silence. Firdaus recalls that her father "would sit eating alone while we watched him. One evening I dared to stretch out my hand to his plate, but he struck me a sharp blow over the back of my fingers (18). As a minor, she was engaged fully in taking care of the animals on the farm and also attended to kitchen matters. Firdaus opens up here, "Once back, I would sweep under the animals and the make rows of dung cakes which I left in the sun to dry" (12). Being subjected to serious domestic chores that are meant for adults and watching the father constantly beat her mother is an indication of the depraved individual in her household.

Firdaus was not often chaperoned as a minor and this exposed her to sexual molestations from her play mate, Mohammedian, and her uncle, who violated her at different points in her life. The "paedophiliac" uncle takes advantage of the neglected little girl to satisfy his carnal craving for the prepubescent. In his degenerate mind, he seeks to satisfy himself creating more confusion in the mind of the little girl who by now sees him as a kinsman and private tutor.

Saadawi gradually unearths the depth of human depravity that ultimately leaves the female victim overly fearless, decisively suicidal, and desperately murderous. Firdaus is introduced as a young Egyptian woman who explicitly shares her horrendous life experience, providing details of her childhood days in the rural village farm to the period of her incarceration in the city prison. In this bildungsroman, shortly before her execution, Firdaus indicates an interest to speak to the female prison psychiatrist (the author, Saadawi), who had relentlessly sought after her own side of the story. Hours before she was taken to the gallows and the hangman's halter, Firdaus accepts to talk to the psychiatrist. As she states her terms, one can clearly see a woman who is emotionally exhausted and mentally drained: "Let me speak. Do not interrupt me. I have no time to listen to you. They are coming to take me at six o'clock this evening. Tomorrow morning, I shall no longer be there" (*Woman at Point Zero* 9).

The psychiatrist Saadawi listens attentively as Firdaus begins her narration from growing up with her peasant farmer parents in the rural village. Her mother was so fixated on her husband and preoccupied with taking good care of him that she completely neglected the little ones at home, including Firdaus. The act of callousness and cruelty perpetrated by her father plagues the mind of this young girl and puts her in doubt if he is really her biological father. This is because he exhibits acts that portray him as insensitive, cold, and heartless. Such atrocious behavioral traits gradually impinged on the sensitivities of the young Firdaus who found them grossly disturbing and unsettling.

Firdaus was just about seven years old when she discovered the pleasure of clitoral stimulation through the playful hands of a friend, Muhammadain.

She recalls: "From some part in my body, where exactly I did not know, would come a sensation of sharp pleasure (12). But this feeling of pleasure was short lived as she was scheduled for circumcision, and after her flesh was mutilated, the pleasurable sensation ceased and seemed like it never existed. Shortly afterwards, her parents pass on and she is left in the custody of an uncle, who takes over the guardianship of the young Firdaus. He decides to take her from the village to the big city of Cairo. While under the guardianship of her uncle, Firdaus recalls her experience, stating how he constantly molests her sexually until he eventually gets married to a wealthy bride. A victim of physical, emotional, and mental battery, the young Firdaus continually groaned in grave pain and agony. It festered in her mind and morphed into an excruciating burden since she could not disclose or reveal her gruelling experience to anyone. She is mandated to live with this terrible domestic violence as there was no body to deliver her from this demon of an uncle. This horrible situation becomes too traumatic for her young mind. Freud is of the opinion that whatever emanates from the mind can be linked to the person's encounters and experience. Glen O. Gabbard et al. also submit:

> Freud found that the memories at the source of his patients' neurotic symptoms were invariably revealed to be sexual in nature . . . despite general scepticism, Freud became convinced that the symptoms of neurasthenia, as well as those of hysteria, were caused by sexual disturbances . . . he decided that early childhood seduction, so frequently reported by his patients, was the source of the sexual disturbance. (3)

Her uncle was doing to her what Mohammadian had started in the fields while playing "bride and groom." In actuality this older uncle according to her, "was doing even more" (13). She could not even attain the pleasure she had known in the fields prior to her circumcision. The "pedophiliac" uncle reminds Firdaus of an old pleasure she once experienced before she was circumcised, but to her frustration and distress, she can no longer recall the "sharp pleasure" or detect where it emanates from, on the geography of her body. This leaves her in pain, misery and anguish. Anthony Storr points out that: "Freud became more and more convinced that the chief characteristic of the neurotic person was lack of a normal sex life and that sexual satisfaction was key to happiness" (25).

Her uncle's new wife is uncomfortable with her presence in the home and insists on sending her to a boarding school. Firdaus performs excellently in her academics and subsequently obtains good grades. She gets the chance to interact with young girls of her age and makes new friends. When she gets attracted to a female teacher, Miss Iqbal who does not quite reciprocate her love, Firdaus is hurt by the unrequited emotions. She clearly recollects her experience: "It seemed to me as though I reached out in the dark and took her hand, or that she reached out in the dark and took my hand. The sudden contact made my body shiver with a pain so deep that it was almost like pleasure, or a pleasure so deep that it bordered on pain" (33). Iqbal's rejection of her love has a tremendous effect on Firdaus's mind. Storr affirms: "Freud's findings made sexual emotions the key emotions, which if repressed, were the cause of neurotic symptoms" (24).

Upon graduation, Firdaus wants to seek employment with her secondary school certificate, but her guardians turn down her request and make arrangements to marry her off to Sheikh Mahmaoud—a man who is not only forty years older than Firdaus but also has a leaking smelly abscess which secretes pus on his face. Firdaus vehemently rejects the offer and takes to her heels into the streets of Cairo. Out there she finds out that the streets are not safe for any woman. Firdaus recounts the nerve-racking incident when she took flight to the streets of Cairo. Firdaus is undoubtedly a most vulnerable victim of patriarchy. Maureen Eke is of the view that, "Patriarchy imprisons women and violates them by denying them rights as individuals and as members of a large collective. Through imposed cultural practices, women are repressed, contained and monitored under the constant gaze of a male, first the father, then the brother (where there is one), husband and sometimes the son" (50).

In due course of Firdaus's tribulations, she returns to her uncle's house, only to be married off to Sheikh Mahmaoud. She is subjected to series of beatings and maltreatment despite the fact that he is a pathological miser and also inflicted with a disease. Unable to withstand the battering any longer, she reports the matter to her uncle and his wife. They try to convince her that it is a normal practice for a man to beat his wife. Consequently, she is promptly sent back to Sheikh Mahmuod, who resumes his assaults on a daily basis. When it gets out of hand, and she can no longer endure the torture, she runs out into the streets again. This is due to the fact that as a psychological wreck, she is constantly miserable and troubled, preferring to remain in the streets away from all the domestic frustrations.

On the streets, Firdaus meets Bayoumi, a coffee shop owner who offers to assist her and also provide her with shelter for a while. He holds her in captivity and organizes a gang of men to rape her for a fee. She finally gets the chance to escape and flees to the bank of River Nile. She encounters a high-class prostitute, Sharifa who decides to take her under her custody until Fawzy (another prostitute), reveals Sharifa's hidden agenda to Firdaus. While they are arguing over the issues of ownership. Firdaus runs off and becomes a boss of her own enterprise.

Upon achieving commercial success as a prostitute, she buys a house and other material things and begins to revel in the semblance of a respectable woman who can now afford to live a life of leisure. She now has free time to "relax, go for a walk or to the cinema, or the theatre, time to read the newspaper and to discuss politics with the few close friends" (74). This new status notwithstanding, she is devastated after a client tells her that no matter her comfort and wealth, she is not respectable in society because she is a commercial sex provider. As she succinctly put it, his words "had cut its way through my ears, and the bones of my head to the brain inside" (76).

This piece of information is unsettling, traumatizing and demeaning for her. It is clearly frustrating that after her financial success as a prostitute, she is still humiliated, debased, and degraded by society. It shakes her to the core because she had previously assumed that her wealth had redeemed her image and given her a semblance of inner peace and that she was finally acceptable in the community where she found herself. She is mentally tormented by that demeaning reference "not respectable" and seeks to remedy it by any possible means. Frantic, desperate and distraught, she seeks employment as an office assistant with the hope of gaining some form of respectability but only ends up disappointed after she made some discoveries about the corporate world. She starts a relationship with Ibrahim, until she finds out that he is engaged to another woman—the boss's daughter. It is, indeed, a catalogue of woes.

The grossly enervated Firdaus angrily resigns from the company and becomes a prostitute again. With time she is admired by many, becomes very popular and equally expensive. To her mind, she has attained self-fulfillment, but the depravity in the patriarchal society has utterly fettered her. The accumulated trauma in her results in mounting anger, hatred for men, and revenge. After an altercation with a pimp, they fight over the issue of control and she kills him. This emboldens her and gives her more confidence and power. Her misplaced aggression descends on her last client, an Arab prince, who offers her 3,000 pounds to sleep with her; she rips the money afterward and slaps him. The prince calls the police who gets her arrested, tried and sentenced to death. Firdaus's successive aggression, and ensuing violence constitute an express onslaught on the symbols of depravity and patriarchy that have over the years continually dehumanized and traumatized her.

By the time Firdaus becomes a death row inmate at Qanair Prison, she has undergone a series of torture that affected her mental health. The uncle, the husband, the lovers, the society, the high-class prostitutes, pimps, and every other person who took advantage of her left her broken, tortured, frustrated, and empty. She develops suicidal thoughts and constantly toys with the idea of destroying the male folk whom she perceives as her sworn enemies. Such a persistent mental torture eventually gives room for an encrusted demonization and ultimate destruction of the extremely repressed Firdaus.

CONCLUSION

In sum, the two protagonists of the novels discussed—Bahiah and Firdaus—are Arab women mentally tortured by the depraved, excruciating instruments and traditions that are normative patterns in a monolithic Muslim society, which is obviously energized by religion and patriarchy. This leaves them guilt-ridden because they cannot talk about their feelings, pain, anguish, misery, sexuality, or trauma. They are expected to keep mute and not breathe a word to the moralistic public, or share a bit of their nefarious ordeal, particularly the recurrence of incest, battery, or rape. They are perennially mentally tortured and have to cope with the emotional stress while their bodies constitute the battlefield in the fiery struggle for female indivuation, self-fulfillment and freedom which are the prominent features of Saadawi's outstanding legacy.

These agonized victims are, unarguably, humiliated as a result of their gender. They are, in the main, encumbered with profound sadness and despair. Such an extreme form of human torture and deprivation evokes strong reactions that are capable of producing a lasting effect on the human psychological state. Firdaus and Bahiah attempt to distance themselves, both physically and psychologically from others. Most times the series of events that have occurred in their lives left indelible marks on their mental health. The negative effect on their well-being, peace of mind, and personality are dexterously depicted by the revered psychiatrist and psychoanalyst, Nawal El Saadawi. Her narratives bare very deep emotional disturbances, mental torture, depression, and anxiety of the two protagonists, occasioned by ingrained depravity. This inevitably leaves these young Arab women utterly fearless, decisively suicidal, and desperately murderous. By treating the issues of sexuality, prostitution, child abuse, early/forced marriage, genital mutilation, domestic violence, and emotional battery Saadawi has excelled at exploring a universal patriarchal tragedy: which has flagrantly stoked the angst and mental torture of both victims resulting in the catastrophic ending of both narratives.

WORKS CITED

Basoglu, M. Ed. *Torture and its Consequences: Current Treatment Approaches.* Cambridge: Cambridge University Press, 1992.

Beauvoir, Simone de: *The Second Sex.* Trans. H. M. Parshley. New York: Vintage Books, 1974.

Eke, Maureen N. "The Inner Life of Beings: Failed Maleness and 'Modern' Love." Ernest N. Emenyonu and Maureen N. Eke. Eds. *Emerging Perspectives on Nawal EL Saadawi.* Trenton, NJ: Africa World Press, 2010.

Gabbard, Glen O. et al. Eds. *Textbook of Psychoanalysis*. Second Edition. Washington: American Psychiatric Publishing, 2021.

Mannoni, Octave. *Freud: Theory of the Unconscious*. London: Verso, 2015.

Mitchell, Juliet. *Psychoanalysis and Feminism.* New York: Vintage Books, 1975.

Opara, Chioma *Her Mother's Daughter: The African Writer as Woman.* Port Harcourt: University Press, 2004.

———. "Woman at a Vantage Point: Deconstructing Androcentricism in El Saadawi's *Two Women in One.*" International Women's Literary Conference, Coppin State University, Baltimore, Maryland, March, 2012.

Saadawi, Nawal El. *God Dies by the Nile*. Trans. Sherif Hetata. London: Zed Books, 1985.

———. *Two Women in One*. Trans. Osman Nusairi & Jana Gough. London: Al Saqi Books 1985.

———. *Woman at Point Zero*. Trans. Sherif Hetata. London: Zed Books, 1983.

Storr, Anthony. *Freud: A short introduction*. Oxford: Oxford University Press, 1989.

Chapter 13

Resurrecting Women from the Margins of History

Feminist Synergy in Selected Works by Assia Djebar

Rose A. Sackeyfio

INTRODUCTION

Assia Djebar's artistry as a novelist, poet, playwright, and filmmaker denotes her iconic status among Arab women writers of the twentieth century. As the first North African woman to publish in French, her legacy as an Arab feminist writer is unsurpassed in Francophone and World Literature. She achieved critical acclaim through creation of dynamic and penetrating novels that chronicle the oppression of Arab women. She is notably one of North Africa's literary giants whose life and works have generated enormous influence and significance within Francophone, Postcolonial and Feminist writing.

This chapter celebrates the legacy of Assia Djebar in selected works that reconfigure Arab women's identity. *Fantasia: An Algerian Cavalcade* (1985) and *A Sister to Scheherazade* (1987) assert feminist themes of resistance against patriarchy and the French colonial intrusion in Algeria that began in 1830. In addition, *Children of the New World: A Novel of the Algerian War* (2005) captures the nature of Algeria's War of Independence through the lens of gender. The political themes in the novel resonate the ways in which women's lives are transformed by the struggle for the liberation of their nation.

Her writing career spans fifty years and although she writes in French, she is also fluent in Arabic and English. The autobiographical elements that pervade her novels, reflect her commitment to expose the obstacles to women's equality in Arab society. Her fiction projects a genealogy of Algerian women caught in the grip of patriarchal domination that is inscribed on women's bodies through various forms of suppression and violence that they experience. The plight of Arab women, as well as their resistance to subjugation is cast against Algeria's colonization by France, and the subsequent revolution that led to the nation's independence in 1962.

ASSIA DJEBAR'S LIFE AND WORKS

Assia Djebar was the pen name of Fatima-Zohra Imalhayene who was born in in 1936 in Cherchell, a small coastal village near Algiers. Unlike her female peers, she did not experience seclusion or veiling, and was educated during a period when few females attended school. She completed primary school at Mouzaiaville dans la Mitidja, a French colonial school where her father taught French language. The French authorities forbade teaching in Arabic at that time. In 1954, she completed preparatory year at the Lycee Fenelon in Paris, after secondary school in Algeria. She is the first Algerian woman to attend the elite *Ecole Normale Superieure de Sevres* in 1955.

Her activism and resistance to the French occupation of Algeria began in 1956 when she participated in student strikes for independence. A born rebel, she was suspended from *Ecole Normale Superieure de Sevres* for one year, reinstated by Charles de Gaulle. As part of her activism, she made contributions to the National Front Liberation newspaper, *El-Moujahid*. This period also marks the beginning of her writing career, and the use of her pen name that she retained all her life. Her first novel, *La Soif* (1957) (*The Mischief*, 1958) was published at the age of twenty. This novel portrays a young woman from an elite French-Algerian family who has an affair with her friend's husband. A *New York Times* review stated that it is the first novel by an Algerian woman published outside her country although it was criticized for its lack of engagement with the revolution for independence.

Throughout her distinguished career, Assia Djebar has displayed a commitment to women's emancipation from the shackles of patriarchy dictated by Muslim society. She has used her writing as a weapon to achieve social transformation and to uplift women. In 2005, in an interview with the French newspaper, *Le Figaro*, she is asked about her career as a female author in the Muslim world and states that: "I am not a symbol, my only activity consists in writing.... Like many writers, I use my culture and I collect several imaginary worlds" (de la Baume 4). Her impressive literary corpus includes more than fifteen works, from the genres of poetry, novels, short fiction, and plays that are translated into twenty-three languages.

Djebar's second novel, *Children of the New World* (*Les enfants du nouveau monde Delete Descants*) was published in 1962 and in the same year she was appointed Professor at the University of Rabat in Morocco. She developed her talent in poetry, theater and fiction and published *The Naïve Larks* (*Les alouettes naives*) in 1967; In 1969 she published a volume of poetry titled *Poems for a Joyous Algeria* (*Poemes pour l'Algerie heureuse*) in addition to *Red is Dawn* (*Rouge l'aube*). While living in Paris she wrote a collection of short stories called, *Women of Algiers in Their Apartment* (*Les Femmes d'Algerie dans leurs apartement*) 1980 that is followed in 1985 by *Fantasia: An Algerian Cavalcade* (*L'Amour, la fantasia*). One of her most well-known works is *A Sister to Sherehezade* (*Ombre Sultane*) in 1987. For ten years during the 1970s she did not write due to her conflict over writing in French which she calls the language of the "Others," instead of her mother tongue Arabic, adopted after Algeria's independence. During this time, she produced films about the lives of North African women, most notably, *The Nouba of the Women of Mount Chenoua* (*La Nouba des femmes du mont Chenoua*) in 1978. In 1991, Djebar resurrects the occluded voices of Arab women "cast out of Medina" in her collection, *Far from Medina: Daughters of Ismael* (*Loin de Medine: Filles d' Ismael*). This is a collection of narratives, and accounts originating from Muslim historians who lived during the early periods of Islam (World Literature Today 800). Assia Djebar publishes another of her major works in 1995, *Vast is the Prison* (*Vaste est la prison*). In the same year she is awarded the Prix Maeterlinck and is named Doctor Honoris Causa by the University of Vienna.

The year 1996 unfolds two significant accomplishments in her career: publishing the final work of the Algerian Quartet, *The White of Algeria* (*Le blanc de l'Algerie*). Secondly, she was awarded the prestigious Neustadt International Prize for Literature, perhaps the most significant in her career. In addition, she has earned other significant awards such as the Yourcenar Prize and the Fonlon-Nichols Prize of the African Literature Association in 1997. She was awarded the International Palmi Prize in 1998, and in 2000 the Frankfurt Book Fair Prize (Salhi 201). Djebar was North Africa's first writer to be accepted into the Academie francaise, an eminent and impressive institution recognized as the custodian of French language and culture. Djebar was often named as a contender for the Nobel Prize, and in the latter years of her professional life in the twenty-first century she worked in the United States at Louisiana State University as Director of the Center of French and Francophone Studies. Her final academic appointment was a Silver Chair Professor of Francophone Literature at New York University. Assia Debar joined the ancestors on February 4, 2015, in Paris, France.

FEMINIST AGENCY THROUGH SISTERHOOD

Written in 1987 *Ombre sultane* (*A Sister to Scheherazade*) is one of Assia Djebar's most well-known works. The novel unfolds the complexities of women's identities, resistance to patriarchy and the stifling restrictions and expectations of Muslim society. This novel is a strong example of Djebar's commitment to subvert patriarchy and according to Maria Cooke, early in her career her novel *Les Impatients* (1958), "claimed to be about the past, yet the message was the same: women must be aware of men's need to rule at home" (214). The women characters in *A Sister to Scheherazade* resonates this theme as well. The author skillfully presents two protagonists, married to the same man, who lead very different lives and who function at opposite ends of the spectrum of behavioral norms for Arab women in society. The two women are Isla and Hajila whose stories are cleverly interwoven to form a contra-positional structure of the novel.

Isla is the narrator who speaks both for herself in first person and for Hajila in second person. Her voice assumes command of the text and represents Assia Djebar's alter ego. The novel alternates between each woman's experiences as their personalities are juxtaposed in ways that confound their individual identities. Isla is a liberated Algerian woman who traverses the social and spatial boundaries of the veiled and sequestered life for Muslim women. She is educated, westernized and middle class. In contrast, Hajila, is secluded and suffers in an empty marriage, veiled, passive, and silenced by patriarchal control. Ironically, Isma arranges her marriage. Despite their differences the two women emerge as mirror images whose lives are interconnected. Isma is the first wife who chooses Hajila in order to escape the bonds of conventional marriage. Djebar contrasts Isma's newly acquired freedom with Hajila's subordination and confinement within domestic space (Hiddleston 89).

As the novel opens, Isla admits to herself that "she had decided to act as matchmaker to her own husband; thinking naively to free herself by this means from her own past—enslavement to passion and love—and from the stalemate of the present" (1). She admits that she is essentially "cutting herself adrift" and she says of Hajila, "to be sure, you were the innocent victim whom I enslaved" (1). It is paradoxical that Isma can only be emancipated by the confinement of Hajila, hence an underlying tension between tradition and modernity, and the past and the present in the novel. Her life as a liberated woman in Paris is conveyed with almost lyrical and haunting imagery as she glides through the streets, aware of her body as the object of the gaze of males, taking delight in her western clothing that symbolizes her freedom from the veil at the expense of Hajila's imprisonment.

In recounting the outward journey of Hajila, and the inward journey of herself, Isla becomes the auto-diegetic narrator of the novel who interprets Hajila's sensibilities and her path to selfhood. The reader follows their journey through binary constructions of similarity and difference, competition and rivalry, to arrive at a semblance of sisterhood at the end of the work. Unlike Isma who recalls instances of happiness in her marriage, Hajila experiences cold indifference from her new husband early in her marriage that is not consummated until after six months. Hajila's marriage is essentially dysfunctional, passionless, and emotionally brutal. Her husband remains nameless and is referred to only as "the man." Mildred Mortimer succinctly affirms that: Although Isma refers to her husband as l'aime`, beloved, she and Hajila both respect tradition; they never call him by his given name. L'homme, il, lui reinforce the omnipresence and omnipotence of the patriarchal order that eventually destroys Isma's happiness and condones Hajila's sequestration and humiliation" (160).

Hajila's life in seclusion spells utter boredom and mindless drudgery. While crying one morning, she laments women's fate as she thinks of how fortunate men are because they can present themselves to the world each day and describes herself as a "Still-life with seated woman" (9). Her transformation begins when, after three months, she goes out secretly. This experience is exhilarating, as she is bathed in the sensory stimulation that public space confers and begins to drink in the "elixir of life," reminiscent of Mrs. Mallard in Kate Chopin's feminist classic, "The Story of an Hour." In the story, set in the Victorian period, Mrs. Mallard, mistakenly thinks that her domineering husband has died in an accident. She imagines a life of freedom from the yoke of patriarchy and the open window in her room unlocks her dreams of a new and unrestricted life outside her home. The setting of the story is springtime and from her window she takes in the sights and sounds of the outside world, and awakening nature. The changes that she observes represent her inner awakening to freedom from domesticity and patriarchal subjugation that is similar to Isla.

Against Islamic taboo, Hajia goes out daily, unveiled and Isla narrates that "you have become a 'woman who leaves the house' and when you return in the evening you are filled with the sensation of the infinity of time" (43). The act of unveiling asserts her resistance because she is "naked" and exposed. Indeed, Hajila is naked to the world and subject to the gaze of strangers. Djebar employs the same strategy as Nawal El Saadawi in *Woman at Point Zero* (1975) in presenting public space as refuge for imprisoned women. Firdaus knows that her only hope for freedom and safety lies in running away into the streets. Throughout the novel this action is repeated a number of times, the first of which is Firdaus's horror at the idea of an arranged marriage to a man in his 60s. Upon running into the street, her feelings echo Hajila's as she recalls: "When I looked at the streets it was as though I was seeing them for the first time. A new world was opening up in front of my eyes, a world which for me had not existed before" (Saadawi 42).

Each time that Firdaus runs away, she escapes brutal treatment, exploitation, and violence at the hands of men. She runs into the streets a second time when her husband beats her with a heavy stick until the blood ran from her nose and ears (Saadawi 47). Later in the novel she is imprisoned by Bayoumi and forced into sex with him and other males, but she escapes again. For Firdaus, the cyclic patterns of escape from danger highlights women's vulnerability, even when they attempt to transform their lives. As public space, the streets become at site of freedom, resistance, and safety. In the same way, Djebar emphasizes this message because of Hajila's preoccupation with leaving the house. For her, the psychological impact is deep and transformative in terms of her identity. Although Hajila does not face imminent danger of violence in the beginning, her husband beats her when he learns she has been going out secretly and without her veil. Susan Andrade succinctly captures the significance of Hajila's unveiling as a form of resistance: "Hajila's self-unveiling is a remarkable act, and we are reminded of just how radical it is under her life circumstances. That she succeeds in remaining unveiled when outdoors is itself a powerful statement. Above all, Hajila's actions are noteworthy because of the type of risk she, a socioeconomically marginalized woman, takes in acting" (195).

The inter-textual elements of *A Sister to Shereherazade* and *Woman at Point Zero* is striking as both women characters seek to move beyond the spatial boundaries through feminist agency. In the context of the Arab Muslim environment, both Hajila and Firdaus develop feminist consciousness of their plight that nurtures their resistance to subjectivity. The spatial-temporal dimensions of the novel codify the idea that women can find freedom, even if only temporary, in the public domain. Both women are willing to risk the dangers of the streets, as they become naked to the world and the vulnerability it poses for them outside the domestic sphere. Mildred Mortimer confirms the significance of Hajila reclaiming public space: "One transformation leads to another; Hajila prepares to leave the enclosure. Djebar's message is clear. Access to public space is the first step toward emancipation; there can be no journey to self-understanding without the experience of entering public space, in other words, without some form of the outward journey" (158). Hajila's transformation is illustrated when Isma remarks that: "Whenever you returned from these excursions the kitchen seemed colder than ever" (17). The return to domestic imprisonment spells retreat into a veiled existence, with no identity beyond the sequestered space of the home and her husband as master.

Weeks later, the narrator observes Hajila's heightened sense of identity: "In the evening when you return with aching legs and the rumblings from the outside world drown the beating of your heart, you tell yourself that you too have a history" (41). For Hajila, reclaiming her sense of self through unveiling to the outside world opens a new and liberated existence, and after dropping the veil, she is "moving about freely with open eyes" (41). Thus, her pathway outward (re) shapes her consciousness to subvert the unyielding grip of patriarchy. This represents the feminist underpinnings of Djebar's message in the novel.

After six months of cold indifference, her husband rapes her brutally. In a patriarchal society there is no such thing as "marital rape" as articulated by Esi in Ama Ata Aidoo's *Changes* (1993). Like Hajila, she feels violated and Esi reflects: "But marital rape? No. The society could not possibly have an indigenous word or phrase for it. Sex is something a husband claims from his wife as his right. Any time. And at his convenience" (12). After the painful rape that shatters her virginity, Hajila echoes Esi's reactions as she thinks: "He can see my legs! He can see my blood! He has paid for this right!" (58). These sentiments resonate in the literature of African women, both Muslim and non-Muslim and illustrate men's control of women's bodies and their sexuality as part of the patriarchal order.

Hajila's resistance to the assault illustrates Djebar's feminist stance. While she is being raped, she recollects her discovery of the new world beyond her apartment. She attempts to fight him off as she anchors her mind: "Must you surrender? No! Think of the streets, they stretch within you, bathed in the sunshine that has dissolved the storm clouds. . . . You can see the space out of doors through which you sail each day" (58). The idea that the "streets stretch within her" indicates her self-discovery and the inward journey that can only be realized by moving beyond her home. Her quest for freedom is both an inward and outward journey to resist subordination. Hajilah's husband eventually discovers that she has ventured outside without a veil and beats her. While interrogating her, he hurls threats and says: "I'll break your legs and you'll never go out again, you'll be nailed to the bed and . . ." (87). His violence speaks to the danger and risks to women's safety inside as well as outside the home.

As part of Djebar's feminist agenda, the dialogic structure of the novel underscores thematic focus on the sisterhood motif. Susan Andrade suggests a "schematic reading of *Ombre sultane's* (*A Sister to Scheherazade*) engagement with Western feminism and education, as well as with local women's emancipation" (188). Speaking for both of them, Isma is sympathetic to Hajilah's plight, and by the end of the novel, she expresses female solidarity by extending herself to Hajilah. The evolution of women's sisterhood becomes a route to women's freedom from the veiled realm of confinement in the domestic prison of marriage. The women connect to each other through a series of exchanges that erodes the barriers between them. The *hammam* (Turkish bath) becomes an alternate space within which women can nurture the bonds of their commonality through alliance. In the bath, women can "communicate by signs; here, a split-second glance, a barely perceptible touch, will seal their secret collusion" (148). According to Gracki, "Hajila begins her healing process in the *hammam* when Isma reaches out to her as sister, daughter, and mother and a bond of solidarity is established between the two" (840). The meeting at the *hammam* is described thus, "*Hammam* the only temporary reprieve from the harem . . . The Turkish bath offers a secret consolation to sequestered women (such as organ music offered in former times to forced religious recluses). This surrogate maternal cocoon providing an escape from the hothouse of cloistration" (152). Mildred Mortimer comments on the significance of their meeting. At the Hammam, Isma participates in liberating the *odalisque*. Giving Hajila the remaining key to the apartment, Isma provides Hajila with the means of transformation. Hajila can subvert her husband's authority; she can choose to enter and leave her apartment at will" (161).

As a recurring motif in the literature of African women, sisterhood appears in the classic *So Long a Letter* (1981) by Mariama Ba. Similar to Isma's gesture, Aissatou's gift of a car to Ramatoulaye is a source of freedom and mobility in her environment. It provides access to another reality beyond the spatial-temporal locus of the home. It opens the door for an independent and self-determined existence through the assistance of a woman who has already achieved a strong measure of freedom and autonomy. The allegorical significance of Aissatou's gift of the car to her friend conveys the novel's message that women's collective strength can re-shape their lives. Similar to Hajila, Susan Ardnt in *The Dynamics of African Feminism* observes that:

> It is clearly implied that in the process of writing her letter ad reflecting upon her life, Ramatoulaye starts to rethink and to change. She has already become dynamic in her thinking and behavior. When for instance, her brother-in-law commands her to become his wife-levirate is the traditional custom she refuses. (121)

Self-reflection as a critical thought process is necessary for consciousness raising that may lead to self-discovery and agency for women. As part of the human condition, sometimes people cannot see beyond their individual circumstances in critical ways until they engage with others to broaden their perspective. Nfa-Abbenyi emphasizes women's inherent potential for transformation, "Women's marginal positions are reclaimed and often shown as spaces of strength within and between which they fluctuate, the position of the Other being reversed and sometimes inverted through the perspectives of those who also become and act as insider-within. (150). Mildred Mortimer notes that Djebar's message in *A Sister to Shereherazade* mirrors Mariama Ba's ideas in that women are charged to support and protect one another in the struggle to dismantle patriarchy (Mortimer 161).

In addition, Sefi Atta in *Everything Good Will Come* (2004) pairs Enitan and Sheri who, like Isma and Hajila, are very different. Enitan is educated and comes from a Christian and middle-class background. In contrast, Sheri is biracial and Muslim from a polygamous family. Their friendship is contested throughout the twists and turns of diverging lives and the choices they make. The subtext of the novel unwinds their sisterhood as Enitan advises Sheri about her questionable relationships with men. She urges her to gain economic independence by starting her own business. Like Isma, Enitan seeks escape from domesticity and questions traditional norms and behavior for women in Nigeria. In the end, both women are transformed, through their growing awareness of female subjectivity within a patriarchal society in Nigeria.

In sum, the development of feminist agency is propelled by the interplay of women's voices in *A Sister to Scheherazade*, even though Isma is the only narrator. Towards the end of the novel, the women's identities are blurred because for Isma, Hajila represents her past life in seclusion, veiled and suppressed. Though they lead separate lives, their connection, and eventual meeting forges their identities into a trajectory of self-realization. As the intercessor, and lead protagonist, not only does Isma free herself, she provides the key to her sister-wife's emancipation. In this instance the "key" may be understood both literally and figuratively. In a literal sense, keys open doors, and unlock that which is hidden and secluded. Likewise, keys also open doors to the outside world to potentially free anyone from imprisonment. Thus, the act of giving Hajila the key to the apartment is not only symbolic but is also a radical development of feminist agency for both women characters.

Hajila's ability to reclaim public space as a site of liberation is an act of sabotage against the patriarchal order. In the avoidance of cloistration, she may recover her identity through self-discovery, especially since she escapes motherhood through the miscarriage of her pregnancy. Djebar suggests the possibility of women's identity and potential fulfillment, beyond the socially prescribed roles of motherhood and domesticity. Western radical feminism expresses these ideas, appropriated and expressed in extremist postures of rejection of males, marriage, and motherhood as forms of slavery for women. Finally, *A Sister to Schereherazade* is a vivid rendering of women's identity and the possibilities for transformation that lies within their grasp.

WOMEN, WAR, AND MEMORY

Fantasia An Algerian Cavalcade (L Amour, la fantasia) is a complex work that skillfully etches the lives and identities of Algerian women from the beginning of the French colonial era in 1830 until independence in 1962. It is the first of the Algerian Quartet that chronicles the genealogy of Djebar's Algerian sisters. The structure of the novel interweaves autobiographical elements, narratives, and testimonies of women that juxtapose the official archival accounts by the French colonists. In this way, she resurrects women's collective autobiographies to (re)inscribe their narrative, and recollections of the war into the history of Algeria. She recalls her own memories from her childhood as a way of reclaiming the past as a testimony of the events of the war, Algerian identity and the representation of women and their participation in the war for independence. One of Djebar's aims in crafting the work was to "give voice or agency to Algerian women . . . to delineate the specificity of Algerian women, oppressed at once by colonialism and by Islamic patriarchy" (Hiddleston 70).

Early in the novel *Three Cloistered Girls* sketches the lives of three young females who subvert their imprisonment and restricted social interactions in a patriarchal culture. This chapter is not about the war, but rather, women's agency, and their success in reconfiguring their identities while in confinement. Although they are unable to escape their seclusion physically, like Isma and eventually Hajila in *A Sister to Scherherazade* they connect themselves to the outside world. For adolescent Muslim girls in the novel, romantic adventures materialize for them through the act of writing. Recalling her childhood, Djebar describes how she encountered three girls when her family spends the holidays in a village in the Sahel. She becomes close to them, especially the youngest and over time they share a secret with her, that they are writing letters, to men: "These girls, though confined to the house, were writing letters; letters to men; to men in the four corners of the world; of the Arab world, naturally" (11). Like Djebar, the girls attend school and are literate in French. Djebar is amazed at their audacity and feared their discovery since she is now part of the secrecy. They are of marriageable age despite their youth and Djebar reckons with the dangerous nature of their behavior: They could be murdered by their male relations under the guise of honor killing. "There had been numerous cases in our towns of fathers or brothers taking the law into their own hands for less than this; the blood of an unmarried daughter or sister shed for a letter slipped surreptitiously into a hand, for a word whispered behind shuttered windows, for some slanderous accusation . . . a secret spirit of subversion had now seeped into the house" (12). These events signal Djebar's commitment to encourage feminist agency and remarkably, this is a true story. It is also unusual given the age of the girls and the constraints of their environment. The closing line of the story expresses the author's insight as she senses that "an unprecedented women's battle was brewing beneath the surface" (13). This illustrates the rebellious nature of youth and the extremes to which females may go to redefine their lives in the face of patriarchal oppression within Arab Muslim society. Thus, feminist themes are woven into the novel against the fabric of Djebar's childhood experiences. Furthermore, the girls were able to appropriate the French language as a medium of negotiation to evade the conditions of their confinement, culture, and behavior codes of Islam for females.

For the three cloistered girls, access to the French language and education confers hybridity and alienation from Arab-Berber language and culture. However, it is also a vehicle through which women may achieve some measure of freedom. Throughout Djebar's career as a writer, she experiences ambivalence about writing in French, the language of the colonizer/oppressor because it presents a paradoxical relationship and a foreign perspective. Moreover, writing in French is antithetical to the cultural, political, and historical significance of the colonized "Other." Much has been written about this conflict and in *Fantasia*, Djebar states: "I know that every language is a dark depository for piled up corpses, refuse, sewage, but faced with the language of the former conqueror, which offers me its ornaments, its jewels, its flowers, I find they are flowers of death—chrysanthemums on tombs!" (181). Nevertheless, the young girls succeed in traversing the social boundaries of their enclosed environment and to capture the romantic yearnings and imaginings of youth.

In *Fantasia*, Djebar focuses her attention on women's accounts of the invasion of Algeria by the French in 1830. Katherine Gracki confirms that: "By appropriating the gendered historical relationship between the colonizer and the colonized, Djebar is ultimately able to reveal the resistance and the screams of refusal muffled by the colonial discourse of conquest" (836). In the final chapters of *Fantasia,* Djebar recovers the vivid, but silenced voices of Algerian women, interviewed as a collective autobiography. The "Voices of the Past" chronicle the untold *her-stories* of the War of Independence between 1954 and 1962. This re-telling of history is interspersed with Djebar's remembrances from her childhood within her community. The accounts of the women invoke the spirit of resistance, the humanity and cultural ethos of Algerians as a colonized people. Ranni Kabanni corroborates Djebar's vivid rendering of the past and says that: "Her novel is a bittersweet evocation of that past, weaving eyewitness narrative alongside personal reflection to tell a story that is as moving as it is macabre. The massacres of her people are recounted as if they were private tragedies" (149). Women's identity and their resistance to oppression elucidate feminist themes and delineate inter-textuality between *Fantasia* and *A Sister to Scheherazade* that is a feature of Djebar's oeuvre. In this way, Djebar is able to connect the past and present that is mis-represented in the annals of French history.

Although Djebar laments writing about Algerian women in the language of the conqueror, she passionately shares her sentiments:

> Writing in a foreign language, not in either of the tongues of my native country-the Berber of the Dahra mountains or the Arabic of the town where I was born-writing has brought me to the cries of the women silently rebelling in my youth, to my own true origins. Writing does not silence the voice, but awakens it, above all to resurrect so many vanquished sisters. (204)

In recounting the women's stories, their voices can now be heard above the cacophony of French his-stories that are rife with distortion, dehumanization, and demonization of Arab peoples cast as the *Other.*

The common thread that connects Algerian women's untold experiences of the War of Independence is the spirit of resistance in the midst of violence. Their contributions to the revolution include hiding people, passing information, storing ammunition, providing food and offering moral support for the war effort in their homes and villages among their fellow countrymen and women. Their accounts of life and death are riveting, and bring to life their voices that were silenced by history. Their stories are a vivid rendering of individual and collective memories. In the novel, Djebar signals to the reader by using the chapter heading "Voice" to indicate an authentic testimonial by a woman character. The first story is about Cherifa, a thirteen-year-old girl who flees her home after it has been razed to the ground by French soldiers. She finds her brother Ahmed who is in hiding in the countryside. When they find shelter, the French soldiers eventually discover them. As they try to escape, the soldiers shoot and kill her brother in front of her. What follows is a disturbing account of her search for his body and how she dragged him away to wash his face. Cherifa's story captures the horror of war and its effect upon an adolescent girl through exposure to the death of a sibling.

Cherifa's experiences are also the subject of a period in the war when she works in a field hospital and is trained in caring for the wounded men of the Algerian resistance movement. She spent a whole year there and despite her skill and the quality of her caregiving, she decides to leave. In response to questions about why she is leaving she tells them: "I've been here a year and I've not seen a single woman, or even a child!" No one except our wounded! And my brother's only been to see me once! (131). These experiences are heart wrenching and illustrate how war can rob individuals of their childhood, familial relationships, education, and normalcy. She recalls weeping, along with the patients when she left, only to be sent to another hospital. As soon as she arrives, she is told she must get married. But she bluntly refuses. (131) Owing to her obstinance, she is finally left alone.

Later, Cherifa and others are captured by the French soldiers. She encounters open confrontation with the guards and soldiers who threaten her repeatedly. She exhibits unusual inner strength, fearlessness, and courage because she is not afraid to die. She is interrogated and admits to herself that she would actually prefer to die. She recalls how: "They brought a whip. They beat me. They switched on the electricity for their machines. They tortured me" (135). They are unable to break her spirit and when she is questioned by a high ranking officer her courage is visibly displayed (139–140). After this encounter, she is allowed to see her parents and her father wept when he saw her. Djebar pays tribute to Cherifa's bravery and says: "I have captured your voice; disguised it with my French without clothing it. I barely brush the shadow of your footsteps" (142).

In another account, Algerian women experience humiliation and dehumanization at the hands of the French soldiers. After burning their homes, they take the clothes worn by the women and leave them naked. This is unimaginable in a society where there are strict religious prohibitions against exposing women's faces, arms, and legs. The idea of complete nudity in public for a Muslim female, regardless of her age is inconceivable. Djebar describes a painful account of a woman who, along with forty-eight hostages, is taken to France. It is 1843 and the unnamed woman is pregnant and alone, without her father, husband, or brother. Her pregnancy is in the final stages and narrating in the second person, Djebar says, "The second night you feel death in your belly swallowing all hope" (189). The woman gives birth to a stillborn fetus but clutches the body, refusing to accept the baby's death. One of the old women takes the infant from her and throws it overboard. The author interjects: "I resurrect you during that crossing that no letter from any French soldier was to describe" (189). This episode is redolent of the story, "Children of the Sea" from Danticatt's collection of stories *Krik Krak* (1995). A young Haitian refugee is on a boat sailing to America. She is delivered of a stillborn infant. She is traumatized and refuses to accept the death of her baby, clinging hopelessly to the corpse before it is thrown overboard.

In recording the stories of Algerian women, Djebar celebrates their resilience and heroism as they struggle to survive the ravages of war and the oppression of patriarchy in their sequestered lives. The recovery of the past opens a window into the lived reality of female subjectivity in ways that only women can narrate for themselves. Algerian women's lives are inscribed onto Djebar's reconstructed genealogy in ways that honor their immense sacrifices and courage. The author has essentially rewritten women into history that becomes a gendered revision(ing) of the past. She has pulled aside the veil that clouds reality and truth, albeit through the French language that is her step-tongue instead of Arabic as her indigenous language. Her literature gives voice to the voiceless to animate the individual and collective memories of Algerian women's identities. Thus, *Fantasia* illuminates the political history of Algerian people through a gendered lens.

Children of the New World (*Les Enfantes du nouveau monde*), unlike Djebar's earlier novels are narrated in third, rather than first person. It was written in 1962, the year of Algeria's independence. It is comprised of nine chapters, each of which profiles a young person, four of whom are women and five of whom are males. Their lives are intertwined, and Djebar draws attention to the relationships between women and men against the background of the revolution. Some of the characters are passionately committed to the war for liberation while others betray their people. Four of the women are briefly sketched here because more than the other characters, they emerge as heroines through displays of resistance to the French colonial authorities (Salhi 206).

Cherifa is an attractive young woman, married to a man named Youssef who is involved with the liberation army. She learns that the French authorities have been informed of his nationalist loyalties. In a dangerous act of revolt, she leaves their home and ventures across town to inform him. Her commitment to the revolutionary cause is stronger than her fear of discovery or danger to herself as a woman unescorted in public. Secretly she wants herself and her husband to join the rebellion in the mountains but is unable to tell him. Youssef goes alone while she remains at home.

Another couple, Lila and Ali, experience tensions related to the revolution. Lila has not healed emotionally from the loss of her baby. Like Cherifa, she is left alone and thinks her husband has abandoned her. She becomes friendly with Cherifa. She also attempts to escape from confinement and is arrested. In prison she meets Salima who has been interrogated and tortured because she belongs to the national Liberation Front. Like many Algerian women during the Revolution, she passed information between the rebels and their families and eventually Lila and Salima become heroines of the revolution (Salhi 206). None of the women that are arrested give information to the police. The female characters exhibit political commitment to free their people as well as to free themselves from patriarchy and confinement. They take risks and surrender themselves to the struggle as a testimony to their strength and courage.

CONCLUSION

In sum, *Fantasia: An Algerian Cavalcade* and *A Sister to Scheherazade* are major works of the *Algerian Quartet* that constitute Djebar's autobiography. They represent her talent at a mature stage of her writing career that began in

1957 and are connected by themes of women's resistance during the Algerian revolution as well as the struggle to free themselves from seclusion and patriarchal tyranny.

In addition, an important aspect of Djebar's legacy is the revisionist stance that motivates and pervades her literature as she pays tribute to women's heroism in *Fantasia* as historical fiction. *A Sister to Scherherazade*, heightens themes of sisterhood, women's identities and subversion of patriarchy. Taken together, intertextual relationships emerge that foreground the importance of feminist expression as a message from the author that connects to both novels.

Children of the New World presents young people that experience tensions over gender roles and who are deeply affected by Algeria's War of Independence from 1954 to 1962. As part of her legacy, Djebar develops her characters to provide insightful portraiture of their humanity as well as their vulnerability to human frailty. What is exemplary in *Children of the New World* is the resilience of the young women, their political consciousness and courage.

Finally, Assia Djebar's works are to be treasured because they demonstrate her commitment to foreground Algerian women's identities that were silenced by their omission from French colonial history. In recovering women's stories, she has pulled aside the veil of ignorance, misrepresentation, and distorted historical accounts that are written from a male perspective by French officials.

Djebar's literature is an authentic replication of women's experiences because she interviewed them, and wove their stories into her literature with passion, feminist commitment and creative artistry. Assia Djebar's oeuvre is emblematic of African women's talent, and insight into the human condition that provides the creative spark to craft great literature. Djebar's greatest legacy is her immense contribution to world literature that celebrates women's intrinsic value as human beings.

WORKS CITED

Aidoo, Ama Ata. *Changes, A Love Story.* New York: The Feminist Press. 1993, Print.
Andrade, Susan Z. *The Nation Writ Small: African Fictions and Feminisms, 1958–1988.* Durham and London: Duke University Press. 2011. Print.
Arndt, Susan. T*he Dynamics of African Feminism: Defining and Classifying African Feminist Literatures.* Trenton, NJ: Africa World Press. 2002. Print.
Atta Sefi. *Everything Good Will Come*. Massachusetts: Interlink Books, 2004. Print.
Ba, Mariama. *So Long a Letter. A Novel.* London: Virago. 1981. Print.
Baume, Maia de la. "Assia Djebar, the Novelist Who Wrote About Oppression of Arab Women, Dies at 78." *New York Times*. Feb. 13, 2015. Print.

Cooke, Miriam. "Telling Their Lives: A Hundred Years of Arab Women's Writings." *World Literature Today*, Vol. 6, No. 2, Literatures of the Middle East: A Fertile Crescent (Spring 1986): 212–216. Print.

Chronology, Assia Djebar, *World Literature Today*, Vol. 70, Assia Djebar: Neustadt International Prize for Literature, Autumn, 1996: 800. Print.

Danticatt, Edwidge. "Children of the Sea." *Krik Krak*. New York: Vintage Books. 1995. Print.

Djebar, Assia. *Children of the New World: A Novel of the Algerian War*. Trans. Marjolijn de Jager. New York: Feminist Press. 2005. Print.

———. *Fantasia: An Algerian* Cavalcade. Trans. Dorothy Blair. Portsmoth. NH: Heinemann, 1993. Print.

———. *A Sister to Scheherazade*. Trans. Dorothy Blair. Portsmouth. NH: Heinemann. 1993. Print.

———. "There is No Exile." *Women Writing Africa*. Ed. Fatima Sadique, Amira Nowaira, Azza El Kholy and Moha Ennaji. New York: Feminist Press. 2009. Print.

Donadey, Anne. *Recasting Post-Colonialism: Women Writing Between Worlds*. Portsmouth: Heinemann. 2001. Print.

Ghaussy, Sohela. "A Stepmother Tongue: 'Feminine Writing' in Assia Djebar's *Fantasia: An Algerian Cavalcade*." *World Literature Today*, Vol. 68, No. 3 (Summer, 1994): 457–462. Print.

Gracki, Katherine. "Writing Violence and the Violence of Writing in Assia Djebar's Algerian Quartet." *World Literature Today*, Vol. 70. No. 4. Assia Djebar: Neustadt International prize for Literature (Autumn 1996): 835–843. Print.

Hiddleston, Jane. *Assia Djebar: Out of Algeria*. Liverpool: Liverpool University Press. 2006. Print.

Kabbani, Rana. "Fragments from a Bittersweet Mosaic." *Third World Quarterly*, Vol. 12, No. 2 (April 1990): 149–150. Print.

Mortimer, Mildred. *Journeys Through the French African Novel*. Portsmouth: James Curry. 1990. Print.

Nfa-Abbenyi. Juliana Makuchi. "African Women's Writing as a Weapon." *Gender in African Women's Writing: Identity, Sexuality and Difference*. Bloomington: Indiana University Press. 1997. Print.

Saadawi, Nawal El. *Woman at Point Zero*. London. 1975. Print.

Salhi Smail, Zahia. "Assia Djebar." *Women Writing Africa*. Ed. Fatima Sadique, Amira Nowaira, Azza El Kholy and Moha Ennaji. New York: Feminist Press. 2009. Print.

———. *Politics, Poetics and the Algerian Novel*. New York: Edwin Mellen Press. 1999. Print.

PART 4

Confronting Containment with Resistance and Freedom

Chapter 14

From Passivity to Defiance

The Portrayal of Women in Yvonne Vera's Novels

Blessing Diala-Ogamba

INTRODUCTION

Notable and prolific Zimbabwean female writer, Yvonne Vera, employs her writing to challenge the negative portrayal of women in African literature. She was born in 1964 in Bulawayo, Zimbabwe. After completing high school, she moved to Canada where she got her doctorate in English from York University in Toronto, Canada. She has written several short stories and five novels. Her novels are: *Nehanda* (1993), *Without a Name* (2000), *Under the Tongue* (2000), *Butterfly Burning* (1998), *The Stone Virgin* (2002). Vera was still on her sixth novel when she became sick with meningitis and died in April 2005 in Canada. Her novel *Nehanda* deals with the uprising against the colonial rule while *The Stone Virgins* focuses on the issues of pre- and post-independence periods in Zimbabwe. The focus of this chapter would be on three of her novels: *Without a Name* (WAN), *Under the Tongue* (UTT), and *Butterfly Burning* (BB). These novels are used to show how Vera astonishingly exposes the atrocities committed against women, in war-torn Zimbabwe, using her unique narrative technique as disguise. Yvonne Vera in her writings treads a dangerous path. It is against the norms of her tradition to speak publicly about rape, incest, abortion, and violence against women. These atrocities are committed under the pressure of war, chaos, loneliness, emotional and physical torture, oppression, and silence. Ravaged by the war,

Zimbabwe gains independence in 1980; patriarchy continues with blatant oppression through internal conflicts and different forms of violence. Since citizens are put to death by hanging for speaking against the colonial government, they go about their business without saying anything in order to remain alive. As in the early portrayal of women by some African writers such as Chinua Achebe and Flora Nwapa, the women in Zimbabwe do not have the opportunity to complain or express themselves even when they are right. Vera, therefore, uses her works to expose the negative treatment of women in her society, by bringing them out from passivity in *Without a Name*, to defiance in *Butterfly Burning*. This chapter, therefore, exposes how Yvonne Vera uses her legacy as a feminist, and her awareness to empower women to rebel and protest the inhuman treatment meted against them. The chapter also argues that it is only through rebelliousness that the women rescue themselves from patriarchal oppression and gain the freedom that they truly deserve.

The committed author employs her feminist stance to stoke awareness and empower her protagonists who transcend from their passive state to defiance and freedom. Baruch and Serrano are of the view that:

> Feminism has come to the realization that the oppression of women does not lie solely in the institutions of the society, the social and economic structure. It now recognizes that something hidden fuels this structure, the unseen and often unspoken but powerful feelings of the unconscious, the entire apparatus of what is called the symbolic order, that is the language, values, myths, images, and stereotypes that influence and are influenced by our psychological life. (11)

Vera presents her protagonist, Mazvita in her novel *Without a Name*, as she leaves her home in Mhondoro after being raped by a stranger who happens to be a soldier. Mazvita is determined to change her situation and forget her past, therefore she moves to Kadoma where she works briefly. Nyenyedi tries to discourage her from going to the city as he plans to take her back to see her parents, but she rejects the proposition and explains that it is better to head to the city, "I cannot live here. We must go to the city and live there. I don't know if we are safe even in this place. The war is everywhere. We must go to the city. It is said there is no war there. Freedom has already arrived" (WAN 30). While people in the land are awfully scared, the city dwellers have no fears in their eyes, Nyenyedi is attached to the land and feels more comfortable within this environment. He tries to convince Mazvita to stay because he loves the land. Besides, he sees the city, Harare, as "a strange unwelcoming place . . . everyone carries a knife there" (30–31). Nyenyedzi is not afraid of the war but fails to tell Mazvita that he is afraid of change, and of losing her in the big city of Harare. He prefers the village where he can exercise superior power and pressure her to do his bidding. Mazvita is able to resist his patriarchal control and insists on seeing this new place with the hope that it will help her unburden her fears and forget her past. She has the awareness to exercise her rights of moving to the city to gain freedom without restrictions. Nutsukpo Fafa observes that "For the African woman, self-awareness is the key to the objective viewing of her choices, which inevitably leads to her physical, social and emotional development and her subsequent emancipation from inequality and male domination" (168).

THE BURDEN OF FREEDOM

On getting to Harare, she observes that freedom meant different things to different people. Freedom is a mask, and everybody wears his or her own comfortably. People bleach their skin from dark to light complexion using Ambi Cream. Their faces are so bleached that they hardly recognize one another. "The people walked the streets without any faces, invisible, like ghosts. Was it a surprise then that they could not recognize one another? Ancestors dare not recognize them" (33). The effect of Ambi Cream makes them happy as they disguise themselves, forget their sordid past, and look forward to a better future. Men have Afro hairstyles while women purchase prepared Afro wigs and assert their independence with men. These men and women move about freely without fear. This is the kind of freedom and disguise Mazvita craves. She discovers that "In Harare, it was best to sell your soul to the first and easiest bidder. In this one case of Ambi Generation at least one received a permanent mark for the exchange, an elaborate transformation" (33). This transformation is also seen in Ayi Kwei Armah's *Fragments* where people with successfully bleached skins are admired. As Mazvita plans on how to integrate herself in this lively city, she hears the whispered words of the stranger who raped her and tries to block the words with silence in her body:

> The silence was a quietness in her body, a deafness to the whispering that escaped from the lips of the stranger. He had claimed her, told her that she could not hide the things of her body, that she must bring a calabash of water within her arms, and he would drink ... She must offer him water with cupped hands. She must kneel so that he could drink. (34)

This silence she tries to muster blocks her feelings, but she remembers her name—Mazvita. "She hated the land that pressed beneath her back as the man lay impatiently above her, into her, past her" (37). Mazvita hates both the land she is raped on, and the oppression that comes with the servitude position she is placed on, thus her determination to change things and take control of her body. Bammer notes that "our bodies have been the nexus of the spheres of reproduction and production (as well as the) interlocking systems of economic and sexual exploitation within patriarchal culture" (153). Mazvita rejects the oppression so she can gain back her sanity.

Reflecting on her experiences, Mazvita's ambition increases; therefore, she prepares to start afresh. She seeks freedom from war, working for foreigners, fighting over land, and especially from fear. As she moves like everyone else, Mazvita meets Joel who gives her a ride on his bicycle: "In the city there were no greetings, preliminaries, or rituals to courtship . . . there was no discussion, no agreement, no proposal. They just met and stayed together" (56–58). Mazvita and Joel live together without knowing anything about each other. Staying together without questions keeps the relationship fresh because no one wants to reflect on the past.

The men work in the city and leave their wives in the countryside to work on the farms. This is a way of oppressing the women, but the men claim that the city is not a place for women because of its crime rate. It is also believed that a woman from the city is no good thus stereotyping city women. According to the sexist discussion on the bus: "If you marry a woman from the city you will have made a fire and sat on it. She will even tell you to cook. She will ask you to help unbutton her bra . . . I prefer a woman whose breasts are true and waiting" (61–62). These claims are borne out of patriarchal conceptions and stereotypes that Vera is fighting fiercely against. The men are chauvinists and want to make sure that women are kept "in their places" to avoid competition. Veit-Wild observes that:

> In the post-independence era inveterate patriarchal attitudes flourished again, female ex-combatants were advised by government media campaigns to return to traditional family roles, and the uncompliant were subjected to blatant intimidation such as the notorious "Operation Clean Up" of December 1983, in which unattended women were randomly rounded up from the public streets and automatically detained on charges of prostitution. (173)

The arrests are all patriarchal schemes to cow the women down, but Mazvita is not bothered. She continues her pursuit of freedom as she plans to identify herself in this vibrant city. Before she can successfully do this, she needs to shed the reservations of timid village life and quickly adjust to city life. She also plans to get a job, because for her, that is another source of freedom. Mazvita cries as a sign of cleansing and releases herself from the silence that engulfed her as a protection. She finds out that she is pregnant but quickly rejects the baby because that was not part of her arrangement with Joel. As she envisages, Joel does not want the baby and insists that Mazvita leaves. The baby arrives but Mazvita has no name for the baby. She maintains that:

> A name could not be given to a child just like that. A name is for calling a child into the world, for acceptance, for grace. A name binds a mother to her child. A name is for waiting, for release, an embrace precious and permanent, a promise to growing life. She has no promises to offer this child. . . . The child grew in a silence with no name. Mazvita could not name the silence. (85)

Knowing that the baby would deter her from achieving her goal and impede her freedom, she decides to strangle the baby using Joel's necktie. A similar infanticide is documented in Toni Morrison's *Beloved* when Sethe kills her child as a way of protecting her from slavery. Reginald Watson sees this act as a "love murder committed by Sethe, who kills her newborn child to keep it out of the hands of slave catchers . . . She deconstructs motherhood by violating the mood and ethical standards that surround the concept" (157). In the same way, Mazvita violates the ethics of motherhood by killing her child in order to be free. She blindfolds the baby and carries her on her back and takes a bus to her hometown Mubaira, where she started her journey. She is indifferent, blind to pain and suffering with the baby on her back. She gets to Mubaira to bury the child without letting anyone know and realizes that "If she has no fears, she could begin here, without a name. It is cumbersome to have a name. It is an anchor. It brings figures to her memory. It recalls this place to her, which, earlier, she has chosen to forget" (WAN 115).

THE HEALING SILENCE

Mazvita takes an extreme measure that portrays her as a tortured soul with no feelings. She is indirectly fighting against the patriarchal society that keeps her down, having been raped and abandoned by her partner. The baby is an unplanned burden she does not wish to endure alone; however, she decides to do away with it, but the secret of killing her baby is a bigger burden that she would have to endure.

Just as Mazvita uses her zeal and determination to liberate herself from the shackles of patriarchy, the protagonist in *Under the Tongue*, Zhizha, finds the courage to express her pain over her sordid violation by her father. The events in this novel are relayed mainly from her point of view. As a child, Zhizha understands that it is wrong for her father to rape her but does not know who to confide in, because of the consequences. She loses her voice because of the shock. This stifles her cry for help as no one hears her. She laments:

> I cry but my cry meets silence. My voice has lost the promises of day. I hear my voice fall like a torrent down into my stomach. My voice meets rock, meets water, grows silent and dead . . . A woman must speak the beauties and the

sorrows of the heart, she must dream a celebration. A woman must not forget, she must not bury her sorrow and her dreams. (UTT 131)

Zhizha remembers her grandmother's words to "choose words not silence" but does not understand what is happening to her. As she sees the "wetness, mucus and blood" between her legs, she thinks she is dying thus she says, "Father . . . between my legs . . . He put blood between my legs" (UTT 228). Hearing her cry makes her happy because she knows she would soon be rescued. She could not tell her grandfather because, "it is death when such things are told" (229). She is not sure if she should tell her grandmother, so she has to wait until morning to tell her mother who takes a drastic action by killing her father. Her mother Runyararo is sent to prison without the consideration that she is fighting for her daughter. With her mother's imprisonment, Zhizha lives under the protection of her grandparents without knowing exactly what happened to her parents. Sometimes, she reminisces and scathing memories flood in like a raging torrent. It is only at the end of the war, when soldiers are coming back and those held in prison are released that her mother reunites with her. Runyararo, not bothered about her action and the consequences, is satisfied that she has done the best thing under the circumstances, since the crime of incest is one of those things that cannot be discussed especially by women. She breaks her silence with a drastic action believing that "a word does not rot unless it is carried in the mouth for too long, under the tongue" (231). Zhizha also breaks her fear and silence by revealing the rape to her mother.

Muroyiwa, Zhizha's father, works in the mines. He does not like the darkness in the mines but continues to work there for lack of a better choice. He is only free when he returns to the surface of the earth. The mine owners prefer people who come from outside the mine location to work for them because they usually accept meager salaries and work longer hours without complaining. It is while in the mountains that he meets and marries Runyararo though her parents did not quite like him because of the way he reasons. Runyararo speaks in a quiet and sorrowful ululation, because her husband taught her to keep silent since she is not a man. A woman must learn to keep silent (152). Muroyiwa, like his male counterparts, tries to enforce the patriarchal law of keeping the women down without realizing that a woman's cry, action, and tears are loaded with a lot of meaning, sometimes more meaning than words can express. We are told that, "grandmother's song finds the world where women gather. It is a place watered with tears. It is a place of remembrance. When the tears have become a river, morning will arrive even in such a place. The river will become a tongue. Under the tongue are hidden voices. Under the tongue is a healing silence" (UTT 163). This affirms that the patriarchal pressure of using traditional laws to determine the role of women in society does not last too long, as women can always revolt.

Toward the end of the novel, the women are shown to be excited in anticipation of the return of the men from war. They have "a new gaiety in their speech and their motions because something they thought had vanished had returned" (221). The men and women who fought in the war come home together. The women have new names which the past did not echo. They are shown to be happy and laugh loud because they share secrets with the men they went to war with, while the women at home are excited for surviving the wait and end of the war. The end of the war is a sign of hope and new prospects. "The cease-fire meant that fear would be turned to celebration . . . a new taste to joy, a new sound to dream . . . Something not yet known, to be almost, felt. A touch. The cease-fire had brought them a burst of hope" (222). The women are happy that they can relate to the men they fought with. The women expect this kind of relationship, collaboration, and recognition to forge a better society. This relationship gives them a sense of self, knowing that they are contributing members of the society.

By 1980, women had started plotting and devising their own ways of perception. They end their loneliness by simply breaking mirrors or glasses in public places. This act gives them the courage to move on with life without fear. "Breaking mirrors in public places became a necessary ritual of abandon. Where mirrors could not be found empty bottles were broken to bring good fortune. There was something unfathomable in this easy act, courageous even. The sound and sight of breaking glass brought sharp edges to existence" (233). The end of the war brings hope, freedom, and courage for women.

This excitement, happiness, and hope for a brighter future takes us to the next level where we are confronted with Phephelaphi, the main character in *Butterfly Burning* who destroys herself in the presence of her estranged lover. *Butterfly Burning* is set in the city of Bulawayo and characterized by poverty-stricken people who toil and suffer from day to day as they eke out a living. At the end of the day, the men drown their sorrows by drinking, dancing, and listening to *kwela* music, pretending to be happy. We find out that:

> The work is not their own: it is summoned. The time is not Theirs: It is seized. The ordeal is their own. They work again and again, and in unguarded moments of hunger and surprise, they mistake their fate for fortune. As for healing, they have Music, its curing harmony as sudden as it is sustained . . . they call it Kwela. (BB 5)

People work and go home unnoticed. They lean on the walls and are full of lies pretending to be happy in the midst of their sufferings. The lies are to disguise the fact that they are suffering, and this keeps life moving, especially when they end their day dancing to the rhythm of Kwela music. The movement and sufferings of the characters here are comparable to the poverty-stricken characters in Alex La Guma's *A Walk in the Night*, who move from place to place, most of the time aimlessly, eking out a living. The men who fight against the white status quo are put in prison and are later hanged. Their bodies are left on the tress where they are hanged for birds to scavenge. Their wives are not allowed to touch them before burial and they are forced to keep anything they know about their dead relatives secret. They call the dead new names and change their children's names thus making them lose their identities and birth history. Richard Taylor observes that, "identity represents an evolutionary articulation of personal capacities, value identification and . . . plans, ideals, expectations, and opportunity" (202). Losing their original value identification to create a new one helps the children to start a new life without remembering their sordid past experiences. The children in this community are also seen to be very poor because they wear tattered clothes and play with make-shift toys such as using pawpaw straws as flutes, empty bottles to make musical instrument, staying under skeleton of umbrella to pretend that it is raining. Pretense is the order of the day for both young and old, especially for women who bear the burden of keeping secrets. It is amidst this chaos that Phephelaphi meets Fumbatha while he is resting by the Umgazana river and she swims towards him. They are both strangers to one another but "he wanted her like the land beneath his feet from which birth had severed him" (BB 28–29). Phephelaphi tells him that her mother gave her the name because "she did not know where to seek refuge when I was born. She slept anywhere. She had no food in her stomach, but her child had to sleep under some shelter. She had hard times" (20–30).

Fumbatha does not want to think about what Phephelaphi is telling him, all he wants is to have her. He is also used to the "chameleon quality that women had with names. A woman could offer a name as a pronouncement of her contempt . . . the name confirmed her suspicion of betrayal, revealed her entire struggle with time. She could wear a name easily like a dress and each moment you looked at her she was checking how well the name fits" (30). Phephelaphi has been staying with Zandile her supposed mother's friend since her mother, Gertrude died. She decides to move in with Fumbatha at Sidojiwe E 2, where he lives. Zandile is happy to see her move because they have been sharing a room with Boyidi, her boyfriend. Since she found Boyidi, Zandile has stopped soliciting for men because she wants a man she could call her own.

Phephelaphi and Fumbatha live happily together but she is a restless soul who is searching for identity and freedom through education. She realizes that education is the only way to achieve her freedom. She therefore determines to empower herself by going to nursing school to train as a nurse. Richard Shaul opines that education enables women to "look critically at the social situation in which they find themselves . . . take the initiative in acting to transform the society that has denied them various opportunities of participation (9). Fumbatha is uncomfortable with the idea because he feels he would lose her. He goes to work, building houses for the whites while Phephelaphi stays at home. He sees it as his responsibility to take care of her and believes that the money he makes is enough for both of them. He sometimes travels for days at a time for his job, so at night, Phephelaphi seizes this opportunity to visit Deliwe, a woman who runs her own shebeen. Her first meeting with Deliwe is at the market where she is laughing at women who sell vegetable, as she sees the women as the laziest women in Africa. Africa for her is Sidojiwe E 2. Phephelaphi immediately connects to Deliwe. Phephelaphi is confronted with a large crowd of men who are drinking alcohol and listening to the rhythm of Kwela music. She is drowned by the music and realizes why Fumbatha does not like Deliwe. He claims that Deliwe makes young men forget about their problems when they go to her shebeen.

Deliwe has had several encounters with the law but that has not deterred her from her business. She has been jailed for selling alcohol in a dwelling place and received several beatings in jail which caused her deafness in the right ear, but she does not tell anybody about it. "She threw her head back and laughed like a madwoman when she was told that this square shelter with its falling roof, its colorless weak walls, and nowhere to make love to a man, was a house" (60). She watches through the window often to see when the police would come to raid her house for evidence of selling alcohol.

Phephelahi is happy whenever Fumbatha travels because she is free to do as she pleases and not caged in. She applies for nursing and becomes the first black woman to be admitted for training. She later finds out that she is pregnant but does not tell Fumbatha. She is highly upset and aborts the child herself to avoid anything stopping her from acquiring the education that would make her independent. She realizes that "a woman's right to control her own body encompasses endless new meanings in feminism, including the right to plan one's own reproductivity" (English 341). Phephelaphi does not want anything to stifle her ambition, thus she makes the decision to abort the child. "Her decision . . . is an outright rejection of male centered values as represented by the oppressive concepts of motherhood and the private sphere and serves as a rebellious and subversive action to take control of her own body and her destiny" (Guzman 319). Fumbatha finds out about the abortion and starts keeping away from the house. Most of the time, he sleeps with Deliwe who has now seduced him. On becoming pregnant a second time, Phephelaphi chooses to die instead of living an unfulfilled and miserable life. She kills herself to spite the patriarchy that has vowed to subdue her through pregnancy. This killing is emblematic of what Firdaus does in Saadawi's *Woman at Point Zero* where killing symbolizes the demise of patriarchy.

Yvonne Vera uses her awareness and feminist stance to empower women to speak out and reach for any goal they set for themselves. This is hinged on the fact that women are denied opportunities that would make them equal to men, Simone de Beauvoir asserts that "Humanity is male and man defines the woman . . . she is the incidental, the inessential as opposed to the essential. He is the subject, he is the Absolute, she is Other" (16). By exposing the sordid details of patriarchal oppression, rape, and abuse in her society, Vera toes the same line as Bressler who opines that "Feminism's goal is to change this degrading view of women so that all women will realize that woman is not a 'non-significant other,' but that instead each woman is a valuable person possessing the same privileges and rights as every man" (103).

DISMANTLING THE STANDARD FORM

Apart from using her feminist stance as legacy to empower her protagonist, Vera exposes the violent and degrading view of women by patriarchy through her unique narrative technique. The way she exposes the sordid treatment of women makes her a non-conformist, as she dares to tread the grounds that most male writers would not. She does this by deviating from the standard rules of a novel in terms of form and structure. According to Wellek and Warren, the structure of a novel is synonymous with pattern or organization (216), but Vera does not use the "regular" set pattern in her works. A writer reserves the right to choose his or her materials and ways of shaping these materials into artistic object in relation to the effect the writer wants to produce in his or her readers. Alan Swingewood observes that the writer does not only strive "to capture the plenitude of human experience, its ambiguity and openness, but actually depicts man's struggle to assimilate the social, historical and natural world to his human process" (264). Vera chooses her materials the way she deems fit because she realizes that she can use and shape them in a way to bring out the desired effect from her readers as evidenced in her works.

Some of the narrative techniques Vera employs in her works are necessary to be highlighted here. She starts her novels by giving us cinematic descriptions of places, people, atmosphere, or events. She uses poetic devices in her descriptions of scenes and events purposely as a disguise, and sometimes makes the protagonist the narrator so that readers can feel the impact of her sufferings. Vera's rigmaroles and difficult narrative style, though frustrating, glues the reader to the story, and helps to expose the themes and her intended meanings in her works. In her novel *Without a Name,* she starts with: "Heat mauled the upturned faces. The bus fierce red. Skin turned a violent mauve. That is how the day was. The faces jostled and hurried, surrounding the bus with shimmering voices" (5). *Under the Tongue* begins as follows: "A tongue which no longer lives, no longer weeps. It is buried beneath the rock. My tongue is a river. My tongue is heavy with sleeping" (122). Just as in the first two, *Butterfly Burning*, also poetic with the same meandering style starts as follows: "There is a pause. An expectation. They play a refrain on hand made guitars; lovers with tender shoulders and strong fists and cold embraces" (3). The novel ends with two words "At midnight" (151). These poetic forms, fragments, phrases and incomplete thoughts used all over her novels are not regarded as flaws or incomplete sentences, rather they are the writer's unique style showing her deviation from the standard norms. Even the incest committed by Zhizha's father is beautifully crafted, but the reader does not find out about it until towards the end of the novel. Vera uses ellipsis to heighten our imaginations and to buttress the fact that the story is told from a child's point of view.

The novels are full of images and metaphors which are used to expose the sufferings and violent scenarios in the texts. We see images of "violent red, pain, silence, tears, death" which symbolize sufferings, hopelessness, and struggle in the three novels (WAN 50). Vera's works are characterized by poor people who are mostly blacks which indicates how they suffered when the country was colonized. The men in *Butterfly Burning* work endlessly and drown themselves in kwela music and drinks, pretending to be happy (5). In *Without a Name*, Mazvita realizes while in Harare that, "It was nothing to see a woman with a blind stare on her face, with a baby fixed spidery on her back. It was nothing to be sorrowful" (WAN 43). Apart from their dwelling places, sediments from the factory run by the white status quo empty into the Umgaza River, contaminating the only source of water for the poor. Here, images of dirt, stench, squalor surround the realities of life where the children play (BB 20). This reflects colonization, and abject poverty is shown to be very intense here, which is shown with no sign of rescue coming their way.

CONCLUSION

There can be no doubt that in Vera's works there is a marked progression from docility to extreme action and communication in the process of rebelling against patriarchy, as more women who show positive awareness and empowerment such as Getrude, Zandile, and Deliwe are introduced in *Butterfly Burning*. Getrude for example, carries her baby on her back on her dates with men. She is indirectly telling the men that her family comes first, and that they should either accept her and her baby or leave. This attitude teaches women like Zandile, Phephelaphi, and Mazvita that they should not have to destroy or abandon their children in order to live a fulfilled life. Her attitude depicts her assertiveness and independence. She is determined to call the shots and not to be dictated to, by men who are humans like her. Deliwe runs her own shebeen and cannot be stopped by the law as she finds a way of avoiding them when they storm her place. Her determination proves that she can own and maintain her business despite her molestation at the hands of the police. Zandile is the actual birth mother of Phephelaphi but gives her away to Getrude because she does not want inhibitions in the process of attaining freedom.

The commercial sex workers who solicit for men at night are not left out in this process of awareness. We are told these women have no resevatiun about voicing anything on their minds. They also detest misunderstandings, arguments, and apologies. Obviously enjoying their freedom, the female residents of Sidojiwe E2 in *Butterfly Burning* bond and encourage one another in this emancipation process. Zhizha's grandmother encourages women to speak their mind. Zandile takes her cosmetics to sell to women in Sidojiwe E2 so they can look beautiful and comely. Phephelaphi believes the real woman is one who loves herself, not the one taken care of by a man. The actions of some of the women are taken to extreme and are comparable to the progressive women in Flora Nwapa's *Women are Different* and *One is Enough*, Abla in Farah's *From a Crooked Rib* and Beatrice in Achebe's *Anthills of the Savannah*. The women's actions indicate that they are delighted in taking control of their lives.

Yvonne Vera's novels are suspenseful from beginning to the end. She uses this style to make sure that her characters successfully achieve the recognition they deserve and reject inferiority status imposed on them as women. Her style is a disguise to avoid getting into trouble with the law while working hard to empower the women. She also does not want her works to be censored before her readers get the information she is disseminating. Her main characters who are driven into silence at the beginning of the novels found their voices at the end through Vera's tenacity and persuasion. They realize that it is only when this "silence" is spoken that attention can be drawn to the multitude of problems in Zimbabwe. Vera therefore uses her style to draw the required attention as she breaks the rules of structure and form of a novel, rules of patriarchy and rigid tradition, as she exposes the absurdity in her country, thus breaking the silence to rebel against injustice like her female characters. Yvonne Vera makes her characters convincing, stubborn, and resolute because that is what the society has made of them. Phephelaphi's death is an indication that women will continue to rebel and find alternative ways to freedom if the rigid laws are not changed. Yvonne Vera has freely transformed her imagination in her works using her legacy as a feminist and her unique narrative style, thereby creating the desired artistic effect on her readers wherever they may be. She understands that for the African woman to change her position to a more "significant other," she needs to assert her womanhood with determination, strength, and courage. This is the path that Mazvita, Zhizha and Phephelaphi take to successfully rebel against patriarchal authority and identify themselves positively as effectual members of society.

WORKS CITED

Achebe, Chinua. *Anthills of the Savannah*. New York: Anchor, 1978.
Armah, Ayi Kwei. *Fragments*. London: Heinemann, 1970.
Bammer, Angelika. "Women and Revolution: Their Theories, Our Experiences." *Literature and Ideology*. Ed. Lewis Bury. Louisburg, PA: Bucknell University Press, 1982.
Baruch, Elaine Hoffman and Lucienne J. Serrano. *Women Analyze Women*. New York: New York University, 1988.
Beauvoir, de Simone. *The Second Sex*. New York: Vintage Books, 1974.
Bressler, C. *Literary Criticism: An Introduction to Theory and Practice*. Upper Saddle River, New Jersey: Prentice Hallm, 1994.
Eagleton, Terry. *Marxism and Literary Criticism*. London: Methuesen, 1997.
English, Deirdre. "The Fear That Feminism Will Free Men First." *Feminist Theory: A Reader*. Eds. Kolmer Wendy and Frances Bartkowski. Mountain View: Mayfield Publishing Co. 2000.
Farah, Nuruddin. *From a Crooked Rib*. London: Heinemann, 1970.
Guzman, Marlene De La Cruz. "Signifying Women's Oppression in Zimbabwe: Feminist Theory in Yvonne Vera's *Butterfly Burning*." *A History of Africana Women's Literature*. Ed. Rose Mezu. Baltimore: Black Academy Press, 2004: 305–325.
La Guma, Alex. *A Walk in the Night*. London: Heinemann, 1970.
Morrison, Toni. *Beloved*. New York: Plume, 1987.
Nutsukpo, Fafa. "Feminist Consciousness and Assertiveness in Ifeoma Okoye's *Behind the Clouds* and *Chimere*." *Nigerian Literature in English: Emerging Perspectives*. Ed. Onyemaechi Udumukwu. Port Harcourt: M&J Grand Orbit. 2007: 165–176.
Nwapa, Flora. *One is Enough*. Trenton, NJ: Africa World Press, 1992.
———. *Women are Different*. Enugu: Tana Press, 1986.
Shaul, Richard. "Foreward." *Pedagogy of the Oppressed*. Paulo Freire. Middlesex Penguin, 1972: 9–14.
Swingewood, A. *The Novel and Revolution*. London and Basing Stoke: Macmillan, 1975.

Taylor, Richard. "Black Youth and Psychosocial Development: A Conceptual Framework." *The Black Family: Essays and Studies*. Ed. Robert Staples. California: Wordsworth, 1986: 201–210.

Veit-Wild, Flora. "Creating a New Sociology: Women's Writing in Zimbabwe," *Journal of Commonwealth Literature*. 22, No. 1. (August, 1987): 173.

Watson, Reginald. "The Power of 'Milk' and Motherhood: Images of Deconstruction and Reconstruction in Toni Morrison's *Beloved* and Alice Walker's *The Third Life of Grande Copeland*." *CLA Journal,* Vol. XL viii, No 2. December, 2004.

Wellek, Rene and Austin Warren. *Theory of Literature*. Middlesex; Penguin, 1973.

Vera, Yvonne. *Butterfly Burning*. Harare: Farrar, Baobab Books,1998.

———. *Opening Spaces*. Portsmouth: Heinemann, 1999.

———. *Under the Tongue*. New York: Farrar, Straus, and Giroux, 2000.

———. *Without a Name*. New York: Farrar, Straus, and Giroux, 2000.

Chapter 15

The Buchi Emecheta Phenomenon

Austine Amanze Akpuda

INTRODUCTION

Florence Onyebuchi Emecheta, mainly known as "a revolutionary Nigerian writer," was essentially very forceful and determined in her dogged attack against socio-cultural and political forces that oppress women in Africa, she also took exception to female complicity and complacency with regard to repressive as well as retrogressive patriarchal institutions. Much as Emrcheta's first novel, *Second Class Citizen* was published in 1974, her writings together with those of other female writers were hardly acknowledged by male critics. As can be gleaned from Femi Ojo Ade's 1983 essay "Female Writers, Male Critics," the critical reception of the female authored text in Africa has always bordered on controversy. One can therefore appreciate the essence of Margaret Busby's thesis: "That Buchi Emecheta's work has been more successful than that of her fore sisters is a phenomenon that must be placed in context" (xv). This is especially because the patronage has never been automatic. For instance, despite recognizing that "a periodic re-evaluation of the African novel is necessary in order to develop a lively critical heritage as a support for its growth" or that "our attitudes to existing novels are constantly being affected by the publication of new ones" (7) and notwithstanding that the major issues deliberated in Dan Izevbaye's 1979 canonical essay, "Issues in the Reassessment of the African Novel," the story of the African by himself; portraits of man and society, on the governance of men as well as form and ideas in the novel are also what are discernible in Buchi Emecheta's first four novels, *In The Ditch* (1972), *Second-Class Citizen* (1975), *The Bride Price* (1976) and *The Slave Girl* (1977), none of these was mentioned in

Izevbaye's essay. Equally, that no African female author is mentioned in the twenty-five-page essay is a worrisome development. One cannot help but wonder: if from such near-critical oblivion Buchi Emecheta would move up in the scale of rating to a platform near that which Bernth Lindfors isolates as the High Canonicals, it then means that some literary critics must have done battles on Emecheta's behalf. Concerning how "some reputations have waxed or waned over time," Lindfors states that "chart two records such changes from 1976 to 1991" ("Accounting" 7). Outside what he notes about the decline and rise of reputations among male African authors, Lindfors' observations concerning the profiling of African women authors in the period between 1976 and 1991 is food for thought. According to him:

> Perhaps the most impressive upward mobility has been achieved by women writers, particularly Bessie Head, Buchi Emecheta and Ama Ata Aidoo. This may signal a growing interest worldwide in the literature produced by women. However, to date only Head has broken into the ranks of the High Canonicals, but if the current trends continue, Emecheta and Aidoo appear destined to join her somewhere up there in the near future. (7)

Part of that ascent in profile is what moved Emecheta from the rear in 1976 to number 16, eight steps lower than Bessie Head in 1991.

FROM THE DITCH TO THE SKIES

In contextualizing the Buchi Emecheta phenomenon, it is pertinent to highlight how four major variables contributed to such a profiling. The first is that before Buchi Emecheta broke into novelistic print, she had attracted attention to herself through her autobiographical writings in such periodicals as *African Weekly Review* and *New Statesman*. Similarly, from April 3, 1978, when her "Out of the Ditch and into Print" appeared in *West Africa* to November 1981 she literally became a household name on the pages of *West Africa,* the highly influential London based magazine. Another strong variable has to do with the profile of the publishing firms that printed Emecheta's novels. Some of these include the London based Allison and Busby which in 1975, 1976, 1977, 1979, 1982, and 1983 brought out six novels by Emecheta. Within the same period the New York–based George Braziller also printed Emecheta's second, third, fourth, fifth and sixth novels. The same George Braziller would in 1983 reprint Emecheta's *Double Yoke* and do the same with *The Rape of Shavi* in 1985 and *The Family (*another version of *Gwendoleen*) in 1990. When one adds that other London based publishers such as Barrier & Jenkens which issued her first novel in 1972, Collins and Heinemann had also published

Emecheta's adult novels alongside Macmillan and Oxford University Press which published her Juvenile novels between 1982 and 1986.

The visibility that Buchi Emecheta gained through her sociological essays and works-in-progress in the late 1960s and early 1970s coupled with the publication of her first five novels between 1972 and 1979, a remarkable feat, brought in its wake the first phase of the critical reception of her works. When one considers the quality and number of literary awards that Emecheta's works garnered in the first few years of her writing one can then justify the rationale for the interviews that she would be granted in the period between 1976 and 1982. For instance, her second novel, *Second Class Citizen*, fetched her in 1975 the Daughter of Mark Twain Award. Similarly, in 1978, her 1977 novel, *The Slave Girl* earned her the New Statesman/ Jock Campbell Award as well as the Best Black Writer in the world. While it lasted, Buchi Emecheta was the only female writer who won the £1,000 Jock Campbell/New Statesman Award. However, of the five writers, she is the one that seems to enjoy the nearest rating to Chinua Achebe's *Arrow of God*. For instance, while by August 26, 2017, Achebe's rating was a 3.80 average rating with 3,359 ratings, Emecheta's 3.74 average rating with 316 ratings can compete favorably with Derek Walcott's supposed high 4.50 average rating and 20 ratings or Wole Soyinka's 3.55 average rating and 323 ratings for *The Interpreters*. She beats Shiva Naipaul's *Fireflies* with a 3.72 average rating and 154 ratings (see "The Jock Campbell Prize"). In the reasoning of Chikwenye Okonjo Ogunyemi, "the first signs of male acknowledgment of women's contribution to Nigerian literature have been the literary prize Buchi Emecheta and the newcomer Ifeoma Okoye have won for their novels" (61). Through interviews granted her by *Africa Woman* (January 1976), *West Africa* (February 1978 and April 1978), *Punch* (Lagos, May 1979), *Opzij* (Amsterdam, September 1981), *The Leveller* (October 1981), *Centrepoint* (1981), *Happy Home* (March 1982) among others, it was easy to see that Emecheta had won recognition that was infectious. One major fall-out of the above critical exposure was the anthologization of an excerpt from *The Joys of Motherhood*, "A Man Needs Many Wives" in Charlotte Bruner (ed.) *Unwinding Threads: Writing by Women in Africa* (1983) which, in the testimony of James Currey "was planned from the start as a teaching anthology" (xxvii).

In view of the foregoing and especially the way the 1970s climaxed with the publication of Emecheta's 1979 novel, *The Joys of Motherhood*, it was not unexpected that the 1980s decade would be awash with a harvest of unprecedented critical attention on Emecheta's works. The 1980s decade which started with an April 1980 African Literature Association Conference paper by Femi Ojo-Ade titled "Buchi Emecheta: *Second-Class Citizen, Second-Sex, Slave*" and Marie Umeh's 1980 *Presence Africaine* essay "African Women in Transition in the Novels of Buchi Emecheta" was quite a huge pile by the end of the decade when essays like Helen Chukwuma's "Positivism and the Female Crisis: The Novels of Buchi Emecheta" (1989), among others, would be published. If a raison d'etre would be sought in accounting for this decade that produced Eustace Palmer's two very canonical essays, "The Feminine Point of view: A study of Buchi Emecheta's *The Joys of Motherhood"* and "A powerful Female Voice in the African Novel: Introducing the Novels of Buchi Emecheta," among other seminal essays and prominent chapters in the books focused on women's writings in Africa and the black world, we could rely on the critical opinions voiced by the quintet of Eldred Jones, Eustace Palmer, Charlotte Bruner, Ernest Emenyonu and Helen Chukwuma. In the Editorial to volume 13 of *African Literature Today (ALT)* and an issue aptly subtitled "Recent Trends in the Novel," Eldred Durosimi Jones asserts that in addressing the shortfalls recorded in *ALT 10* that *"ALT* 13 looks at the latest trends in the development of the African novel or at those aspects of the more established works which have hitherto received scant critical attention" (vii). Furthermore, as if to commemorate the coming-of-age of the Buchi Emecheta generation, Jones affirms without fear of contradiction that "one of the most significant trends in the development of the African novel in recent years is the emergence of a very powerful feminist streak—the rise into prominence of a number of highly accomplished and articulate women novelists like Buchi Emecheta, Mariama Ba and Rebeka Njau" (vii). The critical comments by Eustace Palmer, Charlotte Bruner, Ernest Emenyonu and Helen Chukwuma, among others, show that Jones's idea of "highly accomplished" is not an exaggeration. Any wonder then that for Eustace Palmer, "Emecheta shows great psychological insight in the penetration of her character's thoughts. She is particularly good at the presentation of the feminine psyche. Scarcely any other African novelist has succeeded in probing the female mind and displaying the female personality with such precision" (53). Given Palmer's reputation by 1983 one can appreciate the meaning of this type of endorsement after ten years of Emecheta's novelistic career.

In appreciating Emecheta's distinction, Charlotte H. Bruner recognizes that "Emecheta's life is a record of confidence gained after struggles with dislocation geographic and cultural; after misunderstanding with her traditional society and her conventional, egotistical husband, and after being put down by an ethnocentric and racist alien culture" (48). This profiling of the quintessential Emecheta, is, incidentally a metonymic representation of the portraitures she has beamed to the world in her novels. The realization that Emecheta is a symbol of the new Nigerian female-centered novel is one major reason Bruner insists that "her latest novels all concern the problems Nigerian women are beset by sociological and technological change" (49).

Helen Chukwuma isolates two major tendencies in Buchi Emecheta's novels. one of the instances is establishing that the "theme of economic exploitation and denial of opportunity of the female for the expressed benefit of the male is dominant in Emecheta's novels" ("Positivism" 3). Another is that a recurring aesthetic trend in her oeuvre is the "portrayal of female characters from the slave girl prototype to the career mother and single fulfilled woman" (Chukwuma "Positivism" 3). No doubt, this peculiar curve in her fiction has given a trademark quality to her writings.

A distinguishing feature of Ernest N. Emenyonu's 1988 study of Emecheta's novels is his emphasis on the axiom that "language is an important aspect of Emecheta's fiction" (77). Using three novels as reference points, Emenyonu insists that in *The Bride Price*, *The Slave*, and *Joys of Motherhood*, Emecheta's narrative technique is evident in her profuse use of the figurative language, omniscient comments and irony which she employs to set the mood and tone of the story as well as to define the theme and characters of the novel. In *The Bride Price* the awkward handling of language manifests Emecheta's amateurish beginnings. In *The Slave Girl* Emecheta demonstrates in her language usage the promise of artistic talent whose highest maturity and development are evident in *The Joys of Motherhood* (77).

The prominence that Emecheta gained through the first decade of her novelistic career must have been instrumental to her numbering among the few women invited to the second Stockholm conference for African female writers. Those that attended include Ama Ata Aidoo, Lauretta Ngcobo, and Miriam Tlali. It was at the Stockholm conference that Emecheta in exasperation about being pigeon holed as a feminist asserted that "if I am now a feminist, then I am an African feminist with a small "f" (cited in Ojo-Ade "Tiali" 64).

Without doubt, no study of the Buchi Emecheta phenomenon can dispense with the socio-cultural and literary structures that shaped and sharpened her creative imagination. It is possible to argue that there are no fewer than five major sources of influence on Buchi Emecheta's career as a Novelist. These include the medley between the Judeo-Christian ethos and traditional Igbo culture and its pattern of sexual politics; the familiarity with the structure of narratives woven by mothers and grandmothers and stories connecting the lives lived by highly accomplished, influential Igbo women long before the 1929 Aba women's war; the British complicity in slavery, racism and colonialism; and books—historical, sociological, and literary. For our purpose, it is very important we highlight and discuss how the above listed variables combined to provide the background and consciousness behind Buchi Emecheta's *The Slave Girl*, one of her several bildungsroman.

SOCIO-CULTURAL BACKGROUND OF *THE SLAVE GIRL*

For us to fully understand the triple bind of being an *ogbanje* (spirit child), girl child and orphaned girl in what is presented as an extremely insensitive patriarchal culture such as Ibuza of the early twentieth century, we need to reflect on the fact that despite the empowerment given women in the ancient world through the Hammurabic Code in Babylon (Oputa 6); the political structure in ancient Egypt that allowed the reign of Queens: or Sparta, where "women enjoyed near equality with men, mixing freely with them in public and in sports including joint wrestling between men and women . . . also women had a voice in politics and public affairs" (Oputa 7). The paradigm presented by ancient Israel seems to have merged with some aspects of Igbo culture, especially those relating to the disempowerment of the girl child or woman. Here, one has in mind what Chukwudifu Oputa notes about the retailing in ancient Israel of the expression "women, children and slaves" or its modification in "the male's morning prayer . . . Blessed art thou who has not made me a Gentile, a slave or a woman" (7) and how such a mindset contributed to the denigration of women. Despite the change in "the status of women . . . in modern Israel," Oputa laments how "a close affinity [seems to] exist between the conception of womanhood, the status of woman both in ancient Israel and many Nigerian village communities, especially the Igbos" (8). For illustrations, Oputa reflects that beyond the programmatic thrust of the Talmudic injunction: "it is written, a daughter is a vain treasure, to her father. From anxiety about her he does not sleep at night" (7).

Within the canvas of *The Slave Girl,* the foregoing seem to provide a guiding principle. In the wake of the death of their parents, Okolie resolves to sell off his only sister. Concerning the build-up to his damage of filial bond between him and Ojebeta, we read the following:

> Okolie's heart sank. Should he or should he not go ahead with his plan? But who wanted to be saddled with a little seven-year-old sister? And he did not want her living with Ute, because he did not like Eze. No, let her go to Ma Palagada, and he would collect some money from her. Ogbanje Ojebeta's fate was decided. She must be sold. (36)

At Ma Palagada's home, Ojebeta will become the fifth slave girl in the household. Many years after, even after Ojebeta was married to Jacob, the former "remained legally Palagada property" because "Okolie had finally confessed that he had actually sold his sister for eight pounds" (178). Concerning the ownership that Ojebeta herself readily acquiesces to: "I feel free in belonging to a new master from my own town Ibuza" (178); we are also reminded that it is the product of an amalgam of different cultural practices that cut through a long stretch of time. As the authorial narrator relays,"There was certainly a kind of eternal bond between husband and wife, a bond produced maybe by centuries of traditions, taboos, and, latterly, Christian dogma. Slave obey your master. Wife, honour your husband, who is your father, your head, your heart, your soul." (178)

Here, we are made to come to terms with the life of the average woman as a born slave who when not being owned or married off by her father, uncle, brothers and so on may be under constant threat of subscribing to the tradition of having another marriage arranged for her by characters such as Eze who had desired that Adim or perhaps any man who could cut off locks of her hair will by tradition become Ojebeta's husband. After all, as Ojebeta reminisces: "A girl was owned, in particular, by her father or someone in place of her father or her older brother, and then in general, by her group or homestead" (160).

Ironically, the real freedom of any girl or woman from Ibuza is only attained when she becomes a law breaker. Any wonder then that despite the supposed escape from the prison house of Ma Palagada at Otu Onitsha, Ojebeta painfully recalls that "no woman or girl in Ibuza was free, except those who committed the abominable sin of prostitution or those who have been completely cast off or rejected by their people for offending one custom or another" (160). For entrenching and contributing in expanding the institutionalizing of slavery in Igboland and elsewhere, the authorial narrator is frowning upon blatant complicity on the part of the British. She ends the novel with this moral: "So as Britain was emerging from war once more victorious and claiming to have stopped the slavery which she had helped to spread in all her black colonies, Ojebeta, now a woman of thirty-five, was changing masters" (184). No doubt, in the reasoning of the novelist and her narrator, nothing could be more laughable and ironical.

Even when the preceding may give the impression that the Igbo female had no unique features that granted her a profile in her community this is but one aspect of the total picture. In other words, despite the sense in which patriarchy is appropriated and demonized as a buzz word that assumes a talismanic hold on a somewhat disempowered reader, it is not altogether correct to subscribe to Florence Stratton's reading of Ma Palgada as one of the "active agents of patriarchy, perpetuating female enslavement possibly into eternity" (100). No doubt, this reading which is quite emblematic of several feminist interpretations of *The Slave Girl* tends to overlook the different acts— pre-patriarchy and otherwise—that women have adopted to imprison themselves and others. After all, as A.E. Afigbo has observed, "African women had an honored and recognized place in society which made it possible for the gifted ones amongst them to rise to positions of political, economic and social eminence from which they led and dominated not only their fellow women, but the common run of men" (23). It is this type of context that produced the super mama, Ma Palgada.

Talking about the Igbo, Afigbo notes that the Umuada "were particularly powerful and important. They were feared alike by the men folk and the women" (27). What he says about the significance of the women among the riverine and western Igbo, the setting of Emecheta's *The Slave Girl* gives us a peep into one major complex heritage of the Igbo woman between 1850 and 1950. Commenting on the Omu institution by 1885, *The Church Missionary Intelligence* records that it

> ... is not a merely honorary title, but carries with it its own duties and responsibilities. The Omu is the foundation of all honor to the women, as the Eze, or king, is the foundation of honor to the men in the country. She has the absolute control of the trade in which the women are engaged, and can stop and open as occasion requires. (cited in Ijoma 111–12)

For instance, regarding the political worth of the riverine/western Igbo woman as seen in the Omu Igili position, Afigbo remarks that beyond the creation of the "Omu (queen) as the female counterpart of the Obi (King)," the position of the Omu Igili "was one of the most elevated titles" within the riverine Igbo city State of Ossomari" (27). As Afigbo elaborates,

> the occupant of that title, usually a distinguished woman of wealth, intellect and character, reigned with the Obi as co-sovereign, taking responsibility largely for regulating women's affairs. Apart from being the chairwoman and spokesman of Ossomari mothers' council, she took responsibility for maintaining law and order in the market and for advising the Obi on state matters touching the interests of women. (27)

Allied to the foregoing is the martial involvement of the Omu Igili. In Afigbo's words, the Omu "played a leading military role. According to tradition, her war canoe led the Ossomari fleet into battle as she was believed to be the possessor and keeper of a particularly powerful charm which made her shield impenetrable to enemy arrows and could make Ossomari warriors invisible in battle" (27).

Invariably, as with "the Nri creation legend in which the first man Eri, and the first woman Adanma came down from heaven together" (Afigbo 40), there is a historical basis for recreating women of Ma Palgada's profile as we encounter in Emecheta's *The Slave Girl*. As "a huge market mammy" (*Slave* 66), Ma Palagada reminds one so much of some of the prominent women from the western and Delta Igbo who made a lot of money and wielded unimaginable influence economically and politically. Ma Palagada was described as "one of the richest Onitsha market women at the time" and being part of the coterie designated "the sophisticated, rich, fat mammy traders who formed the backbone of Onitsha market" (*Slave* 52) should be enough to warrant a historical enquiry such as Akachi Ezeigbo has done. As Buchi Emecheta reveals in an interview she granted Ezeigbo,

> The strong woman, Ma Palagada, was recreated in the image of the women my mother served. They called her Ma. My mother always said: Oge ayi bi na be Ma' (when we lived in Ma's house). The picture she painted of this woman was so memorable and vibrant that I had her in my imagination all the time until I recreated her in *The Slave Girl.* (cited in Ezeigbo II)

No doubt, if Buchi Emecheta's mother lived in Onitsha in the 1920s, she would have been familiar with the exploits of Omu Okwei. Felicia Ekejiuba reveals that "up till the 1920's, especially in Onitsha with its agriculturally productive hinterland, this new class of traders was naturally predominantly women since trading in most parts of Igboland was considered a woman's job. And it was the rich among these women who controlled the vast system of wholesale marketing and distribution of the Onitsha market until the economic depression of the 1930's which resulted in the influx of men in the distribution and retail trade" ("Merchant Queen" 213). When Chiago in *The Slave Girl* boasts that the extremely well-heeled and connected "market mammy," Ma Palagada is reputed to have "bought the sole right"(43) to market a variety of abada cloth called "*Ejekom be loya*" ("I have a date with a lawyer") (42) and "for the next four markets from those white UAC people" (43), one is reminded of the monopoly that the famous market queen, Omu Okwei once maintained on the Royal Niger Company, the parent of what became UAC between 1904 and 1918. As Felicia Ifeoma Ekejiuba confirms,

> By 1920, Okwei and one Madam Iyaji, an Igala woman, ranked as the most prominent of women merchants in Onitsha whose field of operation covered trade in palm produce and foodstuffs" retail business centered mainly on textiles, tobacco, hardware" and provisions bought from the trading firms. Okwei in particular became a buying agent for chiefs and influential men from the hinterland who depended solely on her taste in the selection of manufactured goods which they ordered from her through her servants. ("Omu Okwei" 98)

Later on "from 1926, Okwei became a money lender" (98) and according to Ekejiuba, because of her near Machiavellian approaches,

> Okwei's rate of interest on money lent to traders and landowners was very high, ranging from forty to eighty percent. So high were the interests she charged that often her debtors preferred taking her to court to retrieve their land and fishing rights to paying back loan with the unusually high interests. (99)

Concerning how in the period between 1916 and 1936. Omu Okwei exerted a lot of "influence both on Nigerian and foreign traders" ("Merchant Queen" 215) .Ekejiuba observes that she employed a unique trade secret such as the one favoured by the market mamas of Emecheta's *The Slave Girl*. In profiling this aspect of Omu Okwei's mercantilist bent, Felicia Ekejiuba remarks that:

> she acquired beautiful girls—mostly 'adopted' children on children pawned to her by debtors, brought them up and gave them out as mistresses or wives to influential businessmen and others. These were of course expected to come back to Okwei's household when the traders finally left Nigeria. Any children or property the women acquired during the association with the traders reverted to their original owner as they, like slaves, could not own properly as they, like slaves, could not own property. (215)

Any wonder then that "as a result of these marriage links, Okwei enjoyed very special treatment" and would enjoy having "trade partners and agents in all the parts of the Niger Delta—at Brass, Ndoni, Oguta, Port Harcourt and Warri" (Ekejiuba "Omu Okwei" 97). It is the prevalence of women like the Omu Okwei in Onitsha in the period between 1904 and 1938 that must have given rise to the following passage in Emecheta's *The Slave Girl*:

> Many of the market women had slaves in great number to help them with the fetching and carrying that went with being a full-time trader—and also in the vain hope that one day the British people at the coast would go and some of these house slaves could be sold abroad, just as their fathers and grandfathers had done. (53)

There is no doubt that since serious enquiries have not being made about the complicity of women in the domestic and international slavery businesses, the authorial narrator has to jolt us with the feminist thrust of "just as their fathers and grandfathers had done." However, there is a lot of evidence to demonstrate that there were also mothers and grandmothers who were neck-deep in the nauseating culture of the enslavement of both females and males. For instance, as far back as the mid-nineteenth century an Ohambele woman who unfortunately is described as "a promising childless Ohambeli woman" is known to have bought David Okparabietoa and later as she felt "the pinch of financial embarrassment," she had to "sell David for two thousand manilas to Chief Warribi M. Pepple of Bonny . . . in 1860" (see Anyika 84). One wonders what type of "financial embarrassment" could have afflicted childless women by 1860. Concerning the activities of such women, J. O. Ijoma notes that "today, there are compounds in Issele Ukwu, Ibusa, Asaba and other western Igbo communities which are predominantly of slave origin" (119). The fact that by 1854 as revealed in W. O. Baukie's

Narrative of an Exploring Voyage of the Rivers Kwora and Benue (commonly known as the Niger and Tsadda) in 1854, there was a situation where because of "a lucrative trade" of the period "a pair of large Ivory anklets worn by Igbo women cost as much as four slaves" (Ijoma 122) can give us a peep into the complicity of women in procuring enough slaves to take care of their endless request for Ivory anklets. Here, it is instructive to note that in a chapter aptly captioned "Ibo women and their ways" G. T. Basden remarks that "the most valuable, and the most priced of all forms of ornaments, are the anklets and bracelets of ivory" (92).

Despite how extremely heavy, inconveniencing and skin chafing they were, Basden observes that "it is astonishing that they can be endured at all" (92). And to believe that in order to display wealth and rank the women were ready to subjugate those denigrated as slaves to procure such anklets. Happily enough and unlike some other readers, Gloria Chukukere asserts that "through Ojebeta and the other women's experiences, the novelist demonstrates the extent to which women are their own worst enemies" (183). Thus, granted "Ma's perpetuation of the system" of slavery and the complicity of her daughters, especially Victoria noted for "her cruelty to the slave girls" (183), Chukukere argues that their "shortcomings as perpetrators of slavery show the degree to which women contribute to their own dilemma" (184). Of course even when fictionally presented the fact that we have female—authorized structures that encourage the life burial of slaves to accompany their mistresses to the great beyond is an indication that Buchi Emecheta in her novel, *The Slave Girl* is provoking her fellow women to the reality of the atrocities that they have been champions and sustainers of.

The intertexts and echoes in Buchi Emecheta's works are quite revealing about the types of milieu that she was exposed to. For instance, writing about Nuruddin Farahis *From a Crooked Rib*, Derek Wright observes that "in its exposure of the evils of patriarchal power, its elevation of the dignity and status of women, and its targeting of the criminal waste of half the population's potential, the novel contains in embryonic form the vision of much of Farah's nature fiction" (29). This could as well be a reference to what Buchi Emecheta had done in her *Second Class Citizen* and *The Slave Girl*. Invariably, the construction of the feminine self which Farah introduced in the African Novel would give Emecheta a shot in the arm that is more impactful than her exposure to Flora Nwapa's *Efuru*. Within this context therefore, James Currey's testimony that "Nuruddin Farah has always been amused that, when in 1968 he submitted the manuscript of *From a Crooked Rib*, I asked him whether he was a woman. The writer had certainly portrayed the heroine Ebla with a female sensitivity" (155). This is a very moving tribute about the beginning of a new phase that is definitive in its representation of the female in African literature and especially the girl child blatantly appropriated as a commodity. That opening shot from a gynandrist novelist would eventually create a long-expected platform for a woman who had experienced the trauma of an oppressive patriarchal culture, the tragedy of being enslaved in a marriage and the discomforts of being uprooted from the relatively more stable mono-racial environment of her childhood into a multi-racial environment that would equally threaten her womanhood and humanity. In *Second Class Citizen*, Emecheta echoes the dictum of the Somalian proverb that gave birth to Farah's *From a Crooked Rib* by intertextually having her authorial narrator venture into a debate about the epistemology of ribs in creation of the woman. As we read and reason with Adah's assumed visage,

> Francis had said men have more ribs than women. And not only did they have more ribs, but that one of a man's ribs makes all the ribs of a woman. Adah peered again at the drawing of the ribs and concluded that they must be those of a woman. The ribs were too fine, too regular to be a man's. (*Second Class Citizen* 111)

Adah would probably have wondered whether she was actually formed from a man's crooked rib, since the drawing depicted very fine ribs.

CONCLUSION

Assertive. primed and highly political and radical, the very prolific and phenomenal writer, Buchi Emecheta has undoubtedly impacted society with her works which are predominantly hinged on autobiography and history thatspans the colonial, post-independence, and civil war periods in the history of her country, Nigeria. She was in effect bruised by the dynamics of slavery. According to her submission, "her father was a servant to a clergyman, while her mother was a slave girl in Onitsha . . . [*The Slave Girl*] sounds more like the biography of the author's mother, Alice Ojebeta, to whom *The Bride Price* is dedicated" (Opara 133). In the light of the prevalence of slavery at that historical moment, a modest attempt has been made in this chapter on the basis of some historical sources to establish the fact that women in that region at that time wielded enormous authority to avert female slavery. However, it would seem they were as complicit as they were complacent. Evidently, Emecheta is implicitly censuring women rather than the patriarchal/ Biblical concept of the rib for the objectification and subjugation of womanhood in *The Slave Girl*.

It is only logical that Emecheta should be so impassioned about the enslavement of women for she also has been mentally, emotionally, and physically shackled as a culturally subjugated girl child; a less privileged black woman in exile; an abandoned wife and mother who is constrained to go through traumatic experiences due to her subcategory status as a second class citizen living in London. She, as a matter of course, crashes into the ditch. Nevertheless, by dint of hard work and perseverance, she raises her head above water and gradually garners numerous accolades as well as laurels and finally attains enviable canonical heights.

WORKS CITED

Afigbo, A. E. "Women in Nigerian History" *Women in Nigerian Economy*. Ed. Martin O. Ijere. Enugu: Acena Publishers (1992): 22–40.

Anyika, Francis. "The Igbo as Missionaries to other Peoples of Nigeria" *Bigard Theological Studies* 12.2–13.1 (Jan.–June,1993): 76–91.

Basden, G. T. *Among the Ibos of Nigeria.* Onitsha: University Publishing Co, 1983. 1st pub. 1921.

Bruner, Charlotte. Ed. *Unwinding Threads: Writing by Women in Africa.* London: Heinemann, 1983.

Busby, Margaret. Foreword. *Emerging Perspectives on Buchi Emecheta*. Ed. Marie Umeh. Trenton, New Jersey: Africa World Press (1996): xiii–xix.

Chuku, Gloria. "Women in Igbo Society: A Historico-Literary Analysis of Forms of Expressed and Transmitted Knowledge" *A History of Africana Women's Literature: Essays on Poetry, Gender, Religion, Feminism, Aesthetics, Politics, Moral Values, African Tradition & Diaspora.* Ed. Rose Ure Mezu. Baltimore, MD: Black Academy Press (2004): 48–89.

Chukukere, Gloria. "Buchi Emecheta: The Yoke of Womanhood" *Gender Voices and Choices: Redefining Women in Contemporary African Fiction.* Enugu: Fourth Dimension (1995): 164–216.

Chukwuma, Helen. "Positivism and the Female Crisis: The Novels of Buchi Emecheta." *Nigerian Female Writers: A Critical Perspective.* Ed. Henrietta Otokunefor and Obiageli Nwodo. Lagos: Malthouse (1989): 2–18.

Collins, Philip. *Dickens and Education.* London: Macmillian, 1965.

Currey, James. *Africa Writes Back: The African Writers Series & the Launch of African Literature. Suffolk:* Boydell and Bewer, 2008.

Ekejiuba, Felicia Ifeoma. "Omu Okwei of Ossomari." *Nigerian Women in Historical Perspective*. Ed. Bolanle Awe. Lagos: Sankore and Bookcraft, (1992): 91–104.

———. "Omu Okwei: The Merchant Queen of Ossomari." *Nigeria Magazine,* 90 (Sept .1966): 213–220.

Emenyonu, Ernest N. "The Female as a Writer in Nigeria: Technique and Language in Buchi Emecheta's *The Bride Price, The Slave Girl* and *The Joys of Motherhood.*" *Studies on the Nigerian Novel.* Ibadan: Heinemann: 1991, 76–88.

Emecheta, Buchi. *The Slave Girl*. Harlow, Essex: Heinemann, 1995.

Ezeigbo, Theodora Akachi. "Tradition and the African Female Writer: The Example of Buchi Emecheta" *Emerging Perspectives on Bucih Emecheta.* Ed. Marie Umeh. Trenton, New Jersey: Africa World Press,1996, 5–25.

Ijoma, J.O. 'Pre-colonial Trade and Trade Links among the West Niger Igbo" *Odu: A Journal of West African Studies.* New series. 22 (Jan./July 1982): 109–132.

Izevbaye, Dan. "Issues in the Reassessment of the African Novel." *African Literature Today* 10 (1979).

Jones, Eldred. Editorial. *African Literature Today 13* (1983): vii–x.

Lindfors, Bernth. "Accounting for Differences." In *Reconstructing the Canon: Festschrift in Honour of Professor Charles E.Nnolim.* Ed. Austine Amanze Akpuda, Owerri: Skillmark Media 2001: 2–38.

Luciani, Albino. *Illustration: Letters from Pope John Paul 1 (trans)* William weaver. Boston: Little, Brown and Company, 1978.

Mossberg, Barbara Clarke. "A Rose in Context: The Daughter Construct" *Historical Studies and Literary Criticism.* Ed. Jerome J. MCGann. Madison, Wisconsin: The University of Wisconsin Press 1985: 199–225.

Ojo-Ade, Femi. "African Women Writers and Feminism: An Example of Miriam Tiali" *Being Black, Being Human: More Essays on Black Culture.* Ile Ife: Obafemi Awolowo University Press, 1996: 32–68.

Opara, Chioma Carol. *Her Mother's Daughter: the African Writer as Woman.* Port Harcourt: University of Port Harcourt Press, 2004.

Oputa, Chukwudifu. "Women and Children as Disempowered Groups" *Women and Children Under Nigerian Law.* Eds. Awa U. Kalu and Yemi Osinbajo. Lagos: Federal Ministry of Justice, (1989): 1–14.

Palmer, Eustace. "The Feminine Point of View: Buchi Emecheta's *The Joys of Motherhood*" *African Literature Today* 13 (1983): 38–55.

Rioux, Anne Boyd 'Eight Classic Female Bildungsroman you should know about if you don't already" posted Feb. 18, 2016 in *Books.*

Wright, Derek. *The Novels of Nuruddin Farah.* Bayreuth: Bayreuth University Press, 1994.

Chapter 16

Twin Kernels in One Pod

Naming of Nawal and Firdaus in Nawal El Saadawi's A Daughter of Isis and Woman at Point Zero

Chinyere Grace Okafor

INTRODUCTION

Viewed generally as a radical feminist, Egyptian female writer, Nawal El Saadawi comes across as strong, personable, and dynamic.[1] Her commitment to writing her autobiographical works—*A Daughter of Isis* and *Woman at Point Zero*—is personal, cultural, and strategic through its intersection with different hierarchies of power and power relations, especially the patriarchal system that she experienced and exposed in her writing. "Woman" is a name that denotes biological differentiation of female human beings and the cultural connotations of gender construction imposed on bodies that bear that name. Nawal abhors the inscription of the negative on women through institutionalized male dominance empowered with patriarchal authority. This inscription is the basis of the oppression of women and the central theme of her widely acclaimed books, *Woman at Point Zero* and *A Daughter of Isis* which are used to engage the issue of "name" in this essay. The politically conscious author became aware of the vagaries of patriarchy and how it impacted her name as a child:

> Then I learnt my mother's name, Zaynab. I wrote it down next to mine . . .
> But he removed my mother's name from next to mine, and wrote down his

instead ... When I asked him, he said, "It is God's will," ... I wrote a letter to God ... "O God, if you are just, why do you treat my mother and my father differently?" (*Daughter* 1–2)

She treasured the name, Nawal, which means "gift" and wrote her mother's name, Zaynab, beside hers. The sight of both nestling together in Arabic looked beautiful and was one of her fondest memories, but her mother's name was removed and replaced with her father's and great grandfather's name, El Saadawi. She questioned her father about the removal, and he explained it as "God's will." This was unacceptable to six-year-old Nawal and initiated her feminist reaction to gender differentiation and subjugation. She promptly wrote a letter asking why a just God treated her mother differently. The issue of names and naming bothered Nawal most of her life. She pondered on why women's names were not bequeathed on children they labored to birth, love, and nurture. Even at an advanced age of sixty-one, a successful physician, and renowned writer on a distinguished fellowship at Duke University, North Carolina, USA, she pondered on the issue of naming as she wrote in *A Daughter of Isis*.

> Ever since I was born the name of that unknown Al-Saadawi has been carried by my body, inscribed on my schoolbooks, my school certificates, my certificates of merit, printed on my articles in newspapers and magazines, on the covers of my novels and books written with my ink, my sweat, my tears, my blood. (32)

She clearly resented the notion and practice of popularizing the name of a man she did not know instead of a mother that she loved. She wished that she could "efface my grandfather Al-Saadawi from my name and replace it with my mother's name, Zaynab" (*Daughter* 33), whose essence was in union with hers. She constantly recalled her bonding with her mother—how Zaynab used to carry her in her arms and hold her to her breasts, her smell lingering in her nose as if it were the smell of her own body. The role was reversed in Zaynab's last days when Nawal happily cared for her with the skills of a doctor and love of a daughter. "My mother's name was buried forever. She owned no thing ... her children, including me, were her husband's property. Her name was buried with her body and disappeared from history" (*Daughter* 33). In an environment where women were subjected to multiple oppression from cultural, religious, neocolonial, racist, and class hierarchies of power, Nawal's mother's words that "Nawal can scale any fire" formed the rock of Nawal's resilience as she took on the oppressive powers in her writing.

Her criticism of patriarchal erasure of women's names influenced the title of her popular book *Woman at Point Zero* that immortalized the name of the phenomenal woman, Firdaus, whom she met at Women's Prison in Qanatir.

Firdaus was accused of killing a man who was about to kill her. This implied the highest level of criminality for which the justice system, on behalf of society, deemed it right to snuff her out of civilized society forever. On the contrary, it would have been a great loss to humanity to have missed the story, the essence, the wisdom, and panache of this remarkable prisoner whom Nawal celebrates in the semi autobiography, *Woman at Point Zero*, a cryptic name connoting the woman's final hours on Earth. To emphasize the intention to memorialize, she added the woman's name, *Firdaus*, in the original title, *Woman at Point Zero*, or *Firdaus*. Originally rejected by Egyptian publishers, the book became famous and has been published in over twenty-two languages. It has remained the most widely known of Saadawi's books, subject of numerous articles, and a popular read in feminist studies.

The extinction of women's names and personal aspirations through marriage is sarcastically portrayed in *A Daughter of Isis* through Nawal's meeting with her talented school friend, Fikreya, whose dream at school was to use her artistic talent to become a famous artist. Fikreya's eyes expressed sorrow for her unfulfilled dream of not using her talent, a situation comparable to the portrayal of American women in Betty Friedan's *Feminine Mystique* which stressed "The Problem that has No Name" based on the experience of suburban housewives who revealed their unhappiness for not living up to their full human potential and expertise because they were trying to comply with social expectations that wives should achieve fulfillment from taking care of husbands, children, and the home. Fikreya sarcastically verbalized the patriarchal expectation for wives, "My husband is a well-known artist, and he paints for both of us" (*Daughter* 268). Both friends understood the injustice of erasing women's names, dreams, and ambitions through patriarchal matrimonial dictates. This was why Fikreya punctuated her verbalization with a "dry sarcastic laugh" (*Daughter* 268). Nawal extended the mockery to colonial appropriation represented at Gandhi's meeting with the colonial master, King George of England, to negotiate India's freedom. Questioned about his attire consisting of only loincloth, Gandhi replied, "Your Majesty is dressed for both of us" (*Daughter* 268), which was a cynical indictment of British colonialism that sucked the gold of India and wondered why the people starved.

From birth on October 27, 1931, the names of three patriarchs were bestowed on Nawal and legally written beside her name: Nawal Al-Sayed Habash Al-Saadawi. Her autobiography, *A Daughter of Isis*, shows that she did not care about the names of her great-grandfather. Her paternal grandmother's stories about Nawal's great-grandfather, Al-Saadawi, as a brute influenced Nawal's negative attitude to that ancestor. She portrays him as a ruthless polygamist and compares his abuse of his women to land exploitation by farmers who extract from the land and abandon it when it is famished: "The only verses of the Qur'an which he knew were 'Marry as many women as seems good to you. Your women are as land to be plowed by you, so plow them when you wish,' and 'Abandon their bedding and chastise them'" (*Daughter* 30). Her grandmother described him and his son who was her husband as wicked. She refused to shed tears for his death; just performed the required ceremony and went on with her life vowing never to marry again.

Nawal was glad when the name of her horrible grandfather, Habash, was erased from her name through administrative jingoism, but the name of her great-grandfather, El Saadawi, remained beside her name due to the laws of patriarchal authority, and even though she did not like or choose it, she succumbed to its use as her name till her death on March 21, 2021. Thus, Nawal El Saadawi rides high through his illustrious offspring who would have chosen her mother's name, Zaynab. Nawal achieved a lot in her eighty-one years on earth but harbored the regret of not bearing her mother's name. Nawal's daughter, Mona Helmi, gave her a Mother's Day present that she would have loved to give her mother, Zaynab. She gave Nawal the gift of inserting Nawal beside her name and signed her article as Mona Nawal Helmi. She was taken to court because it was considered heresy, but she won the case. In homage to Nawal for bringing attention to the issue of effacing women's names, Nawal El Saadawi is referred to as Nawal in this discourse.

TWO DAUGHTERS OF THE NILE

River Nile is a symbol of life, identity, richness, and pride in the two books, *Woman at Point Zero* and *A Daughter of Isis*, which dwell on Firdaus and Nawal, respectively. One named Nawal, which translates as Gift and the other named Firdaus meaning Paradise, the two daughters of the Nile have symbolic names that speak to their career and impact in life as illustrated in a survey of their background. Achebe's image of twin kernels separated by a thin wall in a palm nutshell, which is used to represent African and European quarters in *No Longer at Ease* is a befitting symbol for the difference between Firdaus and Nawal as well as their striking convergence and co-dependence. It is salient to note the difference between the two kernels in one pod: one kernel was shiny black and alive, and the other was powdery-white and dead (6).

Their interface began in 1974 when Nawal heard about Firdaus as she was researching on the effect of prison condition on women. There were many women prisoners open to the research whose issues featured in her book, *Women and Neurosis in Egypt*, published in 1976, but Nawal was struck by the personality of Firdaus or maybe her audaciousness and was bent on interviewing her. Nawal solicited the help of the woman warder who advised her in a hostile manner to leave Firdaus alone, insisting that even though she had committed murder, she was decidedly innocent and should not be hanged.

The prison warden was not the only advocate for Firdaus. The prison doctor had vouched for Firdaus's innocence and written a petition to have her sentence converted, but she refused to sign it or talk to him. Struck by how they protected Firdaus, disturbed by Firdaus's rejection of her request to interview her, Nawal persisted in seeking her audience.

Her awe for Firdaus began with the frustration of having the condemned criminal on death row snub her, a doctor and researcher, ready to write her story. Representation of their version of truth or leaving a legacy for posterity is a blessing to prisoners especially those on death row, so Firdaus's audacity to reject Nawal's request for interview was quite shocking, especially with Firdaus's interest in writing as indicated by her request for writing material. When she finally conceded to see Nawal, "her voice was steady, cutting deep down inside, cold as a knife. Not the slightest wavering in its tone. Not the smallest shiver of a note" as she dared to order Nawal to close the window, sit down on the floor, and "Let me speak. Do not interrupt me" (*Woman* 9).

This interaction communicated Firdaus's dignity, confidence, and superiority, which intersected with Nawal's personality, but Firdaus appeared superior as Nawal obeyed her. Nawal describes this encounter as having a lasting effect on her (ix–xii). There was an unnamed and unknown bond that drew Nawal to Firdaus; sisterhood borne of the same understanding, an indomitable spirit of resistance, survival, and triumph. This energy drew a privileged married woman, successful doctor, and renowned writer to a prostitute cum prisoner on death row. It appeared ironical but possibly the same unknown factor got Nawal jailed in the same prison seven years after their meeting to experience some of Firdaus's prison life.

Nawal was a doctor and psychiatrist, founder, and president of the Arab Women's Solidarity Association (1982) that became an international organization with branches in many countries as well as co-founder of the Arab Organization for Human Rights. She had numerous interviews, speaking engagements, and over fifty books that created awareness about issues of women's oppression especially female circumcision, exploitation of the peasants, religious hypocrisy, and abuse of people's human rights. She was an awardee of numerous honors including the 2012 Sean MacBride Peace Prize for her human rights advocacy and remarkable courage during the Arab Spring, numerous honorary degrees, and fellowships. Nawal's brilliance, excellence, and achievement benefitted from her personal hard work and support of her family.

She was born in a village called Kafr Tahal in 1931. The greatest inspirations to her young mind were her mother who supported her continued subversion of insubordination, her paternal grandmother who told her that, "God is justice, and we know him by our mind," and her father who taught her to read the Quaran and think with her mind. Thus, her family nurtured her to think critically and encouraged her to aspire to university education. Family members also had assumptions and prejudices that confused Nawal's sense of justice. These members were born into the religious, gendered, and racialized society and, therefore, internalized discriminatory attitudes through socialization in the culture. Members of Nawal's household had some liberal views, but they were not exempted from patriarchal views and tendencies, so young Nawal experienced discrimination particularly of sexist and racial kinds in her family.

Growing up in her middle-class family, she was peeved at the devaluation of girls and women as well as her brother's privilege based on gender. She heard her grandmother verbalize it by saying that "a boy is worth fifteen girls at least . . . a boy lifts his father's head up in the world . . . but girls get married and go off . . . their children carry the names of the men they marry" (*Daughter* 56). In reply, little Nawal stamped her feet saying, "I will never marry" (*Daughter* 56). This proclamation signaled radical feminist abrogation of the system of inequality, but her grandmother who acted as the custodian of culture countered with anti-feminist voice, "Marriage is your destiny, like all girls. It is God's will" (*Daughter* 56). The dialogue between the two foreshadowed Nawal's later engagement of oppressive cultural practices and her retribution from religious and political leaders.

She was brilliant and excelled at school while her brother did not. She did not feel her achievements celebrated as she felt the family's disappointment at the failure of her brother. She was creative and talented, enjoyed school and made school exciting for other students. She and her friends were the live wire of the school, but they were naughty and told by others that they would go to hell. This greatly disturbed Nawal, but her mother freed her from fear of hell by telling her that it did not exist thereby liberating her mind to soar unencumbered. Her mother had unfulfilled dreams and goals that were aborted by her early marriage, but she supported Nawal's aspirations and was her cheerer as she tackled customs that inhibited her development. She wrote and directed plays at school, wrote stories and was good at all subjects. She went on to the university and to medical school. She graduated in 1955 and married Ahmed Helmi, another doctor she met at medical school. They had a daughter, Mona Helmi. They divorced after two years. Her second husband was Rashad Bey.

Nawal worked as a physician in her hometown and was appalled at the level of domestic violence endured by women as well as the recurrence of disease among the poor. She began to research by reading books outside the medical field. She read about politics, arts, and sexuality, and discovered the connection of poverty to disease and oppression of women as well as the connection of poverty to class exploitation, patriarchy, and colonialism. She knew that medicine would not solve the problem, so she began to share her knowledge with the world through her writing. She was an inspiration to women in Egypt and many parts of the world. In 1964, she married her third husband Sherif Hetata, a fellow doctor and human rights advocate who had been a political prisoner for thirteen years. They had a son, Atef Hetata. Nawal rose to become the Director of the Ministry of Public Health.

Nawal's fight for women is personal and focuses on the eradication of circumcision, which she saw as the basis of women's oppression. An epiphany experience in India led to her adult recollection of her gruesome experience of the surgery (circumcision) at the age of six. After some days, the midwife examined her wound and declared, "All is well. The wound has healed, thanks be to God," but Nawal never forgot the experience of pain and the deeper wound "left in my spirit" (*Daughter* 74). She also heard horrible circumcision stories from her aunts, mother, and grandmother who described it as the most painful experience of her life. In 1972, she published *Woman and Sex*, which centers on female circumcision as a nefarious practice. This was considered an affront against powerful patriarchal establishment, and it cost her a lot. She explained:

> At the end of 1972 the Minister of Health had removed from me my functions as Director of Health Education and Editor-in-Chief of the magazine *Health*. This was one more consequence of the path I had chosen as a feminist author and novelist whose ideas were viewed unfavorably by the authorities. (*Woman* 7–8)

The loss of her position led her to a new path of research on women and neurosis. It was through this research that she met Firdaus. She supported the publication of the feminist magazine, *Confrontation* (1981), and the same year, she was put in prison. In an interview with Anthony Appiah, she illustrated the power of writing by citing how other prisoners were allowed writing material, but she was denied that right and the guards routinely searched her room for paper or pen, not gun. It is because of the power of the pen that Nawal constantly encouraged women and all the oppressed to write. The masses regarded Nawal as their hero, so it is not surprising that a woman smuggled an old toilet roll and eye pencil to her prison cell and she wrote notes for her book and formed the Arab Women's Association while in prison.

She and her husband, Hetata, had memorable experiences of travel to numerous countries speaking and energizing people on issues of gender and human rights, but they had many battles with the Egyptian government and religious pundits. Under an Islamic law, a case was filed in court in 2021 to forcefully divorce her from Hetata on grounds of her apostasy. Some religious leaders called for her death by hanging, and she was on the fundamental Islamic death list. She and her husband divorced in 2010 after forty-six years of marriage. In her eighties, Nawal was an inspiration to the youths who engaged in the Arab Springs demonstration for democracy, occupying the park with them for weeks and jubilating for being alive to see such a revolution.

This background of Nawal's life and contribution shows that she portrayed what her name foretold. She is a gift to Egypt and the world as she forced Egypt and the world to engage in difficult conversations about circumcision and other women's issues that would initiate gender and human rights reforms. She was intelligent, strong, courageous, and unafraid. In a patriarchal society like Egypt, these were regarded as masculine qualities ascribed to boys and men. When women with such qualities confidently engaged the public sphere dominated by men, they were castigated, fought, and silenced or they fought back and became stronger and controversial like Nawal. She never succumbed to silence, which she saw as a weapon of oppression.

Unlike Nawal, Firdaus was from a very poor peasant family, but the audaciousness, control, and dignity displayed in her story parallels aspects of Nawal's character. From childhood, Firdaus's family never appealed to her because of the oppression she and her mother suffered under the domestic autocracy of her father who used them as mules that worked his fields, cooked for the family, ministered to him at home, and got constant beating in return. This is a representation of sex-gender system that depends on the exploitation of women's labor, appropriation of their profit, and their subjugation through violence. Her patriarch's insensitivity to the suffering of his family is deftly portrayed through the female gaze reminiscent of Nawal's piercing eyes referred to at the end of this paper.[2] Firdaus's gaze at her father is depicted through ugly animal imagery as his mouth "like that of a camel, with a big opening and wide jaws" appeared inhuman with his upper jaw clamping "down on his lower jaw with a loud grinding noise" (*Woman* 18). Her world in rural Egypt was peopled by peasants primarily defined by extreme poverty, religious hypocrisy, immorality, and disease. Unlike Nawal's parents, her father did not send her to school, but she had an uncle who was studying in the city of Cairo whose stories introduced her to another world that occupied her dreams.

Unlike Nawal with mature adult recollection of her circumcision, Firdaus never forgot the pain she endured as a child because of her circumcision, which consisted in surgical extinction of "a piece of flesh from between my legs" (*Woman* 12). Similar to Nawal who had a lasting damage to her spirit, Firdaus felt like a part of her being was gone. The question of why women still allowed the painful experience to be visited on their daughters is engaged through Nawal's writing and speaking engagements where she articulated the hold of tradition reinforced by capitalist patriarchy through the intersection of culture, women's oppression, and imperialism. She connected George Bush with increased female circumcision. As oppressed men lost grip on their manly pride in wars and political maneuvers of post-colonial and global masters, they resorted to culture and its use to oppress those they considered weaker—women and children—for it assuaged their manly ego weakened by western patriarchal power. Even though women performed the surgery on girls, it was done in the interest of cultural and religious patriarchy that gave men privilege and pride despite their subjugation by neocolonial powers.

While Nawal had her mother as cheerleader urging her to trust her free spirit and not be afraid of anything, a father who took on the principal and prevented her from being expelled from school for leading a demonstration, Firdaus had no advocate. Even though her uncle sexually abused her, she followed him to Cairo when her father died. He became her sole guardian, and this ensured his ceaseless abuse of her body and appropriation of her labor to cook, clean, and iron his kaftan. Firdaus' predicament lends itself to Marxist/socialist feminist concern with gender and class oppression. Her uncle was middle-class and could afford to buy labor, which he later did when he got married, but he chose to exploit child labor because he had the power to do so. There was inequality in assignment of roles on gender basis with Firdaus being disadvantaged as female and minor, performing adult roles including sexual gratification of the master. It was an unequal distribution of duties, sexual exploitation, and child abuse.

Unlike Nawal whose mother told her father that she would not tolerate abuse, Firdaus learnt submission to male authority and abuse from her mother. From her uncle she learnt that it was normal for girls to submit their bodies to men in return for a little favor. He was from the peasant class but devised a plan to move up through exploitation and marriage. His aunt sold her gold to put him to school, but he snubbed her in his bid to move up in the class and color conscious society. He married a "white" girl and daughter of his teacher at El Azhar. At his wife's prompting, he sent Firdaus to board at school where she got her most treasured secondary school certificate. Goaded by his wife, he married Firdaus off to Sheikh Mahmoud, an old man with a disgusting facial bump that sometimes oozed out pus that would smear Firdaus during rape. This was a fitting symbol of patriarchal violence and ugliness. Feminist subversion of oppressive authority is expressed through Firdaus' sexual control. She could not make love to her husband whom she detested and who treated her like trash, starved and constantly beat her, so she developed a technique for withholding self from the sexual act on her body. She described his sexual act in combative not loving terms such as pouncing on her, "like a mad dog" (*Woman* 47). The animal imagery is important in appreciating the ferociousness of her husband and the patriarchal authority he represented. Her seeming submission as one facing a ferocious wild animal is emblematic of calculated passive aggressiveness. She surrendered her body passively without resistance but withheld self and active involvement. His body felt like a piece of wood devoid of life or feeling, "like a piece of dead wood or old neglected furniture" (*Woman* 47). This marriage experience gave her skills for her later life in sex work.

On one occasion of severe beating, she left her husband and went back to her uncles' house, but his wife told her that "the precepts of religion permitted such punishment" and "a virtuous woman should accept it with "perfect obedience" (*Woman* 46–47). On her return, her husband became more vicious, so she escaped to the street. She was "rescued" by a coffee shop owner, Bayoumi, who initially showed her some kindness and in return she cooked, cleaned, and submitted her body to his sexual pleasure just as she did for her uncle, but she yearned for self-autonomy and fulfillment as a person. When she wanted to find a job with her secondary school certificate which would have given her independence, her colonizer resisted by introducing stringent repressive measures. He first used violence. He gave her "the heaviest slap" she ever received on her face, causing her to sway from side to side and she felt the walls and the floor "shift violently" (*Woman* 50). When his blow landed on her belly, she lost consciousness. He began to lock her up in the house, return at night, slap, and rape her. These actions are symbolic of imperial subjugation of colonized Egypt which Nawal and her father fought against by engaging in anti-imperialist, anti-neocolonial demonstrations for which they were punished. Bayoumi prostituted her body to multiple men, which also is symbolic of how the powerful gang up to exploit and oppress. Firdaus has an indomitable spirit of resistance. She escaped to the street and was rescued by Sharifa who housed her in her beautiful home where she was spoilt with delicacies and fine clothes.

Firdaus got confused when she realized that the seemingly benevolent Sharifa was prostituting her and that the gentle postures of a client, Fawzy, whom she was about to fall in love with, were fake. She saw Fawzy beat and rape her mentor, Sharifa, to submission, so she ran away. She refused the advances of a police officer but when he threatened to apprehend and jail her, she submitted to his rape. Her body had become her means of survival and transcendence. Bitter and soaked in the rain, a gentleman stopped his car and persuaded her to "please get out of the rain" (*Woman* 68). He bathed her, put her on his fine bed and raped her. All this while, Firdaus did not know about prostitution, or that she had already become a prostitute under the control of people she regarded as benefactors who housed and fed her. In the morning, she was about to leave the man's house when he slipped a ten-pound note in her hand. It was an epiphany moment in which she realized the power of her body as a money-making machine. Thereafter, she became a prostitute, conscious of her ability. She made a lot of money, lived in style, and had many friends until a journalist client cum friend, Di'aa, said that her profession was not respectable. Although she pointed out Di'aa's complicity in the business,

"My work is not worthy of respect. Why then do you join in it with me?" (*Woman* 77), the issue made her give up the lucrative sex work for a low-paid job in a company.

She moved out of her luxurious home and began life with salary from her low-paid job. She could only afford to rent a small room in a narrow back street without bathroom facilities, so she had to wake up early to line up at the public bathroom. The company job revealed the sexual exploitation of low-paid women who were coerced to use sex to keep their jobs or get promoted even while they were looked at with contempt. She did her work with dignity, did not give in to the sex racket, and had a good reputation in the company. She, however, fell in love with Ibrahim, the leader of the revolutionary committee. For the first time she began "to imagine that I had become a human being" (*Woman* 93). Love gave her a new self and vision of life:

> It was as though I held the whole world captive in my hands. It seemed to grow bigger, and expand, and the sun shone brighter than ever before. Everything around me floated in a radiant light, even the morning queue in front of the toilet . . . When I looked into the mirror my eyes sparkled like diamonds. (*Woman* 89)

Her soul died the moment she realized that her love, Ibrahim, had got engaged to the chairman's daughter and was being hailed as a clever guy with a bright future in the company. She left the company and went back to prostitution with vengeance in her heart. She would not allow any pimp to control her, and she accepted only high-profile clients. She saw how pimps exploited prostitutes and she vowed not to ever have a pimp, but a pimp forced himself on her business. Nawal's view of patriarchy and imperialism helps us to understand the impossibility of a small State to exist in an imperial world without being "protected" (read controlled) by a patriarchal world power. Like a richly endowed country, Firdaus is endowed with irresistible beauty that is a potential money-making machine, which had to be controlled and exploited by a world power (pimp). She refused to be controlled, so the pimp offered to marry her which would still have given him control of her body and money. Firdaus's experience of marriage, love, and sex work gave her an understanding of patriarchal domination and exploitation of women. She believed that "all women are victims of deception" (*Woman* 94).

She refused the pimp's marriage offer, but he still succeeded in colonizing her body through superior physical strength and violent rape. As she said, "I felt the familiar weight pressing down on my breast, but my body withdrew, turned in on itself away from me, like some passive, lifeless thing, refusing to surrender, undefeated. Its passivity was a form of resistance." (*Woman* 94). The appropriation of Firdaus's body is symbolic of the process of colonization—conquest, take over, domination, and exploitation—which gives the master absolute control of the colonized. Her pimp took the lion's share of her earning for as he said, "My capital is women's bodies" (*Woman* 101). He maintained the services of professionals to protect him and his company. He had a doctor who performed abortion when needed, officers in the justice system to advise him and protect his organization, while he guarded his property.

He achieved complete ownership and control of Firdaus' body. Simone de Beauvoir in *The Second Sex* describes the colonized body as corporeal body wallowing in immanence that can only achieve freedom through transcendence. The oppressed must engage the oppressor through empowered mediation or through force. Firdaus saw the only escape in packing her papers and leaving to find another job because "I don't want to be anybody's slave" (*Woman* 103). de Beauvoir's maxim that the oppressor does not give up power willingly is relevant in understanding the stance of the pimp and his refusal to let Firdaus go. He barred the door and tried to use violence to stop her from leaving, but she fought back and was, therefore, forced into unequal power struggle with her pimp. A combination of will power and providence initiated her contentious transcendental journey for as he was reaching his knife, she took it from his pocket and stabbed him on the neck, chest and "almost every part of him" (*Woman* 104). The stabs symbolize blows at patriarchy and vengeance against the men who have hurt her beginning from her father to this pimp that took the physical blow for all her oppressors.

She walked out and chose an Arab prince for a client at three thousand, but when he paid her, the money became a symbol of the process of her prostitution by hypocrites like her uncle who exploited her girlhood, Bayoumi who prostituted her to his friends, clients in the sex work business who looked down on prostitutes but promoted prostitution by patronizing it, and pimps who lived as parasites on the sweat of prostitutes. She tore the three thousand notes to pieces. It was not easy to tear three thousand, but she kept at it like she was destroying all the money she ever earned and men she had slept with, "tearing them all to pieces one after the other, ridding myself of them once and for all" (*Woman* 107). This single act of destroying the money is a ritual of liberation that symbolized the connection of gender oppression with male domination and capitalism. Betrayed, violated, abused, exploited, and demeaned by every man she loved or encountered including her father, uncle, and the love of her life, Firdaus destroyed patriarchy and attained liberation from the patriarchal world. She verbalized her freedom in her prison cell, "I want nothing. I hope for nothing. I fear nothing. Therefore, I am free" (*Woman* 110).

This summary has shown that Nawal and Firdaus are extraordinary daughters of Egypt, and that their lives intersected like twins in a pod of gender construction, but also separated by the class structure that propelled them to different life-paths. Circumstances of her impoverished environment influenced Firdaus' life's story that differ from those of middle-class Nawal, whom she might have heard about since she was an avid reader. Like Nawal, she was intelligent, bold, courageous, and confident. She fought all her assailants losing some, winning some, but growing from a little girl to a strong sensuous young woman conscious of her power over men, contemptuous of oppressors and rejecting oppression. Nawal saw aspects of herself in Firdaus. She saw the qualities which were marginalized or hidden in many women by cultural and religious conditioning of patriarchal systems and for which she urged women to write, talk about women, draw women, and uphold women so that the world could understand the enigma that was hidden and misnamed by proscriptions on women. Lovely names like Gift (Nawal) and Paradise (Firdaus) may allude to parental benediction and good wishes, but there is another inscription by patriarchal power relations that have untold influence on human beings. The following section delineates the impact of group names encoded with negativity.

NAMING TO DENIGRATE

Naming is implicitly linked with colorism. Blackness socio-culturally connotes ugliness and the attendant sub-category labeling. The protagonist of *A Daughter of Isis* muses:

> I was proud of my dark skin. It was a beautiful brown, the color of silt brought down to my land by the waters of the Nile. I never hid it under make-up or powder or pastes of any kind, did not believe in a femininity born with slave society and handed down to us with class and patriarchy." (*Daughter* 7–8)

> My maternal aunts were also not happy with my hair since it was not silky and flowing like theirs. It had frizzy curls which Tante Ni'mat felt was ugly. "The groom will disappear the moment he sees your kinky hair, slave girl that you are. Warwar." She then proceeded to straighten out my hair with an iron rod heated on a flame. (*Daughter* 174)

The above quotations emphasize gender and colorism as Nawal's personal issues that are expressed in her writing and deserve our focus in this discussion of names and naming. Nawal (Gift) and Firdaus (Paradise) have names that can impact a child positively in a non-gendered and non-racialized world. In post-colonial Egypt struggling with colonial superimposition of gender and racial order on a system dealing with its own internal gender and cultural issues, the writing of "woman" or "black" on anybody adds extra layers of subordination on that person.

Unlike Firdaus who was accused of killing a man about to kill her, Nawal was accused of trying to "kill" the oppressive government under the leadership of President Anwar Sadat. Both Nawal and Firdaus knew the face of oppression from different angles. For Firdaus, it was her father who ate and left the family to starve, her uncle who taught her from her childhood to give her body to him in exchange for some attention or little kindness, the pimps that used her body to make money, police officers that used their power to rape and silence her. Firdaus's list of oppressors was enlarged to include rulers that exploited the masses like her father who in turn exploited women, princes who fed on the sweat of the masses while they lavished money on prostitutes, a system with officers in the ring of pimps who exploited those that they—the officers—should protect.

The connection of Firdaus and Nawal goes beyond storytelling to mentorship, and spiritual affinity. They were "partners in crime, love, and beauty." They both committed "crimes" for which they were incarcerated with one executed and the other on death list. From extreme religious conservative societies, both were unapologetic about the path that circumstances made them choose. They were unapologetic about ownership of their bodies as well as having multiple sex partners or what society regarded as prostitution in the case of Firdaus and serial polygamy in the case of Nawal. Of her multiple marriages and divorces, Nawal said, "I've already divorced two husbands before and when the third violated my rights, I divorced him as well . . . I'm a fighter until the last breath, a fighter for women's rights and I will not live with a husband who violates my rights" (El Saadawi, *Daughter* iv). Nawal and Firdaus were very beautiful when evaluated with eyes limited by one standard of beauty. Eyes enriched by diversity would reveal daunting beauty—born to be weak, but achieved boldness, assertiveness, confidence, and independence. Nawal "developed a feeling and admiration" for Firdaus who seemed "exceptional in the world of women to which I was accustomed" (*Woman* xi).

Nawal's feeling and actions after Firdaus's death are akin to what Siegel in *Entwined Lives* describes as survivor's guilt experienced by twin-less twins, those whose twins have died. Her internalization of Firdaus was intense, creating oneness that "vibrated within" her and she seemed to see Firdaus in front of her, and could "trace the lines of her forehead, her lips, her eyes, watch her as she moved with pride" (*Woman* xii). The vibration stemmed from empathy, credibility of Firdaus's story, and admiration. Nawal speaks about the feeling of isolation, silence, and harshness of the iron bars during her incarceration and how she kept looking for Firdaus in the faces of other women prisoners even though she knew that she had been executed. She wanted to have a glimpse of Firdaus, "her head which she always held so high, the calm movements of her hands, or the stern look of her brown eye" (xi). None of the other women looked like her. Nawal felt a powerful and persistent feeling of vacuum and empathy, and eventually oneness that made her see Firdaus when she looked at herself in the mirror.

CONCLUSION

Essentially, the diverse pairs are reminiscent of Achebe's "twin kernels in different pods," the imagery used in discussing the intersection of the two heroines, Firdaus and Nawal. Her creativity, career, and achievement make her a winner and pacesetter as illustrated through her memorable books, *A Daughter of Isis* and *Woman at Point Zero*, and other achievements especially the exposure of the hidden practices to initiate change. Nawal lived to see her portrayal of Firdaus's story reach audiences in over twenty-two languages and a ban on circumcision that they both portrayed as the most painful experience of their lives. Nawal's name as Gift and Firdaus's name as Paradise are vindicated by their achievements which complement each other like twin kernels in one pod.

WORKS CITED

Achebe, Chinua. *No Longer at Ease*. Ivan Obolensky: New York, 1960.
Beauvoir, Simone de. *The Second Sex*. Trans. H. M. Parshley. New York: Vintage Books, 1974.
Friedan, Betty." The Problem that has no Name." *The Feminine Mystique*. New York: W. W. Norton, 1963, 15–32.
Goldsmith, Arthur H, Darrick Hamilton and William Darity. "From Dark to Light Skin Color and Wages among African Americans." *The Journal of Human Resources*, Vol. 2, No. 4 (Fall 2007): 701–738.
Newson-Horst, Adele..Ed. *The Essential Nawal El Saadawi: A Reader*. London: Zed Books, 2013.
Saadawi, Nawal El. Arthur Miller Freedom to Write Lecture: Interview by Anthony Appiah., September 9, 2009. https://www.youtube.com/watch?v=jue04c1_wkY.
Saadawi, Nawal El. A *Daughter of Isis.* Trans. Sherif Hetata. London: Zed Books, 2009.
Saadawi Nawal El. *Two Women in One*. Trans. Osman Nusairi and Jana Gough. London: Al Saqi Books, 1985.
Saadawi, Nawal El. *Woman at Point Zero*. Trans. Sherif Hetata. London: Zed Books, 2007.

Siegel Nancy. *Entwined Lives: Twins and What They Tell Us about Human Behavior.* New York: Plume Books, 2000.

NOTES

1. I first met Nawal El Saadawi in October 1998 at the International Airport in Indianapolis, Indiana USA during the Women in Africa and African Diaspora (WAAD) Conference. She was the keynote speaker, and her affable personality attracted many participants who listened attentively as she emphasized the need to expose issues that keep women and other oppressed groups down. I remember her sharp eyes and parting smile as she stated, "Never cease to tell the stories of women."

2. The author's sharp and piercing eyes are recreated in her alter egos. Clearly, Firdaus's and Nawal's sharp, piercing eyes are redolent of Bahiah's sharp black eyes in her novel *Two Women in One.*

Chapter 17

Women, Tradition, and Resistance in Zulu Sofola's *Wedlock of the Gods*

Irene Isoken Salami-Agunloye

INTRODUCTION

One of the greatest challenges of the African woman today, as with all Nigerian women, is her encumbrance with tradition. Women are put in bondage by scary tales of traditional beliefs and practices, taboos, and evil repercussion of disobedience. In recent times, many critics concerned about the terrorizing effects of these traditional beliefs and values, have challenged the perpetrators, questioning the relevance of these traditions in contemporary times. In the same vein, Zulu Sofola, has been criticized for holding tenaciously to cultural traditions in her plays, without any attempt at recreating them to conform with contemporary situations. A fair critical assessment of Sofola's works looks at the world of first-generation writers, whose main preoccupation was to stop the colonial masters from eroding African culture, or from "contaminating" it. In an attempt to do this, many of them stifled the dignity of African womanhood. Against this background, this paper will explore the role of traditional beliefs and values in Zulu Sofola's play *The Wedlock of the Gods* and the attempt made by her characters at challenging this traditional institution.

Given the fact that Zulu Sofola's debut play was published in 1971, she is regarded as the pioneer female playwright in Nigeria. Expatiating further on this, Olu Obaferni, in his book *Contemporary Nigerian Theatre: Cultural*

Heritage and Social Vision, observes that "Sofola has acquired the 'supernatural' and 'extra effort,' climbing off the 'traditional back seat' of women to steer the wheel of her creative productivity both on the stage and in the publishing houses" (158).

In the account above, Obafemi captures the background challenges and the terrain in which Sofola worked. Appreciating her works meant that they were compared with the works of other post-colonial literary giants like Wole Soyinka, Ola Rotimi, and J. P. Clark-Bekederemo who had already made their mark in the theater by the time she appeared. This in itself was a major challenge for Zulu Sofola that she surmounted over the years. Her experiences in her traditional environment have helped nourish her rich collection of writings. As an avant-garde and pacesetting female playwright as well as one who belongs to the first generation of Nigerian playwrights in the English language, Sofola has an impressive repertoire of writings which include: *The Disturbed Peace of Christmas* (1971), *The Wedlock of the Gods* (1972), *King Emene* (1974), *The Wizard of Law* (1975), *The Sweet Trap* (1977), *Old Wines are Tasty* (1981) and *Memories in the Moonlight* (1986). Her other works include but are not limited to *Songs of a Maiden*, *The Operators, Last Dreams*, and *Queen Omu-Aka of Oligbo*. Viewed from the traditional angle, many have criticized Sofola for being "static, idealistic and restricted to the representation of traditional values. Much as it is impactful in theatricality, *Wedlock of the Gods* is regarded as seriously undermined by its textual ideology" (Obafemi, *Contemporary* 162). Sofola's creativity which she demonstrates in her dramaturgy, carries with it remarkable competence. However, one would have wished Sofola used her theatrical competence, linguistic simplicity, and dramatic spectacle for a positive reconstruction of a new image for the contemporary Nigerian woman (Salami-Agunloye 124). This concern is also shared by Obafemi in his article titled "Zulu Sofola's Theatre." He queries:

> It is high time Zulu Sofola used the position of influence and pre-eminence she enjoys, as a leading female dramatist in Nigeria, to positive and pertinent ends. She must move away from the old school and depict realities of today. Rather than advocate the continued subjugation of the female folk in particular and humanity in general to old, outdated lore and burdens, she should strive towards the emancipation of her sex, in particular, and the liberation of humanity in general, from enslaving codes, icons and ideas. (65)

Similarly, a good number of African critics have commented that Sofola merely reproduces the traditional beliefs without any intervention to place them in their historical perspective. In *Wedlock of the Gods*, Sofola would rather allow Oguoma and Uloko to die in order to prove that tradition is supreme. In most of her works, Sofola advocates the preservation of the old traditional order, and a punishment for anyone who disobeys tradition. In *Sweet Trap*, we see elements of female suppression as a way of appealing to the men in society, in order for peace to prevail. The party ends in a fiasco to prove that insubordination of wives leads to shame and disgrace. Mrs. Sotubo must humiliate herself to assure her husband that she is indeed repentant. She also reinforces the much talked about cliché that women without husbands are dangerous company for a married woman who intends to keep her home This is established in the case of Mrs. Ajala and Clara.

In a discussion with a scholar on the issue of reconstructing the image of women, which was cited in Obafemi's *Contemporary Nigerian Theatre*, Sofola reemphasized that the emancipation of any educated African woman lies in her being obedient to laid down traditional rules and accepting the gender roles society has ascribed to her. Any deviation from this; results in disaster. She accordingly prescribes that "One should do whatever one is committed to do. But once you disturb whatever is there the repercussion will crush you" (cited in Obafemi, *Contemporary 184*). This is the case with Ogwuoma in *Wedlock of the Gods*, who is far ahead of her traditional society. She tries to "outsmart" her tradition, but the tradition outsmarts her for she is "crushed" by the tradition for liberating herself from a marriage which tradition had sanctioned as a mode of enslavement.

In her plays, Sofola openly displays elements of magic, myths, and rituals. In *Sweet Trap*, she finds a place for the Oke-Ibadan festival, an all-male festival that attacks only women. In defence of this Sofola says, "Well, that was how our forebearers felt and so it was" (cited in Obafemi, *Contemporary* 200).

For Sofola, whatever was good for our forefathers should be upheld by us, therefore it must be maintained, preserved, and re-enacted so that the younger generations and generations yet unborn will get to know it and also learn to respect it. This in itself contravenes contemporary discourse on Africa and development, which subscribes that the old must give way to the new if it no longer serves any useful social function.

But as noted by Ayo Akinwale in his article, "Zulu Sofola: Her Writings and their Undermeanings," Sofola's dramaturgy comprises:

> Plays based on the traditional society which if properly diagnosed from the position of one who wishes to see the people within a society examine their plight, their struggles, beliefs, sociological organization, and social control methods, can be seen as really relevant to contemporary society. If the past and the present are but one continuum, if the past can be used to examine the present so as to make projections into the future, then these plays serve a very relevant purpose. (68)

One wonders whether Sofola's traditional plays "serve a very relevant purpose." Viewing Sofola through the feminist lens, it is also obvious that Sofola pays lip service to feminism when one examines the "under meanings" of her supposed feminist plays like *Sweet Trap* for those who read the play superficially and conclude it is a feminist play. Some critics flay Sofola for "framing" and descending heavily on her female characters in order to humiliate as well as admonish them. She would seem to view the entire concept of feminism as completely alien, both to the African man and woman.

Sofola has always seen feminism as a façade, arguing that there is no need for African women to clamor for rights they already have. She has often argued that if women are hardworking enough there is room for them to excel. For her, there is no obvious restriction to the advancement of women, if they abide by the rules. She believes that the problem of women is not with the society but with the women themselves; she claims that women are ignorant of the great legacy of influence handed to them by their foremothers. Differently stated, female liberation is not really necessary in African traditional world where women have visibly been accorded relevance and power. In Westernizing the above, it is important to contextualize the time and space in which these views were upheld and aired. As a first-generation writer, many women though marginalized, were not conscious of it. Patriarchy was the norm and so many women accepted it. Besides, Sofola spoke from a privileged position in an academic institution at a time when being a member of such an institution was next to being a member of House of Parliament.

In most of her plays, Sofola deals with issues concerning women and tradition. She is always unequivocal about her defense of tradition. Her play titled *The Sweet Trap* deals with women, society, and acculturation. We see women struggling for equality with men. In that work, the playwright portrays women as socially active and capable of making decisions independently, we also find them in the anti-pedal stance to what they regard as an oppressive aspect of tradition. Finally, her belief in the tradition in which wives must highly esteem their husband is projected in the play. In her play *King Emene*, there is an attempt by a woman, the King's mother, to usurp authority; carrying out duties which traditionally belong to men. In Sofola's view Emene's mother had no right tampering with tradition in an attempt to work a way out for her son to be king. For doing this she collides with tradition and faces the reparation.

Generally, in her plays, she counterpoises the old against the young, new idea versus old tales. Her attitude seems to favor a preservation of the old even when this is inconvenient or unattainable. This is clearly demonstration in *Old Wines* Are *Tasty.* Akuagwu says to Okebuno who after several years of sojourn in Lagos and overseas has become alienated from his people: "It is old wines that are tasty, not the new. You have tasted in white man's country wines brewed only yesterday, but know our wine so that you may know what mix it is" (44).

Although one may not describe her as a feminist or a feminist writer, her works cannot escape examination from a feminist perspective. In fact, the rural world of her plays that is predominantly enmeshed and driven by traditions provides an enabling platform for such discourse as most of her plays dwell on women's issues either as subject matters or thematic preoccupations. Therefore, as Obafemi further espouses, "Consideration of Sofola's dramatic output from a feminist standpoint provides the second critical category of her theatre" (*Contemporary* 160). The "traditionalist reading of her works" is, glaringly the other category. Likewise in her submission, Nana Wilson-Tagoe upholds the need for a feminist reading of literary works by women as this

> can bring new energy and vitality to this writing and actually inspire a theorization within its own specific context and within the larger context of feminist writing. . . . At one level it permits us to contest and revise misconceptions and narrow representations that trap women within a male literary discourse; at another more liberating level it contextualizes women's creative production within a sphere of difference, of a female experience and perception that asks different questions and draws various significances from a woman writer's texts. (11)

In affirmation, Sofola also makes it clear in an interview with Adeola James that she is always in the business of questioning something because of her inquisitive and questioning mind. In her own words, "I am motivated by human problems that confront us all. It depends on the spirit of a problem before I get the kind of inspiration which makes me want to write about it. Then I do my research" (145). Although she does not, at the time, acknowledge the existence or evolution of a feminist consciousness in the writings of African women, she does however see its possibility (150–151).

Against this backdrop, this chapter will critically subject the play, *Wedlock of the Gods*, to a gender and feminist discourse in light of Ogwoma's fatal but courageous effort to liberate herself from a dehumanizing and oppressive tradition. Having had a traumatizing experience of a forced marriage, Ogwoma goes against tradition while still in mourning for her late husband in an outright move to circumvent being forced into another unwanted marriage prescribed by tradition. In view of women and, characters like Ogwoma who are victims of one form of oppression or the other, Obioma Nnaemeka makes the submission that, "Female characters are victims of multiple oppressions that are internally generated by oppressive customs and practices and externally induced by an equally oppressive, in egalitarian world order" (3–4). The recognition of the existence of several traditional practices across African societies that enslave and debase the African woman and which necessitates the feminist movement towards her liberation is obviously not any way in doubt. According to Emmanuel Ejiofor Ebo in an article titled "Cultural Challenges and Women Liberation in Nigeria: An Analysis of Zulu Sofola's Wedlock of the Gods and Julie Okoh's Edewede":

> Women liberation is the quest for freedom from female subjugation and oppression, obnoxious traditional practices, and sexism in order to achieve their empowerment. These obnoxious practices are the wicked customs and traditions unleashed on women the world over, most especially in the African continent. These traditional practices like female genital mutilation (FGM), widow inheritance, and widowhood rites, among others, are found within African culture. (236)

It is in regard to these degrading traditional practices which women are victims of and against which they seek freedom from its captivity that the play *Wedlock of the Gods* is treated from a gender perspective. While some critics may argue that the play's central conflict is not one of gender that borders on the superiority of the man over the "inferior" woman, one cannot ignore the fact that the play raises and addresses a very fundamental question of women being made insignificant objects of traditions. It therefore amounts to a gender issue that must be grappled with since tradition tends to privilege one segment of the society against the other. Tobe Levin stretches this thought further which, in itself, is a justification for this study:

> Tradition has become a shibboleth in the mouths of men who themselves are quite willing to accept change, provided their own privileges remain intact. Yet tradition can also be invoked with pride where the customs in question are innocuous. In the . . . struggle to extend human rights to women, the need to distinguish between beneficent and malicious practices has become more acute than ever. (208)

We shall in our analysis, investigate the effects of the "malicious practices" on Sofola's most vulnerable and afflicted protagonists.

THEORETICAL FRAMEWORK

African feminism is an interesting all-encompassing field of scholarship that is primarily dedicated to the cause of women with regard to the subjugating experiences of their lives and with the aim of transcending them. Much as feminism is the mother concept and African feminism its offshoot, both share common grounds in gender-related issues in their identification of women's subordinate status. According to Canice Chukwuma Nwosu:

> Feminism is therefore subsumed in genderism since it tilts towards questioning issues of women subjugation and empowerment. Patriarchism, another branch of genderism upholds the traditional society's presentation of natural and conservative images of women rooted deeply in the culturally assigned complementary role of a female folk as a help mate to the head of the family—the man. Unfortunately, this view has been stereotyped over the years and elongated to produce negative and distorted perception of women during different eras in human history. It is this chauvinistic tendency that enables men (in several instances) to lord it over women in marriage and other institutions of most societies. (196)

As an ideology and movement that identifies with and has a more indebt understanding of the African woman and her unpleasant experiences due to an overwhelming societal patriarchal configuration, African feminism looks into the peculiar nature of the various forms of oppression that African women encounter in their daily lives that are often enshrined in traditions as well as cultural practices. In the article "Creating Women's Knowledge: A Case Study of Three African Women Writers," by Wanjiku Mukabi Kabira and Amos Burkeywo, African feminism is presented thus:

> African feminism is reflected in the struggle by African women to be able to take their place in the political arena, exploding myths about male supremacy and interrogating women's lives in areas such as marriage, motherhood, areas traditionally put on the pedestal . . . African feminism is the combination of all the various struggles against social, cultural, political and economic marginalization that have dogged African women. It is the struggle for African women to find their authentic selves, to declare "I am" and "we are" and to demand for a new world that is created by the experiences, aspirations, skills and knowledge of both men and women. African feminists are involved in the twin journey, that is, liberation from all forms of oppression and a return to feel comfortable in their own skins and in their own societies. For women, the second journey is to go back to their authentic selves and begin to create a new world that is friendly to men, women, and African societies. In other words, transforming our societies to create more humane societies. (27)

Carole Boyce Davies who suggests that African feminist consciousness, amongst its other goals, does look "over certain traditional inequities which continue to subordinate African women" (7), also cites Filomina Steady's observed inequities against African women which constitute the focal concerns of African feminism, "Among them, lack of choice in motherhood and marriage, oppression of barren women, genital mutilation, enforced silence and a variety of other forms of oppression intrinsic to various societies which still plague African women's lives and must inevitably be at the crux of African feminist theory" (7).

In the same vein, Omolara Ogundipe-Leslie builds on Mao-Tse Tung's "mountain on the back" metaphor to further accentuate the oppression of African women. In no particular order, these include oppression from the outside world (foreign interference and influence); heritage of (often feudal and subjugating) traditions handed down from generations to generations; men, who are always in the habit of exerting their manliness and dominance over women (especially in abusive ways); her race, which makes her economically vulnerable given that global economic pattern is drawn along racial class; her backwardness, which can largely be attributed to both colonialism and neo-colonialism that privilege the men above the women and, thus, leaving the latter relatively lagging behind the former; finally, herself. On account of the last point, Ogundipe-Leslie makes a noteworthy argument of self-perception being the most crucial test for the African woman since it will ultimately have to decide her own freedom (89).

It is in such respect that bell hooks defined feminism as the woman's "freedom to decide her own destiny, freedom from sex determined role, freedom from society's oppression and restrictions, freedom to express her thoughts fully and to convert them freely into action" (24). Therefore, in *Wedlock of the Gods*, the female protagonist's (Ogwoma's) non-conformity to tradition should not be interpreted or misconstrued as a mere blatant attempt to desecrate a communal traditional heritage but, of course, as an attempt to exert her freedom of choice and also her rights as a human being to be free from an enslaving and strangulating web of tradition. In this way, the playwright makes a bold statement that raises awareness about the state of women in traditional African societies and the urgent need for the reassessment and modification of certain traditional practices. Along this line, Nwosu again asserts:

> The people's tradition as put in place by the family, kinship system and the community is respected and revered even when they appear oppressive or offensive against any group or members of the same society. Traditional societies call the practices against the female folk taboos or restrictions; fortunately or unfortunately, the male child has an edge over the female one as soon as they become members of the society. Thus, these taboos have been there since the beginning of the society. However, while their impact in the West is wound up with civilization; they unfortunately degenerate into instruments of oppression in Africa as we develop. (197)

Against the backdrop of such discrimination and oppression against women, African feminist discourse entered the "debate in an attempt to change supposed women domination and oppression in a 'patriarchal' society. Indeed, it is through debate that feminist theory and practices have evolved to incorporate the discourse on the changing circumstances of women's socio-political and economic conditions" (Obadiegwu 84).

In light of the task before feminist writers who must indefatigably continue to make commentaries on traditional practices that oppress women and which need overhauling Annabella Rodrigues counsels that, "It is easier to eliminate the colonial, bourgeois influences that were imposed on us and identified with the enemy than to eliminate generations of tradition from within our own society" (quoted in Davies 8). This is, however, not to discourage criticisms and clamor for such traditions to be reconstructed along the lines of egalitarianism but to enable feminist conscious critics and writers to be well aware of how deeply entrenched these traditions are, which would require them to be resolutely prepared for the challenge.

Summarizing the nucleus of true African feminism which, according to Davies, is first and foremost a shared struggle with African men towards the obliteration of foreign and European domination and/or exploitation, it challenges men to recognize salient aspects of women's subjugation and the various inequities/limitations against them that are to be found in traditional societies across Africa and reinforced by colonialism. She insists that African feminism examines various institutions in African societies, embracing structures that are valuable and in the interest of women while rejecting detrimental ones. Arising in view of the concrete realities of women's lives in African societies, Davies points out that the privileges accorded to men, especially on marital grounds, at the expense of women need to be attacked for a more egalitarian marriage institution. With respect to women's rights and freedom, African feminism also aims at exploring various traditional and contemporary avenues of choice for women (8–10). Equally, Micere Mugo articulates "a system where all the oppressive institutions are dismantled—politically, socially for the sake of men and women" (quoted in Davies 11).

While literature may enhance our understanding of various African traditions, it equally provides the avenue to tackle traditions that work against women's development and progress. It is therefore no surprise that we are inundated with all kinds of literary texts today that seek to (re)awaken the consciousness of Africans to the various forms of social injustices that are being perpetuated against women in the guise of tradition. From poetry to prose and to drama, literature continues to form the basis for scholarly exploration into an inequitable society that harbors and favors women's traditional subjugation. As cited in Binebai, Calvin Ong expresses this notion:"All authors disguise their frustrations and problems of their time into the book. Although many people may not realize it, sometimes there is a deeper meaning behind the story. For example, a story might be thought of as a struggle between good and evil, but it is really showing the author's protest at a war between two nations" (370).

In the context of this paper, through the purview of feminism and African feminism to be precise, we are dealing with a literary text that is a contestation of traditions that discriminatorily victimize women. Whether or not the play, *Wedlock of the Gods*, has been written under the impulsion of feminist consciousness, the treatment of the work from a feminist standpoint is based on the conviction that Zulu Sofola, as an African woman, did take to the medium of writing for social commentaries. Therefore, for this reason, *Wedlock of the Gods* is viewed as a play that exposes the plights of women in the terrain of tradition and, is thereby, a call for an egalitarian traditional society where there are no discrepancies between a man and a woman in the formulation or application of customs and traditions. On this note, Irene Assiba D'almeida points out that "the language in the writing of African women is necessarily both an aesthetic expression and a powerful weapon, able to convey a committed message" (11) of traditionally oppressed women and their resistance to such oppressive traditions. Consequently, Sofola's *Wedlock of the Gods* portrays horrible traditions like forced marriage, dehumanizing widowhood rites, objectifying widow transfer/inheritance among all other unpleasant cultural practices that continue to plague women's lives. The need then arises for a feminist movement and discourse to advocate women's total emancipation from the whims of such traditions.

WOMEN, TRADITION, AND RESISTANCE IN *WEDLOCK OF THE GODS*

Wedlock of the Gods, as a tragic play, is thematically akin to William Shakespeare's classic play Romeo and Juliet. The plot of the story revolves around two ill-fated lovers who dare to disregard tradition in order to be bonded in marriage. Ogwoma had been forced into marriage with a richer man, Adigwu, without her consent and at the expense of her happiness with "poor" Uloko with whom she is deeply in love. Her forced marriage was predicated on the fact that her parents needed the money from her bride price to treat her younger brother of his ailment. Three years into the marriage, in what Ogwoma later considers to be divine intervention and providence, Adigwu dies a mysterious death with "swollen stomach." As demanded by tradition, Ogwoma is to mourn her deceased husband for a period of three months in confinement with her head shaven and her body covered in ashes after which she would then be inherited as a wife by Adiwgu's brother. By way of resistance, she becomes pregnant for her true love Uloko two months into the stipulated period of mourning. This singular act by these young lovers, which is seen as a taboo, takes the succeeding actions of the play to a whole new dimension of community frenzy. There is resentment, as well as hostility and open feud on the parts of characters, especially the women, who are opposed to one another. Ogwoma's mother, Nneka, faults Uloko and his mother; Uloko's mother, in turn, faults Nneka and her daughter, whereas Odibei is determined to avenge her son's death. In the end, through diabolical and magical means, Odbie succeeds in putting Ogwoma to death and, in a retaliatory move, Uloko kills Odibie and then takes his own life to be reunited with his love by drinking the same poisonous concoction that Odibei had conjured Ogwoma into drinking. In the production note of the play, Zulu Sofola says:

> *Wedlock of the Gods* is a tragedy which finds its roots in the ritual of death and mourning . . . the widow (Ogwoma) expresses a sense of liberation from unwanted marriage while the mother of the deceased (Odibei) performs rites meant to destroy her son's widow as an act of vengeance for supposedly killing her son. (1)

A very decisive yet objective way to begin this analytic exploration as it concerns women's resistance in the face of their victimization by tradition is to state that the traditional system of bride price across African societies like Nigeria has somewhat reduced women to mere objects or commodity to be "sold out" (given out) to the highest bidder. Kabira and Burkeywo rightly observe that "patriarchy looks at women as objects. In the course of negotiating the bride price, it is the men in the community who negotiate and determine how much should be paid. The woman is consequently, reduced to a commodity that can be quantified (29). In the same vein, Helen Chukwuma sees this bride price as exploitation of womanhood, as a woman is supposed to generate income for the family. She regrets that marriage is the most subjugating feature in African womanhood (xix). In support of this Chioma Opara opines that a woman's gendered body is flagrantly immolated on the altar of culture (57).

For some of these parents like Ibekwe and Nneka (Ogwoma's parents) who must use what is at their disposal to get what they want or need, girl-children become sources of income. Ogwoma's friend, Anwasia, attests to this:

> Anwasia: Ogwoma, our people say that a man's daughter is a source of wealth to him. Your parents need the money for a very expensive sacrifice for your brother whom sickness almost killed. You should have been happy that your money saved the life of your own brother. (9)

Without respect for her consent, feelings, and emotional well-being, Ogwoma is forced to marry Adigwu because he can afford the money for her bride price needed so badly by her parents in order to cure Edozie's illness. As a result of this forced marriage, she reluctantly endures for three years a marital union shrouded in unhappiness because she never loved Adigwu but Uloko. Ebo who touches on Sofola's reflection of different cultural practices that are against women in his study has this to say about forced marriages:

> In the play, Zulu Sofola shows that women in Africa are bound everywhere by cultural practices that degrade them. Her exploration of the issue of forced marriage, which immediately brings to mind that of child marriage, is an important aspect of women disempowerment since it reduces women to certain level of powerlessness and displaces them in the scheme of things. It is clear that poverty is the major reason for forced marriages; thus, most parents, especially those in the rural areas, do not bother sending their daughters to school. Rather, they prefer marrying them off to men who are old enough to be their fathers. (241–242)

Ogwoma is denied her conjugal bliss with Uloko because he is not able to raise the money demanded as her bride price. Ogwoma's parents did not even consider enlisting the help of family members to raise such money which would have allowed Ogwoma have her desired marriage. Yet, when Ogwoma's pregnancy for Uloko becomes public knowledge, Ibekwe her father, does not hesitate to call the family together to discuss and find a solution to the sacrilegious situation. Ibekwe claims the type of family he belongs to, perhaps one that is not accustomed to helping one another, is the reason why he refrained from soliciting their help. Possibly, Edozie's critical condition could have tweaked their sympathy/empathy into helping out financially. But without taking the effortless course, he decides to trade his daughter's happiness for money. Okolie berates Ibekwe for giving Ogwoma out in marriage for financial reasons and against her wish rather than calling on the family for help (28).

The manner in which Ogwoma is compelled to become Adiwgu's wife is inhumane in all ramifications; it has no justification of any kind. Ogwoma laments that her parents who were clearly driven by their hunger for money, tied her like a goat and threw her away to a man she hated. (18) She rued the harsh treatment she received before her mother who thinks they did nothing wrong in the way she was given away in marriage.

Her pain is understandable, given that her parents knew how deeply and truly in love she was with Uloko yet they ignored the fact that being married to Uloko would have brought her happiness and emotional fulfillment. Ogwoma endures a marriage that is more of a charade for three years when eventually Adigwu dies of sickness. Adigwu's death means freedom for her even though he will be mourned. She tells Anwasia, "I prayed for the past three years for my God to deliver me from this marriage. My prayers were answered and nothing can stop me this time" (9).

On account of Adigwu's demise, his stricken mother, Odibei suspects that Ogwoma may have murdered her husband. This is a true reflection of the belief system in many traditional African societies when such deaths occur. We can infer that the death of women in many traditional societies in Nigeria and across Africa is often considered to be natural while that of a man is contrastingly often perceived as murder. Not in the least veering from a sexist tradition, Odei is convinced that her son, Adigwu, did not die a natural death. She says, "Adigwu died of a swollen stomach. A man who dies like a pregnant woman did not die a natural death. Somebody killed him" (6). The alleged culprit and murderer is Adigwu's bereaved wife, Ogwoma. Odibei believes her son was killed by Ogwoma either directly with poison or remotely as an aftermath of her alleged harlotry which is deemed a cultural taboo.

As tradition mandates and dictates, Ogwoma is to observe a dehumanizing three months' solitary mourning rite that involves her head being shaven, sitting on the floor and, afterwards, being inherited by her late husband's brother amongst other cultural dictates. Surely, such mourning rites reek of double standard for they are not applicable to widowers. Across Africa, men who lose their wives are often excused from such dehumanizing traditional mourning and purification rites. More often than not, after the necessary burial ceremonies, most men decide for themselves how long they would be in mourning before finding their way around other women who would make them happy.

Clearly and understandably, in an act of resistance to a tortuous and obnoxious tradition that would again compel her into another marriage she does not intend to be in, she makes her own choice by taking that opportunity to be finally (re)united with her true love, Ogwoma does not complete the traditional period of mourning before re-igniting her relationship with Uloko. In an act of adding insult to injury, she gets pregnant for him. As a result, she does not only defile and defy tradition by getting involved with a man while she is still covered in ashes, she also, against all odds, allows herself to get pregnant while she is in mourning. It is a deliberate act and she has no misgivings about her choice of action. Anwasia tries in vain to make her understand the gravity of what she has done in their conversation:

> Anwasia: Look, a woman's honor lies in her name and her sense of shame.
>
> Ogwoma: I don't want to talk about it . . . (8–9)

The severity of the taboo committed by Ogwoma on the African cosmology is stressed by Ejeke:

> The worst form of adultery is that which takes place while a woman is still in mourning for her dead husband. This type of adultery has grave repercussions on the living, the dead, and the unborn members of the family. Severe disorganization is introduced into the family: the dead husband's spirit cannot return to the world of the ancestors; his reincarnation is dreaded for it would disrupt the destinies of the one in whom he were reincarnated; indeed the entire system of transmutation is put in jeopardy: this is the type of illicit affair treated in *Wedlock of the Gods*. (55)

If the assertion above is anything to go by then the extent of its truthfulness is the same measure by which it reflects and underscores the magnitude of Ogwoma's fearless resistance against a tradition that takes delight in her subjugation and unhappiness. Her rebellious act which thus disrupts the transition from one African world view (living) to the other (dead—ancestors) goes to suggest the evolvement of Ogwoma into an audacious and courageous character capable of taking and walking a path other women would normally dread. In view of this, Osita C. Ezenwanebe believes that Zulu Sofola, in *Wedlock of the Gods*, succeeds in,

> Creating strong, central female characters who break women's culture of silence and contend male domination in patriarchal African culture.... Ugwoma, the strong female protagonist, attempts to transgress the sanctity of widowhood rites and wife inheritance, asserting her right to personal choice and self-fulfillment by getting pregnant for her outwitted, soul lover, Uloko, during the period she is mourning the death of her imposed husband, Adigwu. Despite the fact that Ugwoma's act is considered a taboo among her people, because tradition expects her to sit for three months beside the ashes in the fireplace and undergo ritual cleansing before ever having sexual relation with another man, she defiantly argues her quest for self-actualization and personal freedom. Unfortunately, she fails to pull through as she dies with her lover in the struggle. (263)

Ogwoma is very much conscious of what has been done and does not feel any iota of remorse. She does not, for a minute, wish for it to be undone regardless of the repercussions. The penalty for Ogwoma on account of this act is spelt out by her mother as "a swelling of the body with water leaking from everywhere ... even after death no forest will accept your body" (19).

The chastisement tradition has in stock for Ogwoma's partner is very obvious. He must be punished for breaking tradition. In the first place a woman who is mourning her husband must not be visited by any other man until the cleansing rites have been performed on her. Any action against this is an abomination that is frowned upon by the gods. Undaunted, Uloko remains resolute in his battle against a retrogressive tradition.

It is worthy to note that there is hardly any hint on the nature of Uloko's penalty. This omission is rather a true reflection of societal manipulation of traditions that often suddenly become vague especially when men appear to get hit or receive its whips. The story of the adulterous woman in the Bible as contained in John 8:1–11 is a good reference at this point. Ogwoma could be likened to the woman allegedly caught in the act of adultery and about to be stoned to death according to the Law of Moses, before she was finally rescued by Jesus. The adulterous man was never mentioned.

Another aspect of tradition that victimizes women is the levirate marriage, the transfer of widows to brothers of their late husbands. In this instance, a widow who has completed the stipulated period of mourning is to be adopted as a wife by her late husband's brother especially when such a marriage did not yield any child before the death of the man. Ogwoma loathes this levirate marriage tradition of a widow's adoption in her dialogue with Anwasia:

> Ogwoma: Is the woman taken by force? Is she not to choose between her brother-in-law and someone else?
>
> Anwasia: Adigwu had no child by you. His people want a child for him by a woman who was his wife. You are that wife and his brother can have that child for him by you. (21–22)

Ogwoma is as defiant as she is rebellious. Her resistance as well as reaction is well captured by bell hooks when she bares her heart on a similar incident. "Growing up in a southern black father dominated, working class household, I experienced (as did my mother, my sisters and brother) varying degrees of patriarchal tyranny and it made me angry-it made us all angry. Anger led me to question the politics of male dominance and enabled me to resist sexist socialization" (10).

In a similar vein, Ogwoma fiercely resists "sexist socialization." Her outspokenness and willpower to reject a tradition that approves of her being passed on to another man she does not desire can be likened to the defiance exhibited by Ramatoulaye who undergoes a mandatory seclusion of four months and ten days prescribed for Muslim widows.in Mariama Ba's *So Long a Letter* Ramatoulaye is faced with the Senegalese Muslim tradition of widow inheritance which provokes her to reject her late husband's brother who desires to take her as a wife. Coming out of mourning, she tells Tamsir her brother-in-law: that she is not an object to be passed from one hand to another (58). Reacting to the oppressive nature of customs and traditions on marriage, Kabira and Burkeywo once again posit that, "Tradition dictates marriage without considering happiness and love between husband and wife but Ramatoulaye cherishes marriage as an act of faith and of love and it involves the union of body, mind, and spirit. It is not just getting married to bear children and serve a man but there has to be love and commitment (30).

Ogwoma has been trapped in an unwanted marriage which was brutally imposed on her by her parents. Now, the traditional provision for her transfer to Okezie is about to plunge her into another unwanted marriage which implies another period of matrimonial bondage. It is this sense of subjugation that drives her to be even more defiant and courageous in her outright resistance to tradition. For her there is no form of compromise with being inherited as a wife by Adigwu's brother which would definitely be at the expense of her radical relationship with Uloko. Ogwoma is blunt and resolute in her refusal to succumb or conform to a suffocating tradition. Her resistance to tradition has no inhibition; there is just no limit to the extent she would go even if it means losing her life. She intimates her mother with her preparedness to ardently reject tradition without fear:

Ogwoma: Kill me if you like but you cannot stop me from loving Uloko. (20)

Both Ogwoma and Uloko are revolutionary in their stance. From this moment, it is a clear confrontational picture: on one level, it is between the young lovers and tradition that seeks to pull them apart a second time and, on another, it is between them and the diabolical Odibei who seeks to avenge her son's death. Similarly, Osita Catherine Ezenwanebe suggests that "it is a game of circular reasoning in which each party sticks to its gun. The community, laying claims on tradition and customs that privilege communal life, the individuality clinging to the power of the self to assert its uniqueness" (26).

In the end, Odibei nocturnally casts a spell on Ogwoma who, in turn, carries out her commands of drinking from a small pot that has been placed behind her water-pot. In her dying moments, after drinking Odibei's concoction, Ogwoma says to Uloko "Tell them Odibei took me" (54). Ogwoma's death is devastating to Uloko who reacts under a vengeful impulse. According to Christine Odi, "In his pain and anger, Uloko fulfills the biblical injunction 'suffer not a witch to live' (Ex. 22:18) by killing Odibei. He also drinks from the pot Ogwoma had drunk from, and dies beside her" (6).

With their demise, both Ogwoma and Uloko resisted a tradition that is set to pull them apart. Rather than be alive and be bound by some unpleasant tradition, they chose the path of death which ultimately embodies their open and uncompromising revolutionary stance against such traditions. Ogwoma as well as Uloko) died fighting for freedom of choice and freedom from oppression—dying for a noble cause—rather than live as enslaved subjects of a discriminatory tradition. Hence, Obafemi in *Contemporary Nigerian Theatre* opines, "The action of the two lovers in modernist terms, and to a large extent favored in the script, is commendable" (164). He goes on to affirm that in the dramaturgy, even the dramatist is convinced that it is an act of injustice to deprive Uloko of Ogwoma "on account of pecuniary insolvency" (164).

CONCLUSION

In *Wedlock of the Gods*, Zulu Sofola, like most other female playwrights today, consciously or unconsciously reacts to the traditional subjugation of women through her creation of a strong and assertive female character who, in her quest for emancipation from a dehumanizing confinement, doggedly clashes with a tradition that inherently breeds social and gender inequality through various cultural norms and practices. Hence, this study has been able to explore the reality of women like Ogwoma in some African traditional societies who are oppressed and maltreated owing to traditions that often favor men.

In light of this, therefore, we need to re-evaluate upheld traditional practices in our various communities/societies in order to reconfigure or push aside obnoxious traditions that are oppressive and abusive to women and also deprive them of their rights to various freedoms as human beings. If equity must thrive in society, then there should be a paradigm shift in the construction and application of tradition. One section of society should not be unnecessarily made vulnerable as victims of such traditions while the other is protected and positioned in such a way that they are able to evade the penalizing impact of tradition when they are found wanting. Equity and social justice demand that tradition, which should be progressive and for the good of humanity, should be binding on men and women equally and devoid of any form of discrimination. They should be treated equally and not subjected to different traditional rules, privileges or liberties. To this end, Olaghere notes:

> Sofola focused on gender oppression as a social problem. She intended to address gender oppression rooted in tradition by teaching traditional customs to her audience first in order for audiences to make informed and progressive decisions about what to change within traditional practices; and thus, her traditionalist approach to change requires cognizance and recognition of tradition as an initial step. (1)

This clearly explicates why Sofola's legacy as an iconic playwright is deeply rooted in the graphic delineation of hidebound African traditional practices.

WORKS CITED

Akinwale, Ayo. "Zulu Sofola: Her Writings and their Undermeanings." *Nigerian Female Writers: A Critical Perspective*. Eds. Henrietta C. Otokunefor and Obiageli C. Nwodo. Ikeja: Maithouse Press Ltd., 1989, 68–73. Print.

Ba, Mariama. *So Long a Letter*. Trans. Modupe Bode-Thomas. London: Heinemann, 2008. Print.

Binebai, Benedict. "Protest Premise in Drama and Theatre of Africa: A Spotlight on Cultural Nationalism." *The Dawn Journal* 2.2 (2013): 366–379. Print.

Chukwuma, Helen. *Feminism in African Literature*. Port Harcourt: Pearl Publishers, 2003.

D'almeida, Irene A. "Introduction." *Francophone African Women Writers: Destroying the Emptiness of Silence*. Gainesville: University Press of Florida, 199: 1–31. Print.

Davies, Carole B. "Introduction: Feminist Consciousness and African Literary Criticism." *Ngambika: Studies of Women in African Literature*. Eds. Carole Boyce Davies and Anne Adams Graves. Trenton: Africa World Press, Inc., 1990. 1–23. Print.

Ebo, Emmanuel Ejiofor. "Cultural Challenges and Women Liberation in Nigeria: An Analysis of Zulu Sofola's *Wedlock of the Gods* and Julie Okoh's *Edewede*." *Gender Discourse in African Theatre, Literature and Visual Arts: A Festschrift in Honour of Professor Mabel Evwierhoma*. Eds. Tracie Chima Utoh-Ezeajugh and Barclays Foubiri Ayakoroma. Ibadan: Kraft Books Ltd., 2015, 236–248. Print.

Ejeke, Odin Solomon. "The Tragic Vision in *Wedlock of the Gods* and *King Emene*." *African Women. Drama and Performance*. Ed. Irene Salami-Agunloye. Boston: Evergreen Books, 2011, 51–60. Print.

Ezenwanebe, Osita Catherine. "Community and the Individual in the Dramatic World of the Igbo: Conformity and Contestation." *Global Journal of Human-Social Science* 14, 8(2014): 20–30. Print.

hooks, bell. "Feminism: A Movement to End Sexist Oppression." *Feminisms*. Eds. Sandra Kemp and Judith Squires, New York: Oxford University Press, 1997, 22–27. Print.

———. *Feminist Theory, From Margin to Centre* Boston: South End Press,1984.

James, Adeola. *In their Own Voices. African Women Writers Talk*. London: James Curry, 1991. Print.

Kabira, Wanjiku M., and Amos Burkeywo. "Creating Women's Knowledge: A Case Study of Three African Women Writers." *American Journal of Academic Research* 1.1 (2016): 25–37. Print.

Levin, Tobe. "Women as Scapegoats of Culture and Cult: An Activist's View of Female Circumcision in Ngugi's *The River Between*." *Ngambika: Studies of Women in African Literature*. Eds. Carole Boyce Davies and Anne Adams Graves. Trenton: African World Press, Inc., 1990, 205–221. Print.

Nnaemeka, Obioma, Ed. "Introduction." *The Politics of (M)Othering: Womanhood, Identity, and Resistance in African Literature*. London: Routledge, 1997. Print.

Nwosu, Canice Chukwuma. "African Feminism and Zulu Sofola's Paradigm Shift in *The Sweet Trap*." European *Journal of Modern Languages and Literatures* 4 (2015): 193–207. Print.
Obadiegwu, Cyprain C. "From Alternative Ideology to Theatrical Diversities: African Women Rights Advocates and the Politics of Feminism." *Feminist Aesthetics and Dramaturgy of Irene Salami-A gunloye. Idegu, Emmy Unujaed.* Kaduna: TW Press, 2009. Print.
Obafemi, Olu. *Contemporary Nigerian Theatre, Cultural Heritage and Soial Vision.* Ibadan: Krafts Books Ltd, 2001. Print.
———. "Zulu Sofola's Theatre." *Nigerian Female Writers. A Critical Perspective.* Ed. Henrietta C. Otokunefor and Obiageli C. Nwodo. Ikeja: Maithouse Press Ltd., 1989, 60–67. Print.
Odi, Christine. "Concept of Witchcraft in African Drama and Negative Female Stereotyping in Select Nigerian Plays." *International Journal of Language, Literature and Gender Studies* 5.1 (2016): 1–12. Print.
Ogundipe-Leslie, Omolara. "African Woman, Culture and Another Development." *The Journal of African Marxists* 5 (1984): 77–92. Print.
Olaghere, Ajima M., "Change through Tradition in the Work of Zulu Sofola. Rehearsal Presentation Outline." Undergraduate Research Symposium. 2007 Paper 51.1–6. Print.
Opara, Chioma. *Her Mother's Daughter*: *The African Writer as Woman*. Port Harcourt: University of Port Harcourt Press, 2004.
Salami-Agunloye, Irene I. "Challenging the Masters' Craft: Nigerian Women Playwrights in the Theatre of Men." *African Women. Drama and Performance*. Ed. Irene Salami-Agunloye. Boston: Evergreen Books, 2011, 112–167. Print.
Sofola, Zulu. *Wedlock of the Gods*. London: Evans Brothers Ltd., 1972. Print.
Wilson-Tagoe, Nana. "Reading Towards a Theorisation of African Women's Writing: African Women Writers within Feminist Gynocriticism." *Writing African Women.Gender, Popular Culture and Literature in West Africa*. Ed. Stephanie Newell. London: Zed Books Ltd, 1997, 11–28. Print.

Chapter 18

Nadine Gordimer's Multiplex Legacy

Ikeogu Oke

INTRODUCTION

We would all be excused, if our appreciation of a writer's legacy is restricted to their works or if we expect the evaluation of their legacies to be confined to their oeuvre. After all, a writer's primary mission is to write, to create literary works whose beauty can be enough justification for their existence. Even Nadine Gordimer would agree with this; for Stephen Clingman, a Professor of English at the University of Massachusetts observed that Gordimer has echoed Gabriel Garcia Marquez's submission that the best way a writer can serve a revolution is to write as well as he can (Gordimer, Nobel 215).

However, literary works, as evidenced by the works of some of their creators, can also be used to champion causes such as social and racial justice, as Gordimer—and other writers such as James Baldwin and Chinua Achebe—did with their works, defending such and other humanistic values against the interests of powerful systems that would rather profit from their desecration, thereby exposing themselves to persecution by such systems in the form of harassments, arrests, incarcerations, exile, book bans, censorship and whatnot, some of which became Gordimer's lot or that of some of her books—specifically *The Late Bourgeois World*, *A World of Strangers*, *Burger's Daughter* and *July's People*, which were banned by the Apartheid government for periods ranging from one month to twelve years—but in spite of which she became the recipient of the 1991 Nobel Prize in Literature, with the Nobel committee noting that she, according to *The New York Times* has, "through her magnificent epic writing . . . —in the words of Alfred Nobel—been of very great benefit to humanity."

Essentially a writer's legacy usually manifests in two forms, which I would call the legacy of corpus and the legacy of exceptionality. The legacy of corpus, on the one hand, comprises a mere reckoning of the writer's publications and other forms of output, a compilation of the totality of the writer's works in the various literary genres and any other formats. The legacy of exceptionality, on the other hand, is legacy in the form of that which sets the writer's work apart; put differently, it is the type of legacy by which the writer makes a unique impression on the reader or the world.

As the above definitions suggest, every writer leaves a legacy of corpus. It can therefore be described as a common denominator of all literary lives. And having this quality of being universally achievable, as it were, makes it rather unremarkable, by far less important than the legacy of exceptionality, which, as experience shows, cannot be ascribed to every writer, given that only a relatively small fraction of writers—in any generation or for all time—can be said to stand out for the quality or impact of their works or their contributions in other ways to the advancement of the literary vocation or the improvement of the world.

And the reason for this is not far-fetched: as humans we generally value those things that are commonplace less than those that are rare; we tend to take the former for granted, and this cannot but apply to the legacy of corpus in relation to literature.

But then, there are exceptions to this rule when there is a prodigious manifestation of the commonplace through the productivity of one individual, such as a prolific writer who, for instance, and speaking hypothetically, published twenty qualitative novels during a literary career that lasted thirty years, given that the normal expectation would be for a writer, even those believed to possess extraordinary genius and energy, to publish a much less number of novels of such quality within the same period. Therefore, such an exceptional corporal output becomes in itself an index of a unique legacy on the part of the writer, worthy of recognition besides those qualities or other indicators such as stylistic, social, and political impact that must be taken into account in evaluating the legacy of exceptionality.

Speaking of stylistic, social, and political impact, writers have been known for their contribution to improving the sense of literary style either in the form of the aesthetics of language or composition integral to their work. Chinua Achebe, for instance, has earned special recognition as the novelist that pioneered the "domestication" of the English language through his novels by infusing it with Igbo words, phrases, idioms, proverbs, and sayings, thus making it to accommodate the weight of his African experience. Beyond that, it is recognized as one of his legacies as a writer that he inspired a new generation of African writers, as literary disciples who comprised what has been described as the Achebe school, and through his fictional works and essays canvassed for the recognition of the dignity of the African and indeed all those human beings whom he sums up sympathetically in *Home and Exile* as "the kind of 'nothing people' Naipaul would love to hammer into the ground with his well-crafted mallet of deadly prose" (Achebe, *Home* 95)— against their contrived negative depiction by writers from the West.

Again, writers, through and beyond their works, have been recognized for establishing or deepening through practice or association the relevance of literary trends or movements such as classicism, modernism, postmodernism, realism, magical realism, naturalism, existentialism, negritude, and the absurd. This class of influential writers (which includes poets and playwrights) ranges from Giovanni Boccaccio and Thomas More as classicists from the fourteenth and fifteenth centuries respectively to such writers closer to or contemporaneous with our times such as Leo Tolstoy (as a champion of realism), T. S. Eliot (as a propagator of modernism), Emile Zola (as an exemplification of naturalism), Jean-Paul Sartre (as an advocate for existentialism), Samuel Beckett (as a champion of absurdism), Gabriel Garcia Marquez (as a propagator of magical realism), Leopold Sedar Senghor (as a philosopher and promoter of Negritude). Such activities by such writers, depending on the levels of their involvement with such literary trends, can be regarded as having created or deepened the channels of the practice or classification of literature though such literary trends or movements, which is a sort of cultural legacy that can be associated with or separated from the corpus and quality of their works.

In trying to evaluate a writer's legacy of corpus, it would suffice to provide an answer to the question: How many works did the writer produce in the various literary genres and what are their titles? And answering it, as it has been suggested, invites a task that hardly requires more than a bibliographical compilation.

However, in trying to apprehend let alone evaluate a writer's legacy of exceptionality, answers would need to be provided for a far broader range of questions in relation to the writer's works and life. The questions include: What are the unique markers of the writer's style that may have influenced other writers leading to the growth of the literary art through their adoption and propagation of that style? Did the writer found a literary movement or invent a literary trend that attracted a considerable followership and provided a unique platform for the creation and evaluation of literature? Where the writer did not found or invent any such movements or trends, did she or he play a significant role in an existing one, becoming a motivating force in its advancement of the cause of literature? Did the writer through their works or other means fight for the improvement of the world as a social, political, cultural, or moral activist? It may also be the result of finding an answer to a rather personalized version of such questions, namely: Did the writer, again like Chinua Achebe, create for himself or herself some sort of literary manifesto rather as a guide to measuring his achievements as a writer, namely, to show his people where the rain began to beat them, and teach his readers through his novels—"especially the ones set in the past" (Achebe, *Morning* 45), "that their past with all its imperfections was not one long night of savagery from which the first European, acting on God's behalf, delivered them" (Achebe, *Morning* 45), and to champion the establishment of a "balance of stories" (Achebe, *Home* 73) between Africa and the West.

The dichotomy implied by these different sets of questions represents what, in relation to writers generally, would be described as a duplex legacy on account of its being essentially twofold: a legacy of corpus and a legacy of exceptionality. However, when we take into account the fact that the questions associated with the legacy of exceptionality, beyond hinting at a legacy of values, manifests the possibility of extracting many different strands of legacies from a writer's works and life, they become associable with what I would describe differently as a multiplex legacy in relation to some writers, including Nadine Gordimer. In fact, the foregoing have been set down as principles for evaluating Nadine Gordimer's legacy as a multiplex legacy.

DECADES OF CORPUS AND EXCEPTIONALITY

Even for a writing career that spanned over seven decades, Gordimer's oeuvre comprising fifteen novels, one play, four screenplays for adaptations of seven of her short stories, twenty-one collections of short stories, five collections of essays, two edited works, and four other sundry works (including two documentaries)—that is, fifty-two individual works—would, for their number, range and scope, be considered a massive legacy of corpus, vast enough to deserve special recognition for the personal diligence and dedication to the literary vocation which it exemplifies.

However, although the expanse of Gordimer's legacy of corpus deserves recognition as an extraordinary manifestation of the commonplace through the effort of one individual, its significance is less compared to her legacy of exceptionality as reflected in her works and life as an activist.

One of such works is *My Son's Story*, the novel she published the year before she was awarded the Nobel Prize in Literature. It is one of the novels in which Gordimer pits herself against racial injustice as represented by the Apartheid system and by implication fights for racial equality and a more integral humanity. The story begins with the taut, almost austere, elliptical obliquity that partly marks Gordimer's narrative style and from the beginning, thrusts the reader into the racial divisiveness of its spatial setting with the first narrator's mention of his having to "sit in the maroon nylon velvet seat of a cinema in a suburb where whites live" (1). Of course, "a suburb where whites live" (1) bears a hint of racial segregation, of a different class of habitation for non-whites. And presently Gordimer reinforces and clarifies this hint and provides a reason for the segregation, with this introspective reference to its black victims: "Better to keep them at a distance, not recognize any feature in them. And yet they are useful; the self that recognized something of itself in the franchised of the town inherited along with that resemblance the town's assumption that blacks were there to do things you didn't want to do, that were beneath your station; for nothing was beneath theirs" (1).

Shortly after the story opens—and with the narrative voice suddenly shifting to the authorial—it migrates to an oblique introduction of the hero: whose sole documentation was his work paper (2).

Again, "in the area, outside the town, designated by the municipality for their kind" (2), while contrasting with "a suburb where whites live" (2), reinforces the impression of the setting, Johannesburg, as a racially segregated city. And as Gordimer proceeds to inform us, Sonny, the hero, the celebrated "first-born male" (2) of his family, coming from such nondescript backgrounds, "became a teacher" (2)—of whom "everything he was and did evidenced distinction" (3)—and progressed in his career "by ability and gradual seniority during the year he married his wife, Aila, and their two children, a girl followed by a boy, were born" (3).

As her hint at his being a man of culture: He named the boy Will, short for William, after William Shakespeare, whose complete works he owned and read repeatedly with devotion. Also, having enrolled in a correspondence course, he "chose comparative literature and discovered Kafka to add to his Shakespearean source of transcendence—a way out of battered classrooms" (10). With such hints, Gordimer undercuts the prejudice of lack of refinement of the victim that is partly used by some people to justify their feeling of racial superiority over such victims, sometimes branding them as "savages." Here Gordimer's implied message to such champions of racial segregation, of racism generally, is: A savage, lacking culture, cannot be an avid devourer of Shakespeare (who can "quote reams" of King Lear) or a lover of Kafka's works. And Sonny, a symbol of blackness, is; which invalidates the excuse of lack of culture for which he and his kind and brand are segregated against as uncouth or inferior beings.

In Sonny and Aila, Gordimer portrays a compatible, loving, disciplined and virtuous couple who "were not lovers until they were husband and wife," (4) even though, to reinforce the message of their remarkable restraint, she informs us in a tantalizingly erotic description that "there was a real body under her clothes, a lovely body with all the features there for him: the dark nipples like grapes in his mouth, the smooth belly with its tiny well of navel" (4).

The positive characterization of the couple continues as Gordimer further informs us that, "They decided to have children, but not more than two. The fecklessly begotten families of the poor, from which they came. . . . They found that for them both the meaning of life seemed to be contained, if mysteriously, in leaving useful lives" (5).

It is noteworthy that we have gone to this length in delineating some of Gordimer's characters in *My Son's Story* because, to appreciate her art of positive subversion in the novel, we must comprehend her use of characterization as an important weapon in her fight against racial segregation therein. In this sense, she also uses characterization as a tool to reshape perspectives, nudging the reader to see the world and its inhabitants in a new light rather than retain prejudiced notions of them. This motive, with her intention to use characterization as weapon of positive subversion, becomes clearer when we consider the portrayal of some white characters in the novel, in juxtaposition with Sonny and Aila. She obviously implies that she could be accused of subversion by the oppressors who regard subversion as the exposure of the rot in the system. *My Son's Story* is, undoubtedly, a text in which she is relentless in exposing the rot in the Apartheid system, such as its agents planting incriminating evidence—"an RPG-7 rocket launcher and two rockets" (173)—in Sonny's home in order to secure Aila's conviction in what should therefore be a phony trial for "terrorism and furthering the aims of a banned organization."

Thus, earlier in the story we are introduced to the first narrator's father as he leaves a cinema with a woman he introduces to the son as Hannah Plowman, of whom the son later says, "She is blonde, my father's woman" (7). As the couple parts ways with the first narrator at the cinema, he proceeds to describe the blonde in unflattering terms. She is described as decked in pink bottle-calves and clumsy sandals below the cotton outfit composed of a confusion of styles from different peasant cultures. True, Gordimer, through the first narrator, sketches for us the image of an adulterous white woman, in contrast with Aila, with a poor, rather chaotic, sartorial taste (as reflected in her "confusion of styles from different peasant cultures") whose own kind—with "kind" being a categorization by skin color—may in spite of that be driven by the illusion of her inherent racial superiority to consider the former as uncultured and deserving of their contempt, the segregation and other types of formal oppression to which "their kind"—another categorization by a different skin color which bears a hint of otherness—are subjected by the racist white government of their municipality.

OTHERNESS AND SUBVERSION

By such characterizations, Gordimer flips over two types of prejudices, standing them on their heads. One is the prejudice that takes white people's decency and refinement for granted. The other is the prejudice reflected in the presumption of black people's inherent lack of refinement. And we should find it hard to ignore her imputation through such characterizations, apparently using Aila and Hannah as racial symbols, that we are likely to find the racial basis for which we demean others not of our race as unjustifiable, if only we can bear to dispense with our prejudices about them.

Such subversive characterization, with its positive outcome, is only one of the ways in which Gordimer sets up a confrontation with racial segregation and the Apartheid system in *My Son's Story*. For in due course she inaugurates a portrayal of how the system destroys quality in black people as symbolized by Sonny and Aila, a system so decisively rigged that "you can't win against whitey."

Sonny, besides carrying out his responsibilities as a teacher, becomes a political activist, enlisting in the cause of freedom and equality. Not for personal reasons, as Gordimer clarifies—in her authorial, second narrator's voice which repeatedly complements that of Will throughout the story—but understandably for someone who "earned less than a white teacher with the same level of education," even though he was so confident that he "didn't feel himself inferior—inferior to what, to whom?" But he is reluctant at first to take to activism, preferring to devote himself to a life of the mind and improving his lot by acquiring a better education, a decision for which some of "their kind" regard him as not being "really black," something of a sellout. Yet a chain of unpredictable events—beginning with an incident in which "a small boy, running with a crowd of older schoolchildren towards the police, was shot dead, and a newspaper photographer's picture of his body, carried by another child, became the *pieta* of suffering happening everywhere across the veld where the real blacks were" (6). This forced Sonny into becoming a political activist.

With the reenactment of this pieta "in the black areas that were everywhere across the veld outside the towns," and schoolchildren organizing protests against the culpable system, he attracts negative attention from the police for his involvement with the schoolchildren, although "he took responsibility for keeping stones out of their hands," a feat he could not replicate in a later case of petrol and matches in which he backs their protest against the system.

By the time he is dismissed from his teaching job—as a response to his role with the students—and informed that the authorities they would not allow any other school to give him a post, we are meant to grasp Gordimer's indictment of the Apartheid system for also constituting itself into a destroyer of black children, evidenced in the pietas of infant horror it was creating out of them, and for inflicting such an excessive punishment on responsible and a hardworking black man like Sonny by ending his chosen career abruptly and irredeemably.

With the loss of his profession incident on the loss of his teaching job, the people of the committee against removals, which was now his community work, find him a job at an Indian wholesaler's, which implies a sort of career downgrade, with the attendant loss of dignity. They take him to speak on platforms, attend meetings, make speeches, take part in campaigns and as part of delegations to the authorities, which becomes his new profession. Adjusting to the incipient precariousness of his life and its minor shake-up of his home where, thanks to his resolve with Aila not to let such events unsettle the discipline of their lives, he strikes on the idea of their relocating to a better part of town, regardless of the potential of the move to terminate his wife's occupation running a crèche. In an explanatory remark which Gordimer notes as signifying his transformation into a political personality. Gordimer hints at the near impossibility of "their kind" being allowed to make progress under the Apartheid system, their determination notwithstanding, a sort of subtle indictment of the system for racist stultification. Sonny will no longer put up with that. This can be established by his dialogue with Aila, in which his language foreshadows the rise of the rebellious spirit that defines his further engagements in the novel: We are obliquely prompted by Gordimer to wonder at the expense of that system and arrive at the impression that it is an atrocious system that desperately needs to be dismantled in the interest of human dignity. His nascent rebellious spirit propels him to move in among the whites which is usually deemed illegal.

The situation in which Gordimer puts Sonny raises her art of positive subversion a notch, from something rather intangible as an aesthetic (as reflected in her earlier characterization of Sonny) to something concrete as action (as reflected in his tactical move into white residential area). In political-activist- and freedom-fighter terms, the move is comparable to bearding a monster in its cave, a combination of defiance, risk and sacrifice that can prove disastrous to the person involved. In the Homeric epic, Odysseus tricks the cave-dwelling monster from a safe distance to secure his passage with his men. In Gordimer's fiction, which mirrored her country's reality at the time of the publication of *My Son's Story*, Sonny must relocate to the cave in a tactical move (fashioned with his comrades) to confront the monster. But Gordimer's message is that it is only through such acts of strategic daring that Sonny and his comrades, and freedom fighters generally, can earn their liberty. What she does in *My Son's Story* can be summed up as using a character such as Sonny to instigate dissent against an oppressive system, the

Apartheid system to be specific, to prompt victims of the system to organize and take the battle to its doors if they must realize their hope of being rid of its oppression. The courage being exercised by the fictional Sonny is a projection of the type of courage for which Jake Flanagan describes Gordimer as "a lioness of literary activism," a description that also holds true for her in other contexts—such as her activist role as the vice president of PEN defending the right of writers to free expression—and undergirds the various endeavors behind her multiplex legacy.

Even after Sonny is jailed in the story, with his five-year sentence for backing student protests reduced to two on appeal, Gordimer still presents through him and Aila models of calm and determined believers in and organizers for the cause of freedom; her implied message being that even the extreme adversity of their incarceration should not blunt the will of the adversaries of the Apartheid system whose ultimate goal should be its termination. Acting thus as a literary coach of rational insurrection, it becomes easy to understand why other similar books by her were banned or censored by the Apartheid government apparently for being critical of its system. As part of her multiplex legacy, her legacy of exceptionality—a legacy of which writing well was both an end in itself and a means to the end of improving a world she justifiably deemed dissatisfactory. This was consequent upon the fact that society was tainted by the regimented form of racial discrimination represented by Apartheid. The structure that essentially harnessed literary creativity to political struggle derives partly from such use of her work to draw attention to the inhumane world created by the Apartheid system. By implication, it flags the need to improve that world and vacate that system, for it answers in the affirmative the question I posed earlier as a means of apprehending such legacy, namely: "Did the writer through their works or other means fight for the improvement of the world as a social, political, cultural, or moral activist?"

The summit of the self-endangering political activism and its advocacy of liberalism (as dispensing with all sorts of racial prejudice) is reached at the funeral rally in honor of black youths killed for the liberation struggle by the agents of Apartheid—such as the police and the army. Sonny delivers a rousing speech with Hannah with whom he is involved in an adulterous relationship as suggested at the opening scene near the cinema, in attendance with other white people, showing solidarity with black people, the primary victims of Apartheid. In a shocking portrayal of a system whose brutality imposes itself on its weak, defenseless victims even in the midst of mourning, the police discharge teargas at the crowd and shoot them, killing some. But in that crowd are white people whom Sonny acknowledges in his speech as their white comrades. Some of the white men had refused conscription to join the band wagon of police brutality and inhumanity meted out on blacks.

Gordimer's objective here is to reshape perspectives from the point of view of Sonny—a cultured lover of Shakespeare and Kafka—who stands against the trend of racial prejudices. It is, in fact, the whites who now benefit through her characterization of Hannah and some other members of their race that attended the funeral as non-racists. Her thoughts reside on the premise that human beings often err by generalizing against any group out of prejudice, which is basically what racism does. And, in all, both blacks and whites benefit through a better understanding of one other.

Some of the consequences of the show of resistance at the funeral were literally brought home to Sonny and his family by the Apartheid System in other contexts. Not only was there petrol-bombing of their home in the white residential area, there was also the threatening insistence of some of their white neighbors. Sonny exhibits stark defiance which is explicitly prescribed by Gordimer.

Yet it must be said that *My Son's Story* is a fictional work about life in a more general and involved sense than is suggested by the theme of struggle against Apartheid in particular or oppression in general. It is, in a sense, a universal story about the invincibility of the human spirit and its capacity to transcend natural, accidental, or imposed obstacles in its quest for progress and self-determination, as symbolized by Sonny. It is also a novel that can task comprehension. This owes largely to the compactness of Gordimer's prose style: her conflation of narrative voices and the unpredictable switches she executes in the plot. Yet it is a book that rewards diligent reading with such striking insights into human behavior, beyond its preoccupation with racial justice, as, "When a daughter begins to show breasts and a son's voice begins to be mistaken, on the phone, for the father's, there comes a kind of reversal of the clandestinity courting couples have to practice in the house of their parents: the long married now feel an inhibition about making love in the presence—separated only by the bedroom walls—of children who themselves are now capable of feeling the same sexual desires" (48).

It is also a love story about love in a life of struggle in its licit and illicit manifestations that celebrates conjugal affection as embodied by Sonny and Aila and does not cast the usual frown "conventional morality" does on illicit love as embodied by Sonny and Hannah—a representative of an international human rights organization who gets hired by the United Nations High Commission for Refugees—whose affection (and comradeship) complement his life with passion and intellect.

Incidentally, Gordimer's attitude to adultery in *My Son's Story* is reverse-Tolstoyan: In Tolstoy's *Anna Karenina*, Anna's involvement in an adulterous relationship ultimately crushes her spirit, culminating in a chain of events that end in her suicide. But Gordimer's novel does not subscribe to the type of "conventional morality" that will respond to any and every such affair with condemnation. While it does not necessarily approve of adultery (or it would not say that Sonny "knew that it was necessary to forgive himself as well as be forgiven by Aila," implying his affair with Hannah as wrongful), it adopts it in the specific case of Sonny and Hannah to pass the message that things are hardly ever black or white and urge us to endeavor to apprehend them in their complexity, which may make the wrongful explicable even if not morally justifiable. And that for Sonny—who had to take to lying to Aila to cover his tracks with Hannah, but the nobility of whose character was otherwise not questionable. A man does not have to be flawless in order to be considered good, for the real gauge of his character becomes his commitment to the struggle and his willingness to sacrifice his life for the cause of freedom.

The novel also puts the relationship to positive use in subverting the idea of forbidden love (and reminds us of how worse things used to be) under Apartheid, as suggested by Gordimer's remark, "No, the trains on this route were no longer segregated, and there was no law, any longer, against a man of his kind and a woman of her kind sharing a bed" (148). And yet their relationship offered Sonny more than an opportunity for carnal indulgence outside marriage: "With Hannah there was the sexuality of commitment: for commitment implies danger . . . he and Hannah begot no child; the revolutionary movement was to be their survivor. The excitement of their mating was for that" (171).

It is a reflection of the main revolutionary focus of their relationship that even their post-coital conversations would yield such high-minded expressions by both (followed by an authorial comment) as:

> This country's always been way ahead in industrial and technological development, considering its history, and way behind in ideas, political culture. British liberalism tottering on with its form of racism long after it was overtaken by Boer nationalism with its form of racism . . . if the old socialism's dying, let's admit it and make sure we can find our liberation in the new Left that's coming." (151–152)

The author subtly links the liberation of a nation with the unburdening of the mind. This borders on the issues of morality and moral values.

Interestingly, it is to a clergy that Gordimer goes to find an explanation for the relationship between Sonny and Hannah, beyond the limits of orthodox morality—"a militant, worldly priest whose liberation theology would include an understanding of a man's responsibility for loving, inside or outside conventional morality." The clergyman's advice was keenly sought while the pragmatism of his action was underscored (109–110).

For its criticism of racial injustice and segregation, *My Son's Story* lends itself to interpretation as a novel in which Gordimer makes art useful by investing it with a sociopolitical and moral significance in addition to its usefulness as an ornament that can act as a stimulus for intellectual and emotional pleasure. And this bears some relevance to Anne Tyler's remark in her review of July's People that "Nadine Gordimer has always been an admirable writer, combining skill with social conscience";—the skill in the specific case of *My Son's Story* being the capacity to draw such keen observations that transforms what would have been a thematically restricted work into an open landscape of significations. Thus, she adapts Marquez's notion of the writer's "revolutionary duty" to a relevance beyond writing well to writing with a defined moral, social and political purpose without compromising the beauty of her writing, which finds expression in such tropes as "the damp nest of hair in his armpit" (142) and "My heart began to thunder up a troop of wild beasts in my chest" (145).

Now, there are a number of ways in which humans would respond to racism and the attendant injustices or other systemic types of oppression in any society in which they must stake their survival. They include denial, accommodation, connivance, profiteering, revulsion, and opposition, and can be associated with either the perpetrators or victims of such injustices as groups or individuals. Denial shuts its senses to the injustices and pretends they do not exist, usually to enable it to eke out some semblance of survival, even if—and it usually is—undignified, within whatever scope the unjust system may allow it. Accommodation condones it, usually in conspiratorial silence, neither speaking up for or against it, or taking any other form of action against it, usually because it understands itself to have a stake in whatever unfair benefits it confers. Connivance actively works to advance its interests, usually as a known beneficiary of its spoils and not minding being identified as such. Profiteering exploits it for all sorts of material gains and seeks to perpetuate it so long as such gains persist. Aversion, on the other hand, views it with antipathy often expressed as open or tacit criticism while opposition mobilizes, and participates in, struggles to end it.

Writing *My Son's Story* is one of Gordimer's literary gestures of revulsion and opposition to the phenomenon of racial segregation in particular or racism in general. The author lays bare the attendant repression and injustice on such characters as Sonny, Aila, their children Will and Baby, Hannah, their other comrades, and the white people who identify with black people at the funeral of the nine black youths killed by agents of Apartheid. These are of course subjects of her literary objective to achieve peace and freedom at the end of fighting racial injustice through the medium of literature.

CONCLUSION

In all, Gordimer's legacy is proof that literature can be used successfully as a tool for forging racial integration in the social and political spheres, and in so doing create a more just world as well as a more refined and integrated human race. In putting literature to this sort of specialized use, rising to the occasion thrust on her by the moral necessity to dismantle the color bar installed in her home country by the Apartheid government, she became deserving of essential recognition as a literary variant of Nelson Mandela, whose role in the liberation of their home country from the shackles of Apartheid towered in the political sphere, even though her writings and activism were equally useful in strengthening the moral credentials of the political struggle against Apartheid.

Through her work South Africa, and the world, became a sort of laboratory for testing the sociopolitical impact of literature and its capacity for stirring the conscience of humanity and unsettling powers that would rather thrive with obnoxiousness. Such powers were represented by the Apartheid regime in the specific case of her home country—for she was rightly recognized as a citizen of the world due to the reach and impact of her ideas. That they reacted to her writings with hostility, to the point of banning some of her books, is a testimony of the positive impact of her works and the ideas they canvassed, their acknowledgment of her having proven that the pen can be a potent threat to, if not mightier than, the gun.

Hers was a rare exemplification of the relevance of the writer in the social and political space, and of the writer's capacity to assume and fill roles in that space with unflinching moral responsibility. To that end, she fostered those values without which the phrase "our common humanity" would be meaningless. Gordimer also left a legacy of activism beyond the political sphere. She coined the phrase "freedom of the WORD,"[1] which I encountered in one of her letters written at a period the South African government was considering passing a legislation to curb press freedom. She issued a press statement to condemn this move as an avowed adversary of censorship in all its manifestations. The word being the basic unit of human verbal communication, the phrase signifies her firm belief in the right of every human being to express themselves with absolutely no restraint. It stood for something more fundamental than freedom of expression or the related intellectual freedom or creative liberty, to which access may be restricted by one not being educated, creative or intellectual. For her, it stood for the untrammeled right of all human beings to express themselves through the medium of words. And she fought for this right, through her writings and using her influence as the vice president of PEN International, almost to the end of her long and fulfilled life. Through these efforts, she also left a legacy of a world in which censorship would become less of a threat to writers[2] and kindred professionals, like journalists. Thus, her passion to defend the "freedom of the WORD" shone through her words. And her multiplex legacy touched lives on an individual, national and global scale, objectifying her conviction, expressed in *My Son's Story*, that "the strongest purpose in human society" is "to change the world."

WORKS CITED

Achebe, Chinua. *Home and Exile*. New York: Anchor Books, 2000.

———. *Morning Yet on Creation Day*. London: Heinemann Educational Books, 1975.

Ayebia, Nana Clarke and James Currey, Eds. *Chinua Achebe: Tributes and Reflections*. Oxfordshire: Ayebia, 2014, 157.

Clingman, Stephen. "First Time, Last Time: Remembering Nadine Gordimer." Fri. 3 June 2016. http://www.parktownassociation.co.za/wp-content/uploads/20 1 4/07/First-Time-Last-Time.pdf.

Flanagin, Jake. "Remembering Nadine Gordimer, A Lioness Of Literary Activism." *The New York Times*. June 3, 2016. https://op-talk.blogs.nytimes.com/2014/07 /15/remembering-nadine-gordimer-a-lioness-of-literary-activism/. *The New York Times*, 2014.

Gordimer, Nadine. *My Son's Story.* New York: Picador, 1990.

"Nadine Gordimer—Bibliography." Nobelprize.org. Nobel Media AB 2014. Web. May 27, 2016. https://www.nobelprize.org/prizes/literature/1991/gordimer/bibliography/.

Nobel Foundation, ed. "Writing and Being." In *Nobel Lectures from the Literature Laureates 1986–2009*. New York: The New York Press, 2007: 209–219.

Tyler, Anne. "South Africa after Revolution." *The New York Times*, June 3, 2016. https://archive.nytimes.com/www.nytimes.com/books/98/02/01/home/gordimer-july.html. The New York Times, 1981.

NOTES

1. I happened to have had a personal encounter with the passion with which Nadine Gordimer fought for the "freedom of the WORD," with what I would describe as an instinctive aversion for censorship reinforced by the unpleasantness of her serial encounters with book bans and the suppression of her ideas in other less obtrusive ways by the Apartheid government. It was as if, having experienced censorship, she could not bear to see anyone else do so, and would promptly rise like Jake Flanagin's "lioness of literary activism" in defense of its actual or potential victims whenever such was brought to her attention.

2. In 2011 I had already experienced an encounter with the exploitation of writers in my country, Nigeria, in a manner so brazen that it triggered a lyrical poem titled "A Gandhian Prayer," which I sent to Gordimer with its music scores. (It was around the time she issued her well-publicized statement criticizing the said legislation sponsored by the South African government, which she considered as a serious threat to press freedom.).

PART 5

Dynamics of Power and Narrative Voice

Chapter 19

Language Use in the Discourse of Otherness in Bessie Head's *Maru*

Omeh Obasi Ngwoke and Okwudiri Anasiudu

INTRODUCTION

A literary text according to Fowler in *Literature and Social Discourse* is a variety of discourse genre, which represents issues about the material-cum-phenomenological aspects of the human society in general. Language is focal in the discourse formation process in literature as it is one of the areas of overlap between a literary imagination and a society. Not only that, but language is also a vital cognitive tool for construing literary imagination and social tempers. Importantly, every society creates a code system of conceptualization to represent or talk about things, their experiences, and cultural practices.

Through language, the socio-cultural worldviews, mode of knowledge or "the semiotic systems that constitute a culture" (Halliday 2) is represented. This is suggestive of what Halliday and Hasan call "language that is doing some job" (14). And this "language that is doing some job" for instance, in Head's *Maru* is not without a bias, or free from social forces as they encode or reflect forms of discourses wrapped with human, socio-cultural prejudices. Importantly, by examining the linguistic maneuvers in a work of literature, one can ascertain the nature of discourse theme within the novel, which for *Maru* (1971) includes racialism, the power struggle underlying the scheming and quarrel between two close friends and chieftains (Moleka and Maru) over who marries the Masarwa—Margaret Cadmore—and the discrimination of the Masarwa in Dilepe, which crystallizes as a discourse of Otherness. Discourse as used in this context implies a configuration of the world, the processes, and relations, of thoughts, feelings, beliefs and so forth, of the world (Fairclough, *Analysing* 124). M. A. K. Halliday's work in Functional Linguistics and Roger Fowler's pioneering work in Critical Linguistics have opened up new vistas on how language and text encode the kind of discourse explored in this paper, that is, Otherness, in order to reveal the social system of beliefs, ideology, and the reproduction of social relation such as ". . . power—structure and power relations of the society we live in" (Eagleton 13).

Our guiding thesis is that language has a socio-functional role and a functionalist model of language analysis not only acknowledges the correlation between language and social forces, it deepens human understanding of the ways language facilitates meaning creation and ideology in discourse genre like the novel. The crux of the foregoing assertion is that language use in a novel is not just for the linguistic meaning language encode, but also for the social dimensions of discourse that linguistic resources are capable of revealing at the ideological and institutional level since "all discourses are ideologically and institutionally determined" (Birch 35). This view is succinctly explained and captured in Foucault in the assertion that "discourses are composed of signs; but what they do is more than the use of these signs to designate things. It is this *more* that renders them irreducible to the language (langue) and to speech. It is this 'more' that we must reveal and describe" (49). This "more" points to the social power structures within "a discourse [which] defines what can be said, who can speak and who must remain silent, in this way defining their being" (Koul 457).

The implication of the foregoing in our study of *Maru* (1971) is that our analysis of the ways language is engaged in the novel can reveal how the boundaries of subjectivity, autonomous agency is permitted or denied to individuals or groups within the semantic universe or community such as Dilepe as construed in the novel. This type of analysis is what *CDA* does. It is important we stress that the *CDA* employed in this study is not the same as the non-CDA approaches, that is, the generic discourse analysis, carried outside linguistics and without the modifier "critical." The critical approach we employ, shows "how discourse is shaped by relations of power and ideologies, and the constructive effects discourse has upon social identities, social relations and systems of knowledge and belief, neither of which is normally apparent to discourse participants" (Fairclough, *Discourse* 12).

In addition, following Fairclough (2013), the incorporation of the term "critical" into discourse speaks of a methodology of textual analysis that seeks to account for the "relations between discourse and other elements of the social process" through a systematic analysis of texts in order to address "social wrongs in their discursive aspects and possible ways of righting or mitigating them" (*Politica* 110). Fairclough's view of discourse draws from the Social & Critical Theory's conceptualization of discourse by Michel Foucault. But Foucault lacks a critical linguistic basis for the view of discourse he proposed. Thus, what Fairclough did was to incorporate Fowler's critical functional linguistics model to Foucault's discourse to evolve his own strand of discourse analysis which he called *CDA*. According to Fairclough and Fairclough, its main strength is the "critical perspectives on language, drawn from critical theory in the social sciences" (78).

THE DISCOURSE OF OTHERNESS

Otherness is anthropological, and a consequence of ethnocentric bias (Staszak 3). In the words of Childs and Fowler:

> The other is a construct. It is, moreover, a historically and culturally specific construction that is determined by the discursive practices that shape us into what we are [. . .]. Thus, rather than representing the real and diverse qualities of any given group or entity, such constructions reflect the values and norms of the individual or group that constructs it. (164)

Otherness is a topical and "an important concern in postcolonial studies" (Udumukwu 259). Said explored the Otherness of the Orient, where the Orient is configured as an exotic Other in Euro-Western discourses and imagination (1). This imagination of the Orient as the Other undergirds the power and social relation between Europe and Asia that crystallizes as British colonial policy in India. We can also find same in Bhabha's *The Location of Culture*, where he highlights the cultural implications of Otherness due to British cultural imperialism in India. Another scholar, Spivak has also explored Otherness within its gendered form via the question: "Can the subaltern speak? and Can the subaltern (as woman) speak?" (296). "Speak" as a verbal and nominal category engaged by Spivak suggests both an action and an idea. As an action, it implies utterance, while as an idea it implies presence, identity, a position of power and autonomous agency. Also, Mackinnon's *Towards a Marxist Theory of the State* is another text inspired by a sense of female Otherness within the economic sphere. Other type of Otherness is the economic stratification of nations into first, second and the third world (Ahmad 11).

Within African literary imagination, Chinua Achebe's trilogy: *Things Fall Apart*, *Arrow of God* and *No Longer at Ease* reverberate the discourse of Otherness. The conflicts in those novels thrive on the principle of cultural Otherness, between western culture and African culture. Otherness is also captured in Noviolet Bulawayo's *We Need New Names* in terms of the relationship between The NGOs representing western humanitarian interests and extension in Africa (the People of Paradise). Not only that, Western media perception of Africa, in *We Need New Names* is informed by Otherness, that Africa is a waste land. Also, contemporary African women writings are implicated by the discourse of Otherness in its gendered form, in order to uncover the subaltern position of African women in the socio-economic scheme of things in Africa. This is what prompted Molara Ogundipe-Leslie's (2010) essay on Stiwanism that seeks to place African women in the agenda of economic, political, and social conversations.

What the foregoing examples and explanations have in common is the view that the discourse of Otherness is not without politics or interest, as it serves the interest of a given dominant, minority or ideological group within a social framework. This study therefore defines Otherness as identity mapping, a cultural practice encouraged, tolerated, institutionalized, and formulated as a discourse by a social group in position of power over another social group who are narrativized as subalterns through systematic devaluation, resulting in socio-political, economic, spiritual, epistemic, historical, and geographical occlusion and is legitimated through language. Otherness may assume the form of the Osu caste system in Igbo land, gender differentiation in African families where the male child is assumed to be more valuable compared to the female child or the discrimination due to albinism, the ill treatment and the social stratification of the Dalit in India.

OTHERNESS AS A THEME IN *MARU*

Otherness which constitutes one of the themes of Head's novel *Maru* (1971) calls attention to a social anomaly in the cultural practices within the fictionalized representation of Botswana, particularly in Dilepe, where the Masarwa people are treated as outsiders. The Otherness represented in *Maru* is an institutionalized social practice. It thrives because a group such as the Dilepe sees another group such as the Masarwa, as slaves, even if the Masarwa people form part of the community in Dilepe. The Dilepe people treat the Masarwa as lesser humans, outsiders, and "hoi polloi." This also becomes a basis for the discrimination meted out to the Masarwa.

Thus, while the people of Dilepe such as Dikeledi, Moleka, Maru, and Seth, occupy the position of power in Dilepe, they impose their value systems, worldviews, and notions of identity on the Masarwa. By doing this, the people of Dilepe fail to acknowledge the autonomous agency and humanity of the Masarwa, instead, the Masarwa are excluded from positions of social, economic, intellectual, and even spiritual power.

In a situation of Otherness as we can find in *Maru* (1971), the power of the dominating group is legitimated and naturalized while the Other is interpellated and forced to conform or accept subaltern labels through the institutionalization of policies and norms, values, and laws for the interest of the dominating group. Now, we need to stress that the labels on the Other or the Masarwa are not necessarily "truths" or "doxa."

In *Maru*, a type of Otherness is also evident in the name, Masarwa—a term that means "bushmen." The People of Masarwa are a social group or individuals classified as outsiders, who are assumed by the Dilepe people to be fundamentally different, dissimilar, subalterns and separated because of social status, birth, physiology, gender, and social codes. Head's narrative portrayal of the Masarwa as outsiders in *Maru,* foregrounds their powerlessness as a marginal group.

The Otherness of the Masarwa crystallizes as a form of dehumanization and objectification or properties to be owned. This is demonstrated in the refusal of the Dilepe and Totem people who are in positions of power or dominance to acknowledge that the Other (Masarwa) is a subject or a legitimate member of their community. We find this in the representation of Margaret Cadmore, a character in *Maru* who is not accepted into the Dilepe society on the basis that she is fair-skinned, or a Masarwa. Margaret is expected by the society and culture in Dilepe where she finds herself, to remain passive, and invisible as the dominating group refuses to see, acknowledge or recognize Margaret's existence in spite of her intellectual prowess, finesse and beauty.

LANGUAGE USE IN THE DISCOURSE OF OTHERNESS IN *MARU*

We will begin our analysis on *Maru* by calling attention to a kind of otherness we note as territorial Otherness and how language use in the novel represents that kind of discourse theme. By territorial Otherness, we mean an Otherness that speaks or calls attention to territorial distinctiveness or difference that also encourages negative labeling and stereotyping on persons within such a territory. A language form that points to this territorial otherness is the use of place deixis. Deixis "refers to the orientation of the content of a sentence in relation to time, place and personal participants" (Fowler 57). Place deixis points to location or place, or territory. Let us take a look at the excerpt below and pay attention to the words and phrasal groups italicized in the excerpt:

> *In Botswana* they say: Zebras, Lions, Buffalo, and Bushmen live *in the Kalahari Desert*. If you can catch a Zebra, you can walk up to it, forcefully open its mouth and examine its teeth. The Zebra is not supposed to mind because it is an animal.

Scientists do the same to *Bushmen* and they are not supposed to mind. . . . (*Maru* 6, emphases are the author's)

By isolating the italicized phrases, we call attention to a particular interest to us in this paper as shown below:

> Zebras
> Lions
> [*In Botswana*] they say: Buffalo live [*in the Kalahari Desert*].
> Bushmen

The phrase "*in Botswana*" a prepositional phrase composed of PP+NP, "in" (a preposition) + "Botswana" (a noun) and "*in the Kalahari Desert,*" another prepositional phrase made up of a preposition + the definite article, where "Kalahari" the noun component plays the role of an adjective or modifier to the headword "desert" a noun, which speaks of a place, a location, a territory.

The narrative voice represented by the use of the third-person pronoun "they," a person deixis in its plural sense puts the reader on alert to a publicly held opinion which falls within the domain of "a hear say." In spite of that, it is engrafted into popular discourse as a form of truth in Botswana in order to naturalize the view that "Zebras, Lions, Buffalo and Bushmen live in the *Kalahari Desert.*" The statement "they say" constitutes a type of rumor, propaganda or hate speech, for the fact that its source is unidentifiable as we see in the nature of the pronoun which the statement is sourced from. The pronoun which points to the source is indefinite, unclear, and unverifiable which makes it very difficult to hold responsible, or identify, the person the statement emanates from.

We need to note that the person deixis represented by the third person pronoun in its plural sense as we see in the term "they," is used in a collective sense too. It is a plural marker, and it speaks of a view, suggestive of an entire community and their thought and system of belief. It is also important to note that the expression is also crafted in a declarative mood, which makes it have a truth or false value. Furthermore, the statement is projected in such a subtle manner that an unwary reader may see and accept the notion of Otherness it reflects as an established truth, a norm, which should be accepted, whereas it is the view and ideology of an exclusive group in power, the Dilepe, toward the Masarwa.

By the use of the deixis of place or territory, there is a sense of geographical specificity on that statement, "in Botswana," the exact territory which is referenced. A further reading and foray into the novel reveal the particular area of Botswana where such views thrive, the view that zebras, lions, buffalos, and Bushmen or Masarwa live in the Kalahari Desert. This is in the

Dilepe area. For we are made to know in the novel that the "Dilepe village was the stronghold of some of the most powerful and wealthy chiefs in the country, all of whom owned innumerable Masarwa as slaves" (16). Thus, such forms of discourse justify their domination over the Masarwa people.

The implication is that such discourse creates a syntagmatic sequence where the Masarwa collocates in the same semantic order of arrangement with zebra, lions, and buffalos. The presupposition is that the Masarwa people are in the category of animals of the wild; are less humans and are not to be accorded dignity as humans. Also, by projecting the "they say" statement, dominant groups engage the subtle element of language deceptively to justify and legitimize the social alienation of groups they assume as lesser beings or outsiders, as we find in the relationship between the Dilepe people and the Masarwa people. This also is to give legitimacy or normalize the various forms of dehumanization, stereotype or label associated with the Masarwa, such as "the excreta, horror, oddity of the human race, with half the head of a man and half the body of a donkey" (103). Through the use of deixis of place we see the territoriality of otherness where the fringe of the earth, a place of adverse weather condition is projected as the home of the Masarwa.

By using language to represent the Masarwa people as entities sharing abode with wild beasts, in a specific territory—the Kalahari Desert—we can see how language is deployed to naturalize Otherness as normal; to equate and cognitively banish an entire social group or people such as the Masarwa to the sphere of animals of the wild. It is also these senses of Otherness that informed the cruelty to the dead body of a Masarwa which is left on the floor instead of a stretcher as we see in the manner the corpse of Margaret the Masarwa's biological mother is handled (8).

The foregoing, coupled with the encounter with a Masarwa's dead body by Margaret Cadmore, the European, establishes her use of the Masarwa, that is, the daughter of the dead Masarwa woman who she named Margaret Cadmore after herself, for the purpose of her social and behavioral experiment. Hence, Margaret Cadmore (the Masarwa) becomes an experimental object, a lab rat, to ascertain or scientifically verify if the spurious assumption held by both the Dilepe people and white man that the Masarwa, "can't think for themselves. They don't know anything" (88).

Another aspect of language we need to pay attention to is the use of lexico-semantic infraction for exoticism and defamiliarization of the Other. By lexico-semantic infraction, we mean a way language is used to adore a person such that this language use is in contrast with the previous semantic reference to this person, where the previous semantic reference earlier used to label the person is a negative label. We see this in the linguistic structures which underscore Maru's later view of Margaret Cadmore (the Masarwa). This is conveyed in a stretch of utterances which contradicts the labels the

Dilepe people hold towards the Masarwa. Maru views Margaret as "the *sun of his love*" (*Maru* 1).

The above statement semantically infracts on Maru's previous semantic label over the Masarwa. What may seem to have prompted this semantic infraction is the sense of fetishism towards Margaret Cadmore (the Masarwa) when Maru encountered her, which also resulted in a sense of exoticism reflected in the statement "He [Maru] wanted a flower garden of yellow daisies, because they were the only *flowers* which resembled the face of his [Maru's] wife [Margaret] and the *sun of his* [Maru's] *love*" (*Maru* 1).

The linguistic structure that indicates the lexico-semantic infraction constructed above is a complex sentence, made up of a simple sentence that constitutes the main clause and a subordinating sentence introduced by a subordinating conjunction "because." We also need to note the paradigmatic relationship between the phrasal group [the face of his wife] and [the *sun of his love*] which are close substitutes. The *sun of his love* as used in the stretch of utterance, is a linguistic structure whose semanticity is infracted because the referent already has a negative label as a "bushman," away from the context which Maru refers to the Masarwa as an entity which brightens his love, just as the sun brightens or offers vitality to the life of plants and other living organisms.

A focus on the entire narrative will show that it is out of place that Maru refers to a Masarwa (Margaret Cadmore) as the "sun of his love," that is, Maru's love, whereas in several portions of the narrative, Maru (considering his social status as a king) had seen the Masarwa as lesser beings, but encountering Margaret and her education invokes a sense of apprehension on Maru as he sees Margaret as a commodity, a rare commodity for exoticism for the fact that she is an educated, beautiful, fair skinned Masarwa. Staszak notes that "exoticism is characterised by giving value to the other, contrary to ethnocentric bias" (6). We see exoticism demonstrated when Maru marries Margaret. Maru's marriage with Margaret becomes a speech act, which her fellow Masarwa consider as conferring value and humanity on them for, "a door silently opened" with "the wind of freedom" (103).

The foregoing underscored the fact that conjugal relation between Maru and Margaret conferred a level of honour on Margaret, however on a deeper level it unveils the power structure at work. This is because there were other underlying motivations behind Maru's marriage to Margaret. One of the reasons is the exertion of patriarchal power tussle between Maru and Moleka. We are told that Margaret is "the kind of wife everybody would loathe from the bottom of their hearts" (2) as she is Masarwa, "the equivalent of 'nigger,' a term of contempt which means, obliquely, a low, filthy nation" (6). And to complicate Margaret Cadmore the Masarwa's situation, her mother died giving birth to her on the outskirts of a remote village, and she was classified as *untouchable* (8). These negative descriptive adjectives contrast with Maru's statement, that Margaret Cadmore the Masarwa was the sun of his love. Maru's use of language, defamiliarises that which is familiar, that is, the negative labels associated with being a Masarwa.

Clearly for Maru, the eponymous character, and "king in their society" (2), Margaret conjures an exotic imagination. This exoticism of the Masarwa is not that which is derived from real value or respect, but of an awe at meeting someone he assumes to be an outcast demonstrating qualities that those assumed to be true born such as the Dikeledi are associated with such as: refinement and education. This was not the same attitude he expressed earlier towards Margaret Cadmore. In fact, his disdain for Margaret as a Masarwa even without encountering her is captured the moment she heard that Moleka gave a bed to a Masarwa and that Margaret Cadmore the Masarwa sleeps on a bed unlike the typical Masarwa who sleep on the ground with fire as their only blanket (46).

This same Masarwa (Margaret) later becomes a fetish and an object of desire and power tussle between Maru and Moleka. For Maru, owning Margaret as a wife will ensure his victory in the power tussle with Moleka. But what the marriage between Maru and Margaret Cadmore (the Masarwa) reveals is Maru's display of hegemonic power in the guise of love and marriage for Margaret. He sends out a threat and warning to Moleka concerning Margaret Cadmore, "Tell Moleka to remember that he enjoys life on this earth. This is not the end for him. He will have a long life." Moleka replies with a threat, "Since Maru thinks he can send messages to me, through spies, you can also take a message to him. Tell him I say that the day he approaches her, I will burn his house down. He is lucky if I don't kill him too" (62).

Another sense of exoticism of the Masarwa as an Other is evident in the expression by Margaret Cadmore (the European) which identifies a Masarwa as a deity. This Otherness reflects the rarity of the Masarwa and the physiology of the dead body of the Masarwa woman which made Margaret (the European) exclaim that "She looks like a Goddess" (9). By elevating the Masarwa to the status of the divine, the lexical term "Goddess" not only defamiliarizes the social status of the Masarwa, it also reveals a sense of exoticism of the Masarwa as a rare species or commodity. It is this exoticism that instigated the seemingly nice treatment to the corpse of the woman (the mother of Margaret the Masarwa).

TRANSITIVITY STRUCTURES IN THE CONFIGURATION OF OTHERNESS

Another language structure worthy of attention in *Maru* to configure otherness is the use of transitivity structures. "Transitivity structures express representational meaning: what the clause is about, which is typically some process, with associated participants and circumstances (Halliday and Mathiessen 309). It allows the writer, Head, to talk about experiences in the novel as it relates to Otherness. We will look at nominal, verbal, and adverbial group and how they configure such experience. Head configured Otherness through the use of verbal processes, "*She took* in too much . . . *she* really *saw* human suffering, close up, for the first time, but it *frightened* her into adopting that part of the woman.. . . . *She* was also a scientist. As *she* put the child to bed, . . . *She had* a real, living object for her experiment" (9). The In this excerpt the third-person pronoun "she" points to Margaret Cadmore (the European) as an antecedent information. The pronoun speaks of the senser of an experience of hate perpetuated by the people of Botswana on the Masarwa. The process which explains this is evident in the verbal group "took." What this structure reveals is the sense of alienation ascribed to the Masarwa even in death which made Margaret Cadmore (the European) to become aware of the discrimination and treatment of the Masarwa as outsiders. The pronoun also serves to provide a sense of cohesion on the structure. Importantly, the structure above also reveals Margaret Cadmore's (The European's) prejudice over the Masarwa as she sees the baby as an experimental object and not really as a real human being, as we can see in the linguistic structure, "*She* had a real, living object for her experiment" expecting some wonder to be created (9).

Thus for Margaret Cadmore the European, Margaret Cadmore the Masarwa is a lab rat for social experiment. We are told that "The relationship between her and the woman was never that of a child and its mother" (10). Her seemingly acts of kindness were borne out of a sense of superiority of her race over Africans. By her kindness, she seeks to "civilize the native" or provide an education where she assumes there is none, this intrigued fellow, Botswana, for it was thus strange to have a Masarwa, who eats mealie pap in school. (11).

Nonetheless, that was the social experimentation intended by Margaret Cadmore (the European) in proving how an environment conditions an individual. Since the environment proffers the opportunities requisite for learning, Margaret Cadmore the European succeeds in only half her experiment (12). A proof of Margaret Cadmore the European's success in her social experiment is the new identity she conferred on the Masarwa girl Margaret

Cadmore. Such that seventeen years after that eventful evening, some wonder had really been created. We are told that "Margaret Cadmore had *produced* a brilliant student" (12). She was convinced that her brilliance was hinged wholly on social isolation and exposure to books. Attention should be paid to the verbal process "produced" and its usage in the context of the passage. Its semantic implication suggests to make something, to transform through mechanical means, to cause something to bring out something. This implies that Margaret Cadmore, the Masarwa, is a manufactured product, a commodity interpellated with a brand name alien to who she is, but she could do nothing about it. Such an interpellation reveals also the power structure in the relationship between Margaret Cadmore the European and *the produced* Margaret Cadmore the Masarwa which is not based on the principles of equality but on the basis that she is an outcast, marginalized and an outsider who needs help all the time.

INTERROGATIVE MOOD, DISCOURSE TENOR, POWER STRUCTURE AND OTHERNESS

The tenor of discourse speaks of the relationship that exists between the interlocutors in a speech encounter. Apart from the fact that it identifies the addresser and addressee, it underscores the power structure in a speech situation. Let us analyze the speech exchange between Dikeledi and Margaret Cadmore to unveil the sense of Otherness revealed within their conversation and the power structures within it. Dikeledi discovers in the course of the conversation that Margaret is a Masarwa and not a Colored. Shocked at this revelation, Dikeledi advises her, "Don't mention this to anyone else . . . if you keep silent about the matter, people will simply assume you are a Coloured" (16).

Dikeledi wants to know more about Margaret Cadmore. The privileges which Dikeledi enjoys such as her social status, class, and education place her in a position of power such that she does the asking of the questions, "unconsciously" showing off her position and dominance. Meanwhile, Margaret's skin color and education presupposes that she is a new person in the community, and her education offers her privilege too. But when Dikeledi encountered Margaret, her first statement reveals or subtly expresses her display of power in the question "What's your name?" The question speaks of a desire to know Margaret's identity, social background, and stratification all summed in that interrogative sentence. Margaret Cadmore by answering the question reveals her ignorance of the label on the Masarwa and also her openness of mind. But it never ends there. Dikeledi tells Margaret not to announce her identity, "Don't mention this to anyone else." This is a sentence crafted in the imperative mood. What it foregrounds is that Dikeledi expects Margaret to hide her identity as it is derogatory and instead, accepts her Otherness instead of confronting it. Even subsequent questions posed to Margaret by Seth the principal of the School, Leseding, were attempts to define and assign a label to her. When he discovers that she is a Masarwa and not a Colored, "The shock was so great that he almost jumped into the air" (30).

Other interrogative expressions and structures that mark Otherness are: "Tell me," he said. "Since when is a Bushy a teacher?" (34). Such an interrogation serves a purpose of double articulation as it subtly speaks two meanings, that of status and power. Another sentence structure in *Maru* that speaks of Otherness is that which uses allusion as we see in the structure, "He kept noting out of the corner of his eye that the Masarwa (she was no longer a human being) seemed to be extraordinarily friendly with Dikeledi, who, in his eyes, was royalty of royalty (30). This utterance came after Margaret tells Seth the principal that she is Masarwa, and it changes his perception of Margaret and breeds hate and negative allusion of the Masarwa as an object, bushman and not a human being.

Other forms of language used to configure Otherness are in terms of contrastive conjunction, for example: "It was only when they washed the body that they exposed their prejudice, and the reason why the body was not on a stretcher but on the stone floor" (8). The structure "the body was not on a stretcher" contrasts with "on the stone floor," and the use of the contrastive coordinating conjunction "but" captures that. It speaks of how a cultural belief system such as Otherness affects human relationship and also how the dead is treated especially if this dead is the Other. There is also the use of prepositional contrast to mark otherness "she slowly became conscious of her life in the home of the missionaries and conscious of herself as a person. A big hole was there because, *unlike* other children, she was never able to say: "I am this or that. My parents are this or that" (9). The contrastive preposition "unlike" as used in the expression marks the contrast between Margaret the Masarwa and other children, her school mates and those within her immediate environment. From childhood, she felt that sense of difference through the way she was treated.

There are recurring adjectives which play important roles in the discourse of Otherness. This is in terms of recurring words in syntagmatic relations which describe the Masarwa. We see such adjectives in the italicized structures in the excerpt, there is no one "who did not hesitate to tell her that she was a *Bushman, mixed breed, half breed, low breed or bastard*" (5). The structure and arrangement: Bushman, mixed breed, half breed, low breed, or bastard are lexical arrays of labeling which also speak of the Otherness of the Masarwa people.

While the marriage between Maru and Margaret Cadmore the Masarwa may appear to have conferred a sense of value, or dignity to the Masarwa, it is impossible not to note that Margaret Cadmore the Masarwa is powerless and could not say no to Maru. Not because she loves Maru, but because she has come to understand the power dynamics behind Maru's desire to own her as a wife.

CONCLUSION

In this chapter, we have explored the language use in the discourse of Otherness in Bessie Head's novel: *Maru*. Specifically, we have looked at the use of deixis to mark territorial otherness, the deployment of lexico-semantic infraction for exoticism and defamiliarization of the Other, transitivity structures, interrogative structures to reveal the discourse tenor, power structures which naturalizes otherness and recurring adjective as lexical arrays which cognitively describe the Masarwa as the Other. We have shown that language is capable of unveiling the complex realities and regime of social power relations configured in an asymmetrical social power relation. We also note that this chapter significantly contributes to the transdisciplinary synergy between sociolinguistics, theoretical sociology, and literature. Lastly, we submit in this study that Otherness or the treatment of a social group and gender as an outsider as facilitated by the encoding power of language is human-made, and symptomatic of the politics and dynamics of social power relation.

WORKS CITED

Ahmad, A. "Jameson's Rhetoric of Otherness and the National Allegory." *Social Text*, 17 (1987): 3–25.

Birch, David. *Language, Literature and Critical Practice*. New York: Routledge, 1993.

Eagleton, Terry. *Literary Theory: An Introduction*. Massachusetts: Blackwell Publishing Press, 2008.

Fairclough, Isabela. and Fairclough, Norman. *Political Discourse Analysis: A Method for Advanced Students*. New York: Routledge, 2013.

Fairclough, Norman. *Analysing Discourse: Textual Analysis for Social Research*. New York: Routledge, 2003.

———. *Critical Discourse Analysis: The Critical Study of Language.* second edition. New York: Routledge, 2013.

———. *Discourse and Social Change* (Vol. 10). Cambridge: Polity Press, 1992.

Fairclough, Norman. and Holes, C. *Critical Discourse Analysis: The Critical Study of Language.* Harlow: Pearson, 1995.

Foucault, Michel. *The Archaeology of Knowledge and the Discourse on Language.* Trans. A. M. Sheridan Smith. New York: Pantheon Books, 1972.
Fowler, Roger. *Linguistic Criticism.* New York: Oxford University Press, 1989.
———. *Linguistics and the Novel.* London: Methuen, 1977.
———. *Literature as Social Discourse: The Practice of Linguistic Criticism.* London: Batsford, 1981.
Halliday, Michael. A. K. 1978. *Language as Social Semiotics: The Social Semiotic Interpretation of Language and Meaning.* London: Edward Arnold Publishers, 1978.
Halliday, Michael A. K. and Hasan, R. *Language, Context, and Text: Aspects of Language in a Social-Semiotic Perspective.* Oxford: University Press, 1989.
Head, Bessie. *Maru.* London: Heinemann, 1971.
Koul, I. "Politics of Race, Power and Gender: An Analysis of Bessie Head's *Maru*." *An International Refereed/Peer-reviewed English E-journal*, 3(4), 2017: 445–466.
Lloyd-Owen, N. "Pleasure, Autonomy and the Myth of the Untouchable Body in Bessie Head's *Maru*." *Editorial Assistance*, 2011, 46.
Lopang, W. "Curse of the Desert? Magic Realism and the Pitfalls of Setting in Bessie Head's *Maru* and Ben Okri's *Starbook*." *International Journal of Comparative Literature and Translation Studies*, 2(3), 2014: 4–9.
Nichols, L. Bessie Head Interviewed by Lee Nichols. *ReSOUND*, 1999: 1–6.
Odhiambo, E. A., Ogembo, J. and Magak, K. "Literary Commitment in Bessie Head's *Maru*." *Journal of Arts and Humanities*, 2(6), 2013: 83–96.
Ogede, O." Narrating History with a Vengeance: Interracial Marriage as Bessie Head's Doctrine for Racial Harmony in *Maru*." *International Fiction Review*, 1995.
Ogundipe-Leslie, Molara. "Stiwanism: Feminism in an African Context." *African Literature: An Anthology of a Criticism and Theory*, 2010: 542–550.
Pangmeshi, A. "The Utopian Quest in Bessie Head's *When Rain Clouds Gather* and *Maru*." *Rupkatha Journal of Interdisciplinary Studies in the Humanities*, 1(1), 2009: 60–75.
Pucherova, Dobrota. "A Romance that Failed: Bessie Head and Black Nationalism in 1960s South Africa." *Research in African Literatures*, 42(2), 2011: 105–124.
Said, Edward W. *Orientalism: Western Conceptions of the Orient.* Harmondsworth, Penguin, 1995: 105–115.
Spivak, Gayatri C. "Can the Subaltern Speak?: Marxism and the Interpretation of Culture." Cary Nelson and Lawrence Grossberg. Macmillan Education, London, 1988, 271–313.
Staszak, J.F. "Other/Otherness." *Publie dans International Encyclopedia of Human Geography.* Elsevier, Amsterdam, 2008.
Udumukwu, Onyemaechi. *Literary Theory and Criticism: An Introduction.* Port Harcourt: Charles Martins Higher Education and Consulting Company, 2015.
Wilhelm, C. "Bessie Head: The Face of Africa." *English in Africa* 1983: 1–13.

Chapter 20

Synthesis of Binaries
The Mediating Voice in Mariama Ba's Novels

Chioma Carol Opara

INTRODUCTION

African feminist writing, in its capacity as protest literature, is a validation of the African person imbued with dignity and self-worth. In re-affirming the sheer essence of African womanhood, it underlines the inalienable wholeness of the female being. The peculiarity of African feminisms lies in varied negotiating and accommodating strategies in the course of the relentless struggles against a retrogressive, masculinist, and monolithic African culture. Such debilitating traditional patterns evidently denigrate both the female and the feminine in society. Taking a holistic perspective of African cosmology, the African female creative writer, as well as the feminist theorist, seeks a socio-political and cultural milieu propitious to the well-being of women, men and children. Accordingly, African feminist literature is embedded in history, tradition and culture. Small wonder Obioma Nnaemeka has noted "the importance of cultural literacy to any valid theorizing of African literature" ("Introduction" i). A foray into African cosmology encompasses history, philosophy, anthropology, and religion that constitute the seedbed of a rich African tradition reflected in most African creative writings.

Raised in a Muslim culture by her traditional grandparents, Senegalese female writer Mariama Ba descends heavily on a sexist African Muslim culture in her two novels—*Une si longue lettre* and *Un chant ecarlate*—which have evidently put her on a pedestal in feminist literature. In both *Une si longue lettre* (1980) *(So Long a Letter 1981)* and *Un Chant écarlate (1981) (Scarlet Song),* she blazes the trail in taking a swipe at bigoted Muslim tenets. Sharing a similar view, Modupe Olaogun posits that Ba's *So Long a Letter* is "a pioneer work in being one of the first novels by a Senegalese writer to give a close portrait of a woman in an Islamic African context" (178). Again she has been dubbed "a modern Muslim woman who has belligerently adopted Islamic feminism" or feminism in Islam (Latha 26). It is pertinent to note that *So Long a Letter* is one of the twelve fictional works and one play by women, selected at the 2002 Zimbabwe International Book Fair and included on the list of Africa's Best Books of the Twentieth Century (Ogunyemi and Allen 1). This is not, in the least, surprising since the novel had won the first Noma Award for Publishing in Africa in 1980.

Born in Dakar, Senegal, on April 17, 1929, into an educated middle-class Senegalese family, Ba benefited from an early French education while she attended Koranic school. She trained as a teacher and later became a novelist. Her most active years were between 1979 and 1981. She died on August 17, 1981, after a protracted illness. In the vein of her compatriot Nafissatou Diallo who has apparently influenced her, the committed author belongs to the first generation of African female writers. Ba essentially drew a modicum of inspiration from Diallo's *De Tilene au Plateau*: U*ne Enfance Dakaroise* (1975) translated [*A Dakar Childhood*] (1982), the first autobiography by a Senegalese woman. Not only has Ba displayed ample artistic prowess in both the gender-sensitive content and innovative form in her novels, her temperate philosophy resonates with the holistic ideology of negotiation and accommodation immanent in Chikwenye Okonjo Ogunyemi's African womanism, Catherine Acholonu's motherism, Akachi Ezeigbo's snail sense, Obioma Nnaemeka's nego-feminism, Chioma Opara's femalism, Marie Pauline Eboh's gynism and Ada Azodo's di-feminism. The common denominator in these strands of African feminism is the deep concern for African women's perennial subjugation by retrogressive cultural norms. In the same vein they palpably share the vision of a transformed gender relationship in a wholesome nation rehabilitated by the collaborative efforts of both men and women. Nnaemeka aptly observes that, "Power-sharing, complementarity, accommodation, compromise, negotiation and inclusiveness form the foundation of African feminisms and mark their difference from aspects of Western feminisms. Filomina Chioma Steady emphasizes the inclusive and complementary thrust of African patterns of feminism" ("Theorizing African Feminism" 6). Complementarity between men and women, which Mariama Ba explicitly prescribes in *So Long a Letter* (88) is inextricably linked with accommodation and negotiation in a patriarchal culture. Taking a rather radical stance, Molara Ogundipe decries what she views as African feminists' "contradictory loyalties to patriarchy." Ogundipe, whose Stiwanism tenets advocate political, social and economic integration of women in national development, seeks the rational, theoretical and practical resolution of "how one 'accommodates' social negativities for women and the deprivation of basic human rights that are intrinsic to patriarchy" (xv).

This chapter will discuss Ba's literary contributions hinged on bold stylistic imprints on the landscape of African feminisms. Essentially ambivalent in her posture and moderate in her thoughts, Ba excels in the subtle fusion of the paradigmatic angel and the devil, etched by Sandra Gilbert and Susan Gubar (1979), in the female portraiture. Furthermore, her legacies stand out in her distinct philosophies, psychological plumbing of characters, and phenomenal artistry. Antonyms together with overarching binaries are laid out skillfully and ultimately melded. This is a distinct statement of the author's vision which consists in the attainment of a holistic world that traverses and transcends divergent views and oppositions. Her artistic skills are patently laced with her feminist ideologies as well as indices of existentialism and naturalism.

THE POLITICS OF BA'S ARTISTRY

Ba is widely acclaimed for her distinct craftsmanship. It may be appropriate to quote Nnaemeka at length to highlight Ba's artistic feat as a creative writer:

> In my years of researching this extraordinary, gifted Senegalese writer, Mariama Ba, I have come in contact with people who knew her very well and their unanimity on the scores is encoded in the two phrases that I have heard repeated (1) "Elle savait ecrire" [She knew how to write]; and (2) "Elle savait aimer" [She knew how to love]. This beautiful woman with great love in her heart saw deception and wrote a masterpiece against it. Mariama Ba's works stand as an eloquent psychology of deception/deceivers (those captives of the devil-made-me-do-it syndrome that pervades the works). ("Urban Spaces" 188–189)

Evidently, the author underlines the essence of unalloyed love dexterously pitched against ignominious deception. True love is implicitly aligned with real friendship which distinctly defines the essence of enduring relationships. Accordingly, Ba frowns upon unreciprocated affection, particularly unrequited love, in her superbly crafted novels which glaringly testify that not only did she know "how to love" she also "knew how to write." Her writings are, in essence, based on the philosophies of African feminisms that she explicitly espouses.

Ba in *So Long a Letter* moans over men's flagrant betrayal and desertion of women in spite of the profundity of love and care by their wives. The occasion was Ramatoulaye's mourning period of four months and ten days prescribed by Muslim dogma for widows. She ruminates over the gamut of Modou's demise—the fatal blow of death, the Muslim rituals of cleansing and clothing of the dead body—the remains of the love of her youth who had abandoned her for the younger Binetou who, incidentally, is her daughter's friend. Accordingly, Ramatoulaye's vitriolic musings betray the catalogue of binaries—female emotions/male reason; real/ideal; female unalloyed commitment/male egocentric leanings; Muslim tradition/ Western modernity; angel/devil; noise/voice; Femalism (African feminism)/Western feminism.

The African female writer would, as a matter of course, rather identify with Afro-centric feminism than with Western feminism. African feminism has over the years established its own theoretical space. For the African woman, sexism couched in repressive cultural practices, could be more debilitating than racist colonization. An inalienable victim of a politico-cultural imbroglio, the African woman is caught between the historical realities of slavery, colonialism, neo-colonialism, and the menace of stultifying cultural norms. Against this enervating background is the politically conscious woman who may not seem to be as emancipated as her Western counterpart but who is visibly straining at the leash. Appreciating the divergent visions of the two political groups, Senegalese Marxist writer, Sembene Ousmane contends that while the European women revolted against Napoleon code, Christian civilization their African counterparts are rising against so many values (Herzberger-Fofana 56). The clogging values of a masculinist culture, glaringly, not only underline the "patriarchal constructs" of female submission but also endorse double moral standard. This goes a long way in immobilizing the female gender while thwarting potential radical feminism on the African content. Much as femalism, a strand of African feminism, as an ideology is not man-hating, it is concerned with male-institutionalized cultural norms that negate female autonomy. Foregrounding the body and negating gender subjectivity deemed as culturally and socially constructed, the femalist philosophy views the female body as a site of the contrasting sensibilities of pain and nurture. Essentially, the female body is manipulated by the patriarchal hand and revised by the femalist foot—the synecdoche of the itinerant prime African woman, relentlessly seeking self-actualization. The apparent ambivalence in femalism and other hues of African feminism stems from the overwhelming burden of history, racism, colonization, and the attendant clogs of Westernization. Given the reality of daunting colonization and concomitant alienation, Ba, together with most African female writers, is arguably femalist.

Clearly, ambivalence is an offshoot of alienation. The corollary of the ensuing alienation is a split personality. This is dramatized in the figure of Ramatoulaye, Ba's dramatis persona in *So Long a Letter*, who has gone through twelve maternities and chooses to remain married to Modou despite his flagrant betrayal. The schizophrenic mother of nine, obviously torn between tradition and modernity, decides to look after her children in Modou's house. She, nevertheless, hurts profusely and cries out in protest, in the course of the *mirasse* or stripping of the dead and the *tagg* or praise form, challenging an unjust African Muslim religion. Aissatou on her own part divorces Mawdo in spite of the cultural belief that her four sons' future would be blighted without a father to direct them. In a similar analysis, Helen Chukwuma opines that, "The truth of the matter is that Ramatoulaye lacked the guts. and courage of feminism. This is seen in her admiration of her friend Aissatou whom she refers to as the courageous pioneer of a new life" (222). It must be pointed out that narrow socialization process, traditional orientation, cultural beliefs and trammels as well as the repressed individual's make-up diminish guts. It could also be argued that if Ramatoulaye "lacked the guts and courage of feminism," she would seamlessly fit into the pastel hue of femalism which advocates temperance and moderation rather than radicalism. The more courageous and Western feminist-inclined Aissatou stakes the supposed success of her sons by her bold step as she struts defiantly on the radical path. Accordingly, she leaves her marital home, walking out on her husband, but not before dropping a valedictory letter which opens with an epigram:

> Les princes dominent leurs sentiments pour honorer leurs devoirs. Les autres courbent leurs nuque en silence qui les brime. (60)
>
> [Princes master their feelings to fulfill their duties. Others bend their heads and in silence, accept a destiny that oppresses them]. (31)

Aissatou in this singular statement identifies with Simone de Beauvoir's existentialist principles that underline the One, the Subject, which is starkly contrasted with the Object, the Other. In line with the Sartrean tenets of *pour soi / en soi,* she takes her destiny in her own hands by extricating herself from the mud [*le visqueux*]. Her figure adumbrates the new generation of African women—the "trio"—Arame, Yacine, and Dieynaba—who, by virtue of their radical lifestyle, are likely to imbibe Western feminism to the hilt in the future. It is salient to note that Aissatou sojourns in France and later in the United States of America in a climate propitious for her radicalism and ensuing success as well as her distinct achievements. It is indeed Aissatou and not Ramatoulaye who is imbued with what Uzo Esonwanne refers to as enlightenment epistemology or assimilated modernity (82). Ramatoulaye on her own part stays in the hearth, advocating temperance, forbearance, reciprocity, and gender complementarity that constitute the cornerstones of her creator's legacy. Florence Stratton has on her own part noted the distinct likeness between Ba and Aissatou than between Ba and Ramatoulaye. In her own words, "While Ba treats her conservative heroine (Ramatoulaye) ironically, having her tell her story with subconscious evasion and revelation, she explicitly identifies with her radical heroine (Aissatou) who is not only a divorced woman (as Ba herself was) but also shares Ba's last name (138). Therein lie the constituents of the author's ambivalence that manifests in the deft creation of the angel and the devil. The apparently temperate Ba had actually divorced her husband, Obeye Diop, a Senegalese member of Parliament and later took custody of their nine children. It is our contention that Aissatou, Ba's alter ego, is that radical part of the seemingly angelic Ramatoulaye which is submerged by tradition. The author first extricates her from that milieu and allows her to thrive in the Western sphere. Again she names one of Ramatoulaye's children, Aissatou to perpetuate her legacy. Small wonder *l'enfant terrible*, young Aissatou, bears a child out of wedlock in defiance of a restrictive Muslim culture that demands chastity from women before marriage. The schizophrenic Ba/Aissatou, the maddened double, foreshadows Mireille in Ba's second novel.

Ba effectively contrasts Ramatoulaye with Mireille in her second novel *Un Chant écarlate (Scarlet Song)* divided into three main parts. These are further divided into smaller parts. The portrayal of a white female protagonist in this novel is a political stunt pulled to underscore the liberalism of femalism, which is essentially African and not Western. Mireille, an accomplished, educated and intelligent French lady of noble birth marries beneath her. Ousmane on the contrary is rooted in utter grime and filth of the slum. It is probably in a bid to cover his inadequacies that Ousmane flagrantly engages in an illicit affair with an old girlfriend, Ouleymatou, who comes from a similar deprived background. Like poles, as a matter of course, attract. In the vein of Ramatoulaye, the betrayed Mireille loves her husband and has given without stint. Just like Ramatoulaye, Mireille chafes under non–requital of her unconditional love.

The difference, however, lies in the mode of reaction to a conjugal betrayal. While Ramatoulaye forbears to accept her fate with equanimity, the Western feminist Mireille reacts violently. Not only does she descend on her husband with a cutlass, she slays the product of her unwholesome marriage, their son Gorgui in a gory act of vengeance against a patriarchal structure that has institutionalized both polygyny and polygamy[1] to suit men. Sharing a similar view, Nnaemeka asserts that "the contradictions of Mireille's married life take a human form in her mulatto son whom she kills as a rejection and possible resolution of those contradictions" ("Urban Space" 186). Coming from a country where feminism and not femalism is practiced and where polygyny is in the main, regarded as bigamy, Mireille opts out of the marriage but not before destroying a cherished belonging of a perfidious husband. She had initially considered staying in the marriage because of her son. Infused, nevertheless, with feminist consciousness she pondered,

> L'argument "enfant" n'est pas solide. Mais les femmes piétinées, les brandissent et camouflent leur volonté défaillante dans un cri de mère eplorée. C'est par lâcheté, par peur de s'assumer que les mères décus demeurent au foyer. L'habitude de ne plus décider, de ne plus voir et de se laisser vivre les fait prisonnières. (240)

> [The "child" argument is not sound. But down-trodden women thrive and disguise their waning will in this cry of a maudlin woman. It is sheer cowardice and fear of shouldering responsibility that impel cheated women to remain at the marital hearth. The habit of not taking decision anymore and of not looking into things anymore and of leaving things as they are, as them to prisoners.][2]

The Sartrean concept of freedom is applied as Mireille, devoid of the femalist sentiment of culture-bound nurturance, chooses to take her destiny in her hand, which she raises to commit infanticide. That singular act ruptures the marital bond eroded with blood. Ramatoulaye on her own part, is flurried rather than vengeful at the poetic destruction of her treacherous husband, a victim of a heart attack. Ba presents this scene in a passage laden with short and incomplete sentences—fragments. This distinctly bares an agitated woman's excitement, which had reached fever pitch in the wake of the death of a beloved spouse:

> Un taxi héle! Vite! Plus vite! Ma gorge sèche. Dans ma poitrine une boule immobile. Vite! Plus vite! Enfin l'hôpital L'odeur des suppurations et de l'éther mêlés. L'hôpital! (8)

> [A taxi quickly hailed! Fast! Faster still! My throat is dry. There is a rigid lump in my chest. Fast! Faster still! At last, the hospital. The mixed smell of suppuration and ether. The hospital!] (2)

The salvo of moral sensibility in the femalist, Ramatoulaye, for a smitten Modou who had mortified her is most striking. Clearly the contrast in attitude is based on orientation as well as ideology that is spawned by the stoked female voice, a legacy in consciousness-raising.

VOICE AS ANTONYM OF NOISE

The power of the female voice which is contrasted with mere noise, lies in the sonorous exhortation that anticipates the arduous trudge in the path. Given the African traditional society that hardly reckons with female political aspirations but rather tends to dismiss any audible articulation as noise, the distinct female voice which wields authority, respect and rapt attention is deemed reactionary.[3] Female bonding, in effect, stokes the voice as it lends credence to it. Ramatoulaye tells us her story through her celebrated letter to a friend. We know very little of Mireille's tribulations and psychological pains in marriage because we hardly heard her real voice in her vulnerable station as a sequestered housewife. It is only when an anonymous note intimating her with her husband's clandestine affair is sent to her that Mireille's real voice is heard in the gory denouement. She is constrained to emerge from seclusion. Carolyn Heilbrun has noted, "How alone women are, how without close friends are Jane Austen's heroines, and Charlotte Bronte's and George Eliot's. There will be narratives of female lives only when women no longer live their lives isolated in the houses and the stories of men" (47). True both Ramatoulaye and Mireille, in the vein of their Victorian sisters had been isolated in the houses and stories of their men. Armed with the pen and relishing the privilege of a confidante, Ramatoulaye shouts forcefully. Like a lioness in the path that has been caged for too long, she roars at Tamsir's leviratic marriage proposal. It is indeed a moment of sweet revenge. She had been struck dumb by Tamsir's tactless announcement of Modou's second marriage. But now in a stentorian tone she talks back:

> Ma voix connâit trente années de silence, trente années de brimade. Elle éclate, violente, tantôt sarcastique, tantôt meprisante . . . Tu oublie que j'ai un coeur, une raison, que je ne suis pas un object que l'on passé de main en main. (85)
>
> [My voice has known thirty years of silence, thirty years of harassment. It burst out, violent, sometimes sarcastic sometimes contemptuous . . . You forget that I have a heart, a mind, that I am not an object to be passed from hand to hand.] (57–58)

The concept of freedom, choice, and subjectivity is forcefully articulated. The strident voice now stresses the freedom which resides in the very act of choosing. As one critic pithily observed, "A voice that has been repressed for thirty years is finally heard" (Larrier 750). It paradoxically resounds through the cloistered atmosphere of mourning as ascribed by the Muslim tradition. Hooks posits. "Moving from silence into speech is for the oppressed, the colonized, the exploited and those who stand and struggle side by side a gesture of defiance that heals, that makes new life and new growth possible" (9).

It is noteworthy that the distinction between noise and voice is made through the newly resuscitated voice of Ramatoulaye which bares this distinction:

> Chez les femmes, que de bruits: rires sonores. paroles hautes, tapes des mains, stridentes exclamations Des amies qui ne etaient vues depuis longtemps. s'etreignent bruyamment . . . On se transmet les derniers potins. Et l'on s'esclaffe et l'on roule les yeux . . . De temps en temps, une voix virile excédée met en garde, redefinit le rassemblement: cérémonie pour la rédemption d' une âme. (14)

> [In the women's corner, nothing but noise, resonant laughter, loud talk, hand slaps, strident exclamations. Friends who have not seen each other for a long time hug each other noisily . . . The latest bits of gossip are exchanged. They laugh heartily and roll their eyes . . . From time to time an exasperated manly voice rings out a warning recalling the purpose of the gathering: a ceremony for the redemption of a soul.] (6)

In skillfully contrasting the resonant male voice with the jarring female clatter on feminine fripperies, Ba has underscored the need for a challenging female voice in the political quest. Surely women such as those depicted above, on whom the solemnity of obsequies is obviously lost, can only produce clanging noise. Preoccupied with trivialities and gaudy trifles, they are expressly bereft of any political vision that may enhance the status of the African woman. Any babble that is not logical, efficacious, or conceptual is, as it were, noise. Mireille's tirade against Ousmane in her demented state is voice, while the idiophonic squelching of Ouleymatou's shoes 'Thiokète! thiokète! in her seductive steps to lure Ousmane is noise.[4]

In the same vein, the constant whining of Yaye Khady, Ousmane's mother, against her French daughter-in-law is noise. The mothers-in-law, who in the two novels, aid their daughters in ruthlessly supplanting the first wives are noisemakers whose main goal is material acquisition. that would enable them to appear flamboyant at social events, to the horde of idle, parasitic, noisy women. Most of these women are too frivolous to be endowed with any political vision as well as visible means of livelihood. Nadia Youssef has noted that Muslim families are already facing the conflict between the "continued extension of family support to female relatives and increasing economic demands. It will become increasingly difficult for male members to meet these financial obligations" (214). The jealousy and hostility directed against innocent wives by the greedy and overbearing mothers-in-law stem from their culturally assumed rights over their sons' including their daughters-in-law's finances. The daughter-in-law is, as a matter of course, held liable when the son can no longer cope with the needs and wants of the extended family. What makes Mireille a quintessential butt of debilitating ranting of a noisy mother-in-law is the fact that her constant generous contributions are hardly appreciated especially as Ousmane's income had become depleted as a result of his financial obligations to his second wife, Ouleymatou.

The politically conscious author, apparently driven by the ideology of naturalism, sets out at cleaning the Augean stables by underlining cleanliness which is a facet of voice in both novels. Unlike Hercules, the female protagonists, Ramatoulaye and Mireille, are incapable of achieving that Herculean task in one day. Ba, as a form of consciousness-raising, exhorts cleanliness which is as literal as it is metaphorical. Ramatoulaye muses in her long letter,

> Cette netteté de ma personne m'enchante. Point de mire de tant d'yeux, je pense que de qualités essentielles de la femme est la propreté. La plus humble des chaumières plâit si l'ordre et la propriété règnent, le cadre le plus luxeuse ne seduit pas si la poussière l'encrasse. (93)

> [The cleanliness of my body pleases me. I think as she is the object of attraction for so many eyes, cleanliness should be one of the essential qualities of a woman. The most humble of huts is pleasing when it is clean: the most luxurious setting offers no attraction if it is covered in dust.] (63)

She surprisingly, at the darkest moment of bereavement, even notices the dirty habits of some of her visitors paying their last respects in the course of the funeral ceremonies. Similarly, in *Un Chant écarlate* Mireille fusses over the cleanliness of her home which she scrubs and polishes conscientiously since she believes that the environment rubs off on the individual. "Pour elle; le milieu influence le comportment de l'individu" (126). ["As far as she is concerned, the environment influences the individual."]

The author is obviously infused with the philosophy of naturalism which is a "specialized variety of realism" that is akin to materialism. Linking scientific method to philosophy, the behavior of the individual, the "human beast," to borrow Emile Zola's phrase, is essentially deemed a function of the locale or environment. Ba undoubtedly implies in her second novel that since the cleanliness of an individual presupposes that of the environment, both the environment and the individual have to be purged of both physical and moral filth. Noise is viewed as a noisome aspect of that defect as it invariably pollutes the environment and in the long run the individual. Clearly the individual is in one part capable of polluting the environment. Conversely, a fetid environment could incapacitate the individual's mentality, as it does with Ousmane's "retour aux sources"—to his stinking childhood abode at Usine

Niari Tallia and the attendant deception. The total regeneration of the body, mind and surroundings is accordingly advocated as regards the empowerment of the voice. The author seeks a symmetrical and wholesome world which should be united rather than divided by a catalogue of antithetical factors which stand out as stark binaries.

ON BLENDING DIFFERENCES

That *Une si longue lettre* is essentially a novel of binaries is established by a number of antitheses, which serve as a prologue to the novel. Consider for instance the following epigrammatic statements:

> Si les rêves meurent en traversant les ans et les realités. (7)

> [And passing through the realities of life, dreams die.] (1)

Further down the page:

> Les mêmes parcours nous a conduits de l'adolescence a la maturité où le passé féconde le présent. (7)

> [We walked the same paths from adolescence to maturity, where the past begets the present.] (1)

These antithetical constructions anticipate the plethora of binaries in this novel. They are indicative of a narrative strategy that aims at stoking our consciousness by first presenting both sides and expecting us to make a choice which should presumably be in consonance with the author's political thought.

As we have earlier stated, Aissatou is a character Ba creates as a mirror image of the author herself. The radical Aissatou is a veritable foil to the temperate Ramatouloye. In marriage Aissatou's parental background is sharply contrasted with Mawdo's true blood. In the same vein, Aissatou's rejection in marriage by her mother-in-law is contrasted with Ramatoulaye's marriage with Modou that was celebrated under the disapproving look of her father, the painful indignation of her frustrated mother and the sarcasm of her surprised sister. Aissatou, a goldsmith's daughter, is continuously scoffed at by her mother-in-law who is of the view that her son has married beneath him. Aissatou eventually divorces Mawdo, leaving a letter in her wake, which opens and closes with antitheses.

Je me dépouille de ton amour, de ton nom. Vêtue du seul habitvalable de la dignité, je poursuis ma route. (50)

[I am stripping myself of your name. Clothed in my dignity, the only worthy garment, I go my way.] (32)

A dignified Aissatou goes her way with their four sons, none the worse for it. Meanwhile the humiliated Ramatoulaye stays on, ploughing a lonely furrow in the course of her daughters' teenage problems.

The politics of gender is played most skillfully in Ba's characterization. It is not fortuitous that the second wives of the two unsavory old men, Modou and Mawdo are teenagers. To quote Okhamafe "The law of the availability of vulnerable or naïve women guarantees the continuous satisfaction of masculinist desires" (36). The two young second wives are preyed upon by their elderly husbands. The exuding youthfulness as well as immaturity of the vulnerable Binetou is put in bold relief against the ridiculous foppishness of the ageing Modou, presented as a mere caricature striving with his waning looks and flagging energies. The misalliance together with the obvious incompatibility that swaddle the couple is further heightened in a graphic play of antitheses where comparison is made literally by placing two couples side by side. In a contrivance of plot, Modou's daughter, Daba, who had been Binetou's friend before she married Modou, and her young fiancé are made to sit in full view of the elderly Modou and his child bride, eyeball to eyeball. The desired effect of ridiculing the foppish "cradle-snatcher" and his "bewitching" victim is created in the reader's mind's eye in this "grotesque confrontation." The former is described as a well-matched couple, the latter as an ill-assorted couple (50). ["C'était en face grotesque: d' un côté un couple disparate, de l' autre deux êtres assortis."] (75)

Similarly in *Un Chant écarlate* Mireille and Ousmane are seen in the eyes of Guillaume as Beauty and the Beast [La Belle et la Bete]. The ill-assorted couple hardly share much in common. While Ousmane is black and of the Muslim faith. Mireille is white and a baptized Christian who eventually gets converted to Islam in marriage. The filth and grime of Ousmane's childhood existence at the slum referred to as "le quartier" and reminiscent of Alex la Guma's tenements in the title story of *A Walk in the Night*, (1980) is sharply contrasted with the splendor of "l'appartement luxeux" [luxury flat] in which Mireille grew up. In spite of the glaring differences as well as binaries, selfless love sprouts in the beginning of the relationship bonding two fertile hearts, facilitated by the synthesizing fluid:

> Et des fluids se rejoignent pour recréer l'unité, Le couple naît. La mission millénaire s'ébauche. Un homme, une femme ici. Un homme; une femme ailleurs! (28)
>
> [And some fluid collected to recreate unity. A couple is born. The millennial mission is outlined. A man, a woman here. A man, a woman elsewhere.]

This lyrical presentation sets in motion the whirlpool of a love affair with two principal antithetical figures—a man and a woman, here and elsewhere. When a second woman, Ouleymatou appears on the love scene, she is created as a foil. Unlike Binetou and young Nabou who in *Une si longue lettre* were presented as victims, sacrificed on the altar of warped societal values, Ouleymatou is cast in the mold of a temptress who is out to seduce. Villainy is contrasted with ingenuousness. In the main, Ba portrays the diametrically opposed features of life to achieve a didactic end.

In the etching of binaries, Ba proffers the possibilities of tactical bridging occasioned by blending and bonding. This explicates the profusion of water imagery particularly in *Un Chant écarlate* where the author has postulated that fluid is collected "to recreate unity" (28). Water blends various, varied and disparate units in the universe to assume fluidity and create a sense of wholeness. Not only does water douse the tension and rift in Ba's second novel, it refreshes friendship which is substantially underscored. Drawing a fine distinction between friendship and love, Ba implicitly subordinates the latter to the former. According to her philosophical submission, friendship has a code of conduct more established than love. Besides, friendship is not branded by time. Love hardly emanates wholly from the passage. Water in effect constitutes the main component of the acid test.

Ba's two novels constitute an eloquent testimony to the currency of friendship pitted against the transience of love. The aquatic imagery, which looms largely in the second novel nurtures friendship, which flows through individuals as it blends minds. It is not surprising then that true friendship thrives on grounds which have proved infertile for love. The friendship between Ramatoulaye and Aissatou, and also between her and the *griotte*, Farmata, and even between her and her suitor Dieng outlasts Modou's fleeting love for her. Likewise, Mireille's friendship with her sister-in-law Soukeyna, much as it is not in the class of "wolere" (age-old friendship), is more meaningful than Ousmane's professed love for her. By intimating Mireille with Ousmane's secret marriage in a note, Soukeyna demonstrates that she owes more allegiance to a battered friend than to a knavish brother. No doubt, true friendship blends minds and souls because it neither lies, hurts, cheats nor discriminates.

In *Un Chant écarlate* Ba dramatizes the futility in a starkly transient love which hardly blends. Divided into three parts, the first part deals with a blissful courtship that culminates in a turbulent marriage in the second part and the ensuing infanticide in the third part. The dying embers of love for Mireille get fanned into a reckless infatuation with Ouleymatou, which begets lies, betrayal, and eventual tragedy. Structurally the second part bridges the two antithetical parts. And as the second part opens, we are reminded that the huge difference between the two continents has been diminished by the bridging airplane. True the African and Western worlds are two diametrically opposed spheres separated by a colossal ocean. Ba aims at bridging the difference in the idealistic marriage between a Senegalese Muslim of an utterly humble background and an upper class, Christian French lady. In fact the only thing they seem to share in common is the knowledge of philosophy. In an effort to crystallize the union, Mireille is made to bear a child who, in embodying the differing worlds would cement their relationship, their differences notwithstanding. The mulatto, the emblem of their love is butchered as an aftermath of that love which cannot blend. This is definitely not a function of color difference but that of unreciprocated affection. The dirge, a scarlet song of dissipated hope ("un chant profond écarlate d' espérances disperses") (248), which we hear in the wake of the attack on Ousmane is undoubtedly that of the author who had, in the inversion of plot in her second novel, started with a visionary love and ended with a gory tragedy. The optimism evinced by Ba at the end of the first novel degenerates into an unequivocal pessimism tinged with cynicism by the time the second one closes. The dramatic change of authorial vision, manifested in the prevailing disillusionment, is premised on past unreciprocated female love, betrayals, and predicaments.

    True Ba is convinced that the future cannot be built without a well-knit past ("On ne bâtit pas l' avenir sur 'des passés sans liens'") (*Un Chant écarlate* 59).This explains the frequent use of flashback technique by means of the epistolary, diary and album, "fouiller la mémoire" as well as a surfeit of conjunctions—a connecting device. It is pertinent to note that Ba has dexterously blended three forms—epistolary, diary and autobiography. Echoes of Nafissatou Diallo's *De Tilene au Plateau: Une Enfance Dakaroise* [*A Dakar Childhood*] are discernible. Some critics have argued that women use more conjunctions than men (Swacker 76–83). Indeed, in African literature women writers, who are in the main *griottes* in the tradition of their foremothers, sometimes use conjunctions to effect an oral rhythmic flow. This is palpable in *Un Chant écarlate* where the oral form prevails. Conjunctions are also used in Ba's works to link the grueling present with the blissful past. In *So Long a Letter* Ramatoulaye in her cloistered situation and mournful mood reminisces over joyful moments shared in sisterhood:

> Et nous nous gavions des fruits a portée de la main! Et nous buvions l' eau des noix de còco Et nous nous racontions des"hisoires salees"! Et nous nous

tremoussions invites par les accents violents d' un phonograph! Et l' agneau assaisonne de poivre, ail, beurre, piment, grillait sur le feu de bois. Et nous vivions. (37–38)

[And we stuffed ourselves with fruits within easy reach. And we drank the milk from coconuts. And we told juicy stories! And we danced about, roused by the strident notes of a gramophone. And the lamb, seasoned with white pepper, garlic, butter, hot pepper, would be roasting over the wood fire. And we lived.] (23)

The frenzied female speech laden with connectives attests to a smitten woman's attempt to draw some strength from past experiences marked by the repetition of conjunctions employed as an effective blending device.

As with antithesis, Ba in *Scarlet Song* carries out a practical demonstration of linking the grueling present with a seemingly promising past, while blending graphic reminiscences with linking words and conjunctions. In her demented condition, the naked[5] Mireille, who had been pushed over the edge, perseveres to stick the love letters written by Ousmane during their courtship on the living room wall with glue, which serves as a literal connective—gluing the sweet memories of the past to the present angst. Displaced like trophies, the contents of the letters, which profess an unshared and enduring love, cannot be validated by the blatant lie Ousmane is recklessly living at present. Mireille continually calls out for more glue or rather falsehood: "Vite de la colle" (244). It is in this distinct pun that Ba attains the height of her artistic dexterity underset by gender politics. As it becomes more and more frustrating to stick the blatant falsehood to the selfless love it was meant to be, it dawns on Mireille that both cannot blend. This realization is simultaneously made graphic and poignant. in her son Gorgui, the embodiment of that inconsistency. And since there is no visible and viable blend in him, he has to be sacrificed for a more wholesome and stable future. It is salient to note that the depression suffered by the *gnac* Jacqueline an Ivorian who had been continually cheated on by her husband in *So Long a Letter*, escalates to the *toubab* Mireille's total nervous breakdown in the second novel, *Scarlet Song*. Jacqueline had presented with psychological symptoms such as an overpowering lump in her chest. Besides, she had been prescribed some tranquilizers, lived in her "private hell" (43) and later admitted in the neurology ward of a psychiatric hospital. Ba's patent skill at probing the battered psyche of her female characters places her as a leading African figure—in the class of Egyptian writer and psychiatrist, Nawal el Saadawi—seeking the mental well-being of women in stable relationships predicated on symmetrical and equitable cultural norms.

CONCLUSION

It is evident that the femalist, Ba, has in her two novels, in the vein of a real philosopher and psychologist, striven at stoking our awareness to the complexities of life's upheavals which stem from opposing forces. The repletion of binaries not only punctuates this contention but also leaves the option of individual choice open while reaffirming the indispensability of connectives in linking diametrically opposed situations and concepts. Besides, it effects a nexus between the past and the present which is considered a desideratum in the molding of an equitable future. Propriety is seen as a vital ingredient in this vision. The author's idea of propriety is essentially symbolized by a conscious effort at cleanliness, which is germane to the productive voice antithetical to noise. The stentorian female tone remains a privilege of Ba's dynamic female protagonists who obliquely exhort the reader to action. Indeed, the French lady, Mireille, could be said to be speaking up with her black sisters and not against them. For this white lady, the problem is as enormous as it is experiential. In consequence of her traumatic experience in marriage, her voice rather than her reaction, resonates that of an emotionally wounded Ramatoulaye.

The efficacy of the voice presupposes reciprocity, cleanliness, and the blending of minds, irrespective of gender, class, and racial differences. It should be noted that the profusion of aquatic imagery in the second novel, *Scarlet Song*, is probably predicated on the author's conviction that water is absolutely essential to the lofty task of cleansing and blending. Surely only the cleansed, the generous and those capable of reciprocating affections are able to blend in friendship. There can be no doubt that friendship, manifesting in female bonding, fills the yawning gap that unfulfilling love creates in the heart of each female protagonist.

Essentially, in both novels female friendship/bonding, which outlasts marital love, knows no limitations, as we can see in the friendship between Farmata and Ramatoulaye on the one hand and between Mireille and Soukeyna on the other. By creating ideologically, socially, and racially contrasting characters and allowing them to blend in friendship, Ba not only offers a choice in binaries but also proffers a synthesis together with some possibilities of resolving myriad differences. This is graphically dramatized as *Une si longue lettre* draws to a close; Ramatoulaye, the femalist, plays down her victimhood at the hands of man in advocating gender complementarity. She awaits the return of her feminist friend, Aissatou; leans on the crutch provided by her socially inferior friend, Farmata, in the face of her teenage daughters' radical expressions of freedom. The sum total of all these is harmony in adversity and diversity. This underlines the author's tenet which resides in temperance with accommodation. It is the non-existence of this femalist ideal in some strands of feminism that begets the tragic in *Un chant écarlate*. In fact, that is where the point of divergence lies concerning Ba's two political novels that are structurally antithetical.

Ba's enduring legacies are manifest in her inspiring innovations. Her composite political thoughts are deftly articulated with phenomenal craft and artistry. Not only has she been in the vanguard of the application of existentialist and naturalistic philosophies to African women's literature, she has gone ahead to employ an in-depth psychological probing of her female characters. Indices of Sandra Gilbert's and Susan Gubar's maddened double technique—the angel and the devil—are manifest. This device has been signified upon by other female authors such as Nawal el Saadawi and Tsitsi Dangarembga. Clearly Ba's first novel that is reputed to be the "first epistolary novel in African literature," is adjudged "the first truly feminist African novel, skillfully weaving the accounts of individual suffering and dilemmas" (Blair 139). Besides, her singular exhortation for the inevitable and necessary complementarity of man and woman has set the tone for African feminist theory and creative writing.

WORKS CITED

Aidoo, Ama Ata. *No Sweetness Here*. London: Longman Drumbeat, 1979.
Ali, Souad, T. "Feminism in Islam: A Critique of Polygamy in Mariama Ba's Epistolary Novel *So Long a Letter,*" *Hawwa*, Vol. 10, Issue 3 (2004): 179–199.
Ba, Mariama. *Un Chant écarlate*. Dakar: Les Nouvelles Editions Africaines, 1981.
———. *Une si longue lettre*. Dakar: Les Nouvelles Editions, 1980 (trans. Modupe Bode Thomas, *So Long a Letter,* New Horn Press, 1981).
Beauvoir, Simone de. *The Second Sex*. Trans. H.M. Parshley, New York: Vintage Books, 1974.
Blair, Dorothy, S. *Senegalese Literature: A Critical History*. Boston: Twayne Publishers, 1984.
Chukwuma, Helen. "Voices and Choices: The Feminist Dilemma in four African Novels." *Feminism in African Literature*. Ed. Helen Chukwuma. Enugu: New Generation Books, 1994, 215–227.
Diallo, Nafissatou. *A Dakar Childhood*. Trans. Dorothy S. Blair. Essex: Longman, 1982.
Eagleton, Mary, *Feminist Literary Theory: A Reader*. Oxford: Basil Blackwell, 1990.
Esonwanne, Uzo. "Enlightenment Epistemology and Aesthetic Cognition: Mariama Ba's *So Long a Letter.*" *The Politics of (M) Othering*. Ed. Obioma Nnaemeka. London and New York: Routeledge, 1997: 82–100.

Gilbert Sandra and Susan Gubar. Ed. *The Madwoman in the Attic: The Woman Writer and the Nineteenth Century Literary Imagination.* Haven and London: Yale University Press, 1979.

Hartman, Heidi. "The Family as the Locus of Gender, Class and Political Struggle: The Example of Housework." *Signs,* 6, 3 (Spring 1981): 366–394.

Heilbrun, Carolyn. *Writing on Woman's Life.* New York: Ballantine Books, 1988.

Herzberger-Fofana, Pierrette. "Sembene Ousmane, Forgeron de Caracteres: Une Interview Avec Le Romancier Et Cineaste Senegalais." *Komparastistische Hefte.* Heft 8 (1983): 55–63.

Hooks, Bells. *Talking Back. Thinking Feminist. Thinking Black.* Boston, MA: South End Press, 1989.

La Guma, Alex. *A Walk in the Night.* London: Heinemann, 1980.

Larrier Renee. "Correspondance et Creation Litteraire: Mariama Ba's *Une si longue lettre*." *French Review,* Vol. 64, No. 5 (April 1991): 747–753.

Latha, Rizwana Habib. "Feminisms in an African Context: Mariama Ba's *So Long a Letter*." *Agenda: Empowering Women for Gender Equity.* No. 50, African Feminism One (2001): 23–40.

Nnaemeka, Obioma. "Introduction: Imag(in)ing Knowledge, Power, and Subversion in the Margins." In *The Politics of (M) Othering.* Ed. Obioma Nnaemeka. London and New York: Routledge, 1997: 1–25.

———. "Theorizing African Feminisms: Rethinking Epistemologies and Pedagogies." *Ofo: Journal of Transatlantic Studies.* Vol. 5, Nos 1 and 2, June/December 2015: 1–12.

———. "Urban Spaces, Women's Places: Polygamy as Sign in Mariama Ba's Novels." *The Politics of (M) Othering.* Ed. Obioma Nnaemeka. London and New York: Routledge, 1997: 162–191.

Ogundipe, Molara. "Preface." *Critical Issues in African Literature: Twenty-First Century and Beyond.* Ed. Chinyelu F. Ojukwu. Port Harcourt: University of Port Harcourt Press, 2013: xiii–xvi.

Ogunyemi, Chikwenye Okonjo. "Prolepsis: Twelve Telling Tales by African Women." *Twelve Best Books by African Women.* Ed. Chikwenye Okonjo Ogunyemi and Tuzyline Jita Allen. Athens: Ohio University Press, 2009.

Okhamafe, Imafedia E. "African Feminism(s) and the Question of Marital and Non-Marital Loneliness and Intimacy." *SAGE: Scholarly Journal on Black Women,* Vol. 6, No. 1 (Summer 1989): 33–39.

Olaogun, Modupe. "Aesthetics, Ethics, Desire and Necessity in Mariama Ba's *So Long a Letter.*" *Twelve Best Books by African Women.* Ed. Chikwenye Okonjo Ogunyemi and Tuzyline Jita Allan. Athens: Ohio University Press, 2009: 177–198.

Opara, Chioma. "A Matter of Contrasts: The Antithetical as Political in Mariama Ba's Novels." *Journal of Gender Studies.* Vol. 1, No. 3 (Sept. 2001): 119–139.

———. *Towards Integration in Heterogeneity: Poetics, Conflict and Gender Politics in Literature.* 39th Inaugural Lecture, Rivers State University of Science and Technology, Port Harcourt, January 27, 2016.

Raymond, Janice. "Female Friendship: Contra Chodorow and Dinnerstein." *Hypertia: A Journal of Feminist Philosophy,* Vol. No. 2, (Fall 1986): 37–48.

Stratton, Florence. *Contemporary African Literature and the Politics of Gender.* London: Routledge, 1994.
Swacker, Majorie. "The Sex of the Speaker as a Sociolinguistic Variable" *Language and Sex: Difference and Dominance.* Ed. Barrie Thorne and Nancy Henley. Rowley, Massachusetts: Newbury House, 1975: 76–83.
Walker, Alice. *In Search of Our Mother's Garden: Womanist Prose.* New York: The Woman's Press, 1983.
Youssef, Nadia H. "Women in the Muslim World." *Women in the World: A Comparative Study.* Ed. Lynne B Iglitzin and Ruth Ross. Oxford: Clio Books, 1976: 203–217.

NOTES

1. In this study, polygyny refers to plurality of wives while polygamy denotes the acquisition of more than one partner. Accordingly, a monogamous man could be polygamous in his lecherous escapades. Nnaemeka proffers her own definition thus: "Polygyny comes from two Greek words: poly (many) and gyne (woman or wife). Polygyny has therefore two possible meanings—'many women' or 'many wives' . . . The English dictionary sanctifies only one of the two possibilities, 'many wives,' a limitation to which no one seems to object." See Obioma Nnaemeka, "Urban Spaces," p. 184.

2. *Un Chant écarlate.* My translation.

3. See Chioma Opara, "A Matter of Contrasts: The Antithetical as Political in Mariama Ba's Novels," *Journal of Gender Studies,* Vol. 1, No. 3 (Sept. 2001): 125–133.

4. The squeaking tone of Ouleymatou's shoes *"Thoikete! Thoikete"* in her seductive steps, recalls the moralistic song of Mercy's shoes in Ama Ata Aidoo's "Two Sisters" in *No Sweetness Here* (1979). Connie's passivity is markedly contrasted with Mercy's licentious assertion. Her shoes are meant to sing a note of warning to the straying feet: Count, Mercy, count your blessing, Count, Mercy, count, count, your blessing.

5. I have in my N/n Principles distinguished between nudity and nakedness. Nakedness which is linked with the Fall, connotes perfidy, deceit, and shame. Nudity on the contrary evokes the spiritual and the idyllic. Women protest against patriarchy in nakedness while nudity prevails in utopian or spiritual communities of creativity, healing and spirituality. See Chioma Opara, "Towards Integration in Heterogeneity," pp. 62–65.

Epilogue
Un Cri De Coeur

Marie Umeh

When I visited Buchi Emecheta in 2000 in her London home in Cranley Gardens, one of the first places she escorted me to was her reading and writing room where she had on display a fine ebony wood, glass book case, with all her hardcover novels and plays that were translated into many languages around the world, even Arabic. Buchi was so proud of her accomplishments as she was an award-winning Nigerian British author, London University Fellow, an activist for women's rights, among other attributes. But what was it that attracted so many of us to her books and eventually her life, like a magnet attracts everything within reach? What was Emecheta's appeal to critics, feminists, journalists, anthologists, readers, and publishers? Why was she given so many awards, such as "The Best British Writer Award" or the "New Statesman/Jock Campbell Award" or "The Sunrise Award for the Best Black Writer in the World Award"? or "The Daughter of Mark Twain Award," to name only a few of her many accolades? It was her *cri de coeur*—her special appeal for justice for women and girls—who also needed to develop their full potential outside of domesticity, the role patriarchy created for women as mothers and wives. Emecheta would agree with Betty Friedan, author of the 1963 bestseller, *The Feminine Mystique* that marriage and motherhood did not fulfill many women's raison d'etre. Determined to diagnose "the problem with no name," to borrow Friedan's term, and fix it through the power of the pen, as a trained sociologist, with a bachelors of science degree (1974) and a masters degree in philosophy (1976) from London University. Through observation and research, Emecheta came to the conclusion that male and female relationships in *patriarchal* Nigerian society were in trouble and that there was a need for change as the subjugation of African Women, physically, mentally, and psychologically was unacceptable in the twenty-first century. Emecheta called for *social transformation* and the end to the concept that men and women are not equal and that men are stronger and better and more intelligent than women. She refused to *pretend* that the African homestead was a peaceful, happy and loving space where *all* women and girls flourished and everybody could aspire to fulfill their dreams of acquiring the best life they wanted whether it would be a professional career in *aviation*, *diplomacy*, *education*, *finance*, *law*, *medicine*, *social anthropology*, or *writing and publishing*. To demonstrate her message, she created characters in her literary corpus with an omniscient narrator to espouse feminist thought. Her appeal for *change* as delineated in her volumes of books, was her way of demanding patriarchal fathers and their followers, for a *"change of heart!"* If it's true that African men have a need to control women's lives, then the cure is for the society to give women the freedom and independence to choose the life they want to live. Equal opportunities for advancement to both boys and girls at all levels in the society is a right. Equal access to the rich resources throughout Nigeria must be shared. Furthermore, all forms of discriminatory practices and violence against women and girls have to be eradicated. For example, in her novel *The Bride Price*, harmful widowhood practices and a forced marriage brought about the death of the main character, Aku-nna. Again, I ask, "What made Emecheta have such wide, universal appeal?" Definitely, it was her gift of storytelling and penchant for dramatic effect which added to her theme of *feminist consciousness* and *social transformation*, with the contention that "we should all be feminists—both men and women alike (Chimamanda Ngozi Adichie, TED Talk, 2017). In her magnum opus, *The Joys of Motherhood*, Emecheta contends that the popular mantra, "Mother is Gold" is a farce. We give our mothers elaborate funerals, but how well do we care for them in old age? Emecheta's plea for the death of gender constructs where men are socialized to believe that they are privileged to have more access to power than women is another erroneous trend that Emecheta fought to end in her literary works for her vision of a world where everybody in the homestead would be happy to be alive and fulfilled as self-actualized compatriots and human beings. Finally, Emecheta's personal story of success and her message of *hope*, no matter one's circumstances, endeared her to the *hearts* of so many of her readers continentally and globally. Thank you, Buchi, for your personal courage to change the world. You did it!

Long live Buchi Emecheta!

Index

A Walk at the Night 224, 324
African, 1–3, 8, 18, 20–30, 35, 44,
  47–51, 54–58, 61–63, 65, 77–79,
  101–02, 113, 115–16, 117, 119–20,
  128–29, 130–31, 140, 146, 153–54,
  160–61, 162–64, 172–73, 199, 201,
  225, 231, 284, 225, 301–02, 320,
  326, 327, 333–34
  consciousness, 54
  diaspora, 34–35, 164
  female writers, 1, 3, 50, 316
  feminism, 11, 51, 168, 206, 213,
    266–70, 313–16
  feminist, 3, 8, 11, 52, 54,
    70, 77, 168, 235, 267–68,
    313, 315, 329
  fiction, 21, 62, 77, 213
  literary landscape, 2, 11
  literature, 1, 4, 6, 10–11, 16–17,
    30, 33, 37, 44, 47–48, 51,
    52–54, 57, 61, 94, 101, 106,
    112, 115–16, 119–26, 130,
    131, 137, 162, 201, 217, 233–
    34, 241, 313, 326
  modernity, 1, 167, 169,
    170, 173–74
  scholar(ship), 2, 11, 48, 51,
    52–54, 55–57, 112, 167, 175
  standpoint, 286, 291

theorist, 341
tradition and European modernity,
  174–82, 183
womanism, 15, 314
women writers, 11, 16, 35, 38–39,
  47, 50–51, 168, 267
writer, 5, 15, 16, 25, 33, 39, 48,
  53, 106, 115, 117, 121, 128,
  143, 153, 157, 164, 167–68,
  172, 179, 218, 283
Algerian woman, 200–01
alienation and desalination,
  167, 174, 183
Al-saadawi, 246–47
American women, 2, 28, 247
anatomy class, 190–91
animal imagery, 252–53
anthropological, 17, 18, 37, 301
appendages, women as, 37, 87
Arab women, 185, 197, 199–02,
  213, 249, 251
arranged marriage, 187, 203
Arrow of God, 18, 119, 173, 233, 301
artist, 1–5, 10, 35, 79, 83, 91, 92, 103,
  115–117, 119–21, 125–28, 130–31,
  172, 226, 235, 247, 314
artistry, 10, 199, 213, 315, 327

autobiography, 5, 8, 92, 94, 98, 143, 155, 161–62, 170, 179, 209, 212, 242, 247, 314, 326

"between my legs," 222, 252
Black women, 225, 242
burden of history, 4, 47, 54–55, 58, 316
Butterfly Burning, 217–18, 223, 227–28

canonical essays, 231, 234
childhood, 193, 194, 208–10, 242, 252, 258, 310, 322, 324
childlessness, 24, 42, 83–85
Children of the New World, 199, 201, 212, 213
Christianity, 19, 24–27, 30, 63, 155–56, 158, 181
colonial master, 247, 261
    modernity, 168, 172–73, 179
colonialism, 7, 25, 54, 63, 66, 115, 138, 175–76, 208, 235, 247, 250, 268–69, 316
communication, 6, 9, 93, 101–02, 103, 106–09, 112–13, 121, 125, 156, 227, 293
complexity, 167, 169, 291
conflict, 7, 23, 24, 35, 63–64, 82, 101, 167–68, 170–75, 178, 183, 187, 201, 209, 218, 266, 301, 321
courtship, 101, 108, 110, 220, 326–27
creative work, 17–24, 28, 168
    writing, 11, 17, 22, 61, 168, 179, 313, 329
cruelty, 108, 185, 193, 241, 305
cultural imperialism, 51, 301
    Milieu, 130, 172, 313
    value, 49, 51

dehumanization, 1, 210–11, 303–05
depravity, 7, 185–86, 188, 192–93, 196–97
dialogue, 18, 27, 57, 83, 93, 111, 158, 250, 275, 288
dichotomy, 62, 167, 169, 171–72, 284
dictatorship, 122, 129, 130–31

Doduicimi, 188
domestic violence, 187, 194, 197, 250
Double Yoke, 7, 167–80, 183, 232

early marriage, 185, 250
Efuru, 1, 4–5, 16–18, 20–24, 28–29, 33–44, 47–49, 51, 55–59, 61–74, 77–87, 116, 241
Egyptian writer, 9, 185, 327
emblematic, 140, 213, 226, 237, 253
English, 2, 11, 22, 25, 61, 63, 106, 124, 144, 200, 217, 225, 262, 281, 282
    language, 61, 144, 262, 282

enslaved, 6, 128, 202, 242, 276
eponymous heroine, 17, 49
ethnic community, 151, 153–54
European modernity, 181, 185–88, 192–94

father figure, 158, 172
female beauty, 178, 180
    circumcision, 84, 187, 188, 249, 251–52
    folk, 87, 130, 189, 262, 267, 268
    genital mutilation, 199
    victim, 4, 188, 192–93
femalism, 51, 314, 316–319
feminism texts, 2–3
feminist, 2–3, 8, 11, 17, 34, 37, 48–55, 58, 61, 70, 77, 80, 128, 137, 151, 153, 156, 159–60, 168–69, 175, 199, 202–05, 207, 208–09, 213, 218, 226, 228, 234–35, 237, 240, 245–47, 250–53, 264–70, 313–19, 328–29, 333–34
fiction, 2–4, 6, 16–17, 21, 35, 37–40, 44, 49, 57, 62, 64–65, 74, 77, 92, 103, 137, 140, 142, 160, 162, 164, 170, 200, 201, 213, 235, 241, 283, 288, 289
foremother, 1, 3, 33, 48, 56, 264, 326
francophone, 199, 201
freedom, 8–11, 16, 18, 160, 164, 178, 189–90, 197, 202–06, 209, 218–24, 228, 237, 247, 256, 266, 268–69,

272, 274, 276, 277, 287–89, 291–92, 293–94, 306, 319–20, 328, 334
Freud, 187–88, 189, 194, 195
frustration, 38, 170, 187, 194–95, 249, 269

girl, child, 188, 271
grandmother, 85, 148, 222, 228, 235, 240, 247, 248–50
gynism, 314

Hajila, 202–08
high-handedness, 129, 190
hinterland, 56, 239
history, 4–6, 8, 23, 27, 29, 33–37, 48–49, 54, 57–59, 64, 79, 97, 117, 147, 154, 155, 199, 205, 208–13, 224, 242, 246, 267, 291, 313, 316
homeland, 25, 44, 139
Hughes, 158, 160
humiliation, 42, 78, 203, 211
hybridity, 7, 167–68, 172, 183, 209

ideology, 52, 54, 97, 106, 156, 162, 164, 173, 262, 267, 300, 304, 314, 316, 319, 322
imperialism, 51–52, 186, 252, 255, 301
imprisoned, 186, 203–04
Indigenous African, 6, 109, 117, 130
    culture, 6, 117, 130
Industrial Revolution, 35, 50
infanticide, 221, 319, 326
interpretations, 36, 53, 92, 126, 129, 137, 147, 160, 169, 237, 292
interrogate, 4–5, 7, 55, 167, 170, 172, 174–75, 211–12
Isma, 201–08, 226, 238, 288
isolation, 173, 189, 204, 282, 334

jail, 225, 249, 254, 289
juxtaposition, 118, 286

kinship, 25–26, 102, 106, 125, 268

literary, 1, 4, 11, 17–18, 29, 34, 44, 47–48, 49, 50–51, 53, 57, 63, 98, 106, 116, 130–31, 140, 153, 159, 160–64, 187–88, 199–200, 232, 233, 262, 265, 269–70, 281, 284, 289, 292, 293, 301, 315
    analytical, 18, 24
    critics, 17, 24, 30, 232
    landscape, 2, 11, 51, 116
    works, 48, 188, 265, 281, 334
Luo people, 101–07, 109–13

magic, 63, 66, 67, 72, 126, 128, 130, 144, 189, 263, 271, 283
male critics, 2, 37, 44, 231
    folks, 87, 130, 187, 189, 192, 196, 262
    supremacy, 186, 267
manhood, 23, 171
manuscript, 157–58, 241
marketplace, 35, 69, 72, 111
marriage, 5, 17, 19, 21, 23, 24, 26, 28–30, 36, 42, 56, 58, 68, 70–71, 73, 74, 83, 84, 86, 95, 101, 109, 127, 129–30, 138, 140, 147, 154, 161, 175, 182, 185, 187, 188, 191, 197, 202–03, 205, 207, 226, 237, 240, 242, 306–07, 318–19, 320, 325–26
    institution, 58, 269
Marxist, 253, 301, 316
medical school, 186, 250
mental health, 185–87, 196, 197
    torture, 185–88, 196, 197
metaphorical, 36, 102, 110, 120, 322
mirror, 3, 64, 67, 68, 71, 73, 93, 98, 130, 189, 202, 207, 223, 255, 259, 288, 323
misfortune, 36, 41–42, 140, 162
modernity continuum, 7, 167, 172
mother archetype, 62, 67, 71–72, 141, 146–51
mother-in-law, 24, 27, 39, 55, 69, 70, 71, 85, 96–97, 148, 322, 323
motherism, 51, 314
Muslim culture, 189, 313, 318

post-colonial Egyptian
society, 188, 190
tradition, 7, 275, 316, 320
women, 202
My Son's Story, 9, 284, 286,
288, 292, 294

narrative style, 4, 8, 16, 21, 22, 226, 284
narrator, 5, 21–22, 24, 26, 29, 40, 92,
94, 98, 142, 145, 149, 176–82, 202,
206–08, 237, 240, 242, 286–87, 334
nation-building, 21, 26
nego-feminism, 51, 314
ni-feminism, 314
Nigerian civil war, 7, 40, 56
university, 16, 171
novel, 3–10, 16–22, 24, 26, 29, 33–44,
48, 53, 61–64, 70, 74, 78, 81–83,
85, 86, 91, 94, 103, 107, 137–41,
147–48, 151, 153–59, 161–64,
167–76, 178–79, 185–88, 190, 192,
197, 199–201, 202–07, 208–10, 212,
213, 217–18, 221, 223, 226–28,
231–35, 237, 241, 248, 282, 283,
293, 301, 302, 308, 313–18, 321–22,
326–27, 334

Old Wines are Tasty, 262, 264
Oligbo Kingdom, 124, 130, 131
omniscient narrator, 40, 334
oracle, 26, 118, 122, 125, 142
oral literature in Africa, 1, 6, 11, 26,
103, 116, 117, 121, 131

paradigm, 1, 6, 10, 20, 236,
277, 306, 315
patriarchal subjugation, 8, 56, 203
bondage, 51
culture, 55, 188, 208, 220,
236, 242, 314
patriarchy, 7, 35, 48, 51, 55, 57, 163,
169, 185, 188–91, 195–97, 199, 200,
200–03, 205, 207, 208, 211–13, 218,
221, 225–28, 237, 245, 250, 252–53,
255–57, 264, 271, 315, 333

phenomenon, 8, 168, 171, 174, 231,
232–35, 292
playwright, 6, 115–16, 120, 122,
125, 127–29, 199, 261–62, 264,
268, 277, 283
poems, 16, 17, 153, 157–58, 162, 201
postcolonial African, 1, 7, 20
post-independence, 56, 145, 161,
217, 220, 242
prose, 92, 269, 283, 290
prostitute, 195–96, 249, 254–56, 258
protagonist, 5–9, 36, 44, 56, 61, 63,
65–68, 71, 73, 127, 173, 185, 187–
89, 197, 202, 207, 218, 221, 257,
226, 274, 318, 322, 328
proverbs, 94, 103, 121–26, 131, 282

rain, 28, 42, 115, 119, 124, 141–45, 147,
224, 254, 284
Ramatoulaye, 5, 92, 94–98, 206,
275, 316–26
rape of Shavi, 171, 232
reactionary, 127, 128, 131, 320
real imported footballs, 176, 178
rebel, 8–9, 127–30, 200, 210, 212, 218,
225, 228–29, 275, 288
re-creation, 116, 125–26
regular, 41, 92, 103, 190, 226, 242
religious hypocrisy, 249, 252
rhythm, 37, 54, 124, 224, 225, 326
ritual, 84, 94, 103, 126, 128–29, 144,
220, 223, 256, 263, 271, 274, 316
rural village, 104, 193

Scarlet Song, 10, 314, 318, 326, 328
second class citizen, 231, 233, 241
9781793655240 42, 243
self-fulfilled, 40, 189
sexual organs, 190, 192
slavery, 185, 187
sexuality, 187, 191, 197, 205, 250, 291
sisterhood, 84, 202–07, 213, 249, 326
slavery, 7, 138, 185, 187, 207, 221, 235,
237, 240–41, 242, 316
snail sense, 122, 314

socio-political, 4, 21, 25–26, 30, 269, 302, 313
standard, 26, 56, 73, 78, 128, 163, 168, 178, 221, 226–27, 258, 273, 316
stepmother, 145, 148–49
stillborn, 172, 211
Stiwanism, 51, 302, 315
struggle, 7, 8, 20, 28, 35, 48, 54, 63, 81, 86–87, 147, 162, 169, 186–89, 197, 199, 207, 211–24, 226–27, 234, 256, 263, 266, 267, 269, 274, 289–93, 299, 313, 321
subjugation, 7–8, 56, 130, 200, 203, 242, 246, 252, 254, 262, 266–69, 274, 276, 277, 314, 333
subtext, 7, 171, 176, 178
suicidal, 7, 185, 187, 193, 196, 197
suitor, 105, 107, 187, 325
supreme penalty, 119
synopsis, 17, 170, 175–76, 180

The Bride Price, 57, 168, 231, 235, 242, 334
   Collector of Treasures, 154, 162, 163, 169
   Slave Girl, 8, 168, 231, 233, 235–42
   Sweet Trap, 262–64
   Wedlock of the Gods, 120, 261–66, 268, 270–71, 273–74, 277
Things Fall Apart, 1, 4, 16, 18, 21, 25, 38, 101–02, 110, 141, 173, 301
topicality of the story, 167, 169

tradition and modernity, 7, 113, 117, 129, 131, 167, 168, 169–71, 172–76, 180, 182, 183, 202, 313
trajectories, 4, 21, 23
traumatic, 5, 140, 188, 194, 243, 328
tribulations, 195, 320
Two Women in One, 3, 7, 185–87, 188, 190, 260

unique narrative style, 8, 229
uwa oma, 4, 33, 36
uwa umunwanyi, 4, 33, 35, 36–37, 39–40, 41, 44

verisimilitude, 17, 140
village life, 171, 220

war, 7, 82, 85, 93, 120, 137–38, 156, 199, 208–213, 217–18, 220–23, 235, 237, 238, 242, 253, 270
Western Christianity, 19, 25, 30
   civilization, 163, 173, 179
white people, 143, 160, 287, 289, 292,
widowhood, 98, 266, 270, 274, 334
window, 17, 203, 208, 211, 225, 249
Without a Name, 217–18, 226–27
Wolof culture, 98, 91, 96
Woman at Point Zero, 7, 9, 185–87, 192–93, 203–04, 226, 245–47, 248, 259
womenfolk, 38, 51
workplace, 23, 187
world literature, 199, 201, 213

About the Editors and Contributors

ABOUT THE EDITORS

Helen Chukwuma is professor of English in the Department of English and Modern Foreign Languages at Jackson State University in Jackson, Mississippi. She was the first woman to be promoted to the rank of professor in the University of Port Harcourt, Nigeria, in 1993. From 1991 to 1992 she was a Fulbright Research Fellow at the University of Cincinnati in Ohio. A feminist scholar, she has served as the editor of *Journal of Women Studies in Africa*. Her academic areas of interest are African literature—oral and written—feminist theory in literature, contemporary English and American literature, and women's studies. Her current research focuses on indigenous African feminism and meeting points in Black women's literature. She has several publications including eight books, some of which are: *Feminism in African Literature, Igbo Oral Literature, Achebe's Women: Imagism and Power,* and *Meeting Points in Black/Africana Women's Literature.*

Chioma Carol Opara, PhD, is professor of English and comparative literature and the former director of the Foundation Studies Unit at Rivers State University in Port Harcourt, Nigeria where she has taught modern African literature, varieties of English, literary theory and English composition. With specialization in writing, comparative literature and gender, her major research interests are African fiction, world Englishes, women and cultural studies. She has written extensively on African literature and has several publications which include books, chapters in edited volumes and articles in academic journals. Her books include *Her Mother's Daughter, Beyond the Marginal Land,* and *Effective English*. She has served as West African coordinator for the Women Caucus African Literature Association (WOCALA), council member of the International Society for the Oral Literatures of

Africa (ISOLA), and a member of the board of directors for the International Society for Universal Dialogue (ISUD). She was for several years the editor of *Journal of Gender Studies*, a multidisciplinary annual publication.

ABOUT THE CONTRIBUTORS

Anthonia Osayaba Adadevoh obtained her PhD from Clark Atlanta University in Atlanta, Georgia. A tenured professor at Miles College in Fairfield, Alabama, she has been in the field of higher education in the United States for over twenty-eight years. Her career includes serving in executive administrative positions in academic affairs and institutional effectiveness. Professor Adadevoh is also an author; her creative writing is inspired by her children and grandchildren. She particularly takes delight in writing and illustrating children's books. Some of her children's books draw extensively on the Ancient Edo Kingdom of Nigeria. A few of her titles are: *Ekaladeran: A Prince in Exile, Idia the Warrior Queen, Ovoramwen: A King Indeed, Best Friends and the Good Luck Leaves*, and *The Outside Wife and other Short Stories*. Her books are available on Amazon.

Akachi Adimora-Ezeigbo, a multiple award-winning, prolific writer and international scholar is professor at Alex Ekwueme Federal University Ndufu-Alike, Ikwo in Ebonyi State, Nigeria. She was a three-time head of English department at University of Lagos. She has been awarded visiting fellowships in the United Kingdom, South Africa, and Germany. Apart from academic books and scholarly articles in journals, she has published in all genres of literature: she is a poet, novelist, playwright, short story writer, and children's book author, writing under the pen name Akachi Adimora-Ezeigbo. Among her over 50 books are: the trilogy, *The Last of the strong Ones*, *House of Symbols* and *Children of the Eagle*; *Trafficked*; *Roses and Bullets*; *Fact and Fiction in the Literature of the Nigerian Civil War*; and *Gender Issues in Nigeria*. Ezeigbo was a joint winner of The Nigeria Prize for Literature (NPL) in 2007 with her children's novel *My Cousin Sammy*. Akachi Ezeigbo was the vice president of PEN International, Nigeria Centre (2002–2011) and vice president of Women Writers Association of Nigeria—WRITA (1995–1999). In March 2021 she was appointed chair of the advisory board of The Nigeria Prize for Literature and The Nigeria Prize for Literary Criticism sponsored by Nigeria LNG Limited.

Austine Amanze Akpuda is professor of literature and history of ideas in the Department of English Language and Literature at Abia State University in Uturu, Nigeria. Beyond publishing meta-critical essays on Ngugi wa

Thiong'o, Nawal El Saadawi, Sam Ukala, and some other writers, he is the editor of the critically influential *Reconstructing the Canon: Festschrift in Honour of Professor Charles E. Nnolim* (2001). He also edited with Greg Mbajiorgu, *50 Years of Solo Performing Art in Nigerian Theatre, 1966–2016* (2018). Among his other edited books are *Currents in Early American Literature* (2000), *The Black Presence in Caribbean Literature* (2005), *The Literary Response to Modernity* (2014), *Paradigms in Modern Nigerian Drama* (2017) and *Celebrating God's own Robot: The Gani Fawehinmi Phenomenon in Nigerian Poetry (2003)*. He was also part of the college of screeners for the Africa Movie Academy Award in 2015 and 2017.

Queen Albert, PhD, lectures in the Department of English at Rivers State University in Port Harcourt. Committed to writing and literary criticism, Dr. Albert has a number of publications in edited volumes and literary journals. Her research interests center on African literature and gender studies.

Okwudiri Anasiudu received a PhD in English a couple of years after he graduated a first class in English studies from the University of Port Harcourt, Nigeria. His research interests are within the fields of Afropolitan/diasporic discourse, literary stylistics with insights drawn from functional linguistics, and cultural studies with focus on pop culture. He seeks a transdisciplinary synergy in the reading and interpretation of literature. He is published in a number of journals and Working Papers. He is currently working on a Tertiary Education Trust Fund sponsored research in Nigeria with focus on the Metaphorical Representation of Corruption in Selected Nigeria's Newspapers.

Perp St. Remy Asiegbu, PhD, teaches literature in English at the University of Port Harcourt, Nigeria. She majors in African literature and gender studies and has written a number of creative works—*Grandma Dora Goes to Italy, Tripod, The Palm Plantation, Whispers of the Gods,* and *Ifeoma the Virtuous Maiden*.

Ada Uzoamaka Azodo, PhD, is a multidisciplinary scholar, author, literary critic, (co)editor, feminist theorist ("Di-Feminism"), and teaches African and African diaspora literatures, as well as French and Francophone studies. She is currently an associate faculty in the humanities at Indiana University Northwest. Professor Azodo was a nominee for the 2019 Indiana University Northwest Founders' Day Excellence in Teaching award. She was two-term President (2017–2021) and Immediate Past President of the Igbo Studies Association, USA.

Solomon Omatsola Azumurana, PhD, lectures in the Department of English at the University of Lagos in Lagos, Nigeria. His areas of research include the comparative study of African and African American novels, gender studies with particular emphasis on women creative writing, and the interface between literary theories and works of fiction.

Blessing Diala-Ogamba, PhD, is a professor of English and the chair of humanities at Coppin State University in Baltimore, Maryland. She teaches English composition, world literature, and other literature courses. She has published several scholarly articles in books and journals. She holds a Sloan-C certificate in design and delivery, and she is also a QM (Quality Matters) peer reviewer. Diala-Ogamba is the coeditor of *Literary Crossroads: An International Exploration of Women, Gender, and Otherhood* and *Emerging Perspectives on Akachi Adimora-Ezeigbo*. She is author of *Visions of Womanhood in Contemporary African Literature*. Her academic interests are women's literature, world literature, and immigration and migration issues. She is currently working on a manuscript on South African literature.

Anthonia Kalu, PhD, is a full professor in the Department of Comparative Literature and Foreign Languages at University of California-Riverside (UCR). She joined the UCR faculty in the summer of 2015 from the Ohio State University-Columbus, Ohio. She earned a PhD in African Languages and Literatures from the University of Wisconsin, Madison in Wisconsin. In the summer of 2014, she served as a Carnegie African Diaspora Fellow at the University of Ilorin-Ilorin, Kwara State in Nigeria on capacity building, research development, and mentoring for faculty and graduate students. She is a past president (2013–2014) of the African Literature Association (ALA). Kalu has served as president and on the steering committee of the Women's Caucus of the African Literature Association (WOCALA. She has also served as a board member for the African Studies Association (USA). Among her multiple awards is a Ford Foundation postdoctoral fellowship. Kalu's published works include articles in academic journals. Kalu is also a creative writer (fiction). She is the author of *Women, Literature, and Development in Africa*.

Mary S. Lederer received her Ph.D. in Southern African literature from UCLA and was formerly senior lecturer in African literature at the University of Botswana. She resides in Gaborone, Botswana and works as an editor and independent scholar. She is the author of *Novels of Botswana in English, 1930–2006* (2014).

Omeh Obasi Ngwoke, Ph.D lectures in the Department of English Studies at the University of Port Harcourt. He teaches courses in dramatic literature, oral literature, and Shakespeare and Renaissance poetry and literature of the African diaspora, among others. He has contributed essays to a number of academic journals.

Onyemechi Nwaeke obtained a bachelors degree in visual arts from the University of Port Harcourt. She also has a bachelor of arts degree in English studies from Ignatius Ajuru University of Education in Port Harcourt. In addition, she holds a Master of Arts degree in literature and a PhD in literature from the same university. She is an epistolary enthusiast and has presented papers on epistolary aesthetics in seminars and conferences. She is a diarist, poet, and short story writer.

Eunita D. A. Ochola earned a PhD in linguistics from the University of South Carolina, a Master of Arts degree in language studies from the University of Lancaster in the United Kingdom, and a bachelors degree in English and education from the University of Nairobi in Kenya. She has taught English, literature and linguistics at various institutions in the United States and Kenya. Her current research focuses on choices of the use of discourse features in expressing messages in written discourse.

Chinyere Grace Okafor, chair of the Department of Women's, Ethnicity, and Intersectional Studies (WEIS), and director of the Center for Women's Studies at Wichita State University in Wichita, Kansas, USA, is professor of English, women's, and intersectional studies. She teaches theories of feminism, women's writing, intersectional engagement, and fundamentals of diversity. She is a poet, playwright, and short story writer. She has authored ten books and numerous articles in journals and edited volumes. Some of her creative works are: *From Earth's Bedchamber*, *The Lion and the Iroko*, *He Wants to Marry Me Again and Other Stories*, and *Zeb Silhouette*. Her current research focuses on Omumu—an African concept of uniting gender power.

Ikeogu Oke (May 23, 1967–November 24, 2018) was a Nigerian author, journalist, and award-winning poet. He received a masters degree in literature from the University of Nigeria, Nsukka, and a bachelors degree in English and literary studies from the University of Calabar, Nigeria. In 2017, Oke's collection of poetry, *The Heresiad*, was nominated for the Nigeria Prize for Literature, along with two other works. *Heresiad* clinched the prize. In his acceptance speech, Oke described poetry as "healthy narcotics." He died the following year in November of 2018.

Nkem Okoh earned a PhD from SOAS, University of London. He is a professor of English and teaches at the University of Port Harcourt in Nigeria. His research interests straddle such disparate domains as EAP grammar, research writing, orality in a highly technologized or rapidly technologizing age, TESOL, African literature, sociolinguistics, and world Englishes. Not only has Nkem Okoh published extensively in academic journals, he is also the author of such books as *To Use or to Abuse Words in English, Writing Right in English, Preface to Oral literature,* and *Keeping Language Clean: A Guide to Usage and Grammar in English.*

Rose A. Sackeyfio has taught in the Department of English and Liberal Studies at Winston Salem State University for almost three decades. Her areas of specialization and research interests are inter-disciplinary and include the literature of African and African-diaspora women, women's studies, cultural studies and African migration. She is the author of *West African Women in the Diaspora: Narratives of Other Spaces, Other Selves.* She is editor of a volume of critical essays, *Women Writing Diaspora in the 21st Century* and co-editor of a collection of critical essays, *Emerging Perspectives on Akachi Adimora Ezeigbo.* Dr. Sackeyfio's current research examines the experiences of African female students in China and constitutes a larger project on the ways in which African women in China have negotiated gendered spaces within the context of globalization. Dr. Sackeyfio is also the guest editor of a special issue of the *Journal of Post-Colonial Writing* that examines "The African Novel in the 21st Century." In 2012 she produced a documentary, *Building Bridges: The Untold African Story,* that examines the historical and cultural linkages between Ghana and the African diaspora through memory, identity, and reconnection in the 21st century.

Irene Isoken Salami-Agunloye is a playwright, screenwriter, and professor of African drama, women, gender and film studies at the University of Jos in Nigeria. She holds a post-doctoral masters degree in gender, women and sexuality from Georgia State University, Atlanta, Georgia, USA. She is a feminist scholar trained in multiple disciplines; her conversation is fueled by the diversity of her global experiences. She is a recipient of several international grants and awards amongst which are: Fulbright Senior Scholar at the School of Theater, Television and Film and Center for the Study of Women, University of California, Los Angeles (UCLA) (2004–2005), the first and only woman till date in the University of Jos to have received the Senior Fulbright Fellowship award. Agunloye also earned the IWLF Post-Doc fellowship (2011–2012) and became a fellow of the prestigious IWLF (International Women's Leadership Forum) Leadership Foundation. She is the initiator and the pioneering director for Centre for Gender and Women's

Studies, University of Jos. She has become an international authority on street children in Africa. Her project and paper on *Shade Tree Theatre with Street Children* is one of the most assessed academic articles on that subject online. This contributed to University of Jos's first position in webometric ranking in 2010.

Onyemaechi Udumukwu is professor of English at the University of Port Harcourt in Nigeria. A prolific writer, he has published books and contributed to several journals and edited volumes. His research interests include literary theory and African fiction which he has taught over the years.

Marie Umeh received her MA and PhD degrees from the University of Wisconsin-Madison where she was a graduate fellow in the Department of African Languages and Literatures, specializing in African women writers in the second half of the twentieth century. The former chair of the Department of English at Anambra State College of Education (Awka, Nigeria), Dr. Umeh has received PSC-CUNY awards and a National Endowment for the Humanities (NEH) Award in Feminist Theory and Literary Criticism. At John Jay College of Criminal Justice, New York, she has taught literatures of the African world, research methods, writing composition, Western literatures and modern literature. She has authored critical and theoretical essays that appear in journals and books throughout Africa, Europe, and North America. She is also the editor of two anthologies, *Emerging Perspectives on Buchi Emecheta* and *Emerging Perspectives on Flora Nwapa*; she is contributing editor to *Who's Who in Contemporary Women's Writing*.

Kemi Wale-Olaitan, PhD, a multi-talented academic and activist teaches at Obafemi Awolowo University, Ile-Ife, Nigeria. A feminist scholar, she has published widely in the areas of feminism and African literature.

www.ingramcontent.com/pod-product-compliance
Lightning Source LLC
Chambersburg PA
CBHW021340300426
44114CB00012B/1021